The International Political Economy of New Regionalisms Series

The International Political Economy of New Regionalisms series presents innovative analyses of a range of novel regional relations and institutions. Going beyond established, formal, interstate economic organizations, this essential series provides informed interdisciplinary and international research and debate about myriad heterogeneous intermediate level interactions.

Reflective of its cosmopolitan and creative orientation, this series is developed by an international editorial team of established and emerging scholars in both South and North. It reinforces ongoing networks of analysts in both academia and think-tanks as well as international agencies concerned with micro-, meso- and macro-level regionalisms.

Other Titles in the Series

South Africa's Multilateral Diplomacy and Global Change
The limits of reformism
Edited by Philip Nel, Ian Taylor and Janis van der Westhuizen
ISBN 0 7546 1653 3

European Union and New Regionalism
Regional actors and global governance in a post-hegemonic era
Edited by Mario Telò
ISBN 0 7546 1748 3

Crises of Governance in Asia and Africa

Edited by

SANDRA J. MacLEAN
Dalhousie University, Halifax, Canada

FAHIMUL QUADIR
St. Lawrence University, New York

TIMOTHY M. SHAW
Dalhousie University, Halifax, Canada

Ashgate

Aldershot • Burlington USA • Singapore • Sydney

© Sandra J. MacLean, Fahimul Quadir and Timothy M. Shaw 2001

Published by
Ashgate Publishing Limited
Gower House
Croft Road
Aldershot
Hants GU11 3HR
England

Ashgate Publishing Company
131 Main Street
Burlington, VT 05401-5600 USA

Ashgate website: http://www.ashgate.com

British Library Cataloguing in Publication Data
Crises of governance in Asia and Africa. - (The
    international political economy of new regionalisms)
    1. Minorities - Asia 2. Minorities - Africa 3. Asia - Politics
    and government - 1945- 4. Africa - Politics and government -
    1960-
    I. MacLean, Sandra J. II. Quadir, Fahimul III. Shaw, Timothy
    M.
    320.9'5

Library of Congress Control Number: 2001089133

ISBN 0 7546 1410 7

Printed and bound by Athenaeum Press, Ltd.,
Gateshead, Tyne & Wear.

Contents

Part IV: Governance and Conflict

List of Tables

List of Abbreviations

ACLIS	American Center for International Labor Solidarity
Aflife	African Life Assurance Company
AMDP	Accelerated Mahawelli Development Programme
ANC	African National Congress
ANZ	Associated Newspapers of Zimbabwe
ASA	Association for Social Advancement
BN	Barisan Nasional
BRAC	Bangladesh Rural Advancement Committee
CA	Collective Agreement
CBOs	Community-Based Organizations
CC	Constitutional Commission
CEO	Chief Executive Officer
CEWPA	Cape Estate Wine Producers' Association
CGAP	Consultative Group to Assist the Poorest
CHT	Chittagong Hill Tracts
CIO	Central Intelligence Organization
CIWG	Cape (Independent) Winemakers' Guild
CLOB	Central Limit Order Book
CODESRIA	Council for the Development of Social Science Research in Africa
COSATU	Congress of South African Trade Unions
COTU	Central Organization of Trade Unions
CWSI	Cape Wine and Spirit Institute
DAP	Democratic Action Party
DFID	Department for International Development
DP	Democratic Party
DRC	Democratic Republic of Congo
ECA	United Nations Economic Commission for Africa
EE	Eastern Europe
EOI	Export-oriented Industrialization
EON	Edaran Otomobil Nasional
EPF	Employee's Provident Fund
ERWG	Ethnic Redistribution with Growth
ESAP	Economic Structural Adjustment Program
ETI	Ethical Trading Initiative
EU	European Union
FDI	Foreign Direct Investment

FNDL	Five Year National Development Plan
FNLA	Frente Nacional de Libertacao de Angola
FORUM	Forum for Democratic Reform Trust
FSU	Former Soviet Union
FTA	Free Trade Agreement
GB	Grameen Bank
GDP	Gross Domestic Product
GEAR	Growth, Employment and Redistribution
GK	Gono Shasthya Kendra
GLR	Great Lakes Region
GNU	Government of National Unity (South Africa)
GNP	Gross National Product
GSS	Gono Shahajjo Sanghstha
HPD	Health and Population Development
ICA	Industrial Coordination Act
IDRC	International Development Research Centre
IFIs	International Financial Institutions
IFP	Inkatha Freedom Party
IMF	International Monetary Fund
IPE	International Political Economy
IR	International Relations
ISI	Import-substitution Industrialization
ISST	Institute of Social Studies Trust
JSE	Johannesburg Stock Exchange
JSS	Jana Sanghati Samity
KLSE	Kuala Lumpur Stock Exchange
LC	Local Council
LRA	Lord's Resistance Army
LTTE	Liberation Tigers of Tamil Eelam
MCA	Malaysian Chinese Association
MDC	Movement for Democratic Change
MIC	Malaysian Indian Congress
MISC	Malaysian International Shipping Corporation
MMT	Mass Media Trust
MONGO	My Own NGO
MP	Member of Parliament
MPLA	Movimento Popular de Libertacao de Angola
MTUC	Malaysian Trade Union Congress
MWENGO	Mwelekeo wa NGO
Nail	New Africa Investments
NAWO	National Alliance for Women's Organizations

NCA	National Constitutional Assembly
NDP	New Development Policy
NEC	National Empowerment Consortium
NECC	National Economic Consultative Council
NEDLAC	National Economic Development and Labour Council
NEP	New Economic Programme
NFPE	Non-formal Primary Education Program
NGIs	Non-Governmental Institutions
NGOAB	NGO Affairs Bureau
NGO	Non-Governmental Organization
NIC	Newly Industrializing Country
NK	Nijera Kori
NRM	National Resistance Movement
ODA	Official Development Assistance
OPP2	Second Outline Perspective Plan
PAS	Parti Islam Se Malaysia (Malaysian Islamic Party)
PBS	Parti Bersatu Sabah (United Sabah Party)
PCLA	Peace and Conflict Impact Assessment
PCOs	Public Call Offices
PKN	Parti KeADILan Nasional
POs	People's Organizations
PRIA	Society for Participatory Research in Asia
PRM	Parti Raykat Malaysia (Malaysian People's Party)
RDP	Reconstruction and Development Programme (South Africa)
RDP	Rural Development Program
RSA	Republic of South Africa
SA	South Africa
SAB	South African Breweries
SACP	South African Communist Party
SACU	Southern African Customs Union
SADC	Southern Africa Development Community
SAF	South Africa Foundation
SANCO	South African Civics Association
SAP	Structural Adjustment Program
SAPS	South African Police Service
SARDI	South Asian Research and Development Initiative
SAWIT	South African Wine Industry Trust
SAWSEA	South African Wine and Spirit Exporters' Association
SEWA	Self-Employed Women's Association
SMEE	Small and Micro-economic Enterprises
SPARC	Society for Promotion of Area Resource Centers

SPLA	Sudanese People's Liberation Army
TULF	Tamil United Liberation Front
UDI	Unilateral Declaration of Independence (Rhodesia)
UK	United Kingdom
UMNO	United Malay National Organization
UNDP	United Nations Development Program
UNITA	Uniao Nacional para Independencia Total de Angola
UNP	United National Party
UP	Union Parishad
UPC	Uganda People's Congress
VO	Village Organization
VSS	Voluntary Separation Scheme
WFS	Women's Feature Service
WTO	World Trade Organization
ZANU-PF	Zimbabwe African National Union-Patriotic Front
ZAPU-PF	Zimbabwe African People's Union-Patriotic Front
ZCTU	Zimbabwe Congress of Trade Union
ZIMCORD	Zimbabwe Conference on Reconstruction and Development
ZINLWVA	Zimbabwe National Liberation War Veterans Association
ZUM	Zimbabwe United Movement

Contributors

Kenneth D. Bush is a Geneva-based Research Fellow with the Centre for Foreign Policy Studies, Dalhousie University. He received his Ph.D. in International Relations and Comparative Politics from Cornell University and has held teaching positions at Queen's University, Carleton University, and Bilkent University (Ankara, Turkey). He has developed and taught courses on post-Cold War security, international relations theory, conflict management, forced displacement, and foreign policy. He has published widely on issues of peace-building, identity-based conflict, and governance. He is a member of the Consultative Board of the Butterfly Garden in Batticaloa, Sri Lanka and the Advisory Board of the Canadian Peace-building Coordinating Committee.

Tan Beng Hui is a freelance researcher trained in political economy and economic history. She also holds an M.A. in Women and Development from the Institute of Social Studies, Den Haag, the Netherlands. She has been involved in the Malaysian women's movement since 1990 and is a member of two NGOs, Women's Development Collective (WDC) and All Women's Action Society (AWAM).

Sandra J. MacLean is an Assistant Professor of Political Science at Dalhousie University, Halifax where she teaches courses on comparative politics and development, globalization and governance, and African politics. She holds adjunct appointments in the International Development Studies Program and the Department of Community Health and Epidemiology where she has taught courses on development and the political economy of health. Her most recent published work on issues of civil society, peace-building and new regionalisms has appeared in *Third World Quarterly, New Political Economy,* Gills (ed.), *Globalization and the Politics of Resistance* (Macmillan, 2000) and Lawton, et al., *Strange Power* (Ashgate, 2000).

Assis V. Malaquias received his Ph.D. in Political Science from Dalhousie University in Halifax, Canada. He is currently an Assistant Professor of Government at St. Lawrence University in Canton, NY, where he teaches courses in international politics, international political economy and African politics. He has published several articles on the conflict in Angola. His current research focusses on the politics of ethnicity and security in Southern Africa.

Pamela Mbabazi is Head of the Department of Development Studies at Mbarara University of Science and Technology (MUST) and Acting Dean of the Faculty of Development Studies. She was educated in Ghana, Germany and the UK as well as Uganda. She has recently received an IDRC grant for work on civil society in reconstruction in the Great Lakes Region and is co-author of a contribution to David Lewis and Tina Wallace (eds), *After the New Policy Agenda* (Kumarian, 2000).

Maznah Mohamad is an Associate Professor in Development Studies at the School of Social Sciences, Universiti Sains Malaysia and recently appointed Chair for the year 2001 of the Munk Centre for International Studies, University of Toronto, Canada. Her field of specialization is gender studies and development education. She has published a book on *The Malay Handloom Weavers: A History of the Rise and Decline of Traditional Manufacture* (Singapore: ISEAS) and co-edited a volume on 'Feminism: Malaysian Critique and Experience' (special issue of *Kajian Malaysia: Journal of Malaysian Studies*). Her article (co-authored with Cecilia Ng), 'The Management of Technology, and Women in Two Electronics Firms in Malaysia', was published in the *Journal of Gender, Technology and Development* (New Delhi: Sage).

Cecilia Ng is a feminist researcher from Malaysia. She previously taught at Universiti Putra Malaysia and is currently enjoying early retirement. As an Associate Professor at the university, her areas of interest included globalisation, technology and work. She is active in the women's movement in Malaysia and is a founding member of the Women's Development Collective (WDC) and the All Women's Action Society (AWAM).

Alfred G. Nhema is the chair of the Department of Political and Administrative Studies at the University of Zimbabwe. He received a Ph.D. in Political Science from Dalhousie University. He is also the author of a forthcoming book titled *Democracy in Zimbabwe: From Liberation to Liberalization*.

Maria Nzomo holds a Ph.D. in Political Science and International Studies. She has taught for 15 years at the University of Nairobi in the Department of Government and the Institute of Diplomacy and International studies. She has done research and published in the areas of political economy, international relations, and gender. She has also many years of experience working with NGOs/professional associations, engaged in training, advocacy and coordinating research networks. Since 1998, she has been serving as a Senior Program Coordinator at the Council for the Development of Social Science Research in Africa (CODESRIA), managing the institution's Civil Society Empowerment Program.

Abillah H. Omari is a Professor of Defence and Security Management and Director of the Centre for Foreign Relations, Dar es Salaam, Tanzania. He received his Ph.D. in Political Science from Dalhousie University. He has published articles on Southern African security issues. His current research interests are conflict in the Great Lakes Region of Africa and civil-military relations in Southern Africa. He is co-editor of a book entitled *In Search of Human Security in and for Africa* (UNU Press, 2001).

Fahimul Quadir is an Assistant Professor of Global Studies at St. Lawrence University, NY. He received a Ph.D. in Political Science from Dalhousie University with the support of a Social Science Research Council (USA) Dissertation Fellowship and a Killam Memorial Doctoral Scholarship. He has taught Political Studies at Queen's University and International Development Studies at Dalhousie University, Canada and Political Science at the University of Chittagong, Bangladesh. He also held research and consulting positions in both Canada and Bangladesh. He has recently published on such topics as economic liberalization, civil society, democratization, development and human security in *Contemporary South Asia, New Political Economy, Development Review*, Thomas and Wilkin (eds), *Globalization and the South*, Gills (ed.), *Globalization and the Politics of Resistance*, and Poku and Pettiford (eds), *Redefining the Third World.*

Johan Saravanamuttu is Professor from Universiti Sains Malaysia in Penang where he served as Dean from 1994-1996. In 1997, he was appointed Visiting Chair in ASEAN and International studies at the Centre for International Studies, University of Toronto. His published works include the first major study of *Malaysia's Foreign Policy* (1983), *ASEAN Regional Non-governmental Organizations* (1986) and the *Nexus between Industrialization and the Institutionalization of Authoritarian Regimes in Southeast Asia* (1991). He has also published numerous articles on issues pertaining to regional security, foreign investment, the role of major powers, the Cambodian peace process and the rise of the middle class as a factor in politics in journals such as *Contemporary Southeast Asia, Journal of*

Contemporary Asia, Sojourn, Security Dialogue, Interdisciplinary Peace Research, Journal of Oriental Studies and *Asian Journal of Political Science*.

Timothy M. Shaw is Visiting Professor of Development and International Relations at Aalborg University in 2000/1, on leave from Dalhousie University, where he served as Director of the Centre for Foreign Policy Studies. He has recently published essays in *Canadian Journal of Development Studies, New Political Economy* and *Third World Quarterly* as well as co-edited volumes on *Africa's Challenge to International Relations Theory* (Palgrave) and *In Search of Human Security in and for Africa* (UNU Press). He currently serves as Visiting Professor at Mbarara University of Science and Technology, Stellenbosch University and University of the Western Cape and as general editor of Ashgate Publishing's Series on New Regionalisms in the New Millennium.

J.P. Singh is Assistant Professor in the Communication, Culture and Technology Program at Georgetown University. He is the author of *Leapfrogging Development? The Political Economy of Telecommunications Restructuring* (SUNY, 1999) and co-editor (with James N. Rosenau) of *Information Technologies and Global Politics: The Changing Scope of Power and Governance* (SUNY, forthcoming, 2001). He is currently working on another book project titled *Communications and Diplomacy: Negotiating the Global Information Economy* (Macmillan/St. Martin's, forthcoming). He has taught in the past at Scripps College, UCLA, the University of Mississippi, and American University.

Janis van der Westhuizen (Ph.D., Dalhousie) teaches IPE in the Political Science Program, University of Natal, Durban. His research interests include state adaptation and societal resistance to globalization in the developing world; comparative political economy of Southeast Asia and Southern Africa; and South African foreign policy. He has recently co-edited, *Promoting Change? Aspects of Reformism in South Africa's Multilateral Diplomacy* (Ashgate).

Preface

Events and debates at the turn of the century have intensified challenges to both analyses and practices around global development. This volume presents our collective endeavor to both understand and advance these with special attention to prospects for democratic governance at all levels—from local to global through national and regional—given definitions and incidences of conflicts, ethnicities and pluralisms. The last two years which span the millennium have constituted a very welcome and intense period for all of us engaged in the Ford Foundation-supported collaborative project on 'Ethnicities in the Crises of Governance in Asia and Africa: pluralisms in the changing global political economy'.

And our involvement does not end with the publication of this set of original chapters as we will continue to be engaged in network and outreach around these salient issues in terms of both the analysis and practice of governance: how sustainable, accountable, transparent, enlightened at the start of the new century? The interdisciplinary, international project has already generated a series of both proposed and unanticipated products: from workshop and conference papers and discussions in collaboration with several professional associations to curriculum development and graduate theses in several universities. It will continue to inform ongoing discourses and policies, networks and events around state and non-state actors and think-tanks. In short, this volume is but a way station in our quest for improved understanding of and response to this set of important yet problematic issues and processes.

While participants and contributors come from a variety of national origins, theoretical perspectives and disciplinary bases, together we have been able to advance individual and collective analysis and praxis. In particular, we have all come to appreciate the diversity and nuance of definitions and discourses while agreeing that analysis of our central concepts in the new century requires the appreciation of a trio of central notions if we are to understand and advance governance rather than government. The former consists of patterns of discussion/negotiation/decision involving not just (small/large, old/new) states but also companies and NGOs. Therefore, centering our analyses around our two contrasting continents, we recognize and incorporate, for reasons of both analysis and practice, *a variety of actor types* in contemporary global and local development, notably private sectors and civil societies that are generating a range of norms/rules, both inter- and non-state. In short, current patterns of governance are reflective of the new medievalism that involves:

i) *multiple levels* of interactions amongst all three actor types, from cooperation to conflict, not necessarily nesting or compatible; and

ii) *human development/security* rather than national so that basic needs come to be respected and satisfied everywhere in as sustainable a manner as possible, especially in the least developed countries and communities concentrated in the South.

We welcome the timely opportunity which the Ford Foundation grant has provided for such analysis as the centuries changed and we hope that our revised, edited papers will advance both research and practice. We were able to seek and execute such a project because of common interests as well as some prior professional connections, facilitated in recent years by the global electronic highway. And we expect, now that these connections have been reinforced over the last 24 months, that this welcome experience will further advance such collaboration in coming years and months. Indeed, in association with BISA, IPSA and ISA sections, our own informal 'epistemic community' will continue for the foreseeable future, informing academic and applied analysis around national and global policy think-tank networks. Indeed, arising from a follow-up workshop one year after the one from which the present contributions derive, a parallel publication is already in preparation from the graduate student edited *International Insights* (vol. 15, no. 2, Fall, 2000) on 'Globalizations/New Regionalisms/Development'. We anticipate more such meetings and products over the next few years given the centrality of the issues being addressed and the energy of the analysts involved: a continuing concern about how to advance enlightened governance despite conflicts arising out of ethnicities, pluralisms and globalizations.

Finally, it is a real pleasure to recognize a few people without whom neither this volume nor the related events and activities would have transpired: Julius Ihonvbere, the energetic project officer for Governance and Civil Society at the Ford Foundation in New York, Clara Sarson, the indefatigable Administrator at the Centre for Foreign Policy Studies at Dalhousie University, past and present doctoral students in Political Science there, especially Andrew Grant, Ann Griffiths and Zoe Wilson, and last but certainly not least, my co-organizers and -editors, Sandra MacLean and Fahim Quadir, who have carried much more of the administrative and editorial burden than me as I was either striving to direct the Centre or escaping on research leave to northern Denmark: a very big thank you to you all, which I know will be echoed by readers and users of this timely title.

Timothy M. Shaw, Aalborg, June 2001

PART I

OVERVIEW

1 Pluralisms and the Changing Global Political Economy: Ethnicities in Crises of Governance in Asia and Africa

FAHIMUL QUADIR, SANDRA J. MACLEAN
AND TIMOTHY M. SHAW

> The end of the Cold War has certainly changed the nature of international relations. From the point of view of the South, it has both offered opportunities, in new coalitions and trading partners, and provided new constraints, in new political and economic conditionalities. From the discipline of IR (International Relations), the end of the Cold War has opened up the security agenda to new thinking, which has the potential to include concerns about development in a meaningful manner (Dickson, 1997: 149).

Introduction

This collaborative collection derives from an inter-disciplinary and international project that set out to investigate the inter-relationships between ethnicities and governance in Asia and Africa within the context of current transformations in the global political economy at the beginning of the new millennium. To some extent, such a focus of analysis may be seen to be rather traditional as the problem of managing pluralism in society has been a major preoccupation of orthodox political studies in the past. However, we believe that our focus remains timely and, in certain respects, it is even novel. In particular, it appears that ethnicities and ethno-nationalisms have resurfaced at the turn of the century as the critical focal points of various emancipatory and resistance movements *specifically* as responses to the pressures and changes of economic globalization(s). Moreover, the revival of forms of identity such as ethnicity as the unifying principle for political struggle appears to be a worldwide phenomenon.[1] Therefore, while

3

traditional preoccupations with nationalism, national identity and state behavior remain relevant to present discourses on crises of governance and resurgences of ethnicity, they are insufficient to explain fully the contemporary phenomena. Of equal salience are 'new' issues of security and organizational change resulting from the unprecedented rate and extent of transnational economic, technological and cultural exchange associated with globalizations.

Especially in developing areas of the world, these transformations hold profound implications for governance, with increasing potential for authoritarianism and/or anarchy, but also for novel ways of enhancing popular participation and of managing pluralisms. Therefore, this project was initiated as an attempt to explore the diverse and continuing crises of—as well as the opportunities for—sustainable human security and development in peripheral areas of the global economy. It investigates the relationships between ethnicities and governance in the two contrasting regions of Asia and Africa given changing relations, globally, among states, markets and civil societies: that is, the trio of actors that comprise the nexus of governance.

In this chapter, we seek to establish a framework for analyzing a range of factors which we believe to be critical to understanding, interpreting and predicting the ethnic dimensions of these new directions in social relationships and policy. First, we investigate globalizations as the major determinant of changing relationships among state, market and civil society. As the list at the end of this section indicates, the new divisions of labor which are associated with globalizing economies affect a wide range of issues and factors from foreign direct investment (FDI) to credit, labor relations/practices, and technological development/ use/transfer. The altered social behaviors and greater disparities in power and material advantage that are created by these new divisions of labor may produce friction between or among ethnic groups. Furthermore, especially as the state is increasingly more likely to function as a facilitator of global capitalist interests rather than to serve as a buffer protecting its citizens from the adverse effects of globalizations, traditional patterns and structures of 'governance' have less ability to mitigate identity-based rivalries. Hence, in the third section of this chapter we explore the complexities of governance under pressures of globalizations.

In our view, at the present conjuncture 'governance' involves continuous patterns of relations, decisions and/or policies among the heterogeneous trio of state, market and civil society actors over a diverse range of issues and levels. Our conceptualization is therefore rather different from the conventional state-centric view that governance is the manner in which government officials and institutions manage the economic and social resources of a country. Instead, we acknowledge that governance also involves systems of rules and patterns of behavior which are based upon norms and traditions outside formally sanctioned laws and statutes;

that is, 'goal-oriented activities ... backed by shared goals that may or may not derive from legal and formally prescribed responsibilities and that do not necessarily rely on police powers to overcome defiance and attain compliance' (Rosenau, 1992: 4). Moreover, even when the focal point of discussion or analysis is the state's governing structures and policies, it has become increasingly difficult to ignore the impact of broader political economy issues and the multi-level context in which state and non-state players interact on various core issues.

This has been recognized even by the World Bank, although it was this institution which introduced in its political conditionality agenda of the mid-1990s the narrow, state-centric definition of governance that has fuelled much of the present debate on the subject (see the section on governance in the context of globalization, below). Following the early prescriptions for 'good governance' that focussed on the instrumental functioning of the state—that is, on the accountability, transparency and responsiveness of government as the means for creating an enabling environment for the efficient operation of market economies and the advancement of multi-party political systems (World Bank, 1994)—the Bank's 1997 *World Development Report* (WDR) recognized that state capacity can be enhanced most effectively (and in some instances, only) through partnership with and/or sub-contracting to the business communities and civil societies. The Bank's new direction was developed even further in its 1999/2000 WDR which elaborated a 'post-neoliberal' triangular governance framework: a nexus comprised of business, democratic civil society and a 'developmentalist' (neo-Keynesian) state.

In the following two sections of this chapter, we draw on this conception of the governance 'triangle' to elaborate our view of the inter-related issues of governance within the context of global transformations. And, in the following sections, we relate these issues to crucial features of the new international divisions of labor and power in the area concentrated around the Indian Ocean Rim. The inter-related yet heterogeneous crises in the Asian and African continents to which these factors have given rise support the logic of comparative research on a set of issues that will help to show the impact of changing political economy factors on ethnicity as well as the effects of ethnic group politics on economic growth and forms and practices of governance. Therefore, the analyses in this volume are situated within new international political economy (IPE) theories and debates. And, within the overlapping frameworks of governance and economy, governance and civil society and governance and conflict, the authors examine a variety of inter-related issues that includes:

- foreign direct investment (FDI) and foreign exchange rates, industrialization and post-industrialism (for example, textiles/ automobiles, tourism/services);
- technologies (for example, satellites, telecommunications);
- credit (especially micro-ventures);
- labor (flexibilization and feminization/child labor);
- human (in)security (that is, the 'real' IPE of insecurity: issues of health and ecology as well as scarce resources from food and water to energy and diamonds);
- peacekeeping and peacemaking;
- culture (soft power);
- gender;
- human rights; and
- constitutions and administrations.

It is assumed that such issues have an impact upon official governance (elections, political parties, constitutional reform, state-economy interactions and NGO-state relations) as well as informal, 'third sector' systems of governance that have arisen around the regulating power of global capital and the so-called 'second movement'[2] responses to various human insecurities. They also contribute to/are reflective of changes in governance arrangements at the broadest level of world order, in relation to the development of 'growth triangles', 'new' regionalisms and 'new' multilateralisms.

As we discuss further in the final section, this research supports interdisciplinary and transnational approaches to analysis which draw upon and, hopefully, will inform several literatures and fields of study. Through a comparative approach to ethnicity and governance in Asia and Africa, our aim and rationale for this project is to explore new directions and contribute novel explanations in the fields of international political economy, development studies, area studies, foreign policy, new regionalisms, and global studies. Although concepts and problems of ethnicity and governance have been treated rather comprehensively in earlier, orthodox scholarship—indeed, they are central in the modernization paradigm that was hegemonic in the 1960s and into the 1970s—they are inadequately elaborated for the profound global transformation that is occurring at the beginning of the new century.

Re-arrangements in the juxtaposition of state, market and civil society offer unprecedented opportunities as well as challenges for creative analysis and praxis. It is intended that the edited research from this project will extend dialogue and debate on managing pluralism and promoting democratic participation at a time of unparalleled flux in political economies. Furthermore, it is hoped that the research will indicate new directions and options for (re)institutionalization for the twenty-first century so as to contain the complex and inter-related threats to human security while taking advantage of the openings for furthering the ideals of human emancipation and human development/security.

Globalization(s)

Processes of global interaction and interdependence have become impossible to ignore, with the result that the concept of 'globalization' has galvanized academic interest throughout the 1990s and into 2000. As the discourse on globalization(s) has unfolded, there has been a noticeable change in the focus of the debates. Initially, many scholars questioned the degree to which 'globalization' was either new or transformative (Amoore, et al., 1997). Most authors of the current 'second wave' of analysis, however, accept that a fundamental change in world order is occurring or impending and the debate has shifted from questioning *if* to *how* and *how much* globalization processes affect ecological, economic, political and social life (Held, et al., 1999; Jones, 2000; Schaeffer, 1997; Sens and Stoett, 1998; Woods, 2000).

Attempts to understand globalization and its consequences cross analytical disciplines and theoretical perspectives. These have led to a variety of reactions and debates as well as a profusion of definitions which describe globalization variously as a phenomenon of increasing economic interdependence, of technological advances that diminish space and time, of cultural homogenization, and of emerging global social and political identities (Scholte, 1997: 15). In many instances, such definitions imply that globalization is a singular, unilinear and/or inevitable process. However, globalization processes are experienced unevenly. Indeed, given the intense disparity and dislocation associated with the changes in production, socialization and politicization, it is probably more appropriate to speak of globalizations than to refer to a single phenomenon. As Mittelman (1994: 17-18) notes, globalizations involve multiple features and experiences that include 'the worldwide interpenetration of industries, the spread of financial markets, the diffusion of identical consumer goods to distant countries, undocumented workers feeding a resurgence of sweatshops in the United States, Korean merchants coming into conflict with African-Americans in formerly tight-knit neighborhoods, and an emerging global preference for democracy'. Overall, globalizations are profoundly contradictory, combining both 'a fundamental shift towards an integrated and coordinated division of labor in production and trade' and a simultaneous fractionalization of social order, widening of economic disparities and multiplying political disintegrations (Chin and Mittelman, 1997: 25).

The complex interplay of 'material capabilities, ideas and institutions' that determine change in world order (Cox, 1981: 136) precludes the possibility of explaining globalizations by a single, deterministic rationale. Nevertheless, as Mittelman's observations suggest, much of the current social polarization can be traced to the transnationalization of production and related deregulations of financial markets and trade regimes. Moreover, even if the 'idea of "modern times" and a "global" place are the products of historical developments stretching back about five hundred years' (Schaeffer, 1997: vii), a concatenation of events beginning with the collapse of the Bretton Woods monetary order in the early 1970s has increased the rate of speed of globalization processes.[3]

The growing preeminence of neoliberalism[4] as the ordering principle of international relations has been a major factor in economic globalization(s). Amorre, et al. (1997: 181) list several defining characteristics of economic globalization all of which have obvious implications for transforming social relations and political institutionalization. They include: i) an expansion of the process of capitalist accumulation; ii) the tendency 'toward the homogenization of state policies'; iii) 'the addition and expansion of a layer of transnational institutional authority above the states'; and iv) 'the exclusion of dissident forces from the arena of state policy making'. An important consequence of these changes is embodied within Robert Cox's concept of the 'internationalization of the state' which describes a shift in the state's priority away from the domestic constituency in favor of transnational capital. Whereas traditionally it was assumed that the state served principally as the moderator, protector and/or embodiment of citizen (or at least national elite) interests, the 'internationalized' state has become, first and foremost, a facilitator of transnational market interests (Cox, 1991: 337), especially, as we note above, though intermediary-seeking partnerships with compatible or compliant corporate or civil society actors (World Bank, 1997).

The results of the changes in the role and nature of the state are manifold. Among the more positive of these changes has been the resurgence of a democratization momentum. The new social movements and numerous non-governmental organizations (NGOs) that are feature-players in the so-called, 'politics of resistance' and/or 'globalization from below' are often considered to be emancipatory and democratizing forces because of the role they have assumed in promoting the interests and encouraging the political participation of previously marginalized groups. However, while some of the renewed vibrancy in civil societies appears to represent democratic, 'bottom-up' pressures for greater autonomy and more direct and local control of livelihoods and ecologies against the commodifying and regulating power of global capital (Gill, 1995), the increased vigor has an obvious downside as well. In particular, many of the reactions within civil societies reflect heightened levels of social intolerance, often expressed in 'identity-based' conflict and demands (see section on ethnicity and governance below).

Of the various struggles which have erupted within the new international divisions of labor and power (NIDL/P) of the post-Cold War era, increasing ethnic rivalries are perhaps the most apparent, and also the most troublesome to resolve. Over a relatively short period of time and in many parts of the world, long-forgotten (or at least quiescent or quietly simmering) rivalries among various ethnic groups have erupted into brutal and protracted conflicts. Given both the velocity and vehemence of most of these violent eruptions, policy-makers, citizen groups and scholars have been caught somewhat unaware, inadequately prepared to reach sustainable resolutions or even to understand the reasons for the outbreaks. Clearly, increasing economic constraint within several countries has led to political competition and struggles among different social groups which depend upon the same pool of diminishing resources. However, as international peacekeepers in these proliferating conflicts have discovered, neither the causes nor the fallout from these struggles can be easily understood or resolved by traditional modes of analysis or policy. In most, if not all, recent confrontations, the dimensions of the crises extend across national boundaries to the regional and beyond. They include non-state and informal as well as official actors, and they merge complex sets of issues involving ecology, economics, gender, human rights and security as well as group, national, regime and inter- or trans-national interests.

The unprecedented complexity of pressures, issues and actors is a critical feature of a 'new' security environment and an apparent manifestation of a major transformation in world order. And, clearly, traditional thinking on issues of management and governance is destabilized by the fact that the new insecurities can be understood only in terms of the inter-related activities of states, international organizations, business and civil societies. The complications of governance at the present conjuncture are evident at all functional levels. For instance, in recent security crises, confusion has arisen at the level of field operations with regard to issues of appropriate authority, legitimate chains of command, coordination of actors, etc.

More fundamentally, the new security agenda raises questions about the nature of sovereignty, citizenship and political identity and even the continuing relevance and legitimacy of the Westphalian state. As Amoore, et al. (1997: 185) assert, we are witnessing a 'profound disjuncture between the persistence of territorial sovereignty as the organizing principle of international politics and the increasing global structure of finance, production, society and culture'. Local, regional, and global actors are now juxtaposed next to the state at the center of political order and informal as well as formal actors figure prominently in the multiple forms and levels of governance (for example, the 'new' regionalisms, 'new' multilateralisms and new functionalisms) that appear to be emerging (Archibugi and Held, 1995; Finkelstein, 1995; Hettne and Inotai, 1997; Cox, 1997). As well, new analytical perspectives, to which we will turn in the concluding section of the chapter, have evolved in correspondence with the development of these new political arrangements and the myriad signs that:

> the old system is resolving into a complex of political-economic entities: micro-regions, traditional states, and macro-regions with institutions of greater or lesser functional scope and formal authority. World cities are the keyboards of the global economy. Rival transnational processes of ideological transformation aim respectively at hegemony and counter-hegemony. Institutions of concertation and coordination bridge the major states and macro-regions. Multilateral processes exist for conflict management, peace keeping, and regulation and service providing in a variety of functional areas (trade, communications, health, etc.). The whole picture resembles the multilevel order of medieval Europe more than the Westphalian model of a system of sovereign independent states that has heretofore been the paradigm of international relations (Cox, 1992: 36).

Various mixed actor coalitions have emerged as a result of such transformations. Previously unconnected actors and seemingly diverse interests often converge (albeit not always compatibly) in the establishment, for instance, of regional security communities and civil societies as well as regional economies, trading blocs, triangles and corridors.[5] These 'new regionalisms' reflect changing relations (and also have significant implications for future relations) among a wide range of actors, from micro-enterprises to multinational corporations (MNCs). And, they involve various issues including: the advancement, control and exchange of technology; environmental degradation and/or protection; child labor, gender relations, and various other human rights and cultural issues; crime; the privatization of security and proliferating private armies, mercenaries, and gangs; and health—from the transnational spread of both communicable and non-communicable diseases to the migration of health-care workers. They also have important implications for the ways in which people self-identify and co-exist with those they perceive to be different. In short, it appears that multiple and probably fundamental recombinations and reorderings in economic, political and social relations are occurring as the results of exponential globalizations. The management of such changes, especially for the enhancement of human security and sustainable development, will be a function of effective governance. And, given the multi-layered and multi-faceted complexity of contemporary politics, the concept of governance deserves more careful scrutiny than it is often accorded.

Governance in the Context of Globalizations

As the pressures on the Westphalian system have intensified, the lines of convergence and departure between informal and formal governance structures have become both more complicated and more apparent. Governance in both Asia and Africa, as in other regions, has been profoundly affected by changing combinations of states, companies and civil society relations. In short, as one of us has asserted elsewhere (in Shaw and van der Westhuizen, 1999: 257) and as several case studies in this volume show:

> 'Authoritative' decisions are no longer the monopoly of supposedly 'sovereign' states, but may also be made by corporations and/or NGOs, especially within their mixed-actor coalitions as over, say, biodiversity, child labor, land-mines, ozone depletion, tropical forests etc. Within EPZs [export processing zones] and corridors/triangles, governance is almost entirely non-state. Conversely, such triangular relations may lead to novel forms of company or NGO-dominated corporatisms.

Yet, despite the mounting evidence of new and varied forms and dimensions of governance, a state-centric, institutionally-oriented definition tends to prevail—that is, governance is frequently conceived narrowly as governmental processes. Indeed, such a concept was evident in the introductory phase of the World Bank's discourse on 'good governance' which became the locus for policy among the Organization of Economic Cooperation and Development (OECD) donor community and the major organizations of the inter-state system. In the early 1990s, this powerful group of official actors rapidly coalesced around the Bank's 'good governance' project which was embedded in a neoliberal ideology that supported the promotion of liberal democracy, human rights and strong civil societies as essential preconditions for sustainable economic growth and social development (Islam and Morrison, 1996: 5).

Despite the strength of the 'Washington consensus'—the name by which the ideological and policy convergence of these powerful international players came to be known—recent signs indicate that the easy hegemony of neo-liberalism has peaked. As evidenced first by its 1997 *World Development Report* (World Bank, 1997) and more explicitly by the latest edition (World Bank, 1999/2000), the World Bank has begun to move back toward a more Keynesian perspective. Under the leadership of James Wolfensohn and Joseph Stiglitz, a concern within the Bank both to understand and strengthen the links between 'globalization' and 'localization' (World Bank 1999/2000: iii and 4) in a revised, more 'comprehensive development framework' (World Bank 1999/2000: 21) has become apparent (see Shaw, MacLean and Nzomo, 2000: 394). This new direction,[6] recently validated by the cautionary notes on neoliberalism of disparate analysts from George Soros to Gerry Helleiner ('Special Issue in Honour of Helleiner', 1999), provides a strong rationale for research projects such as the one on which this volume is based.

The Evolution in the World Bank Approach to Governance

The increasing nuance in the World Bank's approach to governance throughout the 1990s followed an equally significant change in policy direction in the 1980s that perhaps reflected, but at least coincided with economic trends from Asian miracle to crisis and African crisis to (anticipation of) renaissance. Throughout most of the 1980s the World Bank was primarily occupied with its economic reform programs, popularly known as structural adjustment programs (SAPs), which fostered the assumption that market-oriented reforms were the only means to resolve the debt crisis of the developing world. During that period, the so-called 'Asian miracle' was frequently presented as the result of effective economic policy choice and African countries were instructed to get their macro-economic balances in order. However, by the end of the 1980s, it became quite evident that most developing economies were either not growing, or growing much more slowly than the Bank had originally anticipated. Many of them failed to achieve the macro-economic targets through structural economic reforms, becoming more indebted then ever before (World Bank, 1992a). In addition, much of the developing world experienced a declining living standard for the majority.[7]

Responding to growing criticism arising from the apparent failure of structural adjustment programs (SAPs) to resolve the developing world's myriad macro-economic problems, the Bank published its first major revisionist analysis in 1989. The document, entitled *Sub-Saharan Africa: From Crisis to Sustainable Growth*, dealt with the various factors that were seemingly preventing African countries from implementing successful market-oriented reforms. To the surprise of many, it suggested a link between political and economic reforms, identifying the importance of effective public sector organizations in carrying out successful economic reform programs. The document blamed African public institutions for the region's deepening economic crisis by suggesting that 'a root cause of weak economic performance in the past has been the failure of public institutions'[8]—in short, Africa's contemporary economic misery was a crisis of national governance.

As a consequence of this conclusion, the report came up with the notion of 'good governance'. Defined by the Bank as 'the manner in which power is exercised in the management of a country's economic and social resources for development' (World Bank, 1992b: 3), 'governance' became the policy response to growing developmental problems facing many countries in the region: a goal for the South in the post-bipolar 1990s. The lack of good governance, according to the Bank, not only destroys the ability of a country to develop an enabling environment for sustainable growth but it also intensifies people's suffering.

The Bank's early, orthodox concept of good governance had four main dimensions: i) public sector management (PSM); ii) accountability; iii) a legal framework for development; and iv) transparency and information accessibility (World Bank, 1994: viii). Primarily concerned with the ability of the public sector effectively to manage public programs and to provide an 'enabling environment for the public sector', PSM identifies three key areas—civil service, financial management and the state enterprise sector—where the need for reform is unavoidable (*Ibid*.: 2). By accountability, the Bank means 'holding public officials responsible for their actions' (World Bank, 1992b: 13). Under the title of 'legal framework for development', questions are discussed regarding the setting up of appropriate legal systems for resolving conflicts that might impede the construction of market mechanisms. Finally, the Bank seeks to create governance systems which guarantee that private entrepreneurs will enjoy unrestricted access to relevant information. It has identified three main areas where greater transparency and improved information access enable the economy to become more open and competitive. These areas are: economic efficiency; transparency as a means of preventing corruption; and the availability of credible information that is required for investment operations (*Ibid*.: 39).

The Bank's concept of 'good governance' has drawn criticism from scholars, activists and policy-makers who claim that it is biased toward the promotion of market economies rather than human security or rights. Furthermore, with the 'good governance' project, the Bank continued to put all the blame for the problems and the responsibility for reform on 'domestic institutions and policies' (Islam and Morrison, 1996: 7). It did not admit that structural adjustment programs have been profoundly flawed in terms of distributing the costs and benefits equally (Oxfam, 1995: 6; Schmitz, 1995: 67). Perhaps it was at least partly in response to such criticism, that the Bank's 1997 *World Development Report* (WDR), *The State in a Changing World,* began to revise its concept of governance with the argument that it is possible 'to make every state a more credible, effective partner in its country's development' through a 'two-part strategy'. The first part of this strategy centers on 'matching the state's role to its capability' and recognizing the limits in the state's capacity for fulfilling its responsibilities effectively. The second part involves building capacity through partnership with the business community and civil society. The concept of the governance 'triad', which has been further elaborated in the 1999/2000 WDR is more progressive still, especially with the inclusion of civil society as a partner with the state.

However, the Bank has not yet set a particularly good example in its own dealings with civil society actors, tending, for example, to view NGOs as sub-contractors rather than partners. Moreover, its view of governance remains rather orthodox, being still exclusively focussed on the national level, if not entirely the state. Indeed, according to some critics, the Bank's position on governance has been and still is an ideological product of the dominant liberal perspective. As Bonnie Campbell (2000: 14) argues, for example, in its 1997 Report, the Bank 'advocates not only very specific notions of the state, its evolution and proper functioning, but also a very precise notion of state-market relations—in short, an unrealistic representation given the recognized diversity in the form and nature of the state in the developing world'. Overall, it appears that the Bank's underlying thesis, while encased in more progressive wrappings, may still be subject to the criticisms made previously that it is primarily engaged in replicating the Western—especially American—model of socio-economic development (Moore, 1993). Or, as Geoff Wood (1997: 79) suggests: 'good governance represents a revival of ethnocentric, modernizing ideology, attempting to make the myths of one society reality in another'.

USAID and ODA Variations on Governance

Strong criticisms notwithstanding, the World Bank's 'good governance' project has been responsible for focussing considerable analytical attention on the problematic of governance. Moreover, although the evolving definitions which the Bank has employed have become standards of comparison, variant perspectives on governance have emerged from bilateral donors, NGOs and critics. As partial remedy to the early formulaic conceptualizations of the Bank and the United Nations Development Program (UNDP), for example, major bilateral donor organizations/agencies in the Development Assistance Committee (DAC) of the Organization for Economic Cooperation and Development (OECD), including the United States Agency for International Development (USAID), Norwegian Agency for International Development (NORAD), Canadian International Development Agency (CIDA) and Swedish International Development Agency (SIDA), adopted more interactive approaches to democracy, human rights, civil society and the free market. USAID's 'good governance' programs have been primarily concerned with strengthening the institutions of what it calls 'free societies'. In addition to promoting pluralist, multi-party democracy, its programs aim to develop an enabling environment for civil society. Considering the latter as the forum for protecting and advancing basic individual freedoms, this organization provides financial and technical assistance to the development of vibrant, autonomous civil societies in the developing world (Blair, 1992).

Similarly, the 'good governance' programs of the UK Department for International Development (DFID), formerly Overseas Development Administration (ODA), are designed to improve governmental accountability in order to allow ordinary citizens to play a role in choosing their leaders and policies. In particular, DFID seeks to develop a structure of governance, which is legitimate, efficient and transparent and it directs its development assistance towards the protection of basic human rights, such as freedoms of speech, religion and organization. Like USAID, its policy encourages civil society organizations to participate effectively in various socio-political activities (Glentworth, 1993).

Overall, these major bilateral donors, like multilateral agencies such as the World Bank, have been contributing resources to support democratization and market reform initiatives through their 'good governance' programs in different parts of the world. And although there have been some differences in approach and emphasis, all have tended to channel a considerable amount of their resources through specific civil society organizations in order to promote a variety of related goals, such as human rights, individual liberties and micro-credit activities (Blair, 1992).

Conceptions of Global Governance

The 'Washington consensus' approaches to governance of the World Bank and major bilateral donors have been primarily concerned with events and processes within national boundaries. Nevertheless, they inform (and are informed by) three emerging, competing discourses on 'global governance': i) a neoliberal position on 'global governance' which endorses and reinforces the view that there is a positive correlation between the worldwide extension of capitalist relations and the distribution of Western-style liberal democracy; ii) a counter-view by critical scholars who view the Washington consensus as the driving force behind the establishment of a system of norms and behaviors that is contributing to the exacerbation of global disparities in wealth and power; and iii) a more visionary perspective which interprets 'global governance' to mean a revolutionary change in the structures and relations of governance.

Each of these discourses has particular relevance for this project and collection. First, they situate analysis of changing state, market and civil society relations within the context of an emerging global polity that is constituted by a set of rules and norms (that is, a governance structure) that is distinct from—but nevertheless affects—those that operate at the national level. Second, especially the third concept of global governance offers innovative possibilities for conceiving new institutions of governance for a post-Westphalian order, with some of the more enlightened reflections on the subject being those of Daniele

Archibugi and David Held (1995) on 'cosmopolitan democracy', Anthony Gidden (1999) on 'the Third Way', and Richard Falk (1995) on governance based upon 'laws of humanity' rather than on 'laws of state'.

Of the three concepts of 'global governance' identified above, the neoliberal view has been hegemonic, but it is increasingly challenged. The apotheosis of the neoliberal position on global governance is Francis Fukuyama's (1989) thesis that the world has reached 'the end point of mankind's ideological evolution and the universalism of Western liberal democracy is the final form of human government'. Conceptually and ideologically, Fukuyama's neoliberal ideas of global governance are based upon the Kantian globalist ideal of universal moral principles (Spegele, 1992) and the appealingly humanist project of establishing common ground for peaceful international cooperation and democratic co-existence. Yet, critical scholars argue compellingly that the idealist component of liberal theory envisaging universal, unilinear progress is at odds with empirical evidence indicating that dominant neoliberalism is producing increasing disparities in wealth and security. Therefore, as Sinclair (1997) has asserted, global governance should be conceptualized as a neoliberal project and a process by which elite decision-makers construct popular understandings of the way that the world works.

Emerging debates such as the ones we discuss below on the declining eminence of 'Asian values' and the possibilities of 'African renaissance' hinge on the suggestion in both cases that the neoliberal system of 'global governance' which is emerging is much less benign than its proponents suggest. The emerging changes in the traditional configuration of state, market and civil society relations may have serious negative implications for human security. As Stephen Gill (1994b: 17) points out:

> Centralized state structures and the forms of sovereignty associated with them are changing in ways which are more consistent with the development of a more market-driven form of civil society: statism and social protection are on the retreat and are giving way to a more individualistic, competitive and disciplinary political culture and society.

From a similar viewpoint, Ankie Hoogvelt (1997: 181) argues that 'there is an emerging system of global governance with methods and instruments geared to containing and managing symptoms rather than removing causes'. In short, there appears to be a connection between the escalation in conflict situations and the regulating properties of the new order. Moreover, there appears to be little incentive as yet for dominant players to encourage or support structural changes that might alleviate conditions of underdevelopment that contribute to conflict.

One of the major objectives, then, of the case studies in this volume is to show if and where any connections—existential and theoretical—exist between ethnic conflict or rivalry and political economy change. An important aspect of this research involves investigating the various 'bottom-up' insurgencies which feature centrally in the third conceptualization of 'global governance'. Revived civil societies, in both empirical and theoretical senses, are now established as necessary partners in the governance triad, at least at the national level. However, the roles and relevance for governance of regional and global civil societies is less well understood, although the fact of their existence seems to be less frequently challenged, if nevertheless still controversial. It does appear that multiple groups in civil societies around the world are now collaborating in a variety of interlinked, transnational networks, often in reactions against economic, ecological, political and cultural insecurities.

Interaction among previously disparate social groups appears to be increasing as the inter-relatedness of issues such as gender, health, human rights, ecology, and economic development become more apparent and as improved technology in communications and travel is effectively shrinking time and distance. The 'new' social movements, NGOs and local associations—that is, the various actors which feature centrally in processes of globalization-from-below—have created significant challenges for governance at the turn of the century. To some extent, the activism in civil society may be seen as emancipatory, enlarging prospects for extending democracy to a global level of polity (Held, 1997). Yet, not all of the new energy in civil society is enlightened or progressive: the emergence of anti-democratic, anarchist or otherwise 'dangerous classes' and groups (Falk, 1997: 21) has led in several areas to intense social fragmentation. Such processes are central to the analysis of several of our case studies on ethnicities, as are the corresponding increases in many areas in government authoritarianism and/or the growing phenomenon of private security forces.

The possibilities and problems created by these rearrangements within and among civil societies, states and markets have forced a re-examination of official frameworks for governance, in which case 'global governance' may refer to new directions or experiments in institutional structures or behaviors (see for example, Ku and Weiss, 1998). The systems of the UN and the International Financial Institutions (IFIs) are the most frequently targeted sites for revision, and various recommendations have been made for greater coordination among the actors that comprise these systems as well as for increased participation within them by non-state actors.[9] Yet, although many of the analyses focus on 'improving international governance'[10] as a step toward or an alternative to global governance, others envisage more fundamental restructurings along lines which will reflect the multiple forms and levels of 'governance' that are now emerging. As several of our case studies indicate, new regionalisms and multilateralisms are taking shape, with varying degrees of convergence, overlap and/or competition among the interests which drive them. Diverse informal and/or covert systems of rules of interaction and exchange (i.e., 'governance') co-exist, cooperate or contend with official structures, for example: in 'new' security operations of peacekeeping, peacebuilding and confidence building (Weiss and Smith, 1997); in 'flexible', post-Fordist economic production and exchange schedules (Helleiner, 1994a); in ecology initiatives that involve various combinations of regimes, epistemic communities and 'new' and 'old' social movements; and in the 'covert' world's, 'inter-related activities of organized crime, intelligence services, money-laundering banking, the arms trade and the like' (Cox, 1997: 114; see also Cox, 1999).

Governance, then, at the turn of the century is disturbingly pluralist as already indicated above. In the transformation of the Westphalian order, unprecedented opportunities for extending democratization have developed within the fissures of the dominant neoliberal order, but the circumstances are also ripe for dramatic and painful social upheavals.

Pluralisms and Popular Participation in Decision-Making

At this conjuncture, the notion of 'pluralism(s)' has thus become much more nuanced than is inferred in traditional conceptualizations that are fixated on political realms defined by institutional structures and enclosed by national boundaries. And, while recognizing that expanded, revisionist definitions may lose some explanatory elegance and exclusivity, a broader definition of 'pluralism' is probably more empirically accurate for the present period of globalizations. Moreover, the almost exclusive use of the term to denote a liberal democratic form of governance (within the strictures of Westphalianism) has come about largely by custom. A more exacting application refers to a general philosophical precept, as the following quotation from Dunleavy and O'Leary (1987: 13) indicates:

> Pluralism is the belief that there are, or ought to be, many things. It offers a defence of multiplicity in beliefs, institutions and societies, and opposes 'monism'—the belief that there is, or ought to be, only one thing. Pluralism began as a philosophy which argued that reality cannot be explained by one substance or principle. Similarly, political pluralism recognizes the existence of diversity in social, institutional and ideological practices, and values that diversity.

Clearly, by this conceptualization, 'pluralism' is an apt, if somewhat elusive, concept with which to grapple if we are to understand the present processes of governance, especially if, at the start of the twenty-first century, the world order is in the midst of a transformation towards post-Westphalianism.

The recent resurgence of interest in the concept of 'pluralism' follows the trend toward the emphasis on democracy, free markets, human rights and development. Recalling the ideas which dominated the discussion of many comparativists, including Robert Dahl and Charles Lindblom, during the 1950s and 1960s,[11] much of the recent analysis has focussed on the need for legitimizing various types of activities undertaken by a wide variety of interest and/or pressure groups as natural contrasts to oligarchy. Emerging as a direct challenge to legal formalism, pluralism rejects the assumption that political power is concentrated in the formal structures of the state. Most proponents of pluralism argue that in a democratic setting, political resources are widely distributed among different interest groups. Such a situation allows various associations to play a critical role in decision-making behind the formal and institutional structures of the state on the one hand, and creates the conditions necessary for limiting the power of the state, on the other (Almond 1990). In other words, pluralism is defined as a system of governance in which socio-political groups freely interact with each other and the state in informal and uncontrolled ways (Schmitter and Lehmbruch, 1979).

For the purpose of this volume, however, we identify the importance of taking the conventional agenda of pluralism beyond the interaction of formal interest groups. In particular, this research focusses on the issue of 'diversity' as an important element of pluralism and it suggests that the future of sustainable democracy and development in the South will largely rely upon the ability of different groups and communities to protect and promote their political, cultural, social and economic interests within a context of multiple pressures of local, national, regional and global dimensions. In addition to exposing avenues for representation of various groups in government structures, it seeks to examine the possibilities of greater participation of different ethnic, religious and political communities in decision-making at all levels—local, national, regional and global. A variety of issues such as multilateralism, regionalism and global governance will be reviewed through this collection in order to examine the future of pluralism in both Asia and Africa.

This study makes an effort then to identify the structural and cultural factors and/or issues that have continued to discourage disempowered sections of the population in several countries of Asia and Africa from both asserting their rights and reducing their political vulnerability—in short, enhancing their human security/prospects of human development. Looking at the recent economic and technological changes in the global political economy, this collaborative research also explores the possibility of offering a broader perspective on pluralism that attaches considerable attention to the process of enabling marginalized groups and communities to manage and control their own resources. More specifically, it examines the prospects for developing pluralist frameworks designed to reduce the powerlessness of various disadvantaged groups at the turn of the twentieth century—that is, it includes an explicitly normative dimension.

The normative aspects of governance involve ideas which capture people's imagination and serve as motivation for political action. Recently, in both Asia and Africa, such ideas have emerged and, in the former, a normative discourse has developed around the notion of 'Asian values', and in the latter, around 'African renaissance'. In the following section, and in several of the chapters of the volume, both the ideational power and the empirical implications of these concepts are explored.

The Challenge of 'Asian Values', the Financial Crisis and the Prospects for Democratic Governance

The burgeoning debate over 'Asian values' creates the need for exploring alternative forms of governance within the changing political economy of Asia in general, and Southeast Asia, in particular. Asian advocates, particularly, those in the assertive 'Singapore School',[12] centered in official institutions in the successful but assertive island-state (Mabubhani, 1998), argue that institutional arrangements in the structures of governance vary significantly between governments primarily for cultural reasons. Kaushikan (1997:30), for instance, suggests that, since cultures and values differ from one society to another, the specific forms of political and social organization appropriate to these societies should also differ. In other words, the authors of the Singapore School claim that Western standards of democracy and human rights are inappropriate in societies that are governed by the ethics of collectivity, harmony and hierarchy.

Such cultural arguments inevitably necessitate the search for non-universal and non-Western models of governance that not only promote individual responsibilities rather than individualism, but also focus on the strict maintenance of law and order rather than freedoms. This type of governance structure is capable of, as claimed by the authors of the Singapore School, limiting conflicts between the state and major socio-economic groups. The assumption is that, such a corporatist arrangement (similar to that expressed in the 1997 *World Development Report*) develops a complementary state-society relationship which is vital to the attainment of development goals (Evans, 1995).

However, a variety of civil society groups, both internal and external, began to challenge these cultural arguments, suggesting that the so-called doctrine of 'Asian values' is largely used to limit individual freedoms and rights. The critics of the Singapore School strongly disagree with the commonly used assumption that the most important question is not whether a government is democratic, but rather whether the system works for both the country and its people. Margaret Ng (1997), for instance, claims that the crucial point in the 'good government' debate is the ability of the government to protect the autonomy of human beings. In other words, 'good government' refers to a system that defends fundamental freedoms of speech, assembly and human rights.

Questioning the false dichotomy between Western and Asian cultural standards, the critics of the Singapore School are, therefore, trying to develop a bridge between these cultural divides so that the region can meet the twin challenge of democratization and development in the twenty-first century. In so doing, they focus on the creation of conditions that are conducive to 'a more steady and stable democratization and the entrenchment of human rights' (Chen and Edwards, 1997: 6).

The recent financial crisis strengthens further the position of these critics who seek to overthrow the old, authoritarian political order. Although the crisis did not last long enough to create a momentum for democracy, it certainly exposed, as discussed in the chapter in this volume by Mohamad, et al., the inherent weakness of what is called 'Asian democracy'. What is even more important to observe is that such a crisis brought out the contradictions of the so-called 'Asian miracle' which once inspired the international donor community, especially the World Bank, to replicate the so-called Asian model of development elsewhere (World Bank, 1993a). Van der Westhuizen makes this point in his chapter in this volume, arguing that although Malaysia had been considered to be a 'developmentalist' state at least in part because of the closely collaborative nature of business and government, the recent crisis has exposed some problems with this growth model. As van der Westhuizen argues:

> In Malaysia, the complexity of separating business interests from political players, in combination with the stifled role of labor and relatively firm controls over civil society made for greater capture than collaboration.

Contrary to what many analysts hoped, then, the financial crisis did not create the conditions for democratization in the region. Nor did it help civil society groups to emerge as a real challenge to 'authoritarian states'. Instead, in some cases, such as Malaysia, the crisis actually enabled the state to use the vulnerability of civil society to its own political advantage. Saravanamuttu's chapter in this volume shows how the state in Malaysia under the leadership of Mahathir Mohamad manipulated the crisis to strengthen its position, which was reflected clearly in the comfortable victory of Prime Minister Mahathir's Barisan National coalition government in the general elections in 1999. By contrast, civil society groups, as discussed in the chapter by Mohamad, et al., failed to seize the opportunity to mobilize popular sentiment against the developmentalist state. They were not able to initiate a larger movement for democracy partly because of their relatively weak organizational structures. Their inability to draw support from big business also helped Mahathir to remain in power for at least another term.

Africa: Renaissance or a New Realism?

While the same pattern of growth and decline clearly does not apply, issues involving the aftermath of the Asian crisis resonate in Africa (see Van der Westhuizen's discussion of this). While the phenomenon of the Asian success had been drawn on frequently as a model for integrating Africa into the global economy, lessons from the recent crisis now serve as cautionary notes (Chan, 1999). Similarly, although more intensely than in the Asian cases, the social, economic and political problems associated with the well-documented 'crisis of the state' in Africa are of acute and distressing concern. Also similar to Asia, the sources and consequences of the crisis go well beyond the policy choices of governing elites; both state 'failures' and increases in bottom-up pressures are strongly influenced by the present transformations in world order. Finally, as an interesting comparative point, the idea of 'African renaissance' has some correspondence with the parallel discourse on 'Asian values'.

A major similarity between the African and Asian discourses is the emphasis in both on strategies that will allow the respective continents and communities to engage with the global economy on their own terms. However, opinions differ as to whether the idea of renaissance was intended, or should be interpreted, as a bid for Africa to embrace the neoliberal ideology associated with globalization. Amidst pressures for states, companies and civil societies to conform to the rules imposed by global capitalism, some scholars, as we have already noted, are warning that this unofficial and non-legitimized, but nevertheless authoritative and coercive, system of 'governance' is not only unlikely to support improvements in human security or development, but is actually unsustainable (Gill, 1995: 422). Some even have predicted apocalyptic outcomes, warning that unless we devise new methods for governing in this increasingly pluralist world, we are heading toward a new realism—not the 'realism' which was based upon a regulated hierarchy of sovereign states, but, rather 'an ugly futurism' of ecological catastrophe and social desolation (Kaplan, 1994; Athanasiou, 1998).

Critics of neoliberal globalism continue to search for cracks in the dominant order within which there are some opportunities for advancing in new directions based upon 'an entirely new universe of ideas and values that would provide the basis for human liberation' (Bobbio, 1979: 42). The idea of 'African renaissance' may contain such a possibility from the margins.

Clearly, it would be absurd to underestimate the realities of poverty, insecurity, disparity and cynicism which militate against the probability of rejuvenation. Moving beyond the optimism that accompanied the early days of democratization and reconstruction in the new South Africa, it now seems improbable, as the chapters by MacLean and van der Westhuizen suggest, that the country might be the center of rebirth in Africa. Moreover, if one looks to the neighboring countries of Zimbabwe or those in Great Lakes region, and as chapters by Mbabazi, Omari, Malaquais and Nhema clearly show, the emergence, and/or continuation of conflict and unrest, makes the prospects of sustainable order and democracy quite unlikely for the foreseeable future. Yet, the notion of renaissance has had a galvanizing effect on imaginations perhaps mostly because of the emancipatory imagery it conveys (Vale and Maseko, 1998). And, it is too soon to discount the importance to development of the optimism that generated the debate on renaissance. As with notions of 'Asian values' or the 'Asian way', the idea of 'African renaissance' has opened up avenues for case studies such as the ones of this project to explore alternative and innovative strategies for managing pluralism in the new world order of the twenty-first century.

Overall, for this volume, we employ an analytical framework that places the problematic of managing pluralism within the broad context of both change in the global political economy and in the emergence of new norms and ideas. Informed by these broad frameworks, the individual chapters are set in comparative national contexts in Asia and Africa, using micro- and meso-level analyses to explore the complexities of governance as it applies to ethnic and other identity-based rivalries and struggles.

Identity, Pluralism and the Problems of Governance in Asia and Africa

Continued ethnic conflicts seem to pose a major threat to both democratic governance and development in many countries of Asia and Africa where the recent resurgence of ethno-religious nationalism has begun to undermine the process of creating strong senses of 'nationhood'. The problem is particularly acute in ethnically plural states of these two contrasting regions, many of which have witnessed high levels of violent ethnic conflicts over the past several decades. While it is difficult to generalize on the cause of ethnic movements given the diverse nature of such conflicts, the studies in this volume identify an 'ideology of exclusion' as a major reason for growing ethnic differences in much of Asia and Africa. In most of the case studies, from Angola to Sri Lanka, ethno-religious minorities have been discouraged to look for a political identity beyond the mainstream concept of nationhood. They often confront a complex system of ideological as well as structural subordination and face an incredible challenge of protecting their socio-political rights (Mendelsohn and Baxi, 1994).

Much more pervasive is the widespread use of state structures and public resources for the benefit of dominant ethnic groups. For instance, in Malaysia, as discussed in this volume by Saravanamuttu, although the state has sought to redistribute income and wealth through the adoption and implementation of the so-called New Economic Policy, the 'authoritarian' structure of governance is used shrewdly to ensure the social mobility as well as economic advancement of the dominant Malay ethnic group. In the case of Uganda, the state's support for dominant ethnic groups forces, as Mbabazi's chapter suggests, minorities to pursue their own political ambitions.

In Africa, generally, contemporary politics and discourses are rife with examples of post-colonial 'predatory' states preying on the vulnerabilities of weak civil societies. Moreover, as in Asia, issues of 'identity' have been at the heart of many of the most intense struggles for power—Ethiopia, Somalia, Rwanda, Angola and the Democratic Republic of the Congo being among the most recent and brutal. Yet, there are differences in the African and Asian situations. In particular, in the former—albeit with some exceptions, such as Eritrea—rival ethnic groups have tended not to fight for secession but rather for control of the state within existing boundaries. Second, in Africa, usually the links (illegal, in some cases, as well as legal) to inter- and trans-national capital continue to be through the state, whereas at least in some parts of Asia, for example, links to business may be more important in growth areas surrounding export processing zones (EPZs), growth triangles, etc. Third, while some Asian leaders have been able to consolidate their power by utilizing long-standing ethnic divisions and inequalities, there are differing opinions on the degree to which African leaders have been able to do this. Célestin Monga (1996: 30) for instance, has recently challenged the widely-held view that many African leaders protect their regimes through patrimonial linkages. He argues that the support of a single ethnic group is not sufficiently strong, in most instances, to sustain leadership and, furthermore, recent elections in several countries have shown 'the nonexistence of ethnic voting blocs'.

Monga's argument, which has relevance beyond Africa, is that 'ethnicity' is a somewhat fluid form/basis of identity. While ethnicity is defined in part by empirical aspects of common origins, biological kinship and shared histories, it is also subjective. In short, the degree to which people self-identify and act on the basis of ethnic ties tends to vary considerably over space and time. The emergence of ethnicities as the focal point of political struggle appears not to be a primordial or entrenched symptom of 'natural' xenophobia or sense of 'otherness' but rather a malleable feature of particular conjunctures of structure, agency and contingency (and, hence, providing interesting possibilities of creative forms of governance!).

Several of the chapters in this volume explore this issue. For example, both Malaquias, who examines the Angolan situation, and Omari, who explores the Great Lakes region of Africa, argue that ethnic identities are more deeply entrenched than the above analysis might suggest. They agree, nevertheless, that the *political expression* of identity is rooted in political economy factors that contribute to the constructions as well as the marginalizations and struggles of various ethno-cultural groups. MacLean's analysis upholds the latter point. She argues that economic pressures associated with globalizations have largely defined the changes in ethnic politics in Zimbabwe and South Africa since the introduction of majority rule in those countries. Nhema supports this analysis in his chapter on the growth and development of Zimbabwe's civil society; indeed, he argues that, because of recent and dramatic changes in political economy, ethnicity is no longer even an important political issue in that once ethnically divided country.

In each of these cases, as in the Asian examples, there has been apparent failure of states to articulate 'national goals' and, in many instances, this failure has resulted in the marginalization and then politicization of specific groups in society. Yet, the degree to which states have used, have attempted to use, or have have been successful in using, the 'politics of exclusion' varies considerably among the cases studied. Furthermore, the degree to which currently or previously marginalized groups can take advantage of new opportunities presented by globalization also varies. For instance, Shaw argues that traditional patterns of ethnic exclusion and inclusion are being altered in the South African wine industry; global shifts in production creating 'niche' opportunities for wine producers juxtaposed with post-apartheid pressures for greater social equity are bringing black entrepreneurs into an industry that was previously dominated by white Afrikaners. Similarly optimistic, Nzomo asserts that strongly held ethnic identities need not be a source of tension in a society; instead, ethnic pluralism may even be a source of democratic strength if governance mechanisms allow for the free expression of ideas and the equitable distribution of assets among the various groups.

Such positive observations notwithstanding, however, in most of the cases explored in this volume, the exclusion of certain social groups has dominated the political landscapes. Hence, a major focus of the project has been to explain the escalation of ethnic and religious intolerance in several of these countries. In these cases, we have been concerned to look beyond state-centric approaches to governance by examining the actions of various marginalized groups, themselves. Indeed, in many countries of Africa and Asia, ethno-religious and ethno-cultural groups have come to discover that without organizing themselves into powerful political groups, they may not be able to prevent the overshadowing of their distinct national identities. Although such 'autonomy movements' vary in their programs and objectives, what is common and therefore makes them particularly relevant for this volume is the desire of such initiatives to develop a more appropriate governance framework where minority groups can either reconcile their ethno-religious differences so that they can live with dignity and equality or can maintain their distinct 'identities' beyond mainstream nationhood.

In addition to ethno-religious minorities, a number of other social groups have similar ambitions. Women, in particular, are frequently excluded from the decision-making process. Not only are they underrepresented in the civil service, they also lack the bargaining power essential to challenge various restrictive and cultural practices that keep women subordinate to men in almost all aspects of life throughout much of Asia and Africa. Thus, this volume draws parallels between the identity issues of gender and ethnicity and several of the chapters deal with the issue of governance with regard to women's movements for greater socio-political change. As attempts to highlight connections between identity issues of gender and ethnicity, these chapters explore the women's organizations and other civil society groups intended to improve the status of marginalized groups in society.

One such chapter by Mohamad, et al. discusses how recent changes in the global political economy affect women's struggle for equality, justice, and democracy in Malaysia. The authors suggest that, contrary to what most analysts would claim, the recent financial crisis and the adoption of flexible industrialization strategies did not succeed in enabling women to play a more assertive role in the country's labor movements. While the financial meltdown made the contradictions of Malaysia's so-called developmentalist state crystal clear, the relatively short-lived crisis apparently failed to create the momentum for women workers, who comprise the largest workforce in the electronic manufacturing sector, to emerge as a key political force in the country.

Quadir also questions whether recent initiatives which have been purported to improve the position of poor women have actually done so. His chapter assesses the ability of development NGOs to empower rural women within the changing political economy of Bangladesh. He confirms that NGO initiatives have begun to expand the productive employment of women by involving them in various micro-finance activities, providing grounds for hope. However, his findings cast profound doubt about the democratizing potentials of NGOs, most of which not only lack a democratic culture, but also maintain hierarchical organizational structures, where key decisions are made by the executive director and his/her close associates.

The impact of information networks on India's gender-based NGOs/women's organizations, which comprise some 30% of the country's NGOs, is analyzed in Singh's chapter. He finds that information technology is helping these local NGOs to form larger strategic coalitions at the national, regional and global levels, thus transforming their 'local' identities. The danger is that these networks can actually be used to perpetuate the dominance of major national and international NGOs, which tend to set the agenda. Networking may also create the need for local NGOs to resist the process of globalizing their traditional identities as it often compels them to compromise on various ideological and symbolic issues.

These comparative case studies allow insights into ways in which ethnically plural societies can be managed, especially in ways that enhance the ability of minority groups to make their own decisions. Yet, given the intractability of the tensions that have emerged in many of these cases, as well as the weak economic positions of the actors and countries involved, possible constructions of sustainable democratic systems of governance depend, at least to some extent, upon the ability of donors to play a constructive role in resolving ethnic conflicts. As Bush's chapter on Sri Lanka emphasizes, in association with other actors involved in the conflict, Official Development Assistance (ODA) can help to bring peace and prosperity. Given its central position in the political economies of much of the developing world, including Sri Lanka, the author concludes that ODA can actually act effectively in restoring peace and stability in 'divided societies'.

A further related issue which we have explored in the project, and to which we turn in the following section, is the significance of symbolic debates for processes of governance. In particular, we consider the parallel discourses that have emerged around 'Asian values' and 'African renaissance'. Just as the World Bank's discourse on governance has been a powerful normative force for setting recent policies of national governments, IFIs, IGOs, INGOs and local NGOs, the debates that have developed around the ideas and ideals of Asian values and African renaissance may be sources of motivation for regional development.

Conclusions: Towards Appropriate Research Agendas

The concept of 'governance' at the end of the twentieth century increasingly means sharing power and responsibility among three broad groups of actors: state, market and civil society. Its emphasis is no longer limited to 'the management of development resources' by the state alone. Interest is shifting away, albeit gradually, from the 'successful' implementation of structural economic reform programs as the means to promote sustainable democratic development. Instead, many development agencies now realize that 'good governance' cannot be achieved without ensuring an equitable distribution of power and resources within and between societies and without creating an environment for popular participation in decision-making. Hence, donor policies are beginning to identify the need to create a framework in which individuals, civil society groups, market forces and governments interact with each other at all levels: from local to global through national and regional.

Our collective research therefore takes the concept of governance beyond both official government agendas and the restructuring of the public sector. We attempt to define governance as a process of building a just, equitable and prosperous world for all groups and communities—not just for dominant ethnic and/or economic groups and individuals. In so doing, our research initiatives attempt to identify the impediments and strategies to movement toward the development of a more plural, more secure and more humane world built on the ideals of democracy, participation, transparency, accountability, human rights, justice and equality.

The chapters in this volume is based upon research that adopts a multifaceted approach to governance, one which not only has relevance for the fields of Economics and Sociology as well as Political Science and International Political Economy, but also transcends the traditional, often artificial boundaries of these established disciplines. Overall, we seek innovative approaches to analysis and offer suggestions for future research on sets of inter-related issues, especially in the areas of:

- *international relations*, by moving beyond NIDL/P and states and onto a range of actors in the state, economy and civil society sectors as well as of issues such as human rights, human security and global governance, and of new institutional arrangements such as in Eastern Europe, the former Soviet Union and Central Asia;
- *foreign policy*, by including non-states as well as states, again treating a wide range of issues from new coalitions of actors, to gender, landmines, ozone, bio-diversity and culture;
- *international political economy*, by investigating the inter-related economic, social and political implications of post-Fordist processes of outsourcing/ subcontracting, flexibilization/ feminization and globalizations in association with DFI, EPZs, growth triangles, the demise of the Multilateral Agreement on Investment (MAI), micro-credit, NICs (noting that such arrangements are changing South-South and well as North-South relations), the World Economic Forum as well as Trilateral Commission, Asian values versus African renaissance, etc.;

- *development studies*, by including actors and items such as informal sectors, NGOs, peacekeeping operations (PKOs), human rights, labor, credit, refugees/migrations, green/bio-diversity, as well as transitions such as in Central Asia and new partnerships and strategic alliances;
- *area studies* (especially Asia and Africa), by offering redefinitions and revisionist interpretations of events within the context of globalizing change and then attempting to identify flexible regionalisms and/or solitudes, especially in relation to the impacts on/from diasporic/ethnic communities;
- *comparative regionalisms* by identifying flexible even variable geometries/asymmetrical corridors/initiatives/triangles including informal sectors/mafias as well as conflicts/confidence-building measures (CBMs)/PKOs that appear to be leading to new forms of multilateralisms, international organizations, law or regimes, norms, architectures; and
- human security/development from CBMs, conflict, PKOs, CPEs, humanitarian interventions, small arms, drugs, gangs, etc., to partnership, sub-contracting, security communities but also anarchies and realism (for example, in the Great Lakes and the Congo or in regards to the India-Pakistan arms/missile/nuclear race).

We hope that our collaborative endeavors will be infused with the critical energy displayed by Christopher Clapham (1996: 256) as he concluded in his own recent overview of Africa's international relations:

> Africa's relations with the outside world were privatized not only through their subversion by the private interests of politicians ... but through the displacement of traditional state-to-state relations as a result of the processes of globalization.

Notes

1. Ted Robert Gurr, who has written extensively on the issue of ethnic conflict has concluded recently that 'ethnic warfare (is) on the wane', largely, he argues—contrary to the view of many observers—because international responses have established successful deterrents (Gurr, 2000).

2. The 'double movement', as conceptualized originally by Karl Polanyi, is 'an expansion of market forces and a reaction to it in the forms of demands for self-protection against capital's socially disruptive and polarizing effects' (Mittelman, 1997, xi). The 'second movement' is the latter part of the process and, in the present context, refers to civil society's response to the insecurities resulting from the globalization of capitalism.

3. Several scholars have traced the events leading up to and following the breakdown in the Bretton Woods order and the related demise of the Fordist production schedule, the erosion of the Keynesian welfare state system, and the Third World debt crisis and onset of structural

adjustment programs (for example, see Shaeffer, 1997; Stubbs and Underhill, 1994 and 2000; Helleiner, 1994b; Piore and Sabel, 1984).

4.   The prefix 'neo' is used to denote a recent change in the liberal order which has been dominant in world politics at least since the end of the Second World War. As Beckman (1993: 21-22) asks: 'Why "neo?' Why not just "liberal"?' He explains that '[t]he new strategy is ... neo-liberal, not because it promotes capitalism, commercialisation and markets, which all liberal strategies do, but because of the redefinition of the role of the state in the process.'

5.   For more on these issues, see Adler and Barnett (1998); Hettne and Inotai (1997); Tang and Thant (1994).

6.   Another important sign may be the increasing credence given to the so-called 'Third Way', for example, by Western leaders such as British Prime Minister Blair and US President Clinton. As elaborated first by Giddens (1999: 64 and 66), the 'Third Way' is an approach to 'help citizens plot their way through the major revolutions of our time; that is, globalization, transformations in personal life and our relationship to nature'. It is based upon values of 'equality, protection of the vulnerable, freedom and autonomy, no rights without responsibilities, no authority without democracy, cosmopolitan pluralism, and philosophical conservatism'.

7.   A detailed analysis of the growing problems of development facing countries in Sub-Saharan Africa was first presented in the Berg report entitled *Accelerated Development in Sub-Saharan Africa: Agenda for Action* (World Bank, 1981). In addition to identifying the main reasons for the region's bleak economic future, this report made attempts to develop appropriate programs for managing and resolving Africa's economic miseries. While the report dealt with some socio-cultural issues such as population growth, health and education, it was primarily concerned with the removal of obstacles to economic growth in the region.

8.   Former World Bank president Barber B. Conable offered this argument (World Bank, 1989: xii).

9.   For example, see the journal, *Global Governance*, which was established in 1995. See also Alger, 1994; Archibugi and Held, 1995; Childers and Urquhart, 1994; Coate, et al., 1996; Cox, 1994; Nelson, 1995; Princen, et al., 1994; Weiss, and Gordenker, 1996; Wiseberg, 1996.

10.   This phrase was suggested by the title of an article by Haas and Haas (1995).

11.   Political pluralism emerged in the eighteenth century in the writings of the famous French liberal philosopher Montesquieu. However, the studies of pluralism began only in the 1920s through the publications of Peter Odegard's book entitled *Pressure Politics: The Story of the Anti-Saloon League* and the work of E. Pendleton Herring entitled *Group Representation Before Congress*. These two pioneering works encouraged a number of political scientists to study interest groups and the importance of limiting the power of the state in order to allow important socio-political groups to play a vital role in decision-making in a democratic polity.

12.   In the broadest sense, the aim of the Singapore School is to offer an alternative perspective on the burgeoning debate about 'Asian values', liberal models of democracy and 'Western' standards of human rights. The proponents of this School often reject the ideal of liberal democracy because of its inability to, as they argue, promote national economic development, which remains the major focus of most Asian countries. They claim that 'western' models of democracy are not compatible with Asian cultures, which emphasize the interests of the country and/or economy more than the value of individual rights and freedoms (Chan 1997; Alagappa 1995; Mahbubani, 1998).

PART II

GOVERNANCE
AND
ECONOMY

2 Globalization, Capital and Governance in a Newly Industrializing Plural Society: Malaysia during the 1990s

JOHAN SARAVANAMUTTU

Introduction

This chapter aims at understanding how the current phase of economic globalization has affected Malaysia, a classic plural society in which economic performance has underpinned political legitimacy. Focussing on the 1990s it empirically investigates the role capital has played in this period in bolstering the Malaysian economy as well as contributing to its social cohesion and political stability. Malaysia's 20-year old New Economic Policy (NEP), which deliberately promoted an ethnic re-distribution of wealth, came to an official end in 1990. The chapter takes its departure from the point when the so-called New Development Policy (NDP) and in particular, the 'Vision 2020' policy of Prime Minister Mahathir Mohamad of attaining developed country status became the new guideposts for economic development, social policy and political practice.

This latest phase of Malaysian development has coincided with an acceleration of economic globalization particularly in East Asia of which the Malaysian economy is an integral part. The study already assumes that through an international division of labor in the 1970s and 1980s, Malaysia had taken off along with other East Asian, newly industrializing countries (NICs). However, like most of them, it became mired in crisis and an economic downturn, which is both structural and contingent upon the financial events that began in mid-1997. These events are themselves, ironically symbolic of the final ascendancy of neo-liberalism on the world stage. At the regional and national level, this phase of economic liberalization has been a two-edged sword, Malaysia and other East Asian 'tigers' having discovered to their chagrin that financial liberalization brings both benefits and dangers to rapidly growing economies. The essay looks at the socio-political implications of some of the measures used to contain the crisis, such as exchange control and the restructuring of banks and Malaysian companies spawned by the NEP. It broaches the question of whether the recovery, which is said to have already occurred in 1999, can be sustained in the long term.

The question of political legitimacy has become particularly important with the onset of the financial crisis bringing about the most dramatic and egregious political developments to the Southeast Asian region in recent history. The political fallout from the crisis is examined with an eye to understanding the nexus between Malaysian capitalist discourse and practices and the plural politics of the Malaysian genre. Who are the winners and who are the losers? To what extent will some of the achievements of the NEP period in indigenizing a large proportion of Malaysian capital be affected by the political developments? What are the positive effects on democratization and plural politics in the medium and long term?

Thus far, the Mahathir government and its beneficiaries remain firmly in place in spite of the economic crisis of 1997/98. However, the government maintains only a tenuous legitimacy where ethnic policies and autocratic politics are ameliorated by performance legitimacy rather than political legitimacy anchored within a strong civil society. In light of events occurring at the end of the 1990s, genuine political legitimacy can be said to have eluded the Mahathir government. In particular, *Reformasi* (reform) politics gave birth to a strong challenge by an 'alternative' opposition front, which garnered 44% of the popular votes in the November 1999 general election.

This chapter begins by outlining the major issues and questions of the Malaysian political economy in the 1990s. It proceeds to an analysis of economic globalization in the context of East Asian development and to the 1997/98 financial crisis and meltdown. Finally it addresses prospects for capital, ethnicity, governance and political legitimacy in Malaysia.

Malaysian Political Economy in the 1990s

Malaysia's population of about 9 million in 1963 has more than doubled today to 22 million, comprising both Bumiputera (indigenes) and non-Bumiputera (non-indigenes), and well over one million non-citizens, mostly migrant workers. By the year 2000, the anticipated 23 million Malaysians will comprise 63% Bumiputeras, 26% Chinese, 7.5% Indians and 3.5% various other non-Bumiputera people. The Bumiputeras consist of the Malays and aboriginal groups in the Peninsula and other 'first peoples' such as the Kadazan, Murut and Bajau of Sabah, and the Iban, Bidayuh, Melanau, Kayan, Kenyah, Kelabit, Berawan and Penan of Sarawak, to name some. The most important ethnic groupings on the Peninsula are the Malays (about 55 %), Chinese (30%) and the Indians (9%). There are also sizeable populations of Chinese in both Sabah and Sarawak. This trichotomy of Malays, Chinese and Indians has been the defining characteristic of the original Malayan polity and has colored the way politics and social life have been conducted in the whole of Malaysia today.

While the 'plural society' remains a most important leitmotif of social and political life, one should not forget that Malaysia's immediate post-colonial society exhibited class dimensions and divisions, which by and large coincided with ethnic divisions. At the time of independence, Malay aristocrats took over the reins of power from the British while the local economy was arguably dominated by the Chinese, with the Indians characteristically occupying clerical jobs and working in rubber estates, and the bulk of the Malays forming the peasantry. The commanding heights of the economy with its global linkages were, of course, in the hands of the Europeans. It is a testimony to the success of the social engineering policies of the succeeding Malaysian governments that the deep divisions and cleavages of class and ethnicity have now been greatly eroded and the clear identification of economic function with ethnic groupings has been decisively ameliorated. A quick reference to the 1995 employment figures in Table 2:1 shows that through its policy of positive discrimination in favor of the Bumiputeras, the New Economic Policy (NEP), implemented from the years 1971-1990, has succeeded in redressing the lopsided occupational situation which existed at the time of independence.

Table 2:1   Employment by Occupation, 1995 (Percentages)

	Bumiputera	Chinese	Indians	Others
Professional & Technical	64.3	26.2	7.3	2.2
Teachers & Nurses	72.3	20.5	6.6	1.6
Managerial	36.1	54.7	5.1	4.1
Clerical	57.2	34.4	7.7	0.7
Sales	36.2	51.9	6.5	5.4
Service	58.2	22.8	8.7	10.3
Agriculture	63.1	12.9	7.5	16.5
Production	44.8	35.0	10.3	9.9
Total	52.4	30.3	8.4	8.9

Source: Malaysia (1999)

The 1990s saw the replacement of the NEP by the New Development Policy (NDP). But, more importantly, the 1990s have seen the unmistakable stamp of the Vision 2020 policy of Prime Minister Mahathir Mohamad in propelling Malaysia towards the status of a developed country.

The NDP and Vision 2020: Achievements and Setbacks

The NDP grew out of the somewhat flawed attempt in 1988 by the Mahathir government to set up a National Economic Consultative Council (NECC), with the task to discuss and come up with post-NEP policies for Malaysia. The withdrawal of many opposition and non-governmental members from the NECC suggests that the Barisan national government failed to institute a truly consultative process to do the job. Milne and Mauzy (1999: 72) suggest that the Economic Planning Unit in the Prime Minister's department was responsible for the Second Outline Perspective Plan (OPP2) which forms the core of the NDP.

Coupled with the NDP is the Vision 2020 policy which calls for a doubling of Malaysia's GDP every 10 years, that is from RM115 billion in 1990 to RM920 billion by 2020, at an average growth rate of 7% per annum.

Following the implementation of the NDP over most of the 1990s, the most important developments in political economy may be summarized as follows:

- The Bumiputera stake in the corporate sector in economy rose to 20.6% by 1995 and dipped slightly to 19.4% by 1998, whereas it was a minuscule 2.4% in 1970. This figure is short of the OPP1 of 30% but it is nevertheless a remarkable increase, given the initial base.
- The Chinese share of the corporate sector has steadily risen from 27.2% in 1990 to 40.9% by 1995 but dropped slightly to 38.5% by 1998. Foreigners who in 1998 had 31.8% of the corporate sector have taken up the slack (see Table 2:2).
- Poverty eradication has been a success from the government's viewpoint with the incidence of poverty declining from 8.9% in 1995 to a mere 6.1% in 1998.[1]
- Restructuring of society has also occurred with many Bumiputeras having joined the ranks of the middle class, professional occupations and forming the bulk of the working class. By 1997, the 22,866 Bumiputera professionals constituted 32% of the total number, with Chinese comprising 52.1%, Indians 13.1% and others, 2.7% (Malaysia, 1999: 73-84).

These are clearly no mean achievements on the socio-economic front for the newly industrializing plural society. By the mid-1990s Malaysia had become the developing world's sixth largest exporter of manufactures. More significantly, Malaysia had evidently moved up the technological division of labor, with the manufacturing of products (not necessarily of Malaysian design) becoming increasingly sophisticated (Jomo, 1997: 116). At the macro-level, Malaysia's export-oriented industrialization (EOI) under the Second Industrial Master Plan (1996-2006) saw the following features and developments by the end of the 1990s:

- The manufacturing sector grew at a rate of 12.4% from 1996-1997 but declined by a dramatic negative 10.2% in 1998 because of the financial crisis.
- Electrical and electronic products grew moderately but maintained their number one spot of some 30.8% of manufacturing output in 1998. Average growth was 5% over 1996-98. Resource-based industries, taken together accounted for 50.7% of total industrial output, while the main buyers of manufactures were Singapore, USA and Japan.
- Domestic investment in the manufacturing sector topped RM44.87 billion representing some 51.95% of the total, while foreign direct investment (FDI) stood at RM41.61 billion or 48.1% of the total during the Seventh Plan period. The main sources of FDI were Japan, USA, Singapore, Taiwan and Switzerland.
- Expansion of the manufacturing sector enabled the employment rate to grow at 7.7% per annum but this declined to 3.6% in 1998. The sector contributed the larger number of jobs for the plan period with a total of 243,900 jobs or 47.4% of total job creation. However, it should be noted that 45,150 workers were retrenched in 1998 in this sector, which represented 53.8% of total retrenchments (Malaysia, 1999: 197-205).

Its overall success notwithstanding, critical analyses of Malaysia's industrialization drive have suggested that it could be improved in various ways including by an increased emphasis on import-substitution industries (ISI) and by developing better linkages between ISI and export-oriented industrialization (EOI). Malaysia's technology policy has also been critiqued for being excessively dependent on foreign companies and their operations (Jomo, 1997: 117).

Economic Globalization in the Context of East Asian Development

The process of economic globalization received a tremendous boost in the early 1970s right through the 1980s, wherein in these two important decades of capitalist development, a New International Division of Labor (NIDL) was crafted by transnational corporations working in tandem with states. During this phase of capitalist development, the East Asian region was also supposedly further overlaid with a regional division of labor in which Japanese capital was particularly prominent.[2]

However, recent and present developments suggest that much larger forces of globalization were and still are at work in the East Asian economies. Most tellingly, economic globalization has in the past decade or so seen the unprecedented ascendancy of neo-liberalism as the driving force behind global and regional economic developments. The early supposedly liberal phase of post-World War II capitalist development was thought to have been guided by the emergence in 1944 of Bretton Woods institutions—the International Monetary Fund (IMF) and the World Bank. Newer interpretations of the Bretton Woods institutions suggest that their emergence already bore the markings of the neo-liberal agendas (Stubbs and Underhill, 1994). If these institutions, as conceived by their proponents, were attempts to strike a balance between the operation of market forces and the social responsibility of states, over time they have certainly become less subject to the control of states compared with the influence of market players. With the collapse of command economies of Eastern Europe and elsewhere by the end of the 1980s, the drive to re-establish neo-liberal principles of economic practice and discourse usually purveyed by market-friendly institutions such as the World Bank and the Asian Development Bank has been particularly effective.

Commentators such as Stephen Gill (1994a, 1998) and Eric Helleiner (1994a) have suggested that as the power of states in economic governance has waned, the proponents of neo-liberalism have inversely gained supremacy. By the 1990s, market proponents have virtually been setting the parameters of a 'new constitutionalism' for global governance (Gill, 1998: 30).

It is generally recognized that the Bretton Woods arrangements were overtaken by events by the 1970s, wherein among other things, the fixed exchange rates system based on gold convertibility was replaced by flexible exchange rates. Since then, the world's financial system has been marked by only sporadic attempts to stabilize exchange rates and only among the important currencies such as the US dollar, the German mark and the Japanese yen, during the Bonn summit of 1978, the Plaza Agreement of 1985 and the Louvre Accord of 1987 (Pauly, 1997: 27). The somewhat free-wheeling situation in the financial sector was not unrelated to the ascendancy of neo-liberalism since states, which lacked political will, could hardly institute systematic measures to check the market players, who by the 1990s had grown by proportions that were truly phenomenal. This is not to say that private market players did not try to institute international regimes for the control of financial sub-sectors such as international banking and the securities markets (Coleman and Porter, 1994). However, such regimes were by and large weak and poorly supervised.

These broad economic and financial developments of globalization in 1990s have provided the context, if not the impetus, for the spectacular events of 1997 and 1998 which have come to be called East Asia's financial 'crisis', 'turmoil' and 'meltdown'.

The 1997/98 Financial Crisis and Meltdown[3]

The East Asian economic turmoil began after an extraordinary spate of developments more or less sparked by the devaluation of the Thai baht in June 1997. With hindsight, analysts have come to realize that a major reason for the financial crisis and meltdown was that Southeast Asian countries had been running large current account deficits for several years, with some effects on local financial markets even prior to the 1997 situation. In addition to this, export growth had also ground to a halt by the end of 1996.

In retrospect, the problem of large current account deficits and its concomitant of overheated economies can be traced to the global developments in the financial sector arising out of the 1985 Plaza Accord. Taking Thailand as the template, the accord, which re-valued the yen upwards vis-à-vis the dollar, had the effect of making Thailand (and much of Southeast Asia) increasingly indebted in yen-denominated loans. This proportion reached 52% in Thailand's case, and brought in massive influxes of Japanese capital and an equally large outflow of exports. The Plaza Accord also made credit in US dollars cheap for Thailand allowing for a decade-long boom of the Thai corporate sector. However, as the dollar value rose against the yen in 1995 and 1996 in tandem with a drop in exports as a result of the Japanese slowdown, Thailand's troubles began to multiply.

Some months before the actual meltdown, however, analysts like David Hale (1997) argued that ineffective exchange rate and banking policies could be corrected especially in the Thai case to avert a Mexican-style crisis. One could say that such policies failed to be effected by the Thai government prior to the July 1997 crash but it would be counter-factual to suggest that had such policies been put into place, the crisis could have been averted. Certainly even the stronger economies like Malaysia and Singapore, with their tighter monetary policies, were by no means insulated from the 'contagion' that swept across the region. Virtually all of East Asia has been affected by the financial 'meltdown' with South Korea taking the worst beating in the second phase, after Thailand.

In the event, the Malaysian Prime Minister, Dr. Mahathir Mohamad, went on the attack early in the day and charged that Asian currencies have suffered at the hands of 'rogue speculators', blaming George Soros, the Hungarian-born American financier-international fund manager-cum-philanthrophist, for launching an assault on the ASEAN economies because of ASEAN's decision to admit Myanmar (Burma) into the regional association. Soros has denied this and ironically has himself been promoting the idea that the global economy is in deep crisis and needs fundamental reform (Soros, 1998). Soros and Mahathir had a war of words in Hong Kong during the IMF/World Bank meetings in September in which the former said the Prime Minister was a 'menace to his own country'. Mahathir, meanwhile, has gone to different international fora to suggest his ideas for reforming the international financial system. In September 1998, the Malaysian premier took the high economic road and introduced capital controls for the country and announced the non-tradability (or convertibility) of the ringgit.

Jomo's edited volume (1998) provides one of best and most comprehensive analysis of the Southeast Asian crisis. In the leading article, he argues that the root of the problem was economic vulnerability. The major reasons for this vulnerability were both internal and external, anchored on the twin problems of a quasi-peg of Southeast Asian currencies to the dollar and the unprecedented level of financial liberalization in the region spawning cheap liquidity which became unaffordable when events turned sour for the tiger economies. However, explanations based on the macro-economic and micro-economic vulnerabilities of the Southeast Asian economies only provide part of the picture. The fact of the matter is that global financial markets and the financial sectors in most economies have become effectively de-coupled from their real economies (Saravanamuttu, 1998: 122-123).

Malaysia: Coping without the IMF

Just prior to the crisis, the basic vulnerability of the Malaysian economy to the forces of financial globalization was clearly in evidence despite the usual strong indicators of economic health. Several macro-economic indicators of such vulnerability emerged by the mid-1990s:

- The savings-investment gap—bridged traditionally by foreign direct investment but increasingly by short-term capital inflows—fuelled a current account deficit in the order of RM12 billion since 1994.
- The sourcing of short-term investment flows through the Kuala Lumpur Stock Exchange (KLSE) had reached feverish levels by the early 1990s owing to the establishment of the Securities Commission and passing of legislation allowing for easy credit. This led to the collapse of the market in early 1994 but a rebound by early 1997 wherein market capitalization exceeded by five times the annual national income.
- An explosion of private sector debt, with commercial bank liabilities increasing from RM10.3 billion at the end of 1995 to RM25.2 billion in June 1997 while their net external reserves position declined from negative RM5.3 billion to negative RM17.1 billion over the same period (Jomo, 1998: 181-82).

As reported in the *Mid-Term Review of the Seventh Plan*, the financial crisis impacted on the Malaysian economy as follows:

- The ringgit depreciated from RM2.52 vis-à-vis the USD during July 1997 to RM3.53, before reaching an all-time low of RM4.88 in early January 1998. It was subsequently fixed at RM3.80 on 2 September 1998 along with the introduction of exchange control.
- The KLSE Composite Index fell by 73% and market capitalization decreased by 74% between 1 July 1997 and 2 September 1998. In the banking sector, NPLs (non-performing loans) rose to 11.4% by August 1998.
- Real output of the economy contracted at an unprecedented rate of 6.7% in 1998. The inflation rate rose 5.3% and the rate of unemployment to 3.9%. The federal government account registered a deficit for the first time since 1993. External debt also increased although the current account saw a surplus because of reduced domestic demand causing a drop in imports.

The Malaysian government's initial response to the crisis—and especially Mahathir's own response—was one of denial. Several direct steps were then taken to insulate the domestic interest rate from capital mobility. The offshore, over-the-counter CLOB (Central Limit Order Book) in Singapore was stopped to prevent illegal short selling of Malaysian shares. There was also the step of banning the short selling of 100 blue-chip stocks and the plan to use funds of the Employees' Provident Fund to shore up share prices. This was followed up, most importantly, by the announcement of capital controls on 1 September as indicated earlier. In such a move, Mahathir had supposedly carried the legitimacy of a proposal by MIT Professor Paul Krugman who had argued in an article in *Fortune* magazine that such capital controls could give crisis-ridden Asian economies a breathing space in which to resume growth.

The controls have remained in place at the time of writing and Mahathir and the government have continued to claim that they have made the difference in Malaysia's economy when compared with the other crisis-stricken East Asian economies. It has been argued that, by doing so, and in tandem with various other fiscal and monetary measures, Malaysia has avoided an IMF rescue package. By the middle of 1999, the Malaysian authorities were already trumpeting that the recovery was more than evident, with the stock market showing signs of new life, indicated by the KLSE-CI breaching 800 points by August after a low of about 260 points at the nadir of the crisis. By August, regular monthly surpluses in the current account had also boosted Malaysia's international reserves to US$31 billion, good for seven months of imports. Although 1998 saw a decline in GDP of negative 6.7%, the government toward the end of the year claimed that a 5% growth for 1999 could be expected.[4]

Throughout the handling of the crisis, the Malaysian government and central bank, Bank Negara, have avoided any borrowing from the IMF. Instead, funds have been sourced from Japan, ADB and the World Bank and through the issue of international bonds. In July 1999, Bank Negara issued US$1 billion bond in New York, which although oversubscribed was issued at a rate 330 basis points above that of US Treasury bonds. Other measures include the setting up of an Asset Management Corporation (*Danaharta*) in March 1998 to undertake restructuring and re-capitalization of the banking system. A 'special purpose vehicle', *Danamodal*, was also set up to mop up NPLs and generally to source funding for re-capitalization of companies and to improve liquidity. Bank Negara, which supervises both bodies, has continued to restructure the banking sector and to cushion debt-ridden companies by keeping interest rates low and by injecting liquidity through measures like the bond issues. In a radical banking move, the central bank in early August 1999 announced its intention of having Malaysian banks merge into six major groups. However, by the next month, it became clear that the move was too ambitious and could not be pulled off without problems. By October, Bank Negara was forced to announce that the banks were free to choose their own partners for merger, following upon Prime Minister Mahathir's own statements to the same effect.[5]

Capital, Ethnicity, Governance and Political Legitimacy

In this section, I will draw on the analyses and conclusions of the previous sections to undertake a more general analysis linking capital, ethnicity and political legitimacy as the key elements of a Malaysian political economy.

As noted earlier, Malaysia's plural society has put a particular stamp on its politics and economy. By the 1990s, we noted that Malaysian society had become much more middle class and with a large proportion of Bumiputeras in the working class. The NEP, which was aimed at restructuring society and eradicating poverty, had been greatly successful in the second objective and to some extent in the first as well. The globalization and liberalization phase of Malaysia's political economy since the 1980s, coinciding with the ascendancy of Dr. Mahathir as Prime Minister, has seen some major developments, not least of all the financial crisis and meltdown of 1997/98.

FDI and the Stock Market

Without doubt, the NIC pattern of economic growth will continue to be the mainstay of the Malaysian economy as evidenced by developments in the 1990s. The role for foreign capital will continue to be important despite the incessant rhetoric of the Prime Minister on foreign domination and re-colonization of the Malaysian economy. The fact remains that whether it is in trade or in export-led industrialization, Malaysia has depended and continues to depend on foreign demand, foreign capital and foreign technology. The joint venture form of foreign involvement in the Malaysian manufacturing sector remains the preferred and most effective strategy of garnering both foreign capital and technology. In the 1990s, Japan has remained as a foremost foreign direct investment (FDI) contributor. However, in the late 1990s the USA substantially overtook Japan in FDI. Interestingly, first-tier NICs, especially Korea, Taiwan and Singapore, have become increasingly important as foreign investors. If benefits from industrialization are the basis for a large part of Malaysia's political legitimacy, it is unlikely that there will be a major change to the current model of foreign-propelled industrialization even beyond the 1990s.

There is another level of activity in which foreign capital has become increasingly important in the 1990s. This is in the area of financial flows and portfolio investment. It is apparent that the KLSE has become a major source of capital for many Malaysian companies seeking capitalization. Foreign participation in the Malaysian stock market is not only important for the actual capital brought in but also is highly desired as a boost to the local bourse's long term credibility and performance. In the current era of neo-liberal financial liberalization, the lack of a high performing bourse is itself an indicator of poor economic fundamentals. In 1997, the Malaysian bourse saw a turnover of some RM408.55 billion. Total equity held was some RM117.06 billion with foreigners holding some RM23.35 billion or almost 20%. Again, given the neo-liberal dictates of capitalism, foreign portfolio capital therefore becomes a crucial element for regime legitimacy in Malaysia, notwithstanding the rhetorical pronouncements of the Prime Minister to the contrary. Needless to say, legitimacy took a precipitous slide when the financial crisis struck in 1997/98 and the KLSE collapsed to only a quarter of its pre-crisis value.

Growing Middle Class and Rentier Capitalism

The NDP and Vision 2020 policies with its emphasis on growth has already had an impact on the Malaysian share of corporate assets as reported in the *Mid-Term Review of the Seventh Plan*. The Bumiputera share fell slightly from 18.6% in 1995 to 17.7% in 1998. The Chinese share of 40.9% in 1995 dropped slightly to 38.5% by 1998. The slack has been taken up by foreigners who in 1998 had 31.8% of the corporate sector, which is 4.1% more than in 1995 (see Table 2:2). The growth strategies seem to have had an effect on Malaysian holdings in the corporate sector although it is perhaps still too early to tell. What is evident is that the middle class among Malaysians has continued to expand along with the NDP.

Table 2:2   Ownership of Share Capital (at par value) of Limited Companies 1995 and 1998 (RM million)

Ownership Group	1995	%	1998	%	Ave. Annual Growth Rate
Bumiputera	36,981.2	20.6	57,240.9	19.4	15.6
Individuals & Institutions	33,353.2	18.6	52,044.5	17.7	16.0
Trust Agencies	3,628.0	2.0	5,196.4	1.7	12.7
Non-Bumiputera	78,026.9	43.4	120,985.4	41.1	15.7
Chinese	73,552.7	40.9	113,542.5	38.5	15.5
Indians	2,723.1	1.5	4,599.7	1.5	19.1
Others	1,751.1	1.0	2,843.2	1.0	17.5
Foreigners	49,792.7	27.7	93,667.1	31.8	23.4
Nominee Companies	14,991.4	8.3	22,682.3	7.7	14.8
Total	179,792.2	100.0	294,575.7	100.0	17.9

Source: Malaysia (1999)

In 1997, Bumiputeras professionals roughly kept pace with Chinese and Indian professionals (32%, 52.1%, 13.1% respectively of the total), but the professional and technical categories had some 63.1% Bumiputeras in 1998. Other categories like clerical and administrative workers also show a high percentage of Bumiputeras. Admittedly Bumiputeras predominate as agricultural workers (61%) but so do they as production workers (43.6%). There is no denying that a large Bumiputera middle class and working class along with the other ethnic groups now inhabit Malaysian civil society. This factor has highly significant implications for political legitimacy, which can only be briefly discussed here. Certainly, it would become increasingly evident that the political base of the ruling coalition may shift from its rural and non-urban sectors to more urban locales, given that middle class Malaysians would tend to be found in urban settings. More importantly, for the United Malay National Organization (UMNO), *primus inter pares* in the ruling coalition, such a change may mean erosion of its traditional source of support which has been in rural constituencies.

Recent work on Malaysian capitalism by Gomez (1999), Gomez and Jomo (1997) and Searle (1999) give interesting insights on how the NEP—and to some extent the NDP—has affected capitalist development at the micro-level of political economy. These findings throw new light on how cronyism, defined broadly as the phenomenon of favoring particular individuals in business dealings and contracts, has affected the whole issue of political legitimacy. While the macro-picture of corporate ownership of the economy throws fairly credible light on the achievements of the NEP, and also on the NDP by the end of the 1990s, there have been many disturbing signs that the distribution of the economic cake has been somewhat skewed. Furthermore, these analysts have suggested that the NEP has created 'rentier capitalists' especially among the Bumiputeras (Gomez and Jomo, 1997: 179).

The authors suggest that the Bumiputera holdings in the corporate sector shown in official statistics probably underestimate the share as well as the strategic holdings of particularly influential Bumiputeras. Another interesting point made is that although Chinese businessmen have been able to hold their own and maintain their grip on the economy, the Mahathir era having spawned crony Chinese capitalists who are closely associated with and cultivate close connections with leading politicians. Speculation is rife that many of these not-so-independent Chinese and other non-Malay businessmen have also operated as proxies for certain UMNO leaders, particularly Daim Zainuddin (Gomez and Jomo, 1997: 181).

Gomez gives more evidence of such connections and associations in his book on Chinese business in Malaysia (1999) but we can only touch briefly on some of the material here. The author examines how Chinese capital has withstood or indeed has taken advantage of the era of the NEP and NDP. It is evident from his eight case studies of prominent Chinese businessmen, that although there has always been pressure to ensure Bumiputera participation in their enterprises, these businessmen have been able to maintain personal or family control. By deftly including prominent Malay directors in their respective companies and operations, there has been little necessity to relinquish full control to the state or to Bumiputeras. Such has been the *modus operandi* of Chinese corporate giants such as Robert Kuok (Perlis Plantations Bhd), Lim Goh Tong (Genting Bhd) and Loh Boon Siew (Oriental Holdings Bhd), the older set of more etablished rich, and newer players such as William Cheng (Amsteel Corp. Bhd), Khoo Khay Peng (Mui Bhd), Vincent Tan Chee Yioun (Berjaya Group, Bhd), as well as the more recent crop of Chinese capitalists such as Francis Yeoh (YTL Corp. Bhd) and Ting Pek Khiing (Ekran Bhd). Various names in last two groups of individuals have been known for their close association with the Prime Minister.

Searle's (1999) study of the NEP period takes on the issue of rentier capitalism and concludes that 'there has been a blurring of categories of state, party and private in the development of Malay capitalism, so from that amalgam have emerged both rent-seekers and entrepreneurs and many groups between the two' (Searle, 1999: 246). Searle's more measured conclusion about the character of Malaysian capitalism suggests that the political legitimacy of the Mahathir regime may have remained largely intact. However, the work, which pre-dates the political turmoil in UMNO following Anwar Ibrahim's sacking, does not take into account developments in the corporate sector in the late 1990s. These new domestic considerations will furthermore need to be weighed along with the impact of globalization, via the financial crisis, on Malaysian capitalist development in all its ramifications. We will address some of these questions in the final section below.

Crisis, Bailouts and Legitimacy

If there is one main lesson to be drawn from the 1997/98 financial crisis and meltdown, it is that nation-states especially of the NIC variety are prone and vulnerable to the vicissitudes of the international economic order. The latitude for action for individual states has become extremely narrow. Such was the case of Thailand and Indonesia in Southeast Asia and their Hobson's choice of accepting IMF rescue packages. Malaysia apparently had much more room for maneuver as indicated by its response to the crisis. However, I would argue that the impact of the crisis would have been equally debilitating and constraining for Malaysia were it not for the easy availability to the government of 'cash cows' such as the national oil corporation, Petronas, the Employee's Provident Fund (EPF) and the

Muslim Pilgrims' Fund (*Tabung Haji*). Had it not been for this factor, the political legitimacy of the Mahathir regime may have been seriously or even mortally stricken by the impact of the crisis. Space does not permit any thorough analysis of the above point. As a partial substantiation, we will focus on the role of Petronas in bailing Malaysia out of the crisis, as revealed in recent developments, moves and disclosures.

According to *Far Eastern Economic Review* writer S. Jayasankaran (12 August 1999), for the year that ended in March 1999, Petronas paid more than RM6 billion in federal taxes, plus RM4.1 billion in dividends, which represents a sixth of the total expected government revenue for 1999. It also repatriates some RM250 million monthly to local banks. Petronas posted net profits attributable to shareholders of RM6.8 billion in the last fiscal year, down 32% due to falling oil prices. Recently, the Prime Minister suggested that it might be appropriate for the oil corporation to bail out the ailing national airline, MAS, which suffered pre-tax losses of RM670 million.

In the upshot of the financial crisis, Petronas' most controversial acquisition has been a RM1.8 billion controlling stake in the Malaysian International Shipping Corp (MISC), the country's largest shipper. However, this move was merely a precursor to MISC's buy-up of *Konsortium Perkapalan*, the ailing shipping firm of Mirzan Mahathir, the Prime Minister's eldest son. MISC paid Konsortium RM836 million in cash and also assumed RM1.2 billion ringgit of its debt. At the same time, Petronas raised its stake in MISC to 62% to allow it to undertake the Konsortium acquisition. Needless to say, the deal has raised more than a few eyebrows. The deposed Anwar Ibrahim has filed a report with the police charging nepotism and calling for a full investigation.

A recent non-core acquisition of Petronas occurred in early August 1999. The oil company bought a 27.2% stake in national carmaker *Perusahaan Otomobil Nasional Bhd,* Proton, at a cost of RM1billion (*New Straits Times*, 7 August 1999). Proton is known to be burdened with heavy debts although its distribution and sales arm, *Edaran Otomobil Nasional* (EON), has been reaping profits.

Apart from bailouts, Petronas has been in the forefront of acquisitions and projects of particular interest to the Prime Minister. It bankrolled the US$800 million (RM4 billion) Petronas Twin Towers, the tallest buildings in the world, which it now occupies. Even potentially more awesome is its financial backing for the new RM22 billion hi-tech administrative center of the government known as Putrajaya, situated 25 kilometres from Kuala Lumpur. Putrajaya also houses the Prime Minister's magnificent office and his palatial residence. Petronas is a major shareholder in a fund known as National Heritage Fund, set up for Putrajaya's construction.

It is clear from the foregoing exposé of the recent activities of the national oil corporation that the Mahathir government is heavily dependent on it for not only favorite projects but also to mend fissures and cracks in the economy. The financial crisis and meltdown has led to an even greater reliance on Petronas but the extent to which its funds can be tapped without raising questions remains moot. Increasingly, more questions will be asked and more transparency and accountability will be demanded of the government for its use of the national oil corporation for the bailing out of favored businessmen and companies. From a political perspective, prevalence of such activities has raised the specter of crony capitalism—that is perhaps even more virulent a species of capitalism than rentier capitalism—during the Mahathir regime. Mahathir has facetiously opined that all Bumiputeras and all businessmen are his cronies (*The Star*, 4 August 1999).

Civil Society and its Impact on Political Legitimacy

It can be said that the legitimacy of the Mahathir government may eventually find its nemesis in the emergence of a strong Malaysian civil society. Currently, civil society forces are weak not least of all because of the state's persistent efforts at eroding civil liberties and political freedoms. These actions nonetheless have spurred greater efforts among admittedly a weak middle class civil society to forge interesting new alliances to combat state repression. Political developments following upon the 1997/98 economic crisis have accelerated this sort of politics. We can only touch briefly on these developments for want of space.

In the aftermath of the financial and economic crisis at the end of 1997, an unparalleled spate of events spilled over into the political arena at a remarkable and frenetic pace. These developments have led to yet another crack in the UMNO edifice with the sacking of Anwar Ibrahim as Deputy President and as Deputy Prime Minister and Finance Minister. Even more bizarre has been Anwar's so-called corruption trial of 77 days. At the time of writing, there are still no signs of the political fallout abating, especially after Anwar's sentencing on 14 April 1999 to a six-year prison term. A new political party was been formed on 4 April, headed by Wan Azizah Ismail, Anwar's wife. The PKN now provides the political vehicle for the forces of *Reformasi* to direct their energies for electoral politics and political change, not least of which would be seeking justice for Anwar as well as for other victims of the current onslaught of political repression.

It is clear that Malaysia is in the grips of yet another bout of political turmoil, which raises further questions about the legitimacy of the current UMNO-led political regime. For the embryonic, essentially middle-class, *Reformasi* movement, the current episode also represents yet another imposition of the sinister power of the state, a repressive legislative and judicial power that can so easily be brought to bear on political dissent. On balance, however, the events, wittingly or otherwise, have impelled new awakenings of political consciousness in Malaysian civil society. The actual outburst of peaceful street demonstrations had a sustaining power few would have predicted. Furthermore, more Malaysians are seemingly now choosing to ignore the 'official' media and to pick up information from alternative news purveyors. The PAS weekly newspaper *Harakah* hit a circulation of more than 380,000 before it was forced by the Home Ministry to become a bimonthly paper. Indeed, certain strata of the knowing public have become so politicized that they have created and used a host of alternative news sources to supplement the existing, government-dominated media.

For the 900,000 Malaysian internet users, not only have the number of *Reformasi* internet sites increased by leaps and bounds but the number of hits on the most popular ones have been remarkable. For example, *Laman Reformasi* (Reformasi Website) reported well over 20 million hits from October 1998 until the end of 1999. At the height of the Anwar affair there were at least some 30 *Reformasi*-related sites in cyberspace. There are also a number of ongoing list serves and websites—*freemalaysia, sangkancil, adilnet, saksi*—which regularly carry spirited, often highly cerebral, alternative reports and commentaries on the unfolding events. A new web newspaper, *Malaysiakini* (*Malaysia Today*), has also been launched.

The *Reformasi* movement has brought onto the political centre-stage a new political culture of peaceful, political protest and dissent. Ironically, the reflexive intolerance of the Mahathir government to the *Reformasi* movement has only served to enhance the imperative for political reform. The new Parti KeADILan Nasional (PKN), which is multi-racial in approach and membership, and the other main opposition parties—PAS, DAP and PRM—were all propelled by the political events to band together to form an Alternative Front against the Barison National (BN) government. Although the November 1999 elections returned the BN to power, the BA through PAS captured both the Kelantan and Terengganu state governments. Both PKN and DAP fared poorer than PAS but obtained 10 and 5 parliamentary seats respectively and together with the 27 PAS seats now constitute the strongest opposition in Parliament in the Peninsula since 1969. The PBS in Sabah won three other seats and the opposition bench now has 45 members.

Concluding Remarks

The above depiction of events and developments shows an interesting new trend in Malaysian politics, namely, the increasing involvement of Malays in issues relating to justice and human rights which are universalistic in terms of political discourse. While it cannot be denied that political mobilization on these issues continues and tends to be predominantly through ethnic-cum-religious channels and processes, the formation of PKN, which is multi-ethnic in membership, is a political development that breaks that ubiquitous pattern of Malaysian politics. The formation of Barisan Alternative also suggests that political practices are shifting in the direction of multi-ethnic coalitions, which put the accent on non-ethnic rather than ethnically slanted political discourses.

The broad argument advanced in this essay that political-economy factors have provided the basis for the 'performance' legitimacy of the Mahathir government is contra-indicated by the developments within civil society described above. Genuine political legitimacy remains problematic for a political regime which not only continually fails to redress fundamental economic problems but one which also persistently ignores the demands, interests and rights of civil society.

Notes

1. Poverty estimation in 1997 was based on the following poverty lines: RM460 p.m. for a household size of 4.6 in Peninsular Malaysia; RM633 (4.9 household size) in Sabah and RM543 (4.8 household size) in Sarawak, *Mid-Term Review of the Seventh Plan 1996-2000*.
2. This phase of Japanese-led capitalist development was known by the colorful phrase, 'flying geese' pattern of development. The concept had its roots in the work of Japanese economist Akamatsu Kaname, writing in the 1930s but was popularized in contemporary times by Okita Saburo and Kiyoshi Kojima. The flying geese notion is based on the product cycle view of the migration of industries in the East Asian region, whereby an upgrading of industrial capacities is effected by the latecomers replicating the development pattern of the earlier industrializers. The concept provides part of the explanation to the so-called 'East Asian Miracle'. Until the recent crisis, the countries of East Asia had been doubling their income every ten years whereas it took Britain and the United States 50-60 years to do the same. Furthermore, these countries had rapidly been transformed from initially agricultural economies to manufacture-based economies. For futher discussion of the flying geese concept, see Korhonen (1994), Bernard (1996) and Kojima (1977). See Saravanamuttu (1986, 1988) for an interpretation of how such an NIDL affected Southeast Asia and for an empirical survey of Japanese penetration in the ASEAN states through a regional division of labor.
3. Among the more competent and better accounts are Jomo (1998), Kwan et al. (1998), Rosenberger (1997), Arndt and Hill (1999) and Krugman (1997, 1998). See also my own effort, Saravanamuttu (1998), the recent edited book by Arndt and Hill (1999) and the earlier collection by Kwan, Vandenbrink and Chia (1998).
4. This was the projection of the 1999/2000 Economic Report that was tabled in October. See *The Star*, 30 October 1999. The recovery would essentially be manufactures-led with exports in this sector expected to step up output by an average of 7.9%, driven largely by strong external demand for electronic products and components.

5. At the time of writing, only Bank of Commerce and Bank Bumiputera have successfully merged to become Bumiputera-Commerce Bank. In the new Bank Negara directives, greater responsibility would be passed on to the shareholders of the banking institutions to carry out the merger process. Certain banks, notably RHB Bank and Arab Malaysia Bank, have indicated their interest to become anchor banks and the likelihood is that the final count will go beyond six anchor banks. The exercise is scheduled to be concluded by the end of January 2000 (*The Star*, 9 December 1999).

3 Globalization, Industrialization and Crisis: The Coming-of-Age of Malaysian Women Workers?

MAZNAH MOHAMAD, CECILIA NG AND TAN BENG HUI

Introduction: Crisis of Governance?

The past two decades have revealed that multinational capital is ever ready to go anywhere in the world to maximize profits (Grieder, 1997: 51). Backed by powerful neo-liberal forces and political initiatives like the International Monetary Fund (IMF), World Bank and World Trade Organization (WTO) which pry open previously closed economies, this has resulted in the declining economic sovereignty of many states (Gill, 1994: 80). The increasing influence and control by markets and transnational capital over states results in labor's weakened position in governance (Gill 1994: 82). The Malaysian state, for instance, has no compunction about removing protection for workers to woo foreign investors. At the same time, it is careful to preserve some kind of labor representation, even if this is weak, to check the power of foreign capital (Frenkel and Peetz, 1998: 7, 26-27). Token benevolence also ensures that labor protests are avoided rather than confronted.

   This paper discusses how industrial relations policies used before and during the economic crisis in Malaysia[1] enhanced the imperatives of global manufacturing. Prior to the crisis, the transnational electronics sector used flexibilization strategies because these were conducive for managerial goals, and regulated labor autonomy. At the same time, the dynamic nature of globalization means that the privileging of capital and the autonomy of nation-states can emerge as competing governing interests. Civil liberties groups and social movements demanding more accountability, transparency and participation in governance have emerged in response to these tensions. With globalization breaking down national boundaries, 'governance' is perhaps more accurately viewed as 'patterns of relations, decisions and/or policies among the heterogeneous trio of state, market and civil society actors over a diverse range of issues and levels' (see Chapter 1 in this volume). It should be seen as involving various stakeholders such that control and decision-making issues of nations are no longer the sole prerogative of states (Kofman and Youngs, 1996: 182). The notion of 'governance' used to be understood as 'government officials and institutions [exercising] power in the management of a country's economic and social resources'. Today, however, there is mounting evidence to challenge this 'state-centric' definition.

Frenkel and Peetz (1998) identify two levels of governance: the macro (nation) and the micro (workplace). In the first, they see as significant four forms of labor market governance: 'state unilateralism'; 'state-employer bipartism'; 'state-union bipartism'; and 'national tripartism'. Governments, employers and workers wield different degrees of influence in each of these. Malaysia is said to approximate the tripartite form where these players supposedly share equal power. In reality, as we show later, employers and the state dominate. The latter also exercises extensive controls over unions. Similarly the writers cite four other types of governance at the workplace: 'management unilateralism'; 'collective bargaining'; 'management-state bipartism'; and 'workplace tripartism'. While Malaysian employees have access to the collective bargaining model, the prevailing form of governance in the workplace remains 'management unilateralism' where management reigns supreme (Frenkel and Peetz, 1998: 7-8).

The predominantly female electronics production workforce in Malaysia possesses multiple identities stemming from factors like class, gender and ethnicity. As such, the workforce participates in societal decision-making in different ways. The notion of multiple strategies as forwarded by Chhachhi and Pittin (1996) helps explain why worker protest was absent during the Asian economic crisis, even when their interests were side-stepped. The issue of ethnicity and how it bears on labor movements is discussed in the section on the labor response to the economic crisis. In the end, the Asian economic crisis which indirectly contributed to the precipitation of the Malaysian political crisis[2] was only useful in bringing out the contradictions and frailties of the developmentalist state. The short-lived nature of the economic crisis served to vindicate the efficacy and power of flexible globalization, rendering labor democratization an almost unreachable political goal.

Background to the Malaysian Economy and the
Electronics Industry: Export-Oriented and Female-Led

In the early 1970s the Malaysian government began to pursue a policy of export-oriented industrialization. With the Fordist manufacturing process decomposed (due to automation), it was no longer necessary to concentrate the production cycle within a single location (Henderson, 1989: 31). Under these conditions, the electronics sector quickly grew to dominate the country's industrial sector, becoming a significant contributor to national growth. From just four companies with 577 employees in 1970 it expanded to 850 companies with 321,700 workers in 1998 (MIDA, Industry Briefs, April 1999). The sector now employs 27% of the country's total workforce. The majority of the workforce in the electronics sector is female (Mid-term Review of 7th Malaysia Plan, 1999).

The majority of labor employed was females and first-time rural migrants. Thus, the Asian growth was not only export-oriented but also female-led (Grossman, 1979; Lim, 1978; Ong, 1987). By the late 1970s, 90% of the workers were female (Lim, 1978: 8). The identification of electronic assembly work with supposedly inherent qualities of the female (manual dexterity and small fingers) was touted to be the reason behind the exclusive employment of females (Lim, 1978: 7). However, all of this belied a work atmosphere which demanded severe obedience and compliance, something women were also thought to be able to bear, as opposed to a less docile male labor force (Rasiah, 1994: 13).

Two decades after transnational electronics firms had taken root in Southeast Asia global competition intensified (Rasiah, 1997: 26). American semiconductor firms particularly faced stiff competition from their Japanese counterparts who adopted organizational and technological innovations to surpass their rivals. This had hastened a restructuring exercise in all firms including the offshore companies. Companies were pressured to enhance their manufacturing flexibility and adaptability. Fordism made way to Toyotism, an euphemism to mean production rationalization, of Japanese origins (Ostry, 1995: 8; Rasiah, 1994: 281). To keep up with global competitiveness, shop-floor production features in the Malaysian electronics industry changed widely by the 1990s (Rasiah, 1994: 22). Manufacturing practice and production form was restructured towards the goal of reducing the development time for new products without sacrificing quality or production (Angel, 1994: 196). Product cycles became increasingly shortened to respond to the extreme state of competitiveness (Lim, 1990: 104). Euphemisms such as team-playing, collective trust and integrative problem-solving were used as guiding principles in the productivity-enhancement exercise. In Singapore and Malaysia where labor supply was far shorter than the demand for it, rationalization through automation did not result in retrenchments on any massive scale. Hence the absence of labor unrest.

Flexibility as an Adaptive Strategy in Industrial Relations

Given the intensification of liberalized trade, world market volatility, market fragmentation, heightened demand for 'just-in-time' production and continuous improvements, semiconductor industries would not survive had it not been for flexibility (Deyo, 1994: 214). Flexibility can be specifically examined at three levels, namely changes in relation to organizational structure of the firm, in the pattern of production, and in the labor market involving labor laws, work status and wages (Chhachhi, 1998: 7). By the mid-1990s new human resource strategies were already being employed within Malaysian transnational companies (Ng and Maznah, 1997). Some of the major shifts were in the aspects of labor, organizational systems and machinery utilization, as summarized below:

Table 3:1   Shifts in Labor, Machinery and Organizational System in Malaysian Electronics Firms, 1970s Compared to the 1990s

1970s	1980s/1990s
• Labor-intensive, low-waged.	• Capital-intensive; shift towards high precision computer-controlled automated systems.
• Task of labor limited to single operation and single machinery.	
• Tasks were monotonous, repetitive and based on manual dexterity.	• Multiple tasks and multi-functional machinery.
• Close supervision, intensive and explicit discipline measures.	• 'Vertical tasking'; reasoning, problem-solving, maintenance and machine-repairs, statistical processing, participation in process-improvements.
• Explicitly hierarchical management.	
• Explicitly hierarchical management-labor divide.	• Self-supervisory or peer-supervision.
• 'Despotic' work regime.	• 'Humanizing' of work atmosphere.

A Critique of Flexible Labor Regimes and
Limits to Labor Democratization

Some observers doubted that social and technological change in the production arrangement would result in a more worker-oriented or democratized working process. Essentially the conditions of flexibility were pre-dictated by a centralized management to the extent that it left no room for inputs from labor. In the developed countries during the 1980s, Michael Burawoy (1983) saw the flexible phase as capital moving from a regime which was despotic during its earlier phases to one which he termed hegemonic (Burawoy, 1983: 590).

A critique which is more relevant to the situation of flexibility in the Asian developing economies was presented by Frederic Deyo (1997). He distinguishes 'static' from 'dynamic' forms of flexibility. Deyo noted that many smaller, less resourceful firms would be adopting short-term strategies which generally involve cost-cutting measures. This is the 'static' variety, involving the use of contractual, casual and sub-contracted work, something that is quite predominant in Asian developing economies.

The other form of flexibility, 'dynamic flexibility', is only pursued by large, resourceful firms producing high-end products such as semi-conductors and requiring high levels of quality, batch vs. mass production, and continuous innovations and improvements in process and product technologies. In dynamic arrangements such as this there is a greater chance that worker welfare and security, and enhanced worker participation, will be engendered in these firms. The expectation in this sort of arrangement is that worker commitment and loyalty to the firms would have been augmented, as workers will have assumed greater responsibility in determining the profitability of the enterprise.

Nevertheless, 'dynamic flexibility' is recognized as emanating from two conditions. One is from a situation where there are 'bargained' forms of flexibility. In this situation strong unions participate in determining the acceptance or rejection of new production systems. In contrast, the other situation, 'participative flexibility' will be characterized by a more circumscribed form of worker participation, confined largely to shop-floor problem-solving, rather than one that could have an impact on the imperatives of production.

What existed in transnational electronics firms in Malaysia in the 1990s was not the bargained form of dynamic flexibility but a *participative and autocratic kind of flexible labor regime*. It was participative (rather than bargained) in the sense that production and organizational changes had not occurred at the backing of strong union agendas, but had been determined by managerial prerogatives for organizational improvements, of unspecified duration, though most likely of a short-term nature.

The state labor regimes of countries like Malaysia and Singapore had excluded any possibilities for collective bargaining through their enacted legislations. Transnational firms had a stake in sustaining a union-free industrial climate, and actually used flexibility as a means of circumventing unions through instituting in-house empowerment programs. Furthermore, workers in developing countries functioned in learning-based industries rather than in those that were innovative and at the leading edge of production. Learning-by-doing relied on local adoption of technologies based upon products developed and designed elsewhere (Deyo, 1997: 217). As ascertained by one of the engineers of a local subcontracting electronics company:

> The headquarters in the US transfers technology from overseas to [our] factories here. So, rather than 'research and development', 'technology and development' is carried out. Transfer of knowledge takes place but more in terms of learning techniques only.[3]

In Malaysia, legislation banning the formation of unions is barely challenged as workers succumb to the appeal of management's 'internally charted' agenda. Outside efforts, particularly wielded by unions to resolve labor woes are considered unnecessary in a 'self-sufficient' organizational environment.

Crisis and Labor Retrenchments

Managers of electronics firms agreed that their firms were affected by the East Asian economic crisis.[4] Whatever the effects, electronics firms were already in the business of reorganizing their operations to remain internationally competitive. The Asian economic debacle caused local demand for electronic products to fall further. However, because the Malaysian industry mainly caters to an international market, the loss in local demand did not have hugely negative repercussions on production output. Export-oriented industries also received a temporary boost by the crisis-induced devalued ringgit. The capital control regulations introduced on 1 September 1998, helped companies to breathe easier. According to one development consultant:

> Some companies were already moving out of Malaysia but when the capital controls were announced, they could stay since labour became as cheap as say in China. The capital controls thus resulted in them deferring their decisions to relocate.[5]

Two factors which greatly helped in easing the losses and burdens of the crisis were the advantages of globalized industrial networking and the employment of flexibilization strategies. Globalization, which was the precursor of the Asian crisis, was also its panacea. As most electronics transnationals have an extensive world-wide network to fall back on, this has given them an advantage to share resources and coordinate production shifts in a balanced way. Companies were able to restructure using their shared global resources to reallocate production options.

Overall there were no massive exercises in retrenchments, but statistics reveal the vulnerability of labor to global forces. The section below presents the macro-picture of industrial reorganization as a result of the crisis. In terms of retrenchments in Peninsular Malaysia a total of 93,061 persons, or 20.4% of the total workforce, from all sectors were retrenched from January 1998 until May 1999.[6] If one were to compare this to the total labor force of 9 million in the country, the number retrenched represents only 1.03% of the workforce. However this still represented almost 12 times the numbers retrenched three years earlier in 1996. Then the total number of workers retrenched in the country was only 7,773 (Malaysia, 1999: 100).

Some sectors are more adversely affected than others (See Table 3:2). In terms of quantity of workers, the manufacturing sector is the worst affected with almost one-quarter of the workforce before retrenchment. This is followed by the services sector (16% retrenched) and the construction sector (15.7% retrenched). This could be due to the fact that many were undocumented or unregistered foreign workers. An amnesty of sorts was granted to Indonesian migrant workers who were ferried back to their homeland during this period. As for the agricultural sector, only 3,559 workers were retrenched.

In terms of the gender breakdown, women employees represented 45.3% and men 54.7% of those retrenched. However the data also revealed that more women than men were affected in some sectors. For example, more women workers were retrenched in proportion to men in the agricultural (56.7%) and manufacturing (54.2%) sectors. They also formed a substantial proportion in the financial services sector (42.1%) and in the wholesale, retail and restaurant sector (40.2%). There were also gender differences according to occupational categories reflecting the unequal gender division of labor in the Malaysian employment pattern. More male managerial and professional staff were retrenched compared to women, while more women were retrenched at the clerical and semi-skilled occupational level.

Within the electronics sector, a total of 334 electronics companies with a total workforce of 101,374 workers reported retrenching their workers during the period January 1998 to May 1999 (see Table 3:3). These companies represent about 40% of the total number of electronics companies in Malaysia and nearly one-third of the total workforce in the sector. It is interesting to note that the factories which 'practised' retrenchment comprised 116 Malaysian-owned, 92 Malaysian and joint venture and 126 foreign-owned companies. The majority of the workers were actually employed by foreign companies which accounted for 71.8% of the workforce, compared to 15.1% and 12.9% hired by Malaysian joint venture and wholly Malaysian-owned companies respectively. As for the gender equation, foreign companies seem to have a penchant for hiring women compared to the other companies. For example, 70.5% of the total employees in the foreign-owned companies were female, compared to 50.8% in Malaysian and 34% in joint venture companies.

The data reveal that 26% of their employees were retrenched during the 17 month period. The majority were local workers (93.3%) with women comprising about two-thirds (65%) of the total retrenched. It is also revealing that most of the retrenchment came from the foreign-owned companies with their workers forming 75.2% of the total retrenched. This shows the instability of foreign direct investment (FDI) in the country, despite the government's assurances of the benefits of FDI to the growth and expansion of the economy in terms of investment and employment opportunities. All in all, the companies fired about 22-27% of their workforce with women (and foreign workers) bearing the brunt of the firing.

The electronics companies cited various reasons for retrenchment. Most of them (60%) stated that the main reason was the declining demand for their product, reflecting the overall downturn at the global level as well as increasing competition discussed in the earlier section. The other reasons given were increasing production costs (16%), reorganization/restructuring (8%) and complete closure of their company (5%). Another nine companies reported that they were selling off the companies retrenching 1,422 employees, while eight disclosed that they were relocating to another country and thus retrenched 983 employees.

Table 3:2   Retrenchment by Sector and Gender, January 1998-May 1999, Peninsular Malaysia

Sector	Before Retrenchment Period			Total Retrenched		
	Male Workers	Female Workers	Total	Male	Female	Total*
Agriculture	4,663	3,853	8516	541	2,018	3,559
(% of total)	(54.8)	(45.2)		(43.3)	(56.7)	(41.8)
Mining & Quarrying	2,410	421	2,831	799	83	882
(% of total)	(85.1)	(14.9)		(90.6)	(9.4)	(31.2)
Manufacturing:						
Electronics	38,248	63,349	101,597	9,135	17,026	26,161
(% of total)	(37.6)	(62.4)		(34.9)	(65.1)	(25.7)
Non-Electronics	64,462	50,453	114,915	14,198	10,824	25,022
(% of total)	(56.1)	(43.9)		(56.7)	(43.30	(21.8)
Construction	53,827	12,858	66,685	8,793	1,672	10,465
(% of total)	(80.7)	(19.3)		(84.0)	(16.0)	(15.7)
Wholesale, Retail,	40,191	25,494	65,685	6,915	4,647	11,562
Restaurants & Hotels	(61.2)	(38.8)		(59.8)	(40.2)	(17.6)
Transport, Storage &	12,925	4,186	17,111	1,443	748	2,191
Communication	(75.5)	(24.5)		(65.9)	(34.1)	(12.8)
Financial Services,	21,858	16,451	38,309	4,656	3,389	8,045
Insurance	(57.6)	(42.4)		(57.9)	(42.1)	(21.0)
Community, Social &	27,487	13,557	41,044	3,367	1,699	5,066
Personal Services	(67.0)	(33.0)		(66.5)	(33.5)	(12.3)
Others**	262	217	479	65	43	108
(% of total)	(54.7)	(45.3)		(60.1)	(39.9)	(22.5)
TOTAL	266,333	190,839	457,172	50,912	42,149	93,061
	(58.3)	(41.7)		(54.7)	(45.3)	(20.4)

*   The percentages here are out of the total workforce.
**   These are activities that cannot be fully classified.

Table 3:3   Retrenchment in Electronics Sector by Equity Ownership and Gender, January 1998-May 1999, Peninsular Malaysia

Equity Ownership	Number of Workers Involved in Retrenchment*			% of Total Workforce Before Re-trenchment	Number of Companies Involved
	Male	Female	Total		
Malaysian	1,847	1,292	3,139	23.8	116
(%)	(58.8)	(42.0)	(100.0)		
Malaysian & Foreign Joint Venture	2,529	807	3,336	22	92
	(75.8)	(25.9)	(100.0)		
Foreign	4,750	14,897	19,647	27	126
	(24.2)	(75.8)	(100)		
Total	9,369	17,161	26,122	26	334
	(36.3)	(64.7)	(100)		

* Figures include both local and foreign workers. Total number reported retrenched in above period was 1,754, while the number for local workers was 24,368.

Globalization and Production Rescheduling

The nature and scale of restructuring varied according to individual factories. While some had to downsize or close down operations entirely, others were able to shuffle workers across the production floor until such a time when demand picked up again. The human resources director at one factory suggested two reasons for this organizational change rather than outright retrenchments: first, to preserve a company's public image; and second, to avoid the costs in having to retrain new workers once demand levels picked up. Rather than retrenching their workers, some larger factories preferred to continue employing them at a loss, or asked workers to use up their annual leave.[7] Schemes such as the Voluntary Separation Scheme (VSS) offering hefty compensation in return for 'voluntary termination' were popular with employees, especially women. In many instances the scheme was over-subscribed by those wanting to opt out and at the same time benefit from a substantial payoff.[8] These schemes actually functioned to regulate labor, allowing management to 'get rid' of those no longer needed.[9] Employees who left were not replaced hence resulting in an increased workload for those left behind.[10]

Workers interviewed in this study said that their greatest concern during the crisis revolved around wages. The cutting back of overtime work which had taken place across the industry was noted as a particular loss. For newly employed production operators, overtime work used to mean an extra RM500-600 each month on top of a basic wage of RM300-400. A more outstanding grievance was the matter of management withholding workers' wage increments. In one established transnational factory, workers were aware that despite the company doing well and achieving its production targets, management used the economic crisis as an excuse to deny them their rights. Says one of the leaders of an in-house union:

> The company has been 'dragging on with discussions' and still has not made a decision on latest salary increments even though the Collective Agreement (CA) expired in December 1998. (The CA lasts for three years. The union draws up a proposal and the management studies this and sends it back for discussion until an agreement is reached.) Demands by workers in the CA are based on the company's achievements. The present demand for wages to be increased was based on the fact that prices have risen (8.5%). Previously we asked for a 10% increment, now we are only asking for 8.5% and yet no decision appears forthcoming. The crisis can thus be said to have reduced the union's bargaining power. [11]

Nevertheless, disputes arising out of poor working conditions or unsatisfactory benefits did not become a dire concern among labor. This seemed so in factories that managed to continue the practice of offering bonuses, profit sharing schemes, medical and life insurance, or skills-upgrading opportunities during the lean period. This focus on worker welfare and security had been part and parcel of a new management style that accompanied the switch into high-value added production over the last ten years. Production of such a nature required workers' skills to be enhanced and this in turn called for long-term investment on the part of these companies. As it was also necessary to circumvent the union role in addressing workers' grievances, employers felt that it would be in their interest to view workers as partners rather than adversaries (Ng and Mohamad, 1997: 189).

Subsequently management has actively endeavored to increase the commitment and loyalty of workers by providing some of the above-mentioned 'perks', and portraying themselves as being interested in democratization at the factory floor for the benefit of mutual profitability. In some, a paternalistic work culture was successfully cultivated where workers learnt to regard themselves and their employers as being part of one big 'family'[12] (Frenkel and Peetz, 1998: 22; Deyo, 1997: 216). The crisis had affected workers' ability to exert pressure for wages to be revised upwards.[13] Even if some companies had offered voluntary separation schemes (VSS), in the main, retrenchments were still the preferred mode of cutting down production costs. Labor Department statistics, between January 1998 and May 1999, reported that only 5,128 workers were 'retired' under the VSS whereas 51,183 were retrenched.[14]

Labour, Gender and Ethnicity: Responses to Crisis

The export-oriented industrialization phase introduced new ethnic and gender dimensions within the manufacturing class. When the economy opened up to foreign investment in the 1970s the labor class switched from being Chinese dominated to becoming Malay and female, especially in the electronics industry.[15] Perhaps because of the switch in the ethnic make-up of the working class, the past legacy of women workers' militancy was not carried into Malaysia's new industrialization phase. Thus, apart from episodes like the Mostek strike in 1985,[16] labor protests have been rare in post-1969 Malaysia.

Unionists argue that it has been difficult drawing workers, especially Malays, towards unionism. Presently, just seven percent of the workforce is unionized. Four percent belong to the Malaysian Trade Union Congress (MTUC) and out of its 400,000 members, only 41 percent are women. The fact that MTUC is registered with the Registrar of Societies and not the Registrar of Trade Unions means that it cannot represent its members in trade union disputes. Apart from this technical restriction, there are other explanations for the organization's unpopularity and inability to lead a nation-wide workers' movement.

For one, its scope to mobilize and organize workers For one, its scope to mobilize and organize workers—like others in the country's trade union movement—is severely curtailed by state controls. The *Trade Unions Act* of 1959 and the *Industrial Relations Act* of 1967 are just two of many laws restricting labor rights in this country.[17] Yet the state does not only rely on repressive legislation. During the economic crisis, companies were required to report any retrenchment, lay-off, voluntary separation or salary reduction plans to the Labour Department so that it could monitor these activities and assist in re-deploying affected workers. Although this move appeared motivated by concern for workers, it was in fact more welcomed because of its desired effect in preventing strikes arising out of worker discontent (Interview with Labour Department, 19 May 1999). Clearly, the state has different forms of labor controls at its disposal, subtle or otherwise—like others in the country's trade union movement—is severely curtailed by state controls. The *Trade Unions Act* of 1959 and the *Industrial Relations Act* of 1967 are just two of many laws restricting labor rights in this country.[18] Yet the state does not only rely on repressive legislation. During the economic crisis, companies were required to report any retrenchment, lay-off, voluntary separation or salary reduction plans to the Labour Department so that it could monitor these activities and assist in re-deploying affected workers. Although this move appeared motivated by concern for workers, it was in fact more welcomed because of its desired effect in preventing strikes arising out of worker discontent (Interview with Labor Department, 19 May 1999). Clearly, the state has different forms of labor controls at its disposal, subtle or otherwise.

Membership levels remain low because recruitment has been hampered by changes in the workforce pattern. Previously when the economy was dominated by primary industries, there were many more workers who could join unions. Today's EPZs forbid the formation of unions except in-house ones but even these are discouraged. With the enlargement of service-oriented industries, MTUC has also found itself without the organizational cadre to woo workers as members. Worse still, in 'boom' times, there is little reason for workers to unionize since wages are relatively good. Being a union member would be perceived as disadvantageous to those wanting to job-hop (for more lucrative offers) during this period.

Furthermore, the persistence of ethnic identification has weakened class unity and diminished the role of bodies like the MTUC. Typically, ethnic-based political parties are sought to redress labor woes instead. According to the Research Offices, MTUC:

> Labour grievances are often channelled through UMNO if workers are Malay and MIC if workers are Indian rather than through the trade unions. There is thus a preference to use political party channels.[19]

Apart from the role of the MTUC, the lack of response by electronics workers during the economic crisis relates to the absence of a national trade union in this industry. For close to two decades the government contained labor organizing and only gave the green light for the formation of in-house unions in 1988[20] (Arudsothy, 1994: 110). These unions give workers a chance to articulate their demands but evidently only within the parameters set by management.[21] More importantly, in-house unions prevent them from building important linkages with each other, in the long run undermining the strength of collective labor action (Wad and Jomo, 1994: 215).

Not all in-house unions have failed, however. One of the most active unions that continues to engage management in negotiations is the in-house union of Harris Advanced Technology (HAT). It was formed in 1989. Despite the government's 'favorable' ruling then, the company's management refused to recognize the body set up by its workers. Within a year it sacked some of the union's elected officials. The matter was brought up to the industrial court and, finally, in 1996 the court ruled that the 21 workers be reinstated to their former positions with no loss of seniority, benefits and back wages.[22]

Presently the union has 2,200 members, 90% Malays and 91% female. Organizing has been made difficult by a management that induces racial politics to dissuade workers from joining this union. For example, it has invited Islamic religious leaders to speak against unionism. The ruling Malay political party, UMNO, has done the same using members of its Youth wing. In spite of these, the union representative interviewed was positive about the organization's future. Since the *Reformasi* movement began in September 1998, there seems to have been a shift in political consciousness. Workers, who previously were not interested in union activities, are now singing a different tune. They appear to be giving more thought to their own situations and role in social change.[23] This recent experience supports Wad and Jomo's (1994: 229) proposition that perhaps an in-house union under pressure can emerge vibrant, accountable and responsive to labor needs.

The sustained union activities of HAT employees attest to the determination of workers to seek a voice and representation in their workspace. Other in-house unions belonging to a Japanese transnational company have been actively involved in seeing through their collective agreements on wage benefits as well. The vibrant involvement of women workers in non-governmental organizations outside the confines of the shop-floor also demonstrate that the struggle for democracy, rights and representation is very much happening. For example, some women with long working experiences within the industrial system have developed the personal confidence and social awareness that allow them to be leaders in other organizations not necessarily connected to labor concerns. This was the case of one woman in Penang who is now an active organizer of a women's group called *Wanita Prihatin* or 'Concerned Women'. This group displays a remarkable record of activities, organizational set-up and procedural obeisance.[24]

Should the following statement be seen as management triumph or an overstretched denial that refuses to acknowledge that the labor force will eventually demand more than just surface 'niceties'?   According to the Human Resource Director of Company I, Penang:

> Workers have not formed a union because the company takes care of their welfare very well. For example, besides their good wages and perks, the company provides a cybercafe at the factory, good chairs at the cafeteria which also has a two-million ringgit view (of the sea).[25]

Flexibility is most pronounced in high value-added industrial production sectors (e.g., electronics). However, in the non-electronics sectors such as textiles and garment manufacturing, gendered division of work functions are more pronounced, and flexibility is more static. Companies where automation of production is not at a high level still prefer labor with perceived innate attributes based on ethnicity (Malay) and gender (female) (Elias, 1999: 7-8). The persistence of local ideologies about 'female suitability/docility' and cost-cutting prerogatives of globalized industrialization will thus continue to reinforce mutually the climate for trouble-free/union-free industrialization.

Conclusion

This study has tried to show that globalization and the economic crisis of the late 1990s have not been successful in delivering a new form of labor politics among Malaysia's manufacturing class. There are several factors to explain this phenomenon. First, the adoption of flexibility through the restructuring of technological and human resource capacities created a flatter work organizational structure. However, labor empowerment measures were affected through a directed decision-making process, and limited to shop-floor problem solving and production improvement goals. The form of empowerment programs encouraged among the labor force precluded collective bargaining involving wages or the enhancement of social security benefits. This was made even more unattainable with the economic crisis when some companies backtracked on their earlier plan to institute more 'participative' modes of interaction with labor.

Second, the very nature of flexibility underscored its temporality allowing very little room for the development of any viable, long-term labor movement in developing economies. Workers were mindful that the distance between management and labor had persisted despite efforts to flatten the organization. The configuration of gender and ethnicity in Malaysia's ambit of industrialization had been molded to fit national prerogatives of maintaining a stable, compliant workforce focussed on productivity. Labor democratization which would enable negotiations on wage issues and social and human rights benefits is being curtailed both by state instruments and flexible strategies of labor control. The latter have become more efficacious due to production rationalization premised upon globalized imperatives.

Third, the economic crisis brought out various corrective measures to cope with the sudden flux in exchange and financial systems but not extraordinary factors which could transform the manufacturing class into a force for significant social change. Both neo-liberal globalization forces and the national state collude in their pursuit of profit maximization, even though globalization may at times jolt the sovereignty of national states when the international financial system may work against national gains.

Malaysian women workers, despite being the main transnational workforce for the last three decades have still not come-of-age, at least not in the arena of labor struggles. Most likely they would have to translate their new sense of 'empowerment' derived from shop-floor experiences outside the perimeter of astute global industrial management. This may be the end of ideology but not necessarily the end of some other history, especially the history of continuing nation-building and the quest for a new social governance.

Notes

1. See for example Jomo (1998) and Saravanamuttu (1998) for the origins and discussion of the crisis.
2. A political crisis was brought about by the removal of Anwar Ibrahim, the former Deputy Prime Minister and Finance Minister from the government. He was subsequently charged for various wrong-doings, from corruption to sodomy, and is currently serving a six-year prison term for abuse of power. This event triggered widespread dissent against the present regime.
3. Interview with Mr AL (Process Engineer, Company S), 11 June 1999.
4. The economic downturn may have been sparked off by a sudden and massive flight of short-term capital. Nevertheless there were already worrying long-term trends in the economy which was 'overheating'. There was a current account deficit that was being predominantly financed by volatile and unsustainable short-term capital, and a banking sector that had expanded too much. Exports were also down, in large part because world demand for semiconductors had declined (Mohamed Ariff, et al., n.d.: 4).
5. Interview with Lim Pao Li, Development Consultant, Penang, who had formerly worked with the Penang Development Corporation, a state-owned development enterprise.
6. The macro-picture of restructuring is based on data collected by the Labour Department of the Malaysian Ministry of Human Resources. The government has made it mandatory, starting from June 1998, for all companies to submit a report to the Labour Department of all restructuring exercises, particularly involving the retrenchment of labor.
7. Interview with Human Resources Director in Company I, 10 June 1999.

8. As an indication of how much money was being offered, production line operators who had been working in a factory for 20 years stood to gain RM40,000. These workers also found this a good opportunity to leave for a different job, claiming to be 'tired' and 'bored' with their present employment (Personal interview with employee of Company M, 18 May 1999 and personal interview with the Malaysian Labour Department, 19 May 1999).

9. According to her, while every worker in one line had been given the option of taking up this scheme—and in fact, those who didn't were later pushed into doing any kind of job on the floor—those on other lines were not extended a similar opportunity (Personal interview with employee of Company M, 18 May 1999).

10. 'After the crisis, those on the production line faced "burden and torture" with the increased workload', says Ms R. of Company M, 18 May 1999.

11. Interview with union representatives of Company HC, 19 May 1999.

12. One of the interviewees stated that in her factory, there was no distinction between bosses and workers, that the bosses were in fact 'like one of them ... like friends' (Personal interview with employee of Motorola, 18 May 1999).

13. It is worth pointing out that not all factories have provided their employees with benefits, not even when the industry was doing well (Personal interview with trade unionist in Company H, June 1999).

14. Since June 1998, the Labour Department has made it compulsory for companies to inform of any plans relating to retrenchment, lay-offs, voluntary separation schemes and salary reductions. Those failing to do so risk incurring a RM10,000 fine. Since this policy was instituted, the number of lay-offs in the electronics industry that the department has been notified of has been minimal (Personal interview with the Malaysian Labour Department, 19 May 1999).

15. Industrial policy in the 1970s favored export-oriented industries (e.g., textiles, garments and electronics) which hired thousands of female workers for their 'dexterity' and 'docility'. Thus the number of female workers in manufacturing increased more than four times within 10 years (from 73,058 in 1970 to about 300,000 in 1980) (See Malaysia, 1996, Tables 20-2, 623).

16. See Lochhead (1988) for an account of this incident which was a response by women workers to being retrenched by their transnational employer during one of Malaysia's worst recessions.

17. Under the former, a union is deemed illegal if not registered with the Director General of Trade Unions (DGTU). Also, the DGTU is empowered to approve or reject any application, and can also de-register already existent unions (George, 1999: 34). *The Industrial Relations Act* precludes from negotiation issues such as dismissals and transfers, and stipulates rules for collective bargaining (Jomo, 1990: 87).

18. Under the former, a union is deemed illegal if not registered with the Director General of Trade Unions (DGTU). Also, the DGTU is empowered to approve or reject any application, and can also de-register already existent unions (George, 1999: 34). *The Industrial Relations Act* precludes from negotiation issues such as dismissals and transfers, and stipulates rules for collective bargaining (Jomo, 1990: 87).

19. Personal interview with the Research Officer, MTUC, 23 June 1999.

20. According to Arudsothy (1990: 110), it was the efforts of Malaysian unions and their international counterparts that pressured the government into allowing unions to be formed in the free trade zones. The former had successfully campaigned for Malaysia's special tariff privileges under the General System of Preferences to be made conditional upon this issue.

21. A union representative of Hitachi noted that the management effectively controlled their union. The former had no qualms about reminding them that at the end of the day, the company was still paying their salaries (Personal interview with a unionist at Company HC, 19 May 1999).

22. For a chronology of events, see Report of Extraordinary General Meeting, 28 February 1999, of the Harris Advanced Technology (M) Sdn. Bhd. Workers Union.

23. Interview with Bruno Pereira, executive Company H Union, 22 June 1999. According to him it is easier now to talk to workers about issues using the terms '*keadilan*' (justice) and '*reformasi*' (reforms).

24. One of its leaders, Cik Norsiah has worked for 18 years in the electronics industry. She rose to become a supervisor in her plant and now manages many workers. 'Wanita Prihatin' was registered on 13 December 1996. It has 330 members and has held several Annual General Meetings with professionally recorded minutes and annual reports. Cik Norsiah's 60 year-old mother is the treasurer of the organization. Both are articulate and highly opinionated in matters of current political and social issues.

25. Interview with the Human Resource Director of Company I, Penang. The Company sits on a beautiful stretch of land overlooking the sea.

4 Comparative Responses to the Challenges of Governance and Globalization: Malaysia and South Africa

JANIS VAN DER WESTHUIZEN

Introduction

This chapter compares different strategies for ethnic (or racial) redistribution with growth in two divergent regions, albeit at slightly different time periods, to see if lessons can thereby be learned for public policy/strategy, particularly for the late-developer, post-apartheid South Africa. Despite the high degree of similarity as well as interaction between the South African and Malaysian political economies, key decision-makers responded to the 'Asian crisis' in profoundly different ways, in part reflective of their distinctive regional contexts. Whereas South Africa largely decided to 'bite the bullet' and increase interest rates accordingly, such action would provoke extreme political consequences in the Malaysian case as the subsequent Anwar-Mahathir affair clearly suggested. Yet, in both ethnically deeply divided societies, state elites have sought to pursue or maintain a strategy of ethnic redistribution with growth (ERWG) amidst the constraining features of a globalizing world order. In as much as there are any 'lessons' for South African policy-makers (and possibly others in the developing world) to draw from the Malaysian experience, this comparative analysis suggests that societal corporatism is probably preferable to many other evils which state elites have to face when embarking upon a process of ethnic redistribution with growth amidst globalization. However, the challenge of preventing societal corporatism from degenerating into a form of patron-client rentierism remains particularly problematic and requires a fine balance between various state/societal actors, in order to enhance the prospects for 'embedded autonomy'.[1]

70

Accordingly, this chapter is structured as follows. Before discussing what the process of ethnic redistribution with growth entails, I make the case for the comparability between the South African and Malaysian political economies. Thereafter, the way in which ERWG has been pursued in the two countries is both compared and contrasted before I conclude with a few thoughts on the implications of this comparative case analysis for the wider debate about global governance and the future of the developmental or 'desarrolista' state in the aftermath of the 1997-8 Asian crisis.

The Mandela/Mbeki-Mahathir Axis

Similar dynamics of social stratification, British colonial influences, strong anti-communist histories and federalist pretensions are but a few of the many parallels between the South African and Malaysian political economies.

Today, the African National Congress (ANC), like the United Malays' National Organization (UMNO), presides over a near two-thirds parliamentary majority, and is also the most important political force in a de facto one party dominant system. Secondly, like UMNO in the 13-member Barisan Nasional coalition, the ANC is the hegemonic partner in the Tripartite Alliance between the South African Communist Party (SACP), the Congress of South African Trade Unions (COSATU) and the South African Civics Association (SANCO).

Not unlike South Africa's Government of National Unity (GNU) formed in 1994 following the first democratic elections, the first Malaysian government after independence also consisted of a multi-ethnic alliance between the Malaysian Chinese Association (MCA), UMNO and the Malaysian Indian Congress (MIC). As in South Africa, it was through this coalition that 'the three parties were able to retain their communal identities and bases whilst achieving elitist, multi-ethnic cooperation' (Jomo and Gomez, 1997: 10, 12). Indeed, the so-called 'package deal' through which the Alliance came to be established ensured that—although the positions of Prime Minister and Deputy Prime Minister would almost always be occupied by Malays—the important portfolios of Finance as well as Commerce and Industry, were assigned to members of the MCA.

Post-1994 South Africa also mirrored this technocratic shift, with the politically 'independent' Finance Minister being the former chief executive of a major mining conglomerate and the Governor of the Reserve Bank, appointed by the previous National Party government, retaining his position for a further five years until 1999.

A considerable measure of 'like-mindedness' between Pretoria and Kuala Lumpur is also evident. South Africa stands at the heart of Malaysia's Africa policy and Mahathir's view of South-South cooperation. Malaysia was at the forefront of efforts to suspend South Africa's membership of the Commonwealth in the 1960s, and donated close to US \$5 million to the ANC's 1994 election campaign. Kuala Lumpur is reported to provide quiet advice to Pretoria in developing its links with India and China, whilst it is alleged that Malaysian advice influenced Mandela's decision in November 1996 to switch South Africa's diplomatic relations from Taiwan to China (Africa Confidential, 3 January, 1997).

Malaysia has not only become the second largest investor in South Africa after the United States—accounting for 21% of FDI in 1997—but close diplomatic relationships are also echoed along party lines (Padayachee and Valodia, 1997; Muda, 1996). Indeed, some Malaysian investment deals are shrouded in controversy. The site for the Hilton Hotel in Durban as well as the development of Durban's waterfront for example, 'were sold to Renong (known to act as the investment arm of the ruling UMNO) at a substantial discount at market value, and in spite of higher bids from other developers. In both cases, prominent (ANC aligned) businessman Mzi Khumalo is alleged to have played a central role' (Padayachee and Valodia, 1997: 25). Interestingly, most Malaysian investors avoid labor-intensive investments—with a clear preference for the property sector—since they remain suspicious of the powerful South African trade unions. In fact, COSATU picketed a visiting Malaysian delegation to oppose the 'slave wages' Malaysian workers were being paid (R4, 36 per hour versus the R7, 68 in South Africa, before the appreciation of the ringgit during 1996) (Madi, 1997: 46).

These links in and across civil societies are also reflected in the small Islamic presence in and around Cape Town, but also a decided South African attempt at emulating Malaysia's ascendance into 'NIC-dom' (see for example, Hart 1994; Southall, 1997). The depth of the Malaysian interest, for example, is in turn reflected in Malaysian Prime Minister Mahathir's right hand man, Tun Daim Zanuddin's 'twelve month attachment to the Harvard Institute of International Development, where he advised faculty members on how South Africa's political leadership and economic system might be restructured' (*Asian Business*, March 1993: 48).

There are, of course, a number of differences that could ensure that South Africa does not entirely follow the Malaysian trajectory. The most noticeable of the differences are the greater political power of labor in South Africa, the significance of Islamic revivalism as a political force in the Malaysian case, the extent to which South Africa has more in common with other British settler societies than Malaysia does and, to a lesser extent, the degree to which the military has played a much smaller role in Malaysia than in South Africa. Finally, the power which each exercises in Southern Africa and Southeast Asia constitutes another set of differences particularly in relation to their foreign policies. However, the most obvious similarity is the extent to which the strategy of ethnic redistribution with growth (ERWG) has been pursued in both countries.

When Ethnic Redistribution With Growth Meets Globalization

Milton Esman (1987) contends that, where minority domination of the economy is perceived in ethnic terms with a high likelihood for political mobilization and economic disruption, the newly incumbent regime may follow one of three options. Firstly, they may choose to take no specific action, fearing that any action taken to address economic inequalities could frighten capital away, weaken and disrupt the economy and lead to a serious loss of skilled human resources. Considering that such a strategy could actually inflict more damage on the disadvantaged majority, they may rather choose to tolerate the economic subordination of their constituents in the hope of gradual vindication of such imbalances through 'autonomous but unspecified economic processes'. Alternatively, such governments may believe they can immediately end minority domination and adopt draconian measures to that effect—i.e., through expropriation, or nationalization of assets or even by expelling ethnic minorities. Though these measures may follow a revolutionary struggle, it is not a characteristic consequence of such takeovers. Finally, a strategy of 'ethnic (re)distribution with growth' (ERWG) may be pursued in which the state's allocative apparatus is put to use for explicitly ethnic economic objectives, to provide middle class employment opportunities and acquire economic assets for constituents of the new ethnic masters of the state and thus redress the original, unfavorable ethnic division of labor (Esman, 1987: 395).

The necessary conditions for the positive-sum strategy of ERWG include: i) a demographic majority; ii) economic subordination; iii) political opportunity which allows the majority to gain control. of the state; iv) a nationalist ideology; and v) unoccupied fiscal space (Esman, 1987: 416). These conditions clearly prevailed in Malaysia in the 1960s and—apart from the requirement of unoccupied fiscal space—also in the South Africa of the 1990s. It is predicated on the acknowledgement that the cumulative and reinforcing effects of lack of attributes (skills, capital, confidence and educational opportunities) and of discrimination in the labor market, makes it well-nigh impossible for the economically subjugated group to overcome its inferior position in the national economy and division of labor through sheer competition within the market (Esman, 1987: 415).

Extensive state intervention is crucial since, with very few exceptions, it is almost impossible to address the economic subjugation of a political majority simply through autonomous market forces. Yet the latter is also the very deficiency in Esman's ERWG framework: it stops short of indicating how the strategy of ERWG unfolds in those societies attempting either to continue, or pursue it amidst globalization. Comparing Malaysian and South African attempts at ERWG is therefore particularly instructive, not only because of the similarities between the two, but also to reveal the way in which globalization has had a differential impact on state-society relations in these deeply-divided societies.

According to Esman (1987) the means by which ERWG is pursued include: i) the expansion of higher education; ii) a discriminatory language policy; iii) an extensive affirmative action program; and iv) state employment—not only directly within the civil service and parastatal government enterprises—but also indirectly by enhancing conditions favorable for the creation of a business or entrepeneurial class.

Bumiputeras and the Advance of Malay Capital

When the Alliance lost its psychologically important two-thirds majority during the 1969 elections, though remaining the ruling party, these conditions sparked off the most violent rioting Malaysia had ever seen on 13 May, 1969. The constitutional package deal of the early post-independence period assumed that i) an ethnic balance of power and ii) a high rate of growth would be able to deliver on two policy goals simultaneously. Firstly, it would maintain the equilibrium between Malay aspirations for progress towards parity with other communities as well as non-Malay desires to protect and enhance their existing living standards. Secondly, on the former being achieved, it would secure continued Malay and non-Malay endorsement of the 'Great Bargain' and thereby lay the political foundation upon which both state and market could interact with stability (Osman-Rani, 1990: 3-4). Nonetheless, the 'package deal' failed to address Malays' profound sense of economic insecurity. The New Economic Programme (NEP) therefore had two main goals. The first prong is to reduce and eventually eradicate poverty by raising income levels and increasing employment opportunities for all Malaysians, irrespective of race. The second prong aims at accelerating the process of restructuring Malaysian society to correct economic imbalances, so as to reduce and eventually eliminate the identification of race with economic function (cf. Mid-Term Review 1973, of the Second Malaysia Plan, 1971-75).

To secure rapid upward mobility for Malays, higher education was expanded and made more accessible, a discriminatory language policy introduced and extensive affirmative action programs, particularly in the civil service and parastatals were introduced. At the same time, conditions for the creation of a business or entrepreneurial class were enhanced.

The rapid expansion of educational opportunities is critical for upward mobility of a previously subordinated group. In the late 1960s, Malays comprised only 25.4% of the student population at the University of Malaya, with 58.9% being Chinese and 13.9% Indian students. By vastly expanding the university sector and lowering educational requirements, scholarships and grants were provided to 'nearly every Malay, rich or poor' (Jesudason, 1989: 113). By the mid-1980s, university enrolment was far more reflective of the national population—with 49.9% Malay students, 40.7% Chinese and 9.2% Indian students (Embong, 1995: 46; 1996: 540). In tandem with the expansion of educational opportunity, a state-sanctioned language preference policy also eases entry into the modern economy. The National Language Act of 1967 designated Malay to be the sole official language with English medium schools converting to the Malay medium three years later, starting with grade one. The upward mobility that English afforded to many non-Malays—those who sent their children to English medium schools—was thus severely restricted (Lim Mah Hui, 1998: 23). These drastic measures were aimed at offsetting Malays' disadvantaged educational position, particularly those from the rural sector.

In terms of state employment, the employment ratio of Malays to non-Malays in the public sector was 4:1 (Lim Mah Hui, 1998: 22). Under the NEP, public sector employment grew by an average of 5.5% during 1970-5 and 6.0% from 1975-80. In terms of total employment percentages, employment in the public sector increased from 12.0% in the 1970s to a peak of 15.0% in 1981 (Embong, 1995: 47).

With a buoyant and sustained rate of growth averaging 7.8% annually, in combination with a good banking system, effective tax collection and an excellent international credit rating, the Malaysian government followed a three-pronged strategy to raise funds and acquire assets for Malays (Esman, 1987: 404): firstly, expansion of the state enterprise sector; secondly, government acquisition of major enterprises from private, mostly foreign owners; and finally more aggressive attempts to secure Malaysian equity and employment followed in the form of the Industrial Coordination Act (ICA). By the mid-1970s, state-owned enterprises expanded at a rate of over 100 enterprises a year, contributing up to 25% of the GDP in 1990 (Embong,

1996: 540). The effects of this exponential state intervention already became apparent in 1975: 32% of Malays were now engaged in manufacturing jobs, their share increasing from 25% in 1970; 17% of managers were Malay up from 11% four years previously, with the share of Malay institutional credit standing at 30%, from 14% in 1971 (Bowie, 1991: 97).

A central purpose of the NEP was to accelerate Malay share ownership from 2.4% in 1970 to 30% by 1990. Accordingly, all new public share offerings had to reserve at least 30% for Malays exclusively. Bumiputera share equity in listed share corporations rose from 2.4% in 1970 to 18% in 1983, and 19% in 1990 (but fell again to 18% in 1992). While most of this accumulation was due to public sector asset accumulation by Malays and other share ownership schemes, private share accumulation increased exponentially, particularly under Mahathir: from 39% in 1975 and 41% in 1983 to 68% in 1990 and 87.6% in 1992, suggesting a considerable concentration of wealth (Jomo, 1994: 13). Despite a widespread public perception that the NEP was more about the NEP's second goal, namely 'restructuring' over poverty alleviation, impressive gains had been made in reducing poverty, the latter declining to 18% in 1984 and 15% in 1989.

Although the NEP significantly reduced the inequalities that soured relations between Malays and non-Malays, it also exacerbated the likelihood for a political culture of patronage and rentierism to take hold. Firstly, as a result of British indirect rule, the Malay aristocrats became colonial civil servants who later formed the leadership of UMNO and also provided the first three Prime Ministers (Lubeck, 1992: 188). With the emergence of the NEP state, these 'administrocats' also straddled the public and private spheres as company directors, trust managers and public corporations as part of the ruling bureaucracy/business/politician network.

Secondly, the ascendance and growing power of these 'administrocats' could not be effectively counter-balanced by a rival social force. Labor had a spurious political role to play, historically emasculated since the Malayan Emergency of 1948-1960 and the consequent crush of independent workers organizations and left-wing groups which the government feared might be a cover for Communist activities. In commerce and industry, the NEP state shunned domestic (i.e., Chinese) capital at all costs. Politically, the MCA could no longer command the kind of influence within the ruling coalition that it could in the 1950s and 1960s. In addition, if the established foreign owned firms could counter the growing hegemony of the state, that capacity was significantly eroded by the gradual take-over of these companies.

Thirdly, when state expenditure represents more than half of GDP amidst these conditions, it is hardly surprising that the propensity for patronage and rentier capitalism expands accordingly. This is not to suggest that one of the features of the developmental state—namely extensive state intervention—necessarily reverts to rentierism. Indeed, until the 1960s, Malaysia shared one of the most significant features with other NICs, namely a 'strong state' able to frame development policy without having to take undue account of domestic pressures. The Korean and Vietnamese wars, as well as the confrontation with Indonesia, dislodged considerable social opposition to the development of export-oriented policies. And the effects of war meant that both the coercive and civil capacities of the state were expanded (Stubbs, 1999).

What set Malaysia apart from the other homogeneous NICs however, was its historic ethnic division of labor. Hence, the need to address the Malay sense of insecurity following the 1969 riots also ultimately meant that the kind of 'embedded autonomy' characteristic of South Korea or Taiwan did not arise (Evans, 1997a). Nor would an alliance between the state and capital which had been crucial in the creation of the East Asian NICs emerge, given the political imperative of the Malay state to 'by-pass' Chinese capital. Instead, the developmental state variant that did arise—both in South Africa and Malaysia—approximated what Schneider (1999: 278) calls the *desarrolista* state. In combination with UMNO's overwhelming political dominance, all these conditions heightened the need to build strong bases within the party to secure patronage. Given their close ties to influential politicians, connected business people could expand corporate holdings and were, in turn, expected to support their political patrons financially.

However, with the severe economic downturn in the mid-1980s and again in the late 1990s, it became apparent that the Malaysian political economy remained vulnerable to tensions within the ruling coalition as disjunctures with the global economy meant that the number of business opportunities to be distributed through these networks diminished. Following the massive expansion of the public sector in the 1980s, the federal deficit grew to over five times its 1975 level, reaching 19% of GNP 'one of the highest such percentages in the world at the time' (Bowie, 1991: 135). In addition, Mahathir embarked upon an extensive program of import-substituting heavy industrialization, not only due to the reluctance of private capitalists to undertake the massive risks involved but also due to the NEP-inspired tradition of ethnically 'by-passing' Chinese Malaysians in such projects in favor of foreign investors (Gomez and Jomo, 1997: 78). Accordingly, the heavy industrialization drive was financed with Japanese loans underwritten by government guarantees (Jomo, 1995: 4).

When the major industrial economies agreed to a significant currency realignment in the Plaza Accord of September 1985, the yen appreciated rapidly against the US dollar. Malaysia's yen-denominated foreign borrowings nearly doubled as a result, exacerbating Malaysia's exposure to market volatility. By early 1987, UMNO faced the most decisive political crisis in Malaysia's history since the 1969 riots, with the party fragmenting into two factions, with the Mahathir-led faction prevailing with a bare majority. Leading the defeated faction, Tunku Razaleigh (once UMNO Treasurer and Finance Minister) contended that Mahathir had formed a kitchen cabinet, centralizing decision-making around a select group of supporters who controlled access to most government contracts and business opportunities and distributed these amongst those within the group. Not unlike Anwar's allegations which would follow in 1998, Razaleigh alleged that Daim Zanuddin, as UMNO Treasurer, controlled Fleet Holdings (UMNO's corporate share-holding company), abused his position as party trustee and channelled most of UMNO's assets to holding firms controlled by his family (Gomez and Jomo, 1997: 122).

The contest for hegemony elicited a period of increased authoritarianism, followed in turn by a series of liberalization measures to attract foreign capital. In addition, as currency appreciations forced Japan, Korea and Taiwan to relocate manufacturing plants to Malaysia and other parts of Southeast Asia, Malaysia's economy also benefited from higher commodity prices for its key exports and the economy entered an unprecedented boom period, culminating in eight successive years of annual growth of more than 8% throughout the 1990s. With the gradual downsizing of the state's economic role, following the internationalization of the Malaysian economy since the 1980s, state elites increasingly looked upon the private sector and the Malay business class in order to sustain the strategy of ERWG.

However, as economic growth threatened to decline with the onset of the Asian crisis, in 1997 tensions within the ruling clique emerged once again. Whereas it was the state that borrowed heavily from abroad during the 1980s, it was now banks and the conglomerates which had become indebted, again, in part due to the appreciation of the US dollar (to which many Southeast Asian currencies had been aligned as part of a basket of currencies) and the failure of these governments, especially Malaysia, to depreciate the ringgit accordingly.

Between 1995 and 1997 liabilities tripled with corporate borrowings highly concentrated with the three biggest borrowers accounting for three-quarters of this total (Jomo, 1998: 183). Whereas the Asian crisis also had a profound impact on the South African economy—prompting state elites to simply 'bite the bullet' and send interest rates to a skyrocketing 25% in mid-1998—the powerful grip of Malaysia's business/politician complex meant that state technocrats were unable to do the same. The fundamental obstacle to letting interest rates go up in order to stem the tide were political considerations: to do so risked the collapse of the vast patron-client network upon which the Malaysian political economy had come to depend for its stability. Hence, the Anwar faction's long-standing dissatisfaction with Mahathir's approach to the crisis became quite evident as the crisis escalated towards late 1998. With memories of the 1987 spilt within UMNO and the prospect of the Indonesian situation being revisited upon Malaysia, Mahathir once again, as in the late 1980s, reasserted control by tightening further opportunities for public dissent.

Are there any lessons for South Africa to draw from the Malaysian experience? How similar or different are conditions at the southern tip of Africa and how does the pursuit of ERWG compare in the South African case?

'Buppies' and other *Comrades in Business*

Unlike the pursuit of ERWG by Malay and Afrikaner nationalists[2] in the 1960s and 1970s, coinciding with the heyday of Fordism and Keynesian economic philosophy, ERWG is infinitely more complicated in the 1990s with the dominance of neo-liberal orthodoxy and the increasing salience of post-Fordism. Nowhere is this restricted policy scope as evident as in the difficulty of emulating the kinds of strategies supposed to ensure the economic advance of an ethnic majority as in South Africa in the late 1990s.

One of the few, but most significant, domains through which ethnic economic advance could be assured was state employment. In February 1995, the government announced that the public service would need to be transformed to reflect the composition of the population as a whole. Referring to the Malaysian riots of 1969, Thabo Mbeki argued that South Africa would also 'explode' if the government failed to intervene in order to create a 'non-racial' and 'non-sexist' society (SAIRR Survey, 1996-7: 35).

Government would implement measures to ensure that those who had been disadvantaged in the past would be given the opportunity to develop their talents (SAIRR Survey 1995/6: 267). Accordingly, the White Paper on Reconstruction and Development (RDP) stated that within four years at least 50% of all public service personnel at management level should be black, while 30% of new recruits to middle and senior management levels should be women. It was expected that within ten years 2% of public service personnel should be people with disabilities (SAIRR Survey 1995/6: 269).

However, as ANC economic policy shifted in a more neo-liberal direction, it became evident that such levels of state employment could not be sustained. By December 1996 it was announced that the 'Jobs for South Africa' program which aimed to fill 11,000 government jobs, had to be abandoned due to 'rationalisation and restructuring' of the public service. Not only was the ANC cash-strapped by the severe cost of providing for the early retirement and retrenchment packages of Afrikaner bureaucrats, as well as by the relocation of staff and retraining costs, but constitutional provisions securing the tenure of former state employees (the so-called 'sunset clauses') severely restricted its freedom of action to employ its own appointees. The consequences were significant. For as Kanya Adam (1997: 243) has remarked:

> The more the socioeconomic conditions for the majority remain the same, the more the Government has to fall back on a symbolic demonstration of 'liberation'. This may increase the pressure to emphasise control and power in realms where this can be achieved, be it through bureaucratic 'face-lifts' or symbolic humiliation of former enemies through the Truth Commission in order to demonstrate 'real change'. *A more representative public service can signal such change at little cost to the state* (emphasis added).

No single instance illustrates the difficulties of trying to pursue the policy of ethnic redistribution with growth better than the demise of state-created corporations in post-apartheid South Africa. Not only is the state not creating new corporations, but those already in existence are increasingly subject to pressures for privatization. To be more precise, some semi-state institutions are increasingly involved in 'commercialization'; i.e., joint ventures with private business. Despite the existence of such partnerships, their capacity is incommensurable with the number of state corporations created both in South Africa and Malaysia during and after the post-war boom of the 1950s and 1960s. These original state enterprises could not be founded without incurring fairly high levels of government debt.[3] ANC economic policy, however, has had to increasingly conform to the expectations of the so-called 'Washington consensus'.[4] Societal corporatism underpinned the remarkable smoothness of the South African transition into this neo-liberal order. For this particular form of corporatism became a 'crisis response' in which both elites within the National Party and the ANC realised the need to contain a possible campaign of mass discontent against the largely neo-liberal economic program upon which they were to embark. As Habib (1997: 71) writes:

> A repressive response would have provoked a mass counter-reaction that could have threatened the viability of the transition itself. At the least, the mass reaction which such a response would have provoked would have generated political instability and threatened the much heralded investment that the GNU [Government of National Unity] was so eager to attract. Corporatism thus

seemed the most feasible response for state elites intent on neutralising a potential opposition while simultaneously retaining a sense of political stability.

With a democratic transition, access to capital markets restored and international investment regained, South African conglomerates were as unfashionable as investment vehicles, as conglomerates and *chaebols* had become elsewhere. And, as foreign investors came to play a larger role in the Johannesburg Stock Exchange, they expected more focussed investment vehicles. Accordingly, 'unbundling' became very much in vogue and throughout the 1990s a multitude of South African corporations were restructured: Barlows, Malbak, Servgro, Sankorp, Old Mutual, Sanlam as well as parts of Anglo American to name but a few (Field, 1998: 111).

Ironically, it was Afrikaner capital which made the first move towards the facilitation of black capital when Sanlam and Metropolitan Life created Methold, Metropolitan's holding company which has subsequently become New Africa Investments (Nail). Alongside Real Africa Investments Limited (Rail), Thebe Investment Corporation and Johnnic, it is one of the major stakeholders in the National Empowerment Consortium (NEC)—a group of 23 partners consisting not only of the new black bourgeoisie, but also 15 trade unions (*Financial Mail*, 7 February, 1997; *The Economist*, 15 March, 1997).

Nail has as its core asset one of South Africa's largest life assurance companies and was listed on the JSE in August 1994. Rail was established in February 1994 after the Southern Life Association (Southern Life)—an associate of Anglo American—announced that it would sell 51% of the African Life Assurance Company (Aflife) for R160 million to a black-dominated acquisition group. Thebe, which initially began as the Batho-Batho Trust, with Nelson Mandela and Walter Sisulu on its board in 1992, currently has a turnover of R500 million and unlike the other black investment groups, has focussed on high growth sectors in industry: leisure services, education, medical care, technology and financial services. Thebe consists of four holding companies, Msele Financial Holdings; Alliance Airline; Moribo Investments; and Vuna Industrial Holdings (*Finansies and Tegniek*, 22 November, 1996).

As recently as 1995, market traders were skeptical about the prospects for some of the largest black investment groups such as New Africa Investment Limited (Nail) and Real Africa. But three years later the latter were becoming sought after holdings 'because of their ability to attract deals and because they were favored by government policies in the award of tenders and business' (*Sunday Independent*, 1 February 1998; *Finansies and Tegniek*, 28 February, 1997).

In 1996 the so-called 'black chips' grew at 20% outstripping the JSE all-share index which grew by 6.9%. Their performance was based on the expectation that these shares have 'the ability to corner government contracts and customers in the mass market' (Madi, 1997: 56). The number of listed black companies is also growing at a much faster rate than those fostered by Afrikaner capitalists.

In 1991 there was not a single black-owned company on the Johannesburg Stock Exchange (JSE). In November 1994, eight black-led companies were listed; by May 1995, 11; by April 1996, 14 and by the end of 1996, 17 (SAIRR Survey 1996/7: 262). By early 1998, 53 black companies had a total market capitalization of R111 billion compared to the R57.9 billion at the end of 1996 held by 33 black firms (*Business Day*, 10 February 1998). Towards the end of 1998, the business consultancy Business Map recorded on average, 20 black empowerment deals per month, whilst its database lists over 500 companies that either have, or are participating in, such transactions (Segal, 1998: 79). Many of these 'black chip' companies have outperformed the JSE as a whole. However, much of this advance has been seriously eroded due to often over-geared investments which left these 'black chips' severely vulnerable to the consequences of the Asian crisis.

Despite the evident success and impressive growth of black big business, it has not occurred without severe criticism. Not unlike the Malaysian depiction of 'Ali-Baba' deals, some critics have contended that 'white moguls are the real beneficiaries of black empowerment' and given that 'most black businessmen do not have access to the same level of capital and financing as their white counterparts ... the result is empowerment deals between existing successful white business and emergent black business that favour white business' (*The Sunday Independent*, 15 June 1997). In sectoral terms, black-controlled firms are largely to be found in the insurance sector, as industrial holding companies, and in food as well as retail. The big success stories, however, are to be found in the media and publishing industry, followed by catering (*Financial Mail*, 26 June, 1998). Yet these are sectors with limited potential to create massive job opportunities in a largely underskilled workforce. Not unlike Malaysia well into the 1970s, there are virtually no black-controlled manufacturers. Segal (1998: 82) claims that:

> virtually no black operating company can stand on its own and claim to add the type of value to the economy that creates significant jobs and improves skills. Outside Nail, Real, Thebe, Kagiso and less obviously Capital Alliance, black firms have been unable to go beyond their initial start-up phase and grow into entities able to stand on their own. Most black economic empowerment

deals are little more than investment syndicates taking small equity stakes in firms, only a handful of which are start-ups.

Can the Center Hold?

Many beneficiaries of black economic empowerment programs are accused of being mere 'tokens', richly rewarded for the degree to which their appointment as 'non-executive' directors of the board lends political legitimacy to the firm, whilst ultimate decision-making remains firmly under white control. On the other hand, where newly created firms under the unequivocal control of black entrepreneurs have achieved successes, allegations of nepotism and corruption have become widespread. As the frequency of these allegations is only matched by the numbers of the *nouveau riche*, during a period of stagnant growth and negligible employment, the parameters of public discourse already highlight the manifestation of 'crony capitalism' (Turok, 1998), 'the empowerment of the black fat cats' (Adam, 1998), 'the new Randlords' and the degree to which the new black bourgeoisie 'remain[s] part of the motive forces of liberation or whether they have been co-opted by the former ruling class and therefore become comprador' (Turok, 1997).

With race no longer an obstacle to individual achievement, state elites will emphasize the potential of black empowerment to provide an opportunity for everyone to better their lives. This is more likely if the professed patriotism of the emerging bourgeoisie does in fact serve to unite and bridge class differences through community empowerment and national incorporation. In that case, 'patriotism legitimises the burgeoning black middle class with the ring of fulfilling a duty for the new nation' (Adam, et al., 1997: 217). Consistent with Horowitz' (1985) notion of 'group worth', positive affirmations of ethnic identity may make for considerable political stability. Hence the ANC's landslide victory in the mid-1999 general elections, puts it on par with UMNO's overwhelming parliamentary representation.

However, if black empowerment ultimately comes to be seen as largely benefiting 'the connected elite' (much like the NEP—even among poorer Malays—is seen to have benefited the wealthy few) the intensification of class difference and competition is likely to become more severe. Neither UMNO nor the National Party—which had been most successful in overcoming the *armblankevraagstuk* (poor whites' problem)—could escape similar pressures. The National Party's conversion from *volkskapitalisme* to the more pragmatic view of the Afrikaner corporate world ultimately prompted the reactionaries to abandon their erstwhile political home. Of all the stakeholders, labor faces the greatest dilemma in this regard. Although it may have been co-opted successfully thus far and its continued participation in the alliance has been buttressed by a number of tactical advantages, this situation cannot persist indefinitely without encountering severe legitimacy problems. On the one hand, if it stays in the Alliance but fails to influence policy, labor will become increasingly marginalized and/or incorporated by neo-liberal economic and social policies. Alternatively, if labor opposes neo-liberal measures it risks a confrontation with government 'in which it will be presented as a special interest concerned with a small proportion of the labor force' (Webster, 1998: 58).

It may, as Webster (1998: 59) suggests, embark upon the challenge of engaging in the process of 'strategic unionism'; that is, being committed to the creation of wealth as well as its redistribution and continuing to participate in tripartite institutions. However, this scenario assumes that pressure following disillusionment within the Alliance will largely come from the left. Equally decisive, although currently under-acknowledged, is the emerging black middle class, and with it, burgeoning black entrepreneurship. The claim made by none other than Cyril Ramaphosa—that government assets should be privatized as means to enhance opportunities for black business—flies in the face of consistent efforts by labor to block the sale of state enterprises. Nafcoc (the National African Federated Chamber of Commerce) has made similar suggestions, calling on government to establish a black economic empowerment fund to support black consortiums that want to buy portions of unbundled companies or privatized parastatals and asking government to sell its shares in Sasol and Iscor and use the proceeds to finance the proposed empowerment fund (SAIRR Survey 1996/7: 272).

Moreover, Nafcoc wants government to facilitate the development of small and micro-economic enterprises (SMEE's) through a more flexible labor market, a strong new competition policy and more lenient monetary policy (SAIRR Survey 1996/7: 273). Just as UMNO in the late 1990s made inroads amongst Chinese constituencies as the commitment to redistribution gave way to the pursuit of growth, a more conservative ANC faction is likely to find itself strongly supported by the tiny but vocal White, Indian and Colored middle classes.

However, if the corporatist project fails—due to the difficulty of sustaining labor's strategy of 'strategic unionism'—or if an alternative coalition of counter-hegemonic social forces fails to strike a sustainable domestic bargain, Pretoria may increasingly come to resemble Kuala Lumpur. That is, corporatism may give way to patron-client linkages between the state and business tying otherwise disgruntled but economically influential White,

Indian and Colored elites—with the black bourgeoisie—into a vast network of state patronage.

In addition, if economic growth declines to the extent that the mass of unemployed outsiders threatens the status quo, or a fundamental political rupture occurs within the ruling coalition, both the Malay and Afrikaner Nationalist experiences also suggest that the temptation to reassert political hegemony through authoritarian means is a very real one. Anne Munro-Kua's (1996) analysis of Malaysia as a 'populist authoritarian', or Harold Crouch's (1996) depiction of Malaysia as a 'repressive-responsive' regime, may be one outcome. This comparative analysis therefore prompts a number of questions. What are the policy implications regarding good governance? What are the crucial preconditions to forestall corporatist modes of interest mediation degenerating into a political culture of patron-client rentierism? And can any light be cast upon the developmental state debate in the aftermath of the Asian crisis?

Conclusion: A Fine Balance

If anything, the very different responses by state elites in Malaysia and South Africa to the Asian crisis illustrate the significant influence of patron-client linkages and societal corporatism, upon these states' ability to manage domestic political fall-outs. South African policy makers—no less upset by the degree to which virtually all the emerging markets seem to get the short end of the stick during these financial crises—were much more flexible in the degree to which globalization was seen to offer both opportunity and constraint.[5] Mahathir's by now infamous rant against George Soros and currency traders, stands in stark contrast to the more pragmatic response of his South African counter-parts.

This comparative analysis corroborates Evans' more recent propositions regarding the notion of 'embedded autonomy'.[6] According to Evans (1995: 50), embedded autonomy—'where bureaucrats have close ties to business yet are still able to formulate and act on preferences autonomously—is the key to the developmental state's effectiveness'. However, once the developmental state becomes a victim of its own success—in the sense that business becomes so strong or independent that it no longer requires the state as an intermediary—weakened business support for sustaining a Weberian bureaucracy increases 'the likelihood that connectedness will degenerate into capture' (Evans, 1997b: 67). In Malaysia, the complexity of separating business interests from political players, in combination with the stifled role of labor and relatively firm controls over civil society made for greater capture than collaboration. What is ultimately required is

> some counterweight ... to keep public-private networks oriented toward collective goals rather than particularistic rent-seeking. Building institutionalized ties with groups other than business is a politically difficult but logically plausible countervailing strategy. Institutionalizing a more encompassing set of state-society ties may be the only way to keep embedded autonomy from losing its developmental effectiveness (Evans, 1997b: 67).

In as much as most Newly Industrialized Countries (NICs)—with the partial exception of Singapore—are ethnically homogeneous societies, historically ethnic divisions of labor make it exceptionally difficult to establish meritocratic Weberian bureaucracies in the developing world and even more so where ERWG is pursued. Nevertheless, Evans (1997b: 72) contends that even where the state bureaucracy is fractured by a sea of clientelism, it could approximate the Weberian model and contribute to what he calls 'transformative growth'. Considerable cohesion and professionalism amongst core bureaucratic agencies attending to monetary and fiscal policy (the Central Bank, the Finance Ministry, etc.) can make great strides toward institutionalizing collaborative relationships. On this score, the South African record to date appears to be relatively positive. Also, in as much as joint action in late June 1999 between the South African state, capital and labor to protest the IMF's sale of gold reserves to finance a debt-relief program, signals strong collaborative relations between these three key elements.

Although the degree of generalization beyond these two cases is uncertain, what this analysis suggests, is that ethnically divided societies pursuing or attempting to sustain ERWG amidst the globalizing features of the contemporary world order, are probably better off doing so through corporatism as the lesser of the many other evils state elites in the developing world have to transcend in their attempts to make political and economic liberalizations compatible. A kind of 'domestic bargain' seems to be essential in order to overcome the crisis of governance and manage the immediate challenges posed by globalization. Hence, the utility of an analytical model anchored around the state, civil society and companies—as pursued throughout this volume—to capture the complexities of ethnicity and global governance.

Lest it appear as if I put the blame for the Asian crisis at the door of the developmental state's proclivity for rent-seeking in the IMF style, consider the following: what the post-Asian crisis developmental state debate should be about is not so much the degree to which the prospects for rent-seeking expand, as it should be about the ways in which a particular kind of 'domestic governance bargain' which take ethnicities or race (and/or other 'identities' such as gender, religion or generation) into account can be sustained in order to prevent the concentration of power and enhance the possibilities for 'embedded autonomy'. The excruciating difficulty of striking the fine balance between various state/societal actors which this process requires, ultimately also rests upon the degree to which the global order has to underscore and be supportive of, the indispensable role of the developmental state to the process of industrial transformation in the developing world.

Rather than considering the domestic and the global as dichotomous spheres, a number of studies over the past years have highlighted the extent to which high 'stateness' does more than merely insulate domestic constituents from external disruptions. In fact, high stateness 'may be a source of competitive advantage in a globalizing economy' (Evans, 1997b: 69). Indeed, a considerable number of cross-national statistics corroborate the notion that successful economies with high levels of trade usually also have fairly high levels of discretionary state intervention. Similarly, reducing the role of the state as a provider of public goods does not merely exacerbate inequalities, but ultimately reduces profit prospects for transnational corporations. Moreover, an economy which increasingly relies on the power of ideas and knowledge as a source of wealth requires an agile, competent state capable of enforcing rules (Evans, 1997b: 69, 73, 77). In short, the crisis of global governance remains finding the wherewithal to realign—at least in the developing world—the link between Peter Evans' 'embedded autonomy'at the local/domestic level with John Ruggie's 'embedded liberalism' at the global level, however modified for the next millennium.

Notes

1. According to Peter Evans, '"embedded autonomy" —where bureaucrats have close ties to business yet are still able to formulate and act on preferences autonomously—is the key to the developmental state's effectiveness and the factor that best explains divergent patterns of industrial transformation' (in Schneider and Maxfield, 1997b: 6).
2. Much like Malay nationalists, Afrikaner advancement through similar means prompted one historian to remark that 'perhaps not in history has there been a case in which an entire under-developed people became so affluent so quickly' (Giliomee in Price 1991: 25). See Van der Westhuizen (1999).
3. The South African government has committed itself to target the deficit before borrowing in the 1998-1999 fiscal year to 3.5% of the GDP and maintain tight monetary controls and rates of inflation.
4. Hence, Mandela urged, 'In reality what we have to do is ensure that our country integrates itself within a world community that is evolving under the impact of a

process of globalisation as well as determine the ways by which we can impact on this process to advance the interests of our broad masses. To try to subtract ourselves from these processes would spell disaster' (Report, 1998: 199). For the responses of the South African policy elite to the challenges of globalization, see Nel, Van der Westhuizen et al. (1998).

5.   Business-government connections can either be of a 'growth oriented' or 'rent-seeking' variety. In the case of the former, these 'networks are instruments for the pursuit of collective goals, while rent-seeking networks are vehicles for allowing capital to avoid the risks of transformation in favor of directly unproductive means of securing profits' (Evans, 1997a: 70).

6.   He defines the latter as 'the apparent contradictory combination of Weberian bureaucratic insulation with intense immersion in the surrounding social structure' (Schneider and Maxfield, 1997: 6). Hence, when the state lacks the capacity to monitor and discipline incumbents, every relationship between a state official and a businessperson is another opportunity to generate rents for the individuals involved at the expense of society at large' (Evans, 1997a: 6).

5 South Africa and the Political Economy of Wine: From Sanctions to Globalizations/ Liberalizations

TIMOTHY M. SHAW*

Introduction

South Africa's wine industry is not unimportant yet it has been remarkably understudied, particularly in terms of national and global political economy, at least until the turn of the century and the industry's own Vision 2020 reflections (see Williams et al, 1998; and references below especially Loubser, 1999; Winetech, 1999a and b). This initial overview essay seeks to begin to analyze its significance for both the development of the country and industry as well as its relevance for comparative studies of globalizations and liberalizations, ethnicities and races. The essay is thus an analysis of the political economy of an agri-industry in a period of profound change, with the latter having both local and international roots (see the concluding section below). The 1990s constituted a turning point for wine in South Africa in general and the Western Cape in particular: together globalization pressures (see section below on 'globalizations') and liberalization conditionalities (see section below on 'liberalizations') compound the intensity of the conjuncture at the start of the new millennium (see section below on 'contemporary issues'), as reflected in the industry's own enquiries (Loubser, 1999; Winetech, 1999a and b) and informed sociological analyses (Bekker, et al., 1999; Ewert and Hamman, 1999).

The juxtaposition of local and global in terms of analysis, policy and praxis is never easy in either analytic or existential terms. Such divides or solitudes tend to reflect rather well-established disciplinary silences and traditions; transcending them is always problematic (Stiles, 1999). Nevertheless, it is also essential as neither local nor global analysis alone can

89

explain such transitions (see Chapter 1 of this volume as well as the final section on implications or lessons for several parallel fields or discourses).

This chapter proceeds from an overview of the (local and international) political economy of South Africa's wine industry to a discussion of the inter-related pressures and effects of globalizations and liberalizations. In so doing it raises a set of issues or debates about this industry in comparative perspective—i.e., wine industries elsewhere, other industries in South Africa, and alternative approaches to its analysis (Loubser, 1999; Sphani, 1995). I conclude by highlighting a range of possible insights for both national and sectoral policy discourses as well as for related disciplines.

Overview: From Sanctions to a World of Opportunity and Competition

Histories

South Africa's wine industry has a long *vintage*, dating back to the second half of the seventeenth century and some of the original white settlers such as Jan Van Riebeek and Simon van der Stel. Early favorable international attention peaked in the Napoleonic era of the early and mid-eighteenth century, when Constantia wines were well-regarded in Europe. Vineyards were gradually expanded as successive waves of settlers moved inland, including the French Huguenots to the Franschhoek Valley, but they have never before been as extensive as today (over 100,000 hectares for the first time in 1998 (see SA Wine Industry Statistics, 1999). They increasingly cover the valleys and mountain sides in a broad sweep through the Western Cape's Boland region: from Vredendal in the north, halfway to Namibia, to Montagu and on through the Klein Karoo and Oudtshoorn in the east, north of George. In the mid-nineteenth century the South African industry received privileged tariff-free access to the UK when the latter discriminated against Mediterranean wines as an aspect of its conflict with the continent. And in the 1970s and 1980s it endured the gradual loss of export markets as anti-apartheid sanctions and boycotts—state and non-state—expanded and intensified (Crawford and Klotz, 1999).

But just as Gilbeys was founded to take advantage of the booms of the Napoleonic period and subsequently the Transvaal gold rush, so the post-apartheid era has seen a dramatic expansion and sophistication: in 1995 alone, exports rose 40 percent. Given inter-war instability, KWV was founded after the South African and First World Wars to regulate supply and price, and to provide myriad technical services. Likewise, SFW was established between the world wars (the brainchild of William Charles Winshaw, an American doctor who had accompanied 4,500 horses from the United States for use in the Boer War). Post-WWII, as the Nationalist Party moved to institutionalize apartheid and advance Afrikaner economic interests, an oligopoly was negotiated among Distillers/Gilbeys, Rembrandt and South African Breweries (SAB) over the full range of alcoholic products: beer, spirits and wines. This comfortable yet stultifying arrangement was only dismantled under the twin pressures of globalizations and liberalizations in the late-1990s, when winds of change finally began to blow across the Cape winelands (Ewert and Hamman, 1999). Thus the industry feels increasingly vulnerable again at the start of the new millennium given the continuing, complicated transitions, as reflected in the emerging winelands debate around Vision 2020.

Snapshots

Viticulture in South Africa is now almost a billion rand industry using capital worth approximately R10 billion, with particular economic, ecological, cultural and aesthetic significance in the Western Cape, where it constitutes 15 percent of agricultural production. The whole industry contributes almost R15 billion to the economy. Its 4,500 wine farmers and approximately 50,000 farm workers (average annual income for the latter in the early 1990s was R4,000) (the largest single employer is the Stellenbosch Farmers' Winery with 4,000 employees) cultivate nearly 250,000 acres or 100,000 hectares of land, generating 1,000,000 metric tons or 10 million hectolitres per acre (pa) out of a global total of some 250-275,000,000 tons. The industry's distinctive 'value chain' or 'logistics system' (Winetech, 1999b) includes 69 cooperative, 79 estate and 139 non-estate cellars, which make it more fragmented than most national producers (Bekker, et al., 1999: 10). There are almost 100,000 employed throughout the industry (South Africa Wine Industry Directory 2000: 241-245) or over 350,000 livelihoods, including some 45,000 seasonal workers (Bekker, et al., 1999). Historically, just as the industry was racially restrictive and spatially restricted—an almost exclusively white male Afrikaner preserve (or 'ethnic corporatist' association according to Ewert and Hamman, 1996) in the valleys west and south of the Karoo semi-desert—almost all the production went to a handful of large cooperatives which rewarded quantity rather than quality. Since the impacts of globalizations and liberalizations, as we shall see below, 300 farmers now make wine themselves and about 100 have registered estates. So, at the end of the century, some 80-85 percent of the annual crop still gets produced by ex-co-ops, the pricing structure of which has not served to enhance excellence or innovation: production- rather than market-driven (Ewert and Hamman, 1999; Loubser, 1999). However, these are increasingly privatized, including the centrepiece—KWV (Inc)—which remains the preeminent producer. But unlike most other national producers, the 'mix' in South Africa is wrong for the global market at the start of the twenty-first century: too many whites and too much *vin ordinaire* (Bekker, et al., 1999; Loubser, 1999)!

As the industry has grown so it has expanded its territorial scale and concentrated on half-a-dozen 'noble cultivars', even if these still account for a smaller proportion of South African production than the other new world competitors: less than 20 percent. Similarly, South Africa produces a much lower proportion of reds than comparable producers, leading to an oversupply of whites even to the extent of storing the excess in some years in the late 1990s (Bekker, et al., 1999: 19). Moreover, South African production thus far is concentrated at the lower end of the market, with only a few expensive varieties available in limited supply. One structural challenge in the new millennium is to generate sufficient mid-level, mid-priced vintages for local and global markets recognizing that wine is somewhat 'lifestyle' sensitive and the female drink-of-choice when compared to other alcoholic beverages.

The Western Cape now has a dozen 'wine routes' developed since the first around Stellenbosch in the early 1970s, which can be virtually sampled via the new Wineways center and website. Its largest wine regions (over 10 percent each) are, in descending order of size: Paarl, Worcester, Stellenbosch, Orange River, Malmesbury, Robertson, Olifants River and Klein Karoo. And given global market pressures, it has increasingly abandoned 'bush wines' and fortified versions to concentrate on Cabernet Sauvignon, Merlot, Pinotage, Shiraz, Sauvignon Blanc and Chardonnay. At present, Pinotage and Shiraz yield the highest prices, Sauvignon Blanc the lowest (i.e., over R4,000 to under R3,000 per ton in 1998).

The Cape wine industry like others in South and North has always had forward and backward linkages with suppliers of fertilizer/pesticides and bottles/corks, and with the transport industry from railways/lorries to cargo and now container boats. But post-apartheid it is increasingly pursuing new linkages into the worlds of culture (auctions, food and fashion shows), travel (airlines, especially South African, tourism and wine tastings etc.), conferences and accommodation, golf and retirement villages etc. In short, its employment- and income-generating potential is several times greater than the value of the wine crop alone, and an ability to anticipate and take advantage of aspects of globalizations may facilitate such multipliers (Winetech, 1999a).

Niches

In wine as in other policy worlds/economic sectors/infrastructural and technological capacities, South Africa is something of a 'middle' power/player, even among the so-called 'new world' producers. In terms of production—some three percent of the global total—it trails the majors like Italy, France, Spain, Argentina and the United States. It is presently #7 in terms of wine production just ahead of Germany, Romania, Portugal and Australia. It produces double that of Chile (Casaburi, 1999), although it actually produces only one-sixth as much as Italy or France. In the ranking of countries in relation to grape production, it is #10 after the above, along with Turkey, Iran, China and Chile. And in terms of area under vines, it is #18, just over one percent of the global acreage (Loubser, 1999; SA Wine Industry Directory 2000: 88). South Africa's vineyard yield is also average at some six tons per acre: superior to France and Italy (circa 3-4 tons) and Spain (just one) but inferior to eight in the United States. Symbolically, South Africa has joined the Cairns Group of agricultural powers which seek to limit US and European Union (EU) protectionist tendencies in the sector (see Wolfe, 1998); so it is affiliated with several new world Southern producers, such as Argentina, Chile, Australia and New Zealand. Yet, as we will see below, it ran into serious difficulties around the turn of the century over free trade negotiations with the EU, in part because the Mediterranean wine and fruit producers preferred to see a competitor kept out of such arrangements.

Periodizations

I complete this overview with a tentative periodization of the South African wine industry's relations to local conditions and global competition over the twentieth century, its third. The periods include:

- *inter-war growth*, mainly in exports of *vin ordinaire* to the UK, including some in bulk: from tank cars on railways to bulk carriers on water, so facilitating sanctions-busting in the 1970s;
- *post-war expansion*, with exports to Europe and Canada as well as the UK peaking in 1968 at 13 million litres to decline to less than 10 million

throughout the subsequent two decades given escalating sanctions despite generic exports in bulk (also known as 'wine from multiple sources'!)

- *1970-1990* stagnation under escalating economic and cultural sanctions (Crawford and Klotz, 1999) leading to sanctions-busting through 'generic' 'Cape Wine of Origin' and generic mixed wines for Europe; local market also flat post-WWII on a per capita basis; fall and rise of global sales given transformation in local and global contexts: from negative sanctions to positive engagement in transition era;
- *1990-1995* boom as sanctions lifted, transformation encouraged, and South African wines become a novelty in the global marketplace even by contrast to other new world sources, particularly in the UK—exports tripled in less than five years to 8 million case equivalents or 10% production of some 80-85 million case equivalents; simultaneously the local market rose by almost 25% in the first half of the decade; but
- *1995 onwards* competition from other new world sources, particularly Latin American (Chile then Argentina) but also some new states in Eastern Europe/former Soviet Union (FSU), some of which have greater supply of noble cultivars, as increasingly demanded by the local market also (which remains small: #11 in world in terms of national consumption after states in the EU and Latin America, and the United States). Moreover, South Africa has remained overly complacent because of its ready place in the UK supermarket sector, which renders it vulnerable to fickle buyer and consumer fads, as revealed in the somewhat preemptive move of Ethical Trading Initiative (ETI) (which includes the major supermarkets) to head-off any embryonic opposition by incorporating at least some antagonistic/sceptical voices.

Thus, the negative turning point of 1970—enforced isolation—has been superceded by the positive one of 1990—end of sanctions (see Crawford and Klotz, 1999)—and the challenging one of the mid-1990s. The challenges of the present period include: renewed impact of global competition; decisions as to what niche to fill even within the 'new world'; domestic challenges such as liberalizations, deregulation, unbundling; and demands for improved conditions for workers along with empowerment in terms of capital, distribution, training, etc. Hence the turn of the century conjuncture at both the national and transnational levels: the response of the industry's growing range of stakeholders through Vision 2020 debates and reports, and the inauguration of the ETI, respectively (Minnear, 1999) (see section on 'contemporary issues', below).

In short, the wine industry in the Cape has always been highly cyclical, mainly because of changes in global markets, rather than, say, ecological threats from disease or drought. But even by such standards, the last decade has been especially challenging—initially positively, subsequently more negatively—as indicated in the next two sections (Ewert and Hamman, 1999; Loubser 1999).

Globalizations

Globalizations have been defined differently within distinct analytic genres. Here we take the concept to mean a variety of new forms of accumulation, communication, compression, homogenization, organization, production, regulation, technologies, as well as exponential differentiation so that divergent communities, companies, countries and regions relate to global change unevenly (see Chapter 1). In the case of this industry and region, the following aspects of globalizations seem to be the most salient:

- *internationalization* of information/internet, markets, networks, ownership, personnel, styles, tastes, technologies etc., especially Australian, British, German, Swiss etc., symbolized by 'flying winemakers' from Europe, America and/or Australia which are truly transnational, so the hitherto somewhat 'parochial' culture or aura of the local industry is fast evaporating, symbolized by the launch of Wineways (a new extension of the Converg logistics network) as both tasting center and website in early 2000;
- *new technologies*, from processing and packaging (eg., nouveau bottles with lips or tetra-packs for wine as well as juice/milk) to shipping and distributing (eg., styrofoam forms around bottles and containerization), especially from other new world wineries, leading to private ISO accreditations;
- *new competitors*, from other new world producers to other world suppliers, such as Croatia, Georgia, Japan, Moldova, Russia, Turkmenistan, even Mexico, in addition to established opposition to new world wines from Bulgaria, Hungary and Rumania etc.;
- *new corporate strategies* including own brand labeling in UK and RSA supermarkets (see below) and strategic alliances with compatible corporations or producers (eg., Stellenbosch Wineries alliance of four established local wineries or the (short-lived) Douglas Green Bellingham

consortium) although these increasingly need to be global rather than local or bilateral (Loubser, 1999);

- *new positive sanctions* to supercede old negative ones, notably the ETI; eg., Tesco's partnership with 'progressive' Vredendal Winery in Olifants River—a huge vineyard producing more than the New Zealand national output through black workers as suppliers/farmers and on to 'green', organic producers/packaging? Tesco and other major customers, primarily the all-important UK market, have also encouraged over a dozen smaller black producers or multi-racial alliances such as Freedom Road (with Michael Back), Nelson's Creek's 'New Beginnings', Spice Route (Malmesbury), Thandi (Elgin's Lebanon village near Grabouw), Winds of Change (Charles Back) etc. ETI may advance a novel transnational 'trilateral' form of governance for the sector compatible with the Wine Industry Trust (i.e., a transnational extension of NEDLAC?);
- but, also *new vulnerabilities* given exponential globalizations as changing currency values, images, interest rates, tastes etc., affect supply and demand; ETI and Vision 2020 are intended to help the industry contain and respond to such threats.

And the South African industry has had to absorb the 'shocks' not only of such intense globalizations, but also of profound 'domestic' liberalizations, both economic and political, compounded by the end of apartheid as indicated in the next section: a double whammy indeed!

Liberalizations

South Africa's dramatic political transformation in the late 1980s and early 1990s coincided with the intensification of economic liberalizations and proliferation towards other liberalizations in Africa as elsewhere. The new non-racial, multi-party coalition Government of National Unity had not only to begin to meet great expectations arising from its political supporters but also to recognize the profound pressures for economic reforms from the international financial institutions. These two sets of demands were hardly compatible as revealed in the continuing controversies over the (ultimately incompatible and unsustainable) GEAR (Growth, Employment and Redistribution) compromise! And they are likely to intensify following the second open general election of mid-1999 that returned the ruling African

National Congress (ANC) to power with a slightly improved showing at the polls.

Economic liberalization in South Africa in the 1990s has involved a trio of strands: i) the liberalization of trade following World Trade Organization (WTO) dictates; ii) the de-racialization of the hitherto racially exclusive and monopolistic architecture; and iii) de-monopolization including reductions in the roles of the state to advance internal competitiveness by privatizing, unbundling, demutualization etc., so that insider trading along the lines of the *broederbond* could not be reinstituted for other exclusive communities.

In the wine industry these forms of liberalizations have been concentrated around the design and form of the new *Liquor Act* which seeks to open up the hitherto state-centric, oligopolistic white-dominated industry through insisting that the producers, wholesalers and retailers are quite separate in future, along with post-KWV cooperative innovations like the Wine Industry Trust etc., as indicated further below.

Post-Apartheid/Oligopoly Unbundling

This has led to a continuing reduction in the degree to which KWV/SFW, Gilbeys/Distillers and Rembrandt constitute the commanding heights of the industry by century's end, although Rembrandt bought Drostdy in Tulbagh and SFW Nederburg in Paarl. Instead, a new division of labor is emerging in which smaller, smarter vineyards and related companies are setting trends and discovering niches. The Afrikaner capitalism/corporatism (Ewert and Hamman, 1999) which characterized the industry, especially after WWII, and is apparent in even the geography of Boland towns like Paarl and Stellenbosch, is giving way to a more open and diverse structure in which vineyard alliances and amalgamations like DGB (Douglas Green Bellingham) and Longridge/Spier/Savanha are challenging the now-privatized cooperatives like Boland, Darling Cellar, KWV and Stellenbosch Wineries. This is paralleled in the related fruit industry—deciduous, citrus and subtropical fruits and juices—where Fyffes of Dublin is acquiring 50 percent of Capespan, the joint marketing company of Unifruco and Outspan for the European Union (EU); i.e., a tactical response to the EU-SA free trade agreement. But whether either the fruit or wine industries can compete globally remains problematic as neither have sufficient integration or the 'right' product mix (eg., apple or vintage varieties) for cut-throat markets like the UK and EU at the turn of the century.

Towards New Governance Structures and Practices

For most of the twentieth century—ironically, it celebrated its 80th year in 1998, just as its role was being downsized and privatized!—KWV was almost synonymous with the Cape wine industry as it played such ubiquitous roles: a classic instance of Afrikaner state-supported capitalism structured through exclusive cooperative arrangements (see critique by Fridjhon and Murray, 1986). But in the 1990s, major changes in legislation and institutions along with a range of responsive strategic alliances have begun to transform the industry, centered on the Wine and Spirit Board. Together with the unbundling and unpacking, KWV (Inc) and Rembrandt remain dominant but have lost their hegemony.

The new (1999) South African Wine Industry Trust (SAWIT), chaired by one of the industry's most vocal critics, Michael Fridjhon (1986 and 1992) oversees several previous roles played by the old KWV. Its membership is drawn from major stakeholders in the industry and outside, nominated by the Department of Agriculture and KWV. Its established role of business development is being carried on by the Trust's subsidiary, Busco, and its novel role of 'development' is being advanced by Devco (Development Company). As indicated above, already there are a dozen empowerment joint ventures such as Freedom Road and Thandi.

The Cape Wine and Spirit Institute (CWSI) still represents the corporate establishment, but it is losing influence to new arrangements and associations which advocate estate-based production and distribution rather than cooperatives: from the open Cape Estate Wine Producers' Association (CEWPA) to the elite (presently 26 member) Cape (Independent) Winemakers' Guild (CIWG) which organizes an annual public auction of up-market varieties. And the South African Wine and Spirit Exporters' Association (SAWSEA) and Winetech are filling the void in terms of putting the best face of the sector forward in emerging transnational trilateral governance arrangements like ETI.

Furthermore, the wine industry like others has to play by WTO and related rules, where it is represented by the global industry association, OIV (Office Internationale du Vin) (see Wolfe, 1998). Indeed, its interests have constituted central difficulties in the fraught EU-SA Free Trade Agreement (FTA) negotiations in the late1990s as the former's Mediterranean wine producers have sought to limit the latter's use of generic terms like port and sherry, even grappa. Indeed, 'technical' negotiations over the definition of such products led by Greece, Italy, Portugal and Spain (not the major producers like France and Germany) still threaten the implementation of this vital agreement at the start of the twenty-first century.

Moreover, the industry will be under continued pressure to reflect South Africa's diversities: black empowerment in terms of capital and training, and affirmative actions in terms of hiring management and technical personnel. Hence the trust fund to finance such transitions which need to receive the seal-of-approval from ETI in terms of ensuring continued and/or improved market access and acceptance. Thus far, however; there are very few female or black wine-makers, let alone owners, but, for example, South African Airways is sponsoring black students in wine management and production at Stellenbosch University and the first black female winemaker, Carmen Stevens, is producing at Maluti near Malmesbury. And labor is increasingly being advanced not only by trade unions but also by NGOs concerned about children, ecology, education, health, housing etc., as indicated below on ETI. There are now a dozen black growers typically using land donated by white farmers, such as 'New Beginnings' outside Paarl on the Nelson's Creek estate. However, empowerment strategies involve their own limitations. Thus far, they have worked largely to the advantage of males from the historically 'colored' community so not all ethnic and gender legacies and biases are being addressed yet.

Repositioning

Mounting concern about the end of the external honeymoon for the industry has led to a revitalization of SAWSEA which has now appointed its first full-time CEO: Ms Kim Green, who is acutely conscious of historic legacies as well as global pressures. It is no longer dominated by the oligopoly of Distillers/Gilbeys (i.e., Rembrandt), KWV (Kooperatieve Wijnbouwers Vereniging) and SFW (Stellenbosch Farmers' Winery) (SA Wine Industry Directory 2000: 32-33 and 209-215); symptomatically, Distillers and SFW amalgamated in early 2000 (Eikestad News, May 2000). Similarly, its new Chair, Graham de Villiers (Franschhoek), also chairs the industry's 'Vision 2020' initiative, which focusses on how to position itself in the new millennium with new vineyards, varieties, technologies, communities, markets, etc. (Bekker, et al., 1999): i.e., the mix of local and global, comparable to the Australian industry's 'Strategy 2025'. The mission statement of Vision 2020 is:

To provide grape based beverages for the global market in order to enhance the socio-economic well-being of the South African community (*Wynboer*, June 1998: 25).

This vision for the national winelands and their myriad features is being debated and refined among major stakeholders in an industry bent on reform and restructuring before the end of 2000 (Winetech 1999a and b), leading towards a more open, inclusive and transnational governance architecture along the lines indicated by the pioneering ETI.

Such sentiments are compatible with our analysis below on contemporary issues: for example, how to be externally competitive by maximizing internal advantages, such as use of the internet. Yet pitfalls remain as indicated by the fraught SA-EU FTA negotiations which almost collapsed a couple of times at the turn of the century over the Achilles heel of generic types of strong wines—port and sherry, then grappa (ouzo)—which has only begun to be produced by a trio of farms in the last decade and so hardly entails a threat to large and well-established Greek or Italian producers. Such 'details' are still under consideration in 'technical' committees, which generates nervousness and scepticism among other sectors as well as among South Africa's smaller partners in the Southern African Customs Union (SACU) and the Southern Africa Development Community (SADC).

Relabelling

Finally, evolving corporate linkages are leading to a local reflection of popular wine presentation in the UK (cf Sainsburys, Tesco and Victoria Wine): most large South African supermarkets now sell their own brands, some of which are purchased at the annual, invitation-only, Nederburg auction, as well as those of leading makers, such as:

- Makro—Bubbling Brook;
- Pick N'Pay—Fabulous with Food (Chic with Chicken, Cool with Curry, Fabulous with Fish, Halves to Hogshead, Marvellous with Meat, Perfect with Pasta);
- Shoprite Checkers—Odd Bins;
- Spar—Country Cellars and Carnival;
- Woolworths—own labels.

Before situating this case in broader analytic and policy discourses, I will provide an overview industry of our own local to global perspective on the international political economy (IPE) of the Cape industry.

Contemporary Issues

Together, then, during the last half of the 1990s, globalizations and liberalizations have complicated the future for the Cape wine industry. It has only just begun through a mix of SAWIT/Vision 2020/Winetech/ETI to respond to this combination of global and local/national pressures which challenge its external niche and internal structures (see Williams, et al., 1998). Such initiatives, symbolized by the difficult inclusive, multi-stakeholder Winelands Conferences, would have been inconceivable a decade ago, but how sustainable and efficacious they will be has yet to be ascertained.

On the one hand, *global* competition means: i) informed forecasting and market research so that taste and demand can be anticipated; ii) continuous quest for innovative advertising (eg., ecommerce), processing, packaging, shipping, distributing (eg., the Wineways initiative which permits one-stop shopping from all estates for informed consumers in the EU); leading to iii) divergent corporate strategies, from KWV's mass marketing to craft estates' boutiques; which in turn require; iv) a variety of 'strategic alliances' involving marketing and technology etc., with compatible local to global airlines and supermarkets etc.

On the other hand, *local* forms of liberalizations—the South African sequence being, because of apartheid legacies and anti-apartheid struggles, political then economic, both concentrated in the first half of the 1990s—have meant: i) the simultaneous restructuring/unbundling of historic organizational structures for the industry from state-supported Afrikaner capitalism to new divisions of labor among a diverse range of stake-holders including NGOs; ii) pressures for empowerment measures, not just in regard to labor conditions but also in terms of advertising, capital, consumption, services, training (up to tertiary level) etc.; along with iii) a new awareness of ecological considerations from immediate fertilizer/pesticide use to longer-term water supplies/shortages; iv) internationalization of some patterns of ownership, both foreign corporations and individuals (some 25 vineyards are now foreign-owned), so the language or culture of the industry is shifting from unilingual Africaans to more usage of English and German; and v) introduction of new events in the winelands' calendar since the early 1970s such as dozens of wine routes, the Bergkelder for maturing/storing of upmarket labels, the prestigious Nederburg and Spier auctions, the Cape Hunt(s) and assorted corporate awards from national airline, bank, credit card, wine magazine, etc. (SA Wine Industry Directory 2000: 277-298). Taken together, these begin to enable the industry to improve both its image and practice at the start of the twenty-first century (Bekker, et al., 1999).

The local response to contemporary challenges—SAWIT and Vision 2020—and the transnational reaction—ETI—constitute interesting, inter-related forms of *local to global governance* at the start of the new millennium. They both involve a heterogeneous group of stakeholders, from labor to civil society, capital to government, and together constitute pre-emptive strategies to head-off opposition or sanctions and to enhance image/market. Both gathered strength and legitimacy through the initial Winelands Conferences in the late 1990s. ETI brings together UK supermarkets, NGOs and TUC with the South African industry and is the first pilot project anywhere in the wine industry. There are parallel ETIs in place over equally sensitive sectors such as bananas from Central America, clothing in China, and horticulture in Zambia and Zimbabwe. The wine pilot was animated by Simon Steyne the International Officer at the TUC in England (Minnear, 1999). But ETI-type multiple stakeholder governance has yet to be proven in terms of impacts: onto evaluations and projections before the end of the first decade of the new century?

Implications for Other Disciplines and Debates

Curiously, none of the major contemporary international relations/ (international) political economy analyses or texts treat the wine (or beer!) industry, although globalizations and liberalizations have affected it (them). This is even so for an otherwise invaluable overview of the discipline for the continent (Nel and McGowan, 1999), even though alcohol production, distribution and consumption have been aspects of a well-established formal and informal sector industry almost everywhere. Certainly South African Breweries (SAB) has become one of the top half-dozen global players, building on its near-monopoly in the Republic of South Africa (RSA) and dominance throughout SADC, symbolized by its listing on the London Stock Exchange as well as the Johannesburg Stock Exchange (JSE): quite a contrast with the fragmented RSA wine industry. And even in South(ern) African studies, where beer, both 'traditional' and industrial, has been an essential correlate of the mineral and industrial revolutions, the focus has tended to be on the anthropology or criminology of alcohol rather than its industrial or service sector aspects. Yet the contemporary wine industry, especially in the Western Cape, is inseparable from a set of changes with profound analytic and policy dimensions: employment, empowerment, internationalization, leisure, (niche) marketing, retirement communities, tourism, etc. And just as is occurring globally, there is the dialectic of differentiation at work nationally, between major brands and micro-producers; i.e., KWV and the proliferation of estates.

In this section, I identify ten sets of implications arising from our case study for parallel fields of analysis, debate and policy (see Chapter 1 in this volume; and Shaw 1999a).

First, although statistically quite insignificant in the *global PE*, wine, beer and related agribusiness industries are not insignificant in terms of emerging sectors/players, often with links into other, larger companies and structures. This is especially so for wine in the 'new world' which has to be more creative to become competitive, particularly given the proliferation of such sources as the number of new states proliferates (eg., Croatia to Turkmenistan). And the beer industry has developed in divergent directions: a few global conglomerates including SAB by contrast to the proliferation of micro and craft breweries almost everywhere (except RSA!). As already indicated above, standard texts on IR/IPE should so acknowledge, along with overlapping post-industrial service sectors such as leisure, retirement communities, travel/tourism, etc.

Second, the wine industry is inseparable from several crucial *development* issues, particularly in the South, such as basic needs like education, housing and water, capital, gender, labor, land, technology, etc. Yet virtually no analysis of local to global development mentions either beer or wine, although the latter has been something of a developmental issue since its origins in the Middle East in 5000-6000 BC!

Third, given continuing 'trade wars', even 'farm wars' (Wolfe, 1998), wine cannot be excluded from studies of *foreign policies and international relations*, whether these be conceived narrowly as inter-state or more broadly as transnational, including non-state actors such as companies and civil societies (cf ETI architecture). Wine along with other agribusiness sectors is negotiated regularly in international organizations such as the WTO, and issues of labelling fortified wines as 'sherry' and 'port' figured prominently in the high-politics/stakes confrontation between the EU and RSA at the turn of the century. Such effective agricultural trade 'regimes' are of particular concern to the middle power Cairns Group, of which South Africa is the latest member, along with Argentina, Australia, Chile and New Zealand. While wine is clearly not a 'non-traditional export' from South Africa, its foreign exchange potentials in terms of conference business, direct exports, foreign direct investment (FDI), tourism, etc., are not insignificant, especially for the post-industrial Western Cape, which has already bid for the Olympic Games and now for the World Cup of Soccer. So moderate, managed declines in the value of the rand may be helpful in terms of competitiveness in a range of sectors.

Fourth, wine can be situated as one factor among many in studies of *'new' regionalisms*; i.e., transnational relations among not only neighboring states but also companies and communities (cf SAB throughout SADC). Wine has been an issue in the several enlargements of the EU and is a source of some tension between South Africa and Zimbabwe along with other larger sectors such as furniture, shoes and textiles. Moreover, if we define 'regionalisms' flexibly—i.e., beyond state-centrism—then wine can also become a cross-border issue among sub-national jurisdictions (eg., California, Washington and British Columbia along the West Coast of North America). In South Africa, wine is a much more important part of the political economy of the Western Cape than other provinces, especially when combined with related export and tourist demand along with backward and forward linkages: an aspect of the country's historic Atlantic rather than Indian Ocean Rim orientation?

Fifth, the IPE of wine could lead to the novel yet promising field of *comparative studies*, both contrasting wine with related agribusinesses such as beer and spirits industries, but also comparing 'old' and 'new' worlds' wine industries, even such industries within sub-state regions, such as South and Western Australia, New York and California.

Sixth, wine is recognized in disciplines/professions like agriculture and agribusiness, possibly also marketing, but perhaps not to the extent deserved given its growing scale and sophistication in an increasing proportion of the world, including FSU/EE. Its implications for the study and practice of *ecology* may be of particular importance in the new millennium, given its use of biotechnologies, fertilizers, pesticides, water, etc. There is a related issue of health, particularly among the vineyard workers, where alcohol abuse is traditionally high, along with related incidents of domestic violence, etc., now compounded by fetal alcohol syndrome, tuberculosis and HIV/AIDS.

Seventh, the rapidly changing corporate structure of the industry in South Africa at the turn of the century treated throughout this essay—from exclusive, oligarchic, Afrikaner/Cape corporatist cooperatives to local affirmative, empowerment, unbundling and onto globalizations and strategic alliances, etc.—means that notions of local to global *governance* are becoming central, both public/regional and corporate/private, as indicated in the inter-related SAWIT and ETI initiatives.

Eighth, *security* issues arise in the case of wine as other industries, both white-collar crime around intelligence over techniques, plans, or planting (along with possible money-laundering via apparently legitimate vineyard investments but which do not seem to need to make a profit: such would stretch the South African Police Service (SAPS) and related economic intelligence skills, possibly leading to further privatization!) and blue-collar crime against products in shipment, especially higher priced vintages. This is a particular issue in this case, given the well-known very high levels of violent crime in South Africa.

Penultimately, ninth, reflected particularly in this case, the PE of wine cannot be separated from issues of *transition and transformation, both locally and globally*, as reflected in the rise and fall in the mid-eighteenth century around the Cape. The IPE of sanctions and incentives in this (Crawford and Klotz, 1999) and related cases such as Argentina, Chile (Casaburi, 1999), Turkmenistan, is interesting, even extending to issues of confidence-building, peacekeeping and post-conflict reconstruction and reconciliation.

Finally, tenth, such comparative perspectives could lead towards a series of *alternative projections/scenarios, both existential and analytic*—from exponential to uneven or negative growth, exclusive to inclusive patterns of governance, or isolation, disintegration, anarchy—i.e., sustainable human development/security to unsustainable growth, etc. The industry's own Vision 2020 should both learn from and inform such previews through a variety or consultants' reports and stakeholder discussions. As Bekker, et al. (1999: 21) caution, the still-fragmented industry is ill-prepared to defend itself against globalizations let alone exploit such opportunities until it replaces its inherited 'ethnic corporatism' (Ewert and Hamman, 1996) with a 'shared strategic alignment' or 'strategic alliance'.

* With thanks for a variety of inputs and encouragements from Kim Hoepfl, Tony Leysens and Lisa Tompson.

PART III

GOVERNANCE
AND
CIVIL SOCIETY

6 Transnational, National, or Local? Gender-based NGOs and Information Networks in India

J. P. SINGH[1]

Introduction

Technologies propose change, they do not determine it. This chapter embeds the effects of information networks in the socio-political institutions underlying them. In examining this embeddedness, the chapter's bias is toward the short term where the nitty-gritty of politics is often played out. Transformations, like those promised by information networks, take time, but these transformations must be negotiated at the micro-level and in the short term. This chapter also focusses on non-governmental organizations (NGOs) working on gender issues in India in the context of globalization as defined in the introductory chapter of this volume. Most studies of networking focus on the international level, which is important, but in doing so these studies skirt the micro 'domestic' level. India's moves toward globalization and the importance of information networks in sustaining NGOs are thus both analytically important. Gender-based NGOs which internationally comprise almost one-tenth of international non-governmental organizations (INGOs) (Keck and Sikkink, 1998: 11) and almost one-third of Indian NGOs (www.indev.org) are thus good representatives to test ideas of emerging forms of global governance. Governance here deals with how goals, conceptualized as agendas, are translated into concerted action through networking.[2] The study asks three questions:

- Are information technology networks helping Indian NGOs formulate global identities?

- How are global information exchanges affecting agenda-setting for NGOs? Are information flows and knowledge building controlled by the North, South, or both?
- How are gender-based NGOs and information networks contributing to emerging forms of global governance such as collective action and global civil society formation?

These questions are instructive for analyzing ethnicity in a global context. This volume emphasizes identity, resistance movements and emancipatory struggles in analyzing ethnicity (see Chapter 1). These three concerns are mirrored in the context of gender in the questions posed above on identity, agenda-setting and possibilities for collective action. Parallels between ethnicity and gender, both conceptually and empirically, are numerous. A broader conception of ethnicity could easily accommodate—as well as gain— from including an emphasis on gender. Both at heart are about identity, legitimacy and struggles of entitlement (ethnic elements emphasized by Horowitz, 1985). Just as the impact of technology on ethnicity has long been realized, gendered struggles in the context of information networks and globalization borrow from such analyses. A famous example of the former is the effect of the printing press on encouraging the vernacular in Europe and the rise of language-based nationalism (Anderson, 1983).

To answer the questions above, this chapter first describes Indian women's movements and the historical context in which they have arisen. Following this, it examines the rise of networks and networking among gender-based NGOs in India. Empirical evidence from India detailed in the last two sections does not posit straightforward answers. Network effects, as moderated by socio-political institutions, are context driven. NGOs may or may not welcome being subsumed under global identities or adapt easily to global agendas and advocacy. Instead of being seamless and democratic, networks might be multilayered, overlapping and hierarchical.

Method

The argument made about the effects of networking in this chapter is explained here in terms of three methodological elements: the need for empirical analysis; the case study used in this chapter; and the theoretical explanation.

Empirical Historical Analysis

Historical analysis, which is mostly descriptive, is combined with empirical analysis to account for sources of variation. Neo-liberal scholars such as Keohane (1991, 1988), specifically in the case of gender scholarship, and radical ones like Castells (1996: 4), advocate the empirical method of observation, data collection, analysis and theorizing to uncover sources of variation.[3]

The empirical portion of this chapter thus relies on two means for data collection: a survey of the literature and in-depth interviews conducted in May-June 1999 with representatives of gender-based NGOs and a few related organizations in India.[4] While half the interviews were conducted in Delhi (the hub of NGO activity in India), others were conducted in Calcutta, Hyderabad, Mumbai and remote areas in the province of Himachal Pradesh to avoid geographic and urban bias.

Why India?

Most analyses of networks are top-heavy, noting final outcomes of networking, the global agendas that are set and how global collective action takes place. They miss the first stage of theory building on networking, namely how the network 'nodes' get connected to the main trunks and how their identities, agendas and governance patterns are transformed or not transformed. Keohane (1988: 392) advocates 'paying sufficient attention to domestic politics', to remove an important 'blind spot' in our theories. India, having just opened itself to global markets, not only allows for seeing the influence of global networks but is also big enough to account for a variety of them in different geographical places with different degrees of connectivity to the networks. India thus represents a 'plausibility probe' for candidate theories of network effects but it does not offer any rigorous validity for the arguments (Eckstein, 1975: 108-113). Second, as implied above and argued by King, et al. (1994: 218), even a single case can consist of a number of observations (as in the many NGOs interviewed here) to account for the sources of variation. Third, India has always been a test case of ethnic issues. The diversity of its ethnic groupings is paralleled by the diversity of gender issues and sub-groupings in the country.

The Theoretical Explanation

All kinds of international transactions are now conducted through networked organizations. Various authors refer to these networks in speaking of the virtual state (Rosecrance, 1996), networked security (Deibert, 1997; Arquila and Ronfeldt, 1997), networked marketplaces (Spar and Bussgang, 1996), advocacy networks (Keck and Sikkink, 1998), and all forms of networked organizations as preeminent in world political economy (Aronson, 2001; Keohane and Nye, 1998; Castells, 1996, 1997, 1998). In Castells (1996: 469) words: 'Networks constitute the new social morphology of our societies, and the diffusion of networking logic substantially modifies the operation and outcomes in processes of production, experience, power and culture'.

What is clearly in question is not network ubiquity but 'the operations and outcomes' of this new form of organization. This chapter investigates neo-liberal institutionalist analysis as its point of take-off but borrows elements from other perspectives to moderate its claims.

The liberal worldview posits technology as humankind's 'heroic' endeavor toward resolving its problems (Landes, 1969; Cipolla, 1976; Rosenberg and Birdsell, 1986). Information technology networks cut distances, bring people together and foster communication, cooperation and, at times, conflict (Rosenau, 1990). The networked technologies flatten hierarchies. As Aronson (2001) argues, 'Information is power. New technologies empower people and always threaten the establishment.' Networked NGOs also bring good governance and civil society (The Commission of Global Governance, 1995: 254-55).

Liberal gender research posits similar results. The power of networks in ending the isolation of NGOs and mobilizing collective action are often noted. While many analyses note the lack of access and marginalization of women from information technologies (Farwell, et al., 1998), gender-based NGOs can effect many gains in their favor through network strategy (Karl, et al., 1999). Networks allow for common cause identification and convergence, and for mobilizing collective action. Liberal feminists are themselves employed in several multilateral organizations and international donor agencies linked to NGOs.

But liberal insistence on pre-specifying preferences in highly interactive networking environments is problematic here. Contructivist worldviews help by emphasizing socialization processes (Berger and Luckman, 1966). Wendt's (1992) famous formulation shows how identities and interests are inherently relational interactive processes. The social constructivist and liberal worldviews both show how progressive concerted action results from networked interactions. But instead of attributing such action to rational egotistical individuals, constructivists attribute it to processes of collective meaning formation in which both cooperation and conflict are possible, depending on the context of interactions over time. Keck and Sikkink develop a network theory of information exchanges to show that the 'bulk of what networks do might be termed persuasion or socialization, but neither process is devoid of conflict' (Keck and Sikkink, 1998: 16). They specifically show how networks develop framing techniques to foster collective action and global advocacy. The framing of violence against women issues as human rights issues is an example (Keck and Sikkink, 1998: Chapter 5). They acknowledge that networks being interactive, they are sites of negotiation and may not be symmetrical, as in North-South relations. Youngs (1998) also notes how feminists can create collective meanings and theories capable of accounting for the 'virtual voices' of women on the net through successive network interactions. Such struggles are also noted by ethnic studies scholarship in speaking of the effects of networks of various types of diasporas.

Multiple network effects are also suggested by radical constructivists, such as Castells (1997), who show how various forms of feminist identity are emerging in various parts of the world depending on the socio-historical context and the dominant production structure. The primary function performed by networks is that of sustaining and coordinating global financial, production and distribution flows. Labor, on the other hand, is fragmented (Castells, 1996: 475). Social movements, including feminist ones can challenge dominant structures using subordinate networks through 'conscious, purposive social action' (Castells, 1998: 380) but this is not a fait accompli. Castells posits feminist movements challenging patriarchal structures in favorable light. Gender-based NGOs which this chapter examines, approximate what Castells (1997: 200) calls 'practical feminists' who, apart from their presence in the developed world, represent 'the widest and deepest stream of women's struggles in today's world, particularly in the developing world'. But he also sees them as being quite elitist. In the end networked capitalism, in replacing industrial capitalism, creates fragmented and multiple social identities, including feminist ones.

The radical position on dominant 'structures' is problematical. Gender identities are conceived in this scholarship in opposition to globalization. Patriarchy, in other words, is sustained by various forms of capitalism, including globalization. Critical feminist theorists have also focused on how patriarchal intersubjective meanings are created and sustained by globalization (Peterson, 1997; Peterson and Runyan, 1999).[5] Franklin (1998) examines the similar representations and meanings created by global information networks and capital. What hope do fragmented and manipulated identities offer in the age of networked globalization? At best, Peterson (1997) sums up (without explicit reference to information technologies) changing ontologies of gender roles and socialization as amounting to a 'crisis of masculinity'.

It is not necessary to try resolve the debate on the connection between patriarchy and capitalism/globalization. This debate really is about basic ontological beliefs. This chapter rejects the heroism of both liberal and radical scholarships. However, empirically it does look at micro-structures to examine the possibilities and constraints for emancipatory action. (Maznah Mohamad examines similar micro-issues in another chapter in this volume.) This chapter suggests that patriarchy is being challenged through information networks which themselves owe their existence to patterns of globalization. In terms of ethnic studies, the chapter stands in stark contrast to primordial identities (Smith, 1981) or unchanging structures of capitalism that manipulate ethnicity (Brass, 1991), allowing for both identity and outcomes to be determined by struggles for legitimacy (Anderson, 1983; Horowitz, 1985).

Historical Context: Women's Movements in India[6]

The sources and scope of women's movements in India are varied but four periods may be discerned to provide a background to the current period which is examined later. First, during the colonial and immediate post-colonial period, the women's movement was elite driven. Select male and female reformers argued for female literacy and equality of status, both political and economic. Universal suffrage through the constitution was a result of these efforts.

The second phase, which marks the ascendance of grassroots pressures, developed out of left-wing politics in India, especially in states like Maharashtra, Gujarat and Andhra Pradesh where communist and socialist workers were present at the local level or where trade union activity was strong. However, while they were associated with party ideologies there were no party-based women's organization in the country in the early 1970s.[7]

In 1972, Ela Bhatt helped form the Self-Employed Women's Association (SEWA) as part of the Textile Labor Association in Gujarat. Perhaps, the most famous leftist organization was Stree Shakti Sangathana which arose in the 1970s from Hyderabad and worked on grassroots women's issues such as landless laborers and anti-arrak (alcohol) campaigns (alcohol consumption by men is a major instigator of violence against women).[8] Many anti-caste crusades by low-caste Dalit women drew upon the Chinese revolution and Black women's campaigns in the United States (Angela Davis, the African-American activist, was claimed as a sister by one of the groups in Maharashtra).

The third phase, beginning in the late 1970s, marks both the diversity of women's issues being addressed and the beginnings of formal linkages with global feminist movements. These issues included campaigns against rape, dowry, sati, marriage and divorce laws, alcohol consumption, landholdings, and deforestation. The very first national women's campaign protested a Supreme Court decision acquitting local policemen of rape because the woman had a boyfriend (and therefore was deemed to be of 'loose' character) was carried out during this period. Interestingly, the national mobilization took place through a letter writing campaign (Kumar, 1995: 70). Another important development, in the context of this chapter, is the establishment of women's resource centers the foremost function of which became information dissemination, consciousness-raising and coordinated campaigns in particular issues.

The origins of networking in India must be located in the developments that took place in the third phase. It is also significant that many of the grassroots organizations were beginning to identify themselves as NGOs. The global awareness of NGOs coincides with the UN Decade for Women (1976-1985), the three World Conferences that the UN organized for this purpose (Mexico in 1975; Copenhagen in 1980; Nairobi in 1985), and the many other UN-sponsored conferences which were important for this purpose. Keck and Sikkink (1998: 168) note that the development of international women's networks is inextricably linked with the UN and that the 'Chronologies of the international women's movement are largely a litany of UN meetings'. But the importance of such international networks must not be overestimated. Domestic NGOs in India were quite firmly established by the 1980s and their issues had grassroots origins. International support initially was minimal.

A fourth phase, starting in the late 1980s, coincides with the macro-economic opening of the Indian economy and the consequent deepening of international linkages. Networking among Indian NGOs themselves and with international groups began to take-off during this period through various media, including traditional media like print and voice and non-traditional media such as computer-based communications. NGOs also begin to receive funding from international donors just as globally a shift toward participatory and decentralized development and governance processes took place (Salamon, 1999).

Information Technology Networks and Gender-Based NGOs

The variable effects of information technology networks on identity, agenda-setting and collective action are themselves related to the variation in information technology networks themselves. This section describes the sources of these variations by explaining difficulties surrounding network diffusion, types of network usage, and the various types of networked organizations.

India's Telecommunications Restructuring[9]

Telecommunications was made a development priority in India in 1983, mostly due to pressures from international and domestic businesses as well as from a few reform-minded individuals within the state. Telecommunications infrastructure enhancement accelerated in the 1990s. India's teledensity (number of telephone lines per 100 people) was 0.33 in 1980, 0.6 in 1990 and 2.2 in 1998. Comparing this with 1998 teledensities of 56.2 in Singapore, 19.8 in Malaysia and 7.0 in China makes the inadequacy of Indian telecommunications quite apparent.

In spite of the slow rate of growth of the infrastructure, a powerful shift has come about in the way telecommunication services are perceived by Indian society. Telephone services were a rarity in the 1980s and waiting lists for telephones extended to 10-15 years for Delhi and Mumbai. Now telephone and fax services are seen as necessities. Cynical statements, common in the 1980s, about the possibility of even getting a telephone, are now directed more at the cost and quality of the services than their procurement. Even though telephone densities remain low, the network is accessible. Rural teledensity is only 0.5 but nearly half of the 600,000 Indian villages have public call offices (PCOs) while all of the district and sub-district (bloc level) headquarters have PCOs. Telecommunications services are growing at a rate of 20% annually.

The key to information age networking, although possible through telephone and fax communications, lies in data-based networks which remain limited mostly to urban and affluent areas in India. Although e-mail and Internet services were liberalized in 1992, the entrenched government carriers created several hurdles. It was only in 1998 that private Internet service providers could begin their work. There were an estimated 400,000 e-mail accounts in the country in 1998, with many users or organizations sharing the same account. However, Internet diffusion is taking place at an amazing speed with 1.5 million users estimated for the end of 2000 and 9 million by 2003 (www.cnn.com, 4 August 1999).

Difficulties with Networking

Studies on access of Indian NGOs to e-mail and Internet are lacking. Anecdotal evidence suggests that most medium to large NGOs, especially those receiving international donor funding, have access to these technologies. Of the 19 organizations interviewed for this chapter, 18 had e-mail accounts but this is not generalizable due to the high-profile nature of these NGOs. The one organization lacking an e-mail account was Sutra, located in the lower Himalayan hills. It had to shut down its account due to low reliability.

A number of difficulties are noted by the representatives of NGOs in using their e-mail and Internet accounts. Dedicated lines are expensive, reliability is low and speeds are extremely slow. NGOs note that they must wait for evening or late night hours just to connect. Many NGOs have only one account which must be shared by several people creating organizational problems with simple tasks like replying to e-mails. A few have outmoded computers. However, here entrepreneurship rules. For example, a network called South Asian Research and Development Initiative (SARDI), bringing together gender-based NGOs and women in trade unions, utilizes old computers that it buys and provides to trade union representatives in South Asia. (SARDI is funded by the American Center for International Labor Solidarity (ACILS) based in Washington, DC.) Many other NGOs complain that while the demands on them to communicate domestically and internationally are high, donor agencies provide little in their funds for electronic communications. The English language domination of cyberspace also limits communications in India, especially outside of large towns. Finally, many note that technology is perceived and acted upon as a male-dominated arena. The convener of SARDI noted that most information technology officers in big NGOs, if they have them, tend to be men. These men, in turn, tend to relate to only the top management people in the NGOs. In small NGOs, men make it their concern to familiarize themselves with these communications. (Quadir in this volume notes similar male domination in terms of micro-finance management in Bangladesh.) An official at the Centre for Women's Development Studies in New Delhi noted that when they first received their computers and Internet access, the men in the office tended to dominate their use.

Variable Use

It is not sufficient to stop at the difficulties surrounding electronic communications. Considerable variation exists in types of usage itself. A few of these variations may be summarized as:

Variety of media: Reliance predominantly on electronic communications is rare and limited to the bigger NGOs in large cities. Telephone or fax seems to be the preferred mode of communication within the country. Most NGOs note that one of their biggest budget items is long-distance telephone bills. Print media, especially desktop publishing, is another major form of communication. Newsletters, monthly magazines, resource manuals and other publications put out by NGOs provide important means of information dispersal. (Many ·NGO publications in India have country-wide audience. They have specific expertise which may be desired in other parts of the country.) As marginal costs of information technologies fall, a few are now developing CD-ROMs, floppy disks and videos to distribute information inexpensively.

Types of NGOs and organizations: A few organizations in the country are explicitly high-tech and have made electronic communications their preferred mode of communication in information gathering and sharing. Women's Feature Service (WFS), managed from New Delhi with collaborating centers in North and Latin America, the Netherlands and the Philippines is a typical high-tech NGO. It specializes in producing news stories about women in development for mainstream media by over 120 women journalists based in 60 countries. WFS has also published a comprehensive book on networking in which many gender-based NGO networks are featured (Karl, et al., 1999). SARDI, mentioned above, is another example of a high-tech NGO. Sanhita, a women's resource center in Calcutta, maintains a list of 600 e-mail addresses of which more than 300 are in India. It is used extensively by Sanhita officials in information dissemination. 'Bol!' is a South Asian e-mail list on gender run by an NGO from Nepal. The British Council in India has started, with DFDI funding, a 'one-stop-shop' for development information on India by hosting a website allowing NGOs and other development organizations to put up homepages (www.indev.org). One third of the NGOs listed so far are involved in women's issues. Indev also holds training workshops for NGO staffs to help put up homepages and run their websites.[10] The Indev website includes databases (of NGOs and other organizations, key documents, statistics, and profiles of development projects in India), a development newspaper put out on the web, an e-mail digest, and a discussion forum which allows for cyber-discussion on NGO-related development issues.

It must be noted that while electronic networking exists in India, it must co-exist with other forms of networks (face-to-face, telephone, print media). Electronic media are the preferred media mostly for international and regional communications. One NGO official (interview) cynically noted in reference to e-mail communications that 'Delhi is closer to DC than to Karimnagar'. (Karimnagar, located in Andhra Pradesh's Telangana region, was a well-known site of the women laborers' movement in the late 1960s and 1970s.) Grassroots NGOs do not have electronic information exchange capabilities. Thus NGOs above the grassroots level often have to act as information brokers, a task that is met with varying degrees of willingness as it imposes additional burdens on already resource-constrained organizations. Networks in India thus remain multilayered, hierarchical and clustered around specific activities and NGOs. However, these networks do exist and their potential for political mobilization is significant—much greater, for instance, than that of the letter-writing campaign mentioned above which was used for a nation-wide protest in 1980. The reliance on telephones for social mobilization is taken for granted now and may even be easier with those with access to e-mails.

Effects of Networks

The scale and scope of different types of networking are now acknowledged by all NGOs. What is in question is how this networking specifically affects identities, agendas and possibilities of governance. Rosenau (2001) suggests differentiating between information technologies, which he holds to be value-neutral, and purposive action which arises from technology usage. According to him, 'the distinction prevents the analyst from mistaking second-order for first-order dynamics, for treating information technologies as an unseen hand that somehow gets people, groups, or communities to pursue goals and undertake actions without awareness of why they do what they do and, accordingly, without taking responsibility for their conduct'. Second-order effects in terms of identities, agendas and governance issues are now described.

Identity Issues

Identity politics are analyzed here in terms of the goals and symbols that gender-based NGOs utilize themselves. Until the 1980s, NGOs conceived their identity around grassroots 'social work' or 'economic development' issues. Now these NGOs converge first around the issue of 'violence against women' or 'human rights' issues, and second, around 'participatory development' or 'civil society' issues (the latter is discussed at length in the next section). What accounts for these change in frames and what kind of identity conflicts have arisen as a result?

Both the focus on violence against women as human rights issues and participatory development or civil society issues are global terms and have come about as a result of networking. These 'umbrella' frames developed out of the several international conferences that the UN organized and also because of the interactions of global feminist groups with each other.[11] The Center for Women's Global Leadership at Rutgers is credited, along with its influential director Charlotte Bunch, with starting a Global Campaign for Women's Human Rights in 1989 (see Bunch, 1990; Bunch and Reilly, 1999). The human rights frames were taken up through the 1993 World Conference on Human Rights in Vienna and then at the 1995 women's conference in Beijing. Keck and Sikkink (1998: 178-179) note how a US-based feminist activist was able to correlate the concerns about violence against women in the United States with what she heard from women in the Garhwal region of India who complained about male violence emanating from their alcohol consumption.

But it must be remembered that this framing is an interactive process. Of particular importance, especially for gender issues, are 'catalytic events' like the several UN conferences which have dealt with gender issues. These catalytic events are important for consciousness raising and formation of umbrella frames. NGOs in India note the identity transformation they went through in organizing for the 1995 Fourth World Conference for Women in Beijing.   The event and the preparations for it are recounted by almost all NGOs the author interviewed.   The National Alliance for Women's Organisations (NAWO) was set up to prepare for Beijing and continued thereafter.   NAWO ended the isolation of NGOs in India by giving them a national identity.   For example, NAWO allowed for policy-making agencies in Delhi to have a national body to turn for advice instead of 'two and a half NGOs in New Delhi' like earlier (interview).   India eventually sent the fourth largest 'national' delegation to Beijing.

   In terms of identity and convergence, local politics also remain important. A lot of the telephone and face-to-face networking is in fact carried out at the local level where NGOs working on disparate issues might join hands to confront local authorities or alternatively share their resources if they are working on a particular issue.   The Ford Foundation has, for example, funded a number of NGOs in Karnataka to work on local governance initiatives affecting women.   They regularly network face-to-face or over the telephone. NGOs also point out that while local efforts do not receive global attention, they are crucial for local advocacy mobilization.   An Asmita official, from a Hyderabad NGO, for example, notes that while they participated in the Rutgers-centered process on human rights, they themselves organized a workshop attended by 2,000 women on this issue in Hyderabad.

   On the other hand, there are a few NGOs that deliberately eschew local, regional or international vocabularies in describing their identities.   The Society for Promotion of Area Resource Centers (SPARC) which acts globally on the rights of women slum dwellers consciously constructs its identity around housing rights and does not see this as either a local or global issue but as both.   The Society for Participatory Research in Asia (PRIA), an NGO based in Delhi, sees international advocacy as one of its main goals. One of the five divisions in PRIA is the Centre for Global Alliances that networks consistently with organizations at all levels.

   Identification of local issues by NGOs with the umbrella frame of globalization has not come about without problems.   The shift toward these global identities, supported by neo-liberal international donor agencies, was especially hard for NGOs that arose from the left.   Many people deserted their ranks and now accuse them of 'ideological bankruptcy'.   Those still involved in traditional leftist issues like trade unionism and grassroots protests see the expertise of these NGOs as 'academic'—aimed at 'workshops, posters, organizing celebrity events'—and remain unimpressed with the lack of involvement NGOs show with grassroots practices (interviews).   One NGO official noted that the sense of involvement that NGOs had in the 1970s and 1980s is gone as NGOs now compete with each other for international donor agency funds (see Quadir in this volume for parallel points). On the other hand, the President of Sutra, a self-identified leftist ideologue, criticizes people who think that Indian NGOs will self-destruct if they accept foreign donor funding. (He notes: 'As if we are not capable of destroying our own country.')

Many NGOs are also skeptical of the outcomes of information technology networks. As the editor of the influential feminist publication *Manushi* describes it, 'People think you can send 500 e-mails a day and work is done but it can easily be an incestuous sort of world with very little knowledge of how to press levers of powers' (interview). Others regret the speed and consequent stress that such communications produce. As one interviewee stated, 'You have to reply then and there. Everything is urgent. We are paying attention to what's urgent forgetting what's important' (interview).

Also, a few NGO officials believe that networks are producing fragmented identities. For a few NGOs, many networks are too issue-based thus inhibiting the formation of an encompassing social movement in India. Here again the issue of competition among NGOs for foreign funding is raised in not only making them issue-focussed but also a bit distrustful of each other and hesitant to share information and resources.

Agenda-setting

The previous section noted that interactive processes help with framing or agenda-setting. Other issues involved in these interactive processes may now be noted. First, it is undeniable that most frames come together at the behest of international organizations located in the North. The human rights/violence against women frame developed through Rutgers and several UN agencies. The civil society/participatory development frame arises out of US academia and multilateral development agencies. Second, while framing is an international exercise, the issue included in the frames may be local.

Third, the efforts of particular NGOs and countries in framing issues varies. India has been, for example, instrumental in raising one particular issue within the civil society/participatory development frame, namely the issue of local decentralized governance. This issue in fact defines most of the NGO work done on civil society processes in India. Indian social movements and the women's movement (including NGOs) worked consistently for the 73rd amendment to the Indian constitution to establish Panchayats (local governance bodies) in every part of the country at the village, sub-district (bloc) and district levels. A minimum of one-third of the seats to these Panchayats are to be filled by women. By May 1998, women filled over 30 percent of the seats on average nationally at all three levels of Panchayats (data collected from Institute of Social Studies Trust, Bengalore). However, many women never participate in decisions (being a mere front for their husbands who could not contest elections because of the quotas for women) or are barred from participating by the other men in the Panchayats. NGO programs are now training women to participate effectively at Panchayat meetings and tackle issues as diverse as water politics, violence against women and corruption (*Uma Prachar*, 1992). Global framing around participatory development and civil society issues has allowed these NGOs to receive international support from agencies like the World Bank and the Ford Foundation. For example, the 73rd amendment to the Indian constitution coincides with the drive within the World Bank since the late 1980s to measure and advocate development through effective decentralized governance mechanisms (World Bank, 1997, 1989).

India is one of the first countries to implement such a wide-scale local governance program, leading to policy emulation elsewhere. NGOs working in this area regularly refer to the number of international observers they receive, especially from countries in sub-Saharan Africa, South and South East Asia, and from within India itself. Best practices in one part of the country may be repeated or remodelled in another part of the country. Just about every NGO interviewed notes the importance of networking within India to gain knowledge of such practices. Workshop materials, newsletters and other publications are especially important in this context.

On the whole, however, NGOs remain concerned about hegemonic information flows, too. Many NGOs distinguish between sharing information and dumping. As one interviewee commented, 'Ford and World Bank dump on us rather than get from us' (interview). Most databases on women's issues are located in the North. Another interviewee said, 'The Bank is a knowledge center. There is a monopoly of knowledge in downloading' (interview). The dissemination of research done by Indian academics on gender-based issues is still in its infancy and research findings are seldom published in academic journals of the North. The Indev initiative mentioned above is trying to correct this by building a database of NGO efforts in India. The National Foundation of India, a New Delhi-based NGO, is similarly concerned with building such databases. Many NGOs setting up women's resource centers around the country are also considering building information databanks.

NGOs are also concerned that Delhi NGOs dominate information flows for the country as a whole. The formation of national networks, like NAWO mentioned earlier, helps to get around this problem but Delhi NGOs still predominantly have the ears of policy-makers and donor agencies. The Institute of Social Studies Trust (ISST) gets around this problem ingeniously by concentrating on international networking through its Delhi office (which also handles most of its theoretical work) while using the Bengalore office for its training programs and empirical work.

A few bottom-up information flows which affect agendas positively may also be mentioned. First, field-level realities get issues on the agenda of NGOs. The HIV/AIDS prevention programs are being enhanced by the field-level stories being circulated by NGOs working at the grassroots level. Second, Indian NGOs feel especially confident that they have a lot to document in terms of 'best practices' and 'success stories'. India has a lot of technical expertise which is contributing to global efforts. However, the latter issue is also sometimes lost in the information flows dominated by agencies from the North. Third, as mentioned above, bottom-up initiatives (like local governance programs in India) are beginning to contribute to global agenda formation.

Governance

Collective action and civil society (national and international) as networking issues are about governance. Collective action becomes easier through networking for the following reasons. First, networks often overlap and intersect and bring disparate parties together. Networking among Indian NGOs over the preparations for the 1998 Beijing Conference is one such example. Networks dealing with violence against women also bring many issues together. But networks are also multilayered (especially those including several types of media and NGOs). For example, networking dominated by donor agencies or 'super NGOs' can be hierarchical and undemocratic.

Second, networking allows for mobilization around specific causes and issue advocacy. Anecdotal examples from India, covering just about every NGO interviewed, include the story of a woman from Surat in western India who was dragged for eight kilometers by Hindu fundamentalist men for trespassing her 'caste-barriers'. Just as this woman was being dragged, the story began to circulate over SARDI's violence against women network. Support rushed in and the woman was rescued. SARDI also mobilized support for a teenage Muslim girl who was sold from Hyderabad to an Arab man. Working with Middle Eastern networks, the girl was brought back and rehabilitated in New Delhi. Other stories include the help that the women's resource center Sanhita in Calcutta provided to a group in Zimbabwe over e-mail for setting up their resource center. ISST in New Delhi is participating with other NGOs in South Asian countries in an IDRC-sponsored study looking at the effects of economic liberalization on violence against women. Mahila Dakshita Samiti has even set up branches in the United States, Europe and Turkey to help Indian women with their specific problems, and its Indian offices regularly interact with these offices through e-mail. Organizations like Sakhi and Manavi in the United States have come about to help South Asian women cope with problems of domestic violence. Sakhi estimates that it has helped 2,000 South Asian women with domestic violence issues (*India Today*, North American edition, 23 August, 1999: 24m).

Third, the international dimension is now explored thoroughly by NGOs in mobilizing support for their goals. Framing techniques allow for a number of local issues to be included in global umbrella terms. While redefining NGO identities, this also provides them with legitimacy and global visibility. SPARC, which acts globally on the rights of women slum dwellers (through networks such as National Federation of Slum Dwellers, the Asian Coalition of Housing Rights and Slum Dwellers International), sees its main source of strength in its global counterparts with whom it shares information, project designs and other strategies. NGOs also note how their international funding and linkages increase their legitimacy and resource mobilization with local governments.

Finally, networking ends NGO isolation in particular issues. At one time, notes a SPARC official, they were 'so socially marginalised that we could hold hands with only other crushed human beings. Now international advocacy for producing cross-linkages has played an important role in breaking these barriers.'

Recent democratizing actions in civil society (Sakamoto, 1997; Nhema in this volume) can easily be attributed to networking. Working toward ending violence toward women or introducing effective governance at the grassroots level can only help to deepen civil society. Increasing networking and information sharing also allows NGOs to develop trust in each other and contribute to deepening gender-based movements themselves. The 30-50,000 representatives gathered in Beijing in 1995 or the one million signatures presented to the United Nations by the Global Campaign for Women's

Human Rights are examples of the interactive power of emerging global society.

Conclusions

By analyzing 'domestic' 'nodes', this chapter calls attention to crucial elements surrounding networking. Although the empirical evidence, based on in-depth interviews, remains anecdotal and country specific, a few preliminary conclusions can be advanced. The question posed in the title of this chapter can be answered first for the effects of networking on identity formation, agenda-setting and governance. The answer would have to be 'all of the above' in choosing between transnational, national or local.

Empirical evidence from India suggests the following answers in the context of both gender and ethnicity. A mixed bag of identities and a variety of transnational linkages suggest that Indian NGOs are only now beginning to see themselves as part of transnational imagined communities. While a few NGOs are aware of their global linkages and how they may benefit from them, others resist or are in conflict about being subsumed under global identity formation. In terms of agenda formation, umbrella vocabularies (as frames), like the global focus on human rights, allow for the convergence of disparate agendas but this very convergence also allows for an entirely new agenda to develop and be shaped by transnational actors. Umbrella vocabularies may also change specific local concerns into global ones in terms of pre-existing vocabularies. This is the case of decentralized governance initiatives in India being understood in terms of civil society and participatory development issues. Eventually, a redefinition of issues takes place. According to Keck and Sikkink (1998: 19), stories are retold and people lose control over their own stories. It is not always easy for all NGOs to adjust to this new 'reality'. As with global identity issues, many forms of conflict and resistance may be observed. In terms of governance, networking remains multilayered, overlapping and hierarchical but concerted action and civil society are still made possible. These findings are supported by the work of those who note that local struggles—including ethnic ones—take place within the context of globalization (Rosenau, 1997; Barber, 1995). This chapter contributes to such understandings in showing the malleability of identities as well as the variations in the outcomes that follow.

Theoretically, this chapter substantiates many conclusions put forth by liberal internationalist analyses. Although technology is not seen as enabling global cooperation and governance, its role in proposing such change is nonetheless important. Constructivist analyses deepen the picture further by pointing out the interactive processes underlying collective meaning formations while radical analyses help to alert us to the many conflicts which underlie them.

Networks capture the governance dilemmas of the information age. While technologies may not be instrumental in furthering human emancipation, they do propose a path toward it. The specificity of this path is littered with institutional cooperation and conflict—as usual.

Notes

1. The author sincerely thanks the editors of this volume for help throughout the project. Geeta Chowdhary, Chuck Johnson, Spike Peterson, Mark Robinson and representatives of many NGOs in India also provided valuable assistance.
2. 'Governance refers to activities backed by shared goals that may or may not derive from legal and formally prescribed responsibilities and that do not necessarily rely on police power to overcome defiance and attain compliance' (Rosenau, 1992: 4).
3. Gill (1997: 8) poses a similar challenge by asking gender theorists to historicize 'patriarchy' and its ontological underpinnings.
     Representatives from the following NGOs were interviewed : Asmita, Resource Centre for Women, Hyderabad; Centre for Environmental Concerns, Hyderabad; Centre for Social Research, New Delhi; Centre for Women's Development Studies, New Delhi; Institute of Social Studies Trust (ISST), New Delhi; Institute of Social Studies Trust (ISST), Bengalore; Mahila Dakshita Samiti, New Delhi; Manushi, New Delhi; National Foundation for India, New Delhi; Sanhita, Gender Resource Centre, Calcutta; Society for Participatory Research in Asia (PRIA), New Delhi; Society for Promotion of area Resource Centres (SPARC), Mumbai; South Asian Research and Development Initiative (SARDI), New Delhi; Sutra, District Solan, Himachal Pradesh; Women's Feature Service, New Delhi; Women's Policy Research and Advocacy Unit, National Institute of Advanced Studies, Bengalore.
4. Among those interviewed were representatives from the following *governmental bodies*: Delhi Commission for Women, New Delhi; and National Cooperative Union of India, District Solan Office, Himachal Pradesh and from the following *international agencies*: Indev, The British Council, New Delhi; and Ford Foundation, New Delhi.
5. Critical theory historicizes the structures of radical theory to understand their evolution and purpose (Cox, 1996). The structure here consists of material/technological capabilities, institutions supporting these capabilities, and ideas. A civil society which supports a liberal democratic state in its compact with capital is an example. Rival critical ontologies are offered as possibilities for human emancipation (Gill and Mittelman, 1997).
6. This section draws extensively from interviews but especially from Kumar (1995) and Shah (1990).

7. An exception was Mahila Dakshita Samiti or MDS (Women's Self-Development Organization) which came from the initiative of socialist-aligned women in the Janata Party in 1977. Interviews with members of MDS were conducted for this chapter.
8. Members who started their activist careers in Stree Shakti Sangathana were interviewed for this chapter.
9. This section draws upon Singh (1999).
10. A workshop conducted by Indev in collaboration with Centre for Development Studies in New Delhi invited representatives from about 50 NGOs from the New Delhi area. A CWDS official noted that only about 15 of them had e-mail addresses.
11. Among the global umbrella frames and possible gender issues included from India are the following: human rights/violence against women; amnio-centesis/abortion; beggars' issues; caste issues; counseling for couples; dowry issues; gender-sensitization training—especially directed at police; gender resource centers; girl-child survival; health: reproductive rights; HIV/AIDS issues; housing rights; incest; liquor related violence; marriage laws; mothers' rights campaigns; rape; sati; sex workers' rights and issues (Devdasi groups); sexual harassment; slum dwellers rights; and trafficking. Among the issues of *civil society/participatory development* are: eco-feminism (patent rights for seeds, deforestation); gender equality; labor relations and disputes; lands for grazing/common lands; lobbying; micro-credit; public protests/ demonstrations/ (gherao); and women in politics. (Note that a few issues might fall in both categories.)

7 Promoting Democratic Governance at the Grassroots in the Twenty-first Century: Myths and Realities of NGO Programs in Bangladesh

FAHIMUL QUADIR

Introduction

The 'success' of some Bangladeshi non-governmental development organizations (NGDOs)—notably the Grameen Bank (GB) and the Bangladesh Rural Advancement Committee (BRAC)—in poverty alleviation, building people's organizations, grassroots democratization[1] and empowering rural women has become a popular subject of discussion among development practitioners and policy-makers globally. These indigenous NGOs are widely acclaimed for their innovative development strategies focussing on group-based mobilization, beneficiary participation, micro-enterprises and the involvement of women in various income-generating activities. Inspired by the success of some Bangladeshi NGOs, particularly the GB, many developing countries in Asia, Africa and Latin America are now engaged in undertaking similar programs (Hulme, 1990: 278-300). Indeed, the performance of the GB and BRAC, as well as Proshika and the Association for Social Advancement (ASA) is so 'amazing' that even many developed countries, including the United States and Canada, have already begun to replicate these models in order to promote development at the grassroots in their own communities and countries.[2] Furthermore, the 'achievements' of some Bangladeshi NGOs in helping the poor alleviate poverty through micro-finance initiatives have drawn attention of the donor community, especially the World Bank. In addition to encouraging many of its member countries to replicate the GB model, the World Bank has already established a forum called the 'Consultative Group to Assist the Poorest' (CGAP) to coordinate micro-credit programs across the globe (Grameen Trust, 1996: 1-3).

Most authors and development practitioners praise the few Bangladeshi NGOs which have established micro-credit programs for initiating successful 'participatory development' strategies. The latter are assumed to enable marginalized groups, particularly rural women, to manage their own development (Westergaard, 1996: 28-57). Also, these NGOs are widely acclaimed for effectively raising the issue of female oppression in a male-dominated society, giving women the power to challenge traditional patriarchal values and encouraging them to participate effectively in various socio-political activities that affect their lives.

Given such apparently remarkable achievements by the NGO sector in Bangladesh, this chapter explores the role of NGOs in promoting democratic governance at the local level, including by defending and promoting the rights of ethnic minorities. The chapter centers on two major questions: i) Can NGO programs promote democracy at the grassroots? and ii) To what extent do NGO programs enhance self-management capabilities of the poor in general, and women in particular? In other words, do NGOs really open up opportunities for the poor to both establish and retain the control over the development process?

The chapter has five parts. First, it provides a general understanding of the role of NGOs in grassroots democratization and empowerment of the poor.   Second, it reviews the history of the proliferating NGO sector in Bangladesh over the past 25 years, examining the shift in focus by NGOs from relief and rehabilitation to empowerment of the poor and grassroots. Third, it provides a brief overview of the role of development NGOs in defending the rights of ethnic minorities. Fourth, it critically examines different models of micro-credit provisions and their ability to empower the rural poor and contrasts this with the role of advocacy NGOs in mobilizing disadvantaged groups to manage their own development. The final section summarizes the findings of this study.

While this chapter acknowledges[3] that the proliferation of development NGOs in Bangladesh has created the necessary political space for promoting democratic institutions in rural Bangladesh, it finds very little empirical evidence to support the widely held claim that NGOs have enabled disadvantaged groups, especially women, to be empowered in a sustainable manner. Nor does it support the thesis that NGOs defend and promote the rights of ethnic minorities. It argues, contrary to the belief of the donor community and many development practitioners, that NGOs which implement programs designed by NGO executives in consultation with their major donors tend to manipulate the vulnerabilities of marginalized groups, especially women, rather than enable them to manage their own development. Thus, I conclude that the ability of NGOs to promote democratic governance and development at the grassroots is more limited than many analysts claim.

NGDOs[4] and Democratic Governance

Many authors and organizations claim that NGOs have a comparative advantage over governments in alleviating poverty, building democracy at the grassroots, protecting the environment and promoting the interests of vulnerable groups at global as well as national levels. It is widely believed that, unlike governments, NGOs successfully adapt to local needs and diversity and often adopt strategies that allow the poor to get involved in decision-making. Also, because of their grassroots associations, NGOs are often viewed as a force for democracy and/or empowerment (Edwards and Hulme, 1992: 24). In addition to helping the poor gain access to credit, NGOs make efforts to create a political space for enhancing popular participation in decision-making (Westergaard, 1996: 29). It is assumed that such 'democratization/empowerment strategies' enable the poor to achieve the eventual goal of managing their own development by taking part in designing and implementing development projects and by influencing those institutions that shape their lives. Overall, it is believed that democratization and/or empowerment programs develop the ability of the poor to emerge as influential political actors thereby reducing their dependence upon the prevailing power structures, which are often seen as the major source of oppression. Consequently, those development NGOs which attempt both to improve people's livelihoods and to represent the interests of the poor in both local and national decision-making structures are viewed as an impetus for grassroots democratization and development.

NGOs in Bangladesh: From Relief and Poverty Alleviation to Grassroots Democratization

After the independence of Bangladesh in 1971, the country witnessed a phenomenal growth of the NGO sector.[5] The immediate task of reconstructing the country's social and economic structures that were totally destroyed by the war of liberation in 1971 prompted the emergence of local, regional and national NGOs. In responding to the crisis situation, quite a few local activists set up NGOs in order to accelerate the on-going relief and rehabilitation efforts undertaken jointly by the government and the donor community, including international NGOs. These 'first generation' NGOs (Korten, 1987: 145-59) moved gradually to adopt broader development programs and became increasingly involved with poverty alleviation, community development, gender equality and grassroots democratization as they began to face a new challenge of ensuring development at the local level (Shailo, 1994: 10).

By the late 1970s, however, it became quite evident that without enhancing the socio-political consciousness of the rural poor, NGOs would not be able to achieve the goals of sustainable development. As well, it was realized that, without helping the poor to form their own organizations, NGOs might not succeed in ensuring popular participation in planning and implementing development projects (Proshika, 1995: 1). Thus, a number of local non-governmental organizations, namely the BRAC, *Proshika Manobik Unnayan Kendra* (Proshika) and the *Gono Shasthya Kendra* (GK) began to undertake programs for mobilizing the rural poor and building people's organizations.[6] This coincided with the coming into operation of the GB, which popularized the concepts of micro-credit and group-based lending in rural Bangladesh.

These new innovations soon drew widespread attention from both international non-governmental groups and other members of the donor community. As well, the preliminary success of these pioneering Bangladeshi NGOs encouraged many other local groups, particularly leftist activists, to direct their efforts toward strengthening the position of the poor. Adopting various approaches to targeted development, many of the latter subsequently formed NGOs in order to promote development at the local level. Relevant to the subject of identity politics with which this volume is concerned, it is interesting to note that from the late 1970s, Islamic groups have been implementing their own developmental programs in different parts of the country, forming a number of voluntary organizations, mainly mosque-based, to deliver alternative support services to the poor (Shailo, 1994: 10).

Bangladesh, therefore, has experienced what is often called 'the NGO revolution' over the past few years. By one estimate, the country has more than 19,000 voluntary social welfare organizations that are registered with the Department of Social Welfare (World Bank, 1996: 3). However, it is believed that only those NGOs which receive external funds from both official and unofficial sources have an active presence in various development programs. Such organizations are required by law to register with the government's NGO Affairs Bureau (NGOAB). According to a government estimate, over 1,200 development NGOs are registered with the NGOAB and are participating actively in national development.

As shown in Table 7:1 below, the numbers of NGOs that receive external funds have increased dramatically from 382 in 1990 to 1,225 in 1998. Of significance is the fact that their annual foreign support has grown from US$37 million in 1990 to approximately US$ 367 million in 1995-96, reflecting a positive donor interest in channeling funds to the growing NGO sector in the country (NGO Affairs Bureau, 1998: 1).

Table 7:1   Growth of Foreign Funded Development NGOs in Bangladesh

Period	Numbers of Active NGOs		Total	% of Local
	Local	Foreign		
Up to 1990	293	89	382	76.70
1990-91	395	99	494	79.95
1991-92	523	111	634	82.49
1992-93	600	125	725	82.76
1993-94	683	124	807	84.63
1994-95	790	129	911	86.72
1995-96	882	132	1014	86.92
1996-97	997	135	1132	86.98
1997-98	1083	142	1225	88.40

Source: NGO Affairs Bureau, Flow of Foreign Funds through NGOAB, 1998.

Most development NGOs rely heavily upon external sources to finance their various programs and cover their office expenses. By one estimate, funds generated and/or received from local sources constituted less than four percent of the total budget of non-governmental organizations in the 1980s. While NGO efforts to mobilize local resources have reduced somewhat their excessive dependence upon foreign funding, it is estimated that foreign sources accounted for some 94 percent of the total budget of ten large, leading NGOs in 1991 (World Bank, 1996: 33-4).[7] In most cases, development NGOs receive these resources as grants and low interest loans. Also, donors provide subsidized funding in order to help NGOs to build their organizational structures (Khandker, et al., 1995: 21-2).

Ethnicity and Development in a Country of 'Ethno-Linguistic Homogeneity'

Unlike most states in South Asia, Bangladesh is often regarded as a country of ethno-linguistic homogeneity as some 99% of Bangladesh's total population belongs to a particular ethnic group called 'Bengali'. While the Bengali-speaking people appear to share a sense of solidarity based upon a common culture, history and tradition, they are divided along religious lines. According to one estimate, approximately 88% of the country's population is Muslim. The Hindus make up about 10.5% and the Christians and Buddhists together represent 1% of the total population (Baxter, 1997: 6). Such religious divisions, however, did not appear to be a major threat to the country's nation- and state-building initiatives. Most religious minorities have lent their support to the process of building a common national political identity for the people of the country.[8] In particular, they have been able to avoid the use of religion as the basis for promoting separate political identities. This is precisely why Kabir claims that 'Bangladesh is perhaps the only country in the region and one of the few in the world where the "state" and "nation" appear to be approximately synonymous' (Kabir, 1998:10).

Nevertheless, Bangladesh faces a formidable challenge in implementing its nation-building project (as a comparison, see Nhema in this volume for an analysis of how civil society groups have challenged the state's drive for hegemony in Zimbabwe, where the Mugabe regime used its nation- and state-building programs to create an authoritarian stucture of governance after the independence of the country). Some 700,000 indigenous peoples of the Chittagong Hill Tracts (CHT)[9]—that is, less than 1% of the country's 130 million population—not only have placed themselves beyond the so-called Bengali/Bangladeshi national political identity, they also have sought 'self-determination' through a violent insurgency movement. Although their autonomy movement goes back to the 19th century, it took a new shape after the liberation of Bangladesh in 1971 when the indigenous peoples of the CHT refused to identify themselves as 'Bengalis'. Viewing the process of constructing the Bengali nationhood as a direct threat to the promotion and protection of the rights of ethnic minorities, the CHT geared up the secessionist movement which was designed primarily to create an alternative government framework for the indigenous peoples.

Successive governments of Bangladesh—both military and civilian—responded to this growing crisis of national identity by attempting to crush the insurgency movement militarily rather than by working out a political formula for resolving the rather complex dilemma of state- and nation-building processes. Rather than reducing the armed resistance, the government's action has further fueled it.

The conflict drew widespread attention from a variety of international human rights organizations (Levene, 1999: 340). However, to the surprise of many analysts, most mainstream Bangladeshi development NGOs chose not to defend the cause of self-determination of ethnic minorities but to continue to operate as the representatives of the dominant Bengali ethnic group. Furthermore, NGO leaders made virtually no attempt either to bring people together or to force the state to adopt a conciliatory approach to solving the ethnic conflicts. Most NGOs appeared to act on the assumption that the Bengalis constitute one single nation and the process of constructing a Bengali/Bangladeshi nationhood does not necessarily pose a threat to the rights of ethnic minorities.

However, two inter-related factors dramatically changed the role of mainstream Bangladeshi NGOs in defending the principle of self-determination. First, the Peace Agreement signed on 2 December 1997 between the Government of Bangladesh and the Jana Sanghati Samity (JSS) created the ground for NGOs to expand their networks to the indigenous peoples of the CHT. In other words, the massive rehabilitation and peace-building tasks have encouraged NGOs to offer development assistance to the people of the area. Secondly, and perhaps more importantly, because of new interest among key external donors in the socio-economic development of the CHT, resources have been made available to NGOs to undertake various programs in support of the implementation of the Accord.

Thus, Bangladeshi NGOs are beginning to make efforts to address the ethnic dimension of democracy and development. For instance, the Program for Research on Poverty Alleviation of the Grameen Bank has started organizing dialogues with the leaders of different ethnic groups to explore the ways in which the GB can contribute to the process of bringing lasting peace and sustainable development in the CHT. Similarly, BRAC has taken on the CHT Integrated Development Project to empower the people of the area. The project aims to improve the standard of living of ordinary people of the CHT through micro-credit, social development and health and education programs (BRAC, 1999: 23).

Poverty Reduction, Grassroots Democratization and Empowerment through Micro-Credit Programs

Programs on behalf of ethnic minorities are but a small part of the efforts being made for the poor in Bangladesh. Many of these initiatives center on micro-credit schemes as the lack of access to financial resources is often viewed as a major impediment to economic advancement by the poor. Several NGOs now organize poor individuals into groups to provide them with small amount of unsecured credit to start up micro-enterprises and provide skills training and other programs to assist in making productive use of the loans. Empirical studies of micro-credit clearly suggest that such lending programs improve significantly the productivity and income of the poor. They also ensure high loan recovery rates, which remain over 90%—one of the highest in the world. More importantly, most studies suggest that micro-credit programs have contributed to the creation of political space for the poor, particularly women living in rural Bangladesh. In brief, micro-finance is seen as a commercially viable strategy for both poverty reduction and democratization, where marginalized groups have begun to make systematic efforts to reduce their vulnerability (Zaman, 1998: 1).

The GB first invented the group-based lending programs called 'credit without collateral' in the country. Unlike conventional banking practices, its credit operations center on the concept of 'collective action of the borrowers' that fosters both group solidarity and peer responsibility. The recipients take loans in groups and agree to monitor the activities of one another in order to ensure strict financial discipline. The process of delivering credit therefore begins with the formation of basically the landless or assetless people into groups of five.

Only two of the group members get loans at one time, with the neediest members usually receiving their loans first. Upon receiving applications for loans, the group meets to select the loan recipients. This selection is then discussed at a center meeting in the presence of a GB employee, following which the final recommendation is submitted first to the branch and finally to the area managers of the GB, who forwards his/her decision to the area program officer for an opinion. If the proposals are found acceptable, the program officer submits his/her recommendation to the area manager. Apparently, this lengthy bureaucratic procedure is put in place in order to minimize the risk of defaults (Khandker, et al., 1995: ix-x).[10]

Yet defaults on individuals' loans are rare as they affects the entire group. If a member fails to repay on schedule, the whole group loses the opportunity to receive any future loans from the GB. This encourages all of the members to closely guide, assist and monitor the activities of one another. When any member faces difficulty repaying his/her loan, the other members of the group try to resolve the issue within the group without involving the GB employee (Holcombe, 1995: 40). In other words, 'peer responsibility' and/or 'peer pressure' ensures on-time recovery of the credits.

In addition to facilitating lending operations, the GB model also focusses on a social development program known as the 'Sixteen Decisions' that seeks to promote socio-cultural awareness among the rural poor, especially women. One of the main components of this program is to free members from the 'curse' of dowry by having them pledge that they will neither take dowry in their sons' weddings nor will they give dowry in their daughters' marriages. The 'Sixteen Decisions' also encourages its members to implement the four GB principles, namely discipline, unity, courage and hard work, this through commitments to a variety of programs involving planting trees, growing vegetables and waste management. The program also emphasizes collective involvement in community development projects in order to realize common socio-political objectives.

The GB has witnessed a remarkable expansion since 1983 when it formally emerged as a rural credit institution. As of May 1996, it has been serving 2,060,761 members with its 1,056 branches located in different parts of the country. The GB's lending activities currently cover a total of 35,726 villages—more than half of Bangladesh's rural area. The cumulative amount of disbursements in 1996 was about US$2 billion. Its average loan repayment rate is 98%, which is comparable with the repayment rate of the Chase Manhattan Bank (Bornstein, 1996: 40). More important perhaps is that about 94% of its members are women, who received some 92% of its credits (Grameen Bank, 1996.)[11]

Like the GB, BRAC's twin objectives are poverty alleviation and empowerment of the poor. However, unlike the GB, its activities are not confined to credit operations, but are focussed on three umbrella programs: the rural development program (RDP), health and population development (HPD) and the non-formal primary education program (NFPE). The RDP, which 'provides the basic framework for the rest of BRAC's activities' (Novib, 1993: 12), comprises the three somewhat inter-related programs of institution-building, rural credit and savings, and income and employment generation (this last through micro-credit provisions).

Like the GB, this program also begins with the mobilization of the poor into 'Village Organizations' (VOs). However, unlike the GB's program, VO members can apply for either small-scale loans for various income-generating activities (maximum amount Tk 9,000) or large-scale loans to facilitate building entrepreneurship (amounts ranging between Tk 20, 000 and 40,000). Although the VO identifies the projects and makes recommendations for credits, BRAC officials make the final decision. Like the GB, peer responsibility/pressure also plays a vital role in BRAC's credit programs. If a member is in default, the group is supposed to manage the funds for repayment. When the group fails to work out a solution, BRAC automatically deducts the outstanding loan from the savings of the group known as 'group fund' which is planned for emergency use (Khan and Stewart, 1994: 57).

Since the rural credit program began in 1979, it has extended its operation significantly (Lovell, 1992: 75-6). By one estimate, some 54,000 VOs were serving about 1.8 million members in 1996. These members had saved a total of about one billion taka and had borrowed over five billion taka in 1996. Like the GB, the RDP's main focus is on the participation of women in various productive enterprises (Chowdhury, 1997: 7). For instance, female members, who are involved primarily in poultry projects, run some 70% of its VOs (Khan and Stewart, 1994: 55) and numerous jobs for women have been created in the silk industry.

Proshika, the second largest NGO after BRAC, also identifies credit programs as a means to achieve empowerment and sustainable development. It operates all of its development programs, including lending activities,[12] through 'people's organizations', which are composed of about 20 poor members of the community (Proshika, 1995: 13-6). While the members can borrow from the Revolving Loan Fund (RLF) of Proshika, they are encouraged to pool their own resources to initiate income-generating programs (Hedrick-Wong, et. al., 1997: 147). Regardless of how they finance their micro-enterprises, the group is held responsible for ensuring strict financial discipline. Proshika retains total control over the loan disbursement process and, in case of default, group members are likely to face a legal action. Like the procedures of the GB and BRAC, a high level Proshika official, usually the Zonal Coordinator, always makes the final decision.

Most studies suggest that the credit programs of the GB, BRAC, Proshika—as well as several other smaller, but similar organizations—make positive impacts on the lives of a considerable number of poor people, especially women. Observers argue that they have achieved amazing success in creating jobs for disadvantaged groups, particularly women (Wahid, 1994: 5-6), contributing to slight increases in wage rates. These programs have improved technical knowledge among the poor and enhanced the latter's bargaining power. Finally, the ability of women borrowers—who were not previously employed—to earn money through their involvement with income-generating activities is starting to change the traditional child-bearing role of women in Bangladesh.

Many authors and development practitioners regard such dramatic changes in the role of women in poverty reduction as clear examples of empowering female in a society that is largely dominated by patriarchal values and restrictive practices. They believe that micro-finance programs not only create opportunities for women to participate in development programs, they also give them the 'power' to resist all sorts of malpractices against their gender (Mizan, 1994: 152). From observations during field visits, it was my impression that women's involvement with income-generating activities had significantly increased their self-confidence, given them greater awareness of their legal and political rights, enhanced their enjoyment of more freedom in making their own decisions, provided them with the confidence to come forward to protest violence against women, improved their capacity for mobilizing to protect their fundamental socio-political rights, and created more bargaining power to protest unfair wages given to them by land owners. Significantly, several NGO members had run in the *Union Parishad* (UP) elections thereby increasing their voice in local decision-making and enhancing their self-image.

These rather optimistic analyses ignore, however, that women remain unable to establish control over the loans or other resources they acquire through their involvement with micro-finance activities. Although there is no doubt that women take much pressure on themselves to repay the loan on schedule and shoulder the responsibility for answering all the questions about the utilization of the credit, in most cases, they lose control of the loan as their husbands and/or male guardians often consume the borrowed money. In interviews with several female loan recipients, I found that most were either encouraged or forced by their husbands to borrow from NGOs so that they (the husbands) could use the loans for their own businesses. A recent study conducted on BRAC's credit programs supports my findings. It states that 'husbands permit their wives to become VO members because they know that BRAC provides loans' (Mannan, 1998: 6). This practice became rampant as the focus of NGOs increasingly shifted to women.

While most NGOs are quite aware of this phenomenon, they seem to overlook the problem, possibly because they regard women as more reliable than men in terms of making repayments. Two inter-related factors actually compel and/or encourage NGOs to focus more on the issue of timely recovery of credit than anything else. First, because most NGOs work under tremendous pressure from donors to prove that their micro-finance activities are 'commercially viable', their primary concern is to improve the repayment performance and keep the default rates low. Secondly, because micro-finance NGOs compete with each other for scarce donor funds, they are forced to show that their model produces better socio-economic results. In short, the need to stay competitive in the micro-credit business encourages NGOs to target women because 'women are better credit risks than men and are more eager to properly use' the loans (Khandkre, et.al, 1995: 12). NGO field workers have relatively easy access to women in rural Bangladesh since they tend to be found at home. Also, women are more reliable both in attending group meetings and fulfilling financial commitments. Thus, the monitoring tasks become much easier for NGOs if loans are given to women members (Goetz and Gupta, 1994: 6).

By targeting women as the primary beneficiaries of their projects, however, NGOs ignore that these credits place enormous burdens on women for ensuring repayment of the loans that are often used by their male so-called 'guardians'. This raises serious doubts about the claim that micro-finance NGOs are engaged in reducing women's socio-cultural vulnerability. Such doubts have been strengthened further by the observation that the organizations of the micro-credit NGOs are male-dominated. It seems strange that while all micro-finance NGOs, including the GB, BRAC, Proshika and ASA, maintain that their primary objective is to empower the poor, particularly women, the people occupying the important positions in their organizations are men. Similarly, despite their assertion of implementing bottom-up development models, all these organizations were found to be highly hierarchical in delivering services to the poor. As discussed before, not only do they make sure that they retain total control over the disbursement and collection of credits, but also their field level staff often 'guide' the programs of so-called 'people's organizations' (Khan and Stewart, 1994: 58-9), which negatively affects people's self-management capacities.

Furthermore, most of these organizations lack a democratic culture. In my field research, I found that the control over key decisions rested solely in the hands of the 'executive director' and his close associates. One reason given for the discrepancy between democratic objective and undemocratic practice is that NGOs operate 'in a hostile institutional environment' that forces them to remain hierarchical. In other words, the lack of democratic process within NGOs is blamed on the existing hierarchical social structure of the country within which the NGO sector pursues developmental activities; i.e., 'NGOs cannot easily insulate themselves from the prevailing organizational culture' (Wood, 1994: 548).

Yet NGOs cannot be absolved so easily; after all, they claim to be different, often representing themselves as forces for democracy and popular development. In fact, however, the latter may be more rhetorical than actual, and as Singh argue in this volume, NGOs' use of popular and jargonist terms such as 'democratization', 'empowerment', 'participation' and 'gender-balanced development' are inspired/compelled by their excessive dependence upon external funding. As one NGO executive states:

The primary purpose (of an NGO) is to make its donors satisfied. The concern is not so much about the invention of something that suits well into our context. The priority of all NGOs is to ensure a smooth access to foreign funds. In particular, if asked by the donors, NGOs do not hesitate to include anything in their program.[13]

Mobilizing the Poor for Strengthening Democracy at the Local Level: The Role of Advocacy NGOs

In sharp contrast to micro-finance NGOs described above, a few Bangladeshi NGOs have begun to organize the landless and powerless marginalized groups in different parts of the country since the late 1970s. In order to both reduce poverty and to empower disadvantaged groups, they aim to improve the bargaining power of the rural poor. This section deals with two such NGOs—Gono Shahajjo Sanghstha (GSS) and Nijera Kori (NK)—which are known for their ability to successfully organize marginalized groups in rural Bangladesh.

GSS began its operation in 1983 as a local NGO based in the Khulna Division. In less than a decade, it has become a national NGO, operating in 11 districts that cover some 300,000 landless people. Considering empowerment as a process of improving people's ability to make and enforce decisions, GSS seeks to improve poverty conditions by institutionalizing people's ability to organize themselves into powerful groups. It has assisted landless people to establish their own organization called Gano Sangothan—that is, people's organizations (POs)—to increase their representation in institutional decision-making at both the local and national levels (GSS, 1993: 14).

Bringing together groups of approximately 20 agricultural laborers—both male and female—GSS organizes functional education programs which focus on the structural causes of both poverty formation of POs (Westergaard, 1996: 38-9). GSS also provides legal and organizational support to establish the legal and political rights of PO members in areas such as inheritance laws, share-cropping, divorce settlement, wage bargaining and land and water rights. It offers legal aid to enable the POs to increase their bargaining capability. GSS also encourages PO members to contest the UP elections and assists the candidates to launch successful election campaigns (GSS, 1993: 14).

NK is similarly engaged in building grassroots organizations by involving the landless people in promoting local development. Like GSS, it does not consider micro-finance activities to be an effective means either to reduce poverty or to empower the poor. Indeed, it views micro-credit programs as 'anti-developmental' and suggests that

> We must choose our roles; we cannot tell the people to fight for their dues and then oppress them by collecting loans; a factory owner cannot be a trade unionist at the same time (Chowdhury, 1989: 174).

NK therefore focuses on the need to prepare people for resisting the forces of exploitation and oppression. Like those of GSS, the programs of NK begin with offering organizational help to the landless and marginal farmers to form self-help groups (Westergaard, 1996: 42). These include: training sessions for both awareness-building and skill-development; encouragement to people to mobilize their own resources to undertake collective economic programs; legal help to lease *Khas* (government) land and water; assistance in actions by members such as protest meetings against different forms of injustice prevalent in rural Bangladesh, namely violence against women and corruption.

A number of studies done on these mobilization efforts show that they have enabled the poor to participate effectively in local politics, thereby giving a greater degree of political autonomy and bargaining power (Streefland, et. al., 1986: 49). Indeed, the poor have emerged as an important political force in rural Bangladesh. This was manifested in the past few UP elections when a considerable number of group members nominated by a variety of NGOs, including GSS and NK, were elected (Westergaard, 1996: 41-5). In addition to reducing the political vulnerability of the poor, the activities organized by GSS, NK and other advocacy groups proved to be effective in both acquiring and redistributing *Khas* land to landless laborers (Holloway, 1998: 162) as well as in reducing violence against women, curbing corruption and giving the rural poor a voice in resisting socio-economic injustice (Chowdhury, 1989: 184-85).

During my visits to POs, however, it appeared to me that most of these groups achieved very little in terms of managing their own development. While their involvement with a variety of advocacy NGOs certainly enhanced their social awareness, most of the POs still relied heavily on the NGO staff to identify their development needs. Indeed, they relied upon the NGO worker for just about everything—from selecting the agenda of the meeting to writing the minutes. The group meetings were mainly used to discuss issues that the NGO staff raised. Moreover, I observed that, when discussing any problem or issue, group members repeatedly made references to concepts such as 'class', 'oppression' and 'exploitation' without apparent understanding of the meanings of the terms they used. When asked why they used these terms, one group member replied: 'I am a poor, illiterate peasant. How can I tell you what do they mean. I will lose my membership if I don't use them.' In other words, the whole question of participation seemed nothing more than what Najam calls 'a look good, feel-good exercise' for the NGOs (Najam, 1996: 346).

I also observed that the activities of these groups frustrated the planners who hoped that their political programs would generate both political and economic benefits. Although the mobilization initiatives created group solidarity and enabled them to emerge as a vote bank, the programs proved to be ineffective in creating tangible economic benefits. This seemed largely to be due to the ambivalent attitude of the NGO executives toward the generation of both income and employment through micro-credits. During interviews, quite a few group members expressed to me their utter dissatisfaction with the inability of these programs to generate immediate economic benefits for the poor. One group member asked 'why should I keep my membership if I cannot arrange three meals per day for my family?'

This problem was further compounded by the inability of the elected UP officials to respond positively to the needs of the groups. Indeed, the assumption that the representation of the rural poor in the institutional decision-making bodies would increase significantly the bargaining power of the poor is based on a false assessment of the complex dynamics of rural power structures in Bangladesh.[14] In many cases, the elected representatives of the poor did not use the newly achieved political status to benefit the group. Part of the reason for this is the strong presence of the co-optation process in rural Bangladesh, where elites strive to retain their traditional control over the decision-making mechanism by granting undue financial favor to opposition members. The benefits are so attractive that most people find it extremely difficult to resist the temptation of using political power to gain personal advantages. Thus, it does not take long before a significant number of elected representatives of the poor simply forget their mission. This is no wonder that many of them do not even bother to attend the group meetings.

The highly hierarchical organizational structures also adversely affect the ability of advocacy NGOs to generate popular power. All the important decisions for the organization are made at headquarters, particularly by the executive director. Not only is he or she reluctant to share the decision-making power but the high command rarely tolerates criticism from subordinate staff regarding the organization's policies, programs and priorities.[15] The problem is even more acute at the field level. As one field-level NGO worker commented, 'How can I possibly try to empower the members when I know that I am not empowered enough to make my own judgement in dealing with the poor? I do exactly what I have been told to do.'

Conclusions

This chapter observes that most development NGOs in Bangladesh have virtually ignored an important finding of the research project which prompted this volume—that is, that both democracy and development have ethnic dimensions. Until recently, the programs and activities of most NGOs were limited largely to poverty reduction within the dominant ethnic group. Instead of enabling minorities—particularly the indigenous peoples of the CHT—to protect and promote their political consciousness and cultural distinctiveness, their activities were directed primarily toward the improvement of the status of the Bengali disadvantaged groups in society. In other words, few development NGOs sought to develop an alternative nation-building strategy in order to address the issue of 'self-determination' in a relatively homogeneous country.

However, such an observation does not dispute the claim that the proliferation of development NGOs in Bangladesh has created hope for democratic governance at the turn of this century. This chapter finds that the financial and institutional interventions of both micro-credit and advocacy NGOs have improved significantly the living standards of a variety of disadvantaged groups, including women, the landless, marginal farmers and slum dwellers. Their innovative programs have enabled them to reduce the burdens of poverty. As a direct result of their participation in NGO programs, their employment opportunities have expanded, wage rates have increased, and the ability to assert their socio-political rights has strengthened. As well, NGO interventions have enabled the marginalized to become more articulate and candid. NGO programs, particularly the group-based mobilization strategy, have increased social awareness, helping 'people's organizations' to take collective actions against social injustice. The rural poor also have acquired the necessary bargaining power to realize their socio-economic expectations.

Contrary to popular assumptions, however, this chapter finds very little or no empirical evidence that the programs of development NGOs have enabled marginalized groups, particularly women, to be empowered politically and economically in a sustainable manner. Part of the reason for this is the inability of development NGOs to make solid efforts to improve women's status in a highly patriarchal society like Bangladesh. Almost all development NGOs, especially micro-finance organizations, are concerned primarily with the recovery of loans. Taking advantage of women's vulnerable situation, they appear to have chosen women as the borrowers in their micro-credit programs. Similarly, while many NGOs pay 'lip service' to popular participation in development, their programs seldom allow the members to become self-reliant in both financial and organizational terms. If the current trend continues, it is very unlikely that the poor will soon become capable of managing their own development and concepts of 'democratization', 'empowerment', 'participation' and 'democratic development' will continue either to be misused or used to exaggerate the 'success' of NGO activities.

This chapter also finds very little evidence to support the assumption that NGOs are the primary force for formal democracy. While it is observed that NGO interventions have created political space for greater politico-economic mobilization of the rural poor at the local level, their top-down development models also impede grassroots democratizing initiatives. Major barriers to promoting democracy at the local level include both the hierarchical and non-democratic organizational framework in Bangladesh within which most NGOs operate and the structural requirements of the international donor community. The excessive reliance of the NGO sector upon external funding creates the imperative for them to focus more on donor suggestions and/or instructions than to meet the challenges of democratic governance in the twenty-first century.

Notes

1. By grassroots democratization we refer to the process of enabling ordinary citizens, particularly vulnerable groups such as women and the rural poor, to gain access to key resources—both financial and political—and to establish control over the institutions that profoundly affect their lives. Such a concept focusses on the need to improve people's livelihood through the creation of both new opportunities and creative spaces within and outside of the framework of the market on the one hand, and it seeks to enhance popular participation in decision-making, on the other.
2. Drawing upon the GB model, the Royal Bank of Canada has begun to help community organizations in different parts of Atlantic Canada to get involved in various micro-enterprises. The program is designed to offer small loans to women to improve their entrepreneurial ability (see Stackhouse, 1998).
3. The data and insights were collected for this study through combining the methods of document observation, field visits and individual in-depth interviews. In consultation with various government and non-government organizations, field visits were organized in three different phases between June 1996 and December 1999.
4. Given the diversity in the NGO sector, the focus of this paper is limited to the operations of those voluntary organizations which are popularly known as non-governmental development organizations (NGDOs). It is widely assumed that not only do NGDOs

make efforts to alleviate poverty, more importantly, they also try to give the poor and disadvantaged groups a voice in decision-making.

5. This analysis focuses only on what are called development NGOs, which can be divided into the two broad categories of micro-finance and advocacy. The majority—about 1,000 NGOs—including the GB, BRAC, Proshika, and ASA, are engaged primarily in reducing poverty and empowering the people by providing credit and organizational help to the poor. But a minority of NGOs, namely Gono Shahajjo Sanghstha (GSS) and Nijera Kori (NK), are organizing disempowered groups such as the landless, marginal farmers and rural women for enhancing their social consciousness so that they emerge as important political actors. Like micro-finance NGOs, the programs of most advocacy NGOs, including GSS and NK, are funded and supported by key donor organizations such as the Canadian International Development Agency (CIDA), Danish International Development Agency (DANIDA), Norwegian Agency for Development Cooperation (NORAD), Swedish International Development Agency (SIDA), and Oxfam (UK). Both groups of NGOs, however, claim that their main objective is to empower vulnerable groups.

6. Of particular significance is that the new international context of development which emerged in the 1980s brought dramatic changes in donor policies and priorities. Abandoning their traditional emphasis on macro-economic aspects of development, most major donors began to undertake broader development programs that address a variety of issues, such as empowerment, participation, gender and human rights. Given such major shifts in the aid paradigm, most development NGOs in Bangladesh began to re-define their roles in development.

7. The lack of information and or records on funds channeling to NGOs makes it very difficult to provide a comprehensive picture of NGO finance. In order to analyze the issue of financing NGOs, this research relies upon a few sample studies conducted mainly by the World Bank.

8. This is not to say that religious minorities always subscribed to the narratives of Bengali and/or Bangladeshi political nationhood. On the contrary, they always questioned and challenged effectively the process of developing a national identity solely on the basis of Islam.

9. The Chittagong Hill Tracts is an area of approximately 13,231 square kilometers, the 18th century. These ethnic groups speak their own language and practice a variety of religions, notably Hinduism, Buddhism and Christianity (Hague, 1998: 47-74).

10. Most financial institutions regard lending in rural areas as a high-risk activity. This is largely because 'rural credit markets are characterized by imperfect information and imperfect enforcement'.

11. These statistical data are gathered from personal visits to the Bank's head office located in the Capital City, Dhaka, between July 1997 and December 1999.

12. As of June 1998, with a membership of 1,571 million, Proshika has been serving over 6,939 villages and slums. It has some 81,627 primary groups of which women constitute about 56 percent. The organization has distributed a total credit in the amount of 6,774 billion taka (Proshika, 1998).

13. Confidential interview, Dhaka, 21 June 1998.

14. Most advocacy NGOs rely on the analysis of village society, known as the differentiation and polarization thesis, which became popular among academicians and left political activists in the 1970s. Such a thesis focuses on the importance of understanding rural Bangladesh through a Marxist framework of class struggles. Although recent socio-political changes in rural Bangladesh have already reduced the ability of such a thesis to explain the current dynamics of rural Bangladesh, NGO

executives seem to have ignored the need to develop a more appropriate understanding of the ways in which NGOs can help the poor achieve their developmental goals.

15. A number of mid-level NGO officials expressed this view to me on a number of different occasions during my field visits in Dhaka between September 1997 and December 1999.

8 Prospects for Democratic Governance in Africa: Impacts of Civil Societies and Ethnicities

MARIA NZOMO

Introduction

Most sub-Saharan African countries have entered the twenty-first century poorer than they entered the last millennium. The combination of numerous factors—poor governance, undemocratic structures and processes, war and famines, the oil crisis of the 1970s, unfavorable international trade and investment regimes, as well as the globalization trends of the 1980s and 1990s—have contributed to the rapid downward slide for Africa since the early 1970s.

Having enjoyed fairly reasonable economic growth rates averaging 5.9% in the 1960s, the annual growth rates began to decline in the 1970s and reached an average of 4.1% by the end of the decade. They declined further to an average of 2% during the 1980s (Botchwey, 1999; Enemuo, 1999; Chole, 1997). By the beginning of the 1990s, many African countries were not only experiencing negative growth rates, they had become so marginal in the global arena, that some scholars grimly concluded that Africa has, for all practical purposes, been dropped from world affairs (Adedeji, 1993).

The deterioration in economic conditions in Africa has been exemplified most dramatically by the increasing impoverishment of the majority of the citizens of this region. Despite some modest improvements registered in the overall economic performance of Africa during the second half of the 1990s (Enemuo, 1999: 6-7), analysts caution that human development indicators for Africa remain abysmally low. Moreover, predictions indicate that the number of the poor will increase in the twenty-first century (Enemuo, 1999: 6; Chole, 1997: 4-6).

The deterioration in African economies has moved in tandem with bad governance and authoritarianism. Despite the introduction, officially, of political pluralism in most countries during the 1990s, a continuing lack of

148

democratic governance, in actual practice, has been manifested in authoritarianism, decay of government institutions and widespread and unchecked corruption in public life. This situation has been further compounded by natural disasters and intra- and inter-state conflicts.

The major international political and economic actors, particularly the Bretton Woods institutions and the Western countries that dominate them, have aggravated this situation. Having previously propped up undemocratic African regimes, both economically and politically, these Western actors began in the 1980s to impose unfavorable economic policy frameworks and conditionalities, especially through structural adjustment programs (SAPs). As Richard Sandbrook (1993: 87) observes, when SAPs were introduced, they were justified on the grounds that they would promote democracy and economic development, but instead they have aggravated the African crisis. Politically, the already authoritarian African state has had to become even more repressive in order to force unwilling African populations to comply with cutbacks on social services and to accept lower incomes and higher costs of living. Furthermore, as Mkandawire and Soludo (1999: 88) point out, during adjustment, the external debt of sub-Saharan Africa escalated, the infrastructure deteriorated and the formation of human capital was reduced. The problem was compounded by a massive brain-drain and demoralization of the civil service caused by sharply declining real wages and massive retrenchments. Overall, poverty has intensified and human development indicators have worsened dramatically while the already fragile industrial base has shrunk even further in many countries.

Africa has also had to endure the impact of the momentous changes in human existence engendered by the advent and rapidly expanding phenomenon of globalization (Aina, 1996; Nnoli, 1998; Goldblatt, 1997; Rosenau, 1997). Notwithstanding globalization's generally positive contribution to improved global communication and increased availability of goods and services, opinions differ over whether the majority of African poor people whose buying and selling power is minimal and who lack access to modern computerized information technology and infrastructures can be considered beneficiaries of globalization (Enemuo, 1999; Campbell, 1999). Indeed, one is hard pressed to see what benefits poor, illiterate and semi-literate African women and other marginal minorities and children can derive from the World Wide Web (Internet). Bazaara and Oloka-Onyango (1999: 2), for instance, argue that it serves as an '"invisible barrier" embracing the connected and silently, almost imperceptibly, excluding the rest'. Shaw (1999), on the other hand, sounds a more optimistic note, arguing that Africa has a third chance to move from regression to renaissance in the new millennium and that it can benefit from globalization 'if the continent moves towards a new form of governance; not just formal local, national and regional government but more diverse and informal relations among states, companies and civil societies at all levels: from local/urban through national and regional to continental and global'.

Whatever perspective one wishes to adopt, it stands to reason that after four decades of failed development and governance paradigms in Africa, there is a critical need to explore new and more innovative strategies for and approaches to governance. To advance the elusive project of 'development and democratic governance' demands the development of collaborative partnerships among a diverse set of actors including African civil societies, government policy-makers, development practitioners, intellectuals, donor agencies and individual African citizens in a collective attempt to combat poverty in Africa.

This chapter is premised on the argument that civil societies and ethnicities are two important social factors that have significant impacts on modes and trends in governance in Africa. My argument is that the attainment of democratic governance in Africa is a long-term project that involves not only the reconfiguration of the African state but also combined pressure for change from non-state actors within civil societies and ethnically-based community action. This chapter examines both strengths and weaknesses of civil societies as agents of democratic development. I argue that civil societies are important change agents but are not necessarily always democratizing agents. The chapter also seeks to review some of the literature that has assessed the role of ethnic-based associational life, with a view to determining the extent to which the latter can be regarded as a hindrance to democratic governance and the extent to which it can be viewed as an asset that can be harnessed to become the cornerstone for building democratic pluralism and good governance.

Conceptualizing Civil Society

The term 'civil society' has a long history in political philosophy, and its definition had been altered with Roman, Lockean, Hegelian, Marxist and Gramscian interpretations long before it was resurrected in the 1990s. Indeed, disentangling those debates has become an intellectual industry of its own in recent years (CIVICUS, 1999; Nyang'oro, 1999; Van Rooy, 1998). As one observer has noted:

> Civil society has wandered its way through the academic world on a torturous path. Ideas have been attached and detached, origins have been ascribed and

divorced, social meanings have been generated and debunked (Van Rooy, 1998: 7).

In the context of this debate those from a neoliberal perspective seek to push a notion of civil society in contradistinction to the state, and as the 'bearer' of market-based political and economic reforms. Others are more focussed on how civil society can be mobilized along the lines of an alternate people-centered 'grassroots' paradigm of development and governance. Most, however, focus on the 'political' role of civil society in relation to human rights, democracy and minority rights rather than on its role in development and the provision of social/welfare services.

Larry Diamond (1994: 5) has described civil society as:

> the realm of organized social life that is voluntary, self-generating, (largely) self-supporting, autonomous from the State, and bound by a legal order or set of shared rules. It is distinct from society in general in that it involves citizens acting collectively in a public sphere to express their interests, passions and ideas, exchange information, achieve mutual goals, make demands on the State and hold State officials accountable.

Casting doubts on the 'civicness' of most civic associations, Thomas Callaghy (1993: 23) points out that

> much associational life has very little to do with the creation of norms, especially civil ones.... In fact, group interaction ... may easily lead to the development of norms that do not further the development of the public sphere, much less a civil, open, tolerant, and participatory one based on established rights, as commonly presumed.

This view is shared by several other scholars including Bangura and Gibbon (1992) and Fatton (1992: 6) who insist that civil society is not necessarily as democratic as many conventional arguments affirm. Indeed, civil society can be reactionary, anti-democratic and the prime depository and disseminator of reactionary forms of knowledge and codes of conduct. Civil society is an arena of class, political and ideological contestations of which members of the ruling class and their political cronies are also prominent actors. In other words, civil society has no determining essential properties, either 'democratic' or 'undemocratic' (Bangura and Gibbon, 1992: 21). Secondly, although civil society is defined by its plurality, its activities should not be conceived in terms of homogeneity and cooperation, but rather in terms of conflict and conflictual relations within itself and between it and the state (Gibbon, 1996).

Beckman (1991) and Mamdani (1996) both interject cautionary notes into the uncritical embracing of civil society as the alternative to the pervasive crisis of the African state, and point to growing skepticism over whether African civil societies have any of the capacities and qualities the African state lacks for democratic governance. Mama (1999: 32) concurs and asserts that the Nigerian situation suggests that there are good grounds for rejecting any simple polarization of 'state' and 'civil society' and suggests that both state and civil society are imbued with gender politics, and that they produce gendered discourses.

Mamdani (1994: 523) insists on a distinction being made between NGOs and what he terms 'popular organizations' like cooperatives and trade unions. The constituency of the latter is its formal membership; as such, the membership always has the possibility of struggling to change the leadership—even the very nature—of the organization. However, as the former is outside the formal membership of the NGO, its constituency is structurally precluded from waging any struggle for rights, thus making the spread of an NGO culture and the growth of an NGO movement a rather mixed blessing.

Clearly, there is still no common understanding of the phenomenon of civil society. Indeed, grave misunderstandings remain about the role civil society plays or should be playing in Africa. Some still idealize African civil society and view it as the redeeming alternative to corrupt and ineffective African governments. The other extreme view is to caricature civil society as an arena inhabited by self-serving, opportunistic individuals who represent nobody but themselves and whose mission is self-enrichment, through exploiting the misfortunes of poor people. Furthermore, there is still no consensus on the demarcation of the 'space' that defines the limits of civil society especially when the gender debate over the overlapping linkages between the 'private' and 'public' spheres is introduced. There is also no consensus on what types of institutions are civil society institutions. For example, are political parties and government-sponsored associations, etc., part of civil society? Does the existence and type of civil society depend on the existence/type of state; that is, do authoritarian/collapsed states result in 'weak' or 'strong' civil societies?

Some scholars have suggested that one way of breaking through the conceptual paralysis that pervades the civil society debate is to move away from a preoccupation with formal organizations and institutions to *an activity view of civil society*. This school of thought argues that such a view allows us to include within civil society activities which would otherwise be invisible. For instance, much that is articulated by ethnic and kinship groups, such as families and clans, is easy to ignore, dismissed as non-civic activity, since these groups hardly meet the orthodox definitional criteria of civil society (Musambayi and Maina, 1999).

Naidoo and Tandon (1999) also attempt to break through this conceptual paralysis by making a clear distinction between civil society organizations and associational life in general. They argue that associational life includes all types of voluntarily-formed and autonomous organizations, while civil society narrows down this universe to those demonstrating civic norms (tolerance, inclusion, non-violence, and commitment to promoting public good). In other words, while associational life includes all civil society organizations, civil society does not include all organizations that comprise a society's associational life. While Naidoo and Tandon make an important and useful distinction between civil society and associational life, the question still remains as to whether indeed the majority of civil society organizations demonstrate the civic norms he identifies.

Civil Society: The Rising 'Star'

> Governments cannot lead, they are lost and almost completely helpless, they can only do crisis management at best. Corporations are resigned to fatalism because they are trapped in the hole of market fundamentalism. But we have the civics with us to show us the way out.... Civics are a bunch of activist idealists in a great hurry. They are in a great hurry to put a stop to runaway, negative globalization. Civics are a driving factor for the creative disintegration of the present system (Serrano, 1999: 164).

Although the concept of civil society remains problematic, the period beginning in the early 1990s, more than any other period before, has witnessed unprecedented attention directed to civil society, by donors, development practitioners, scholars and governments. Donors' disillusionment with the development failures of post-colonial states for over three decades led them to embrace civil society as an alternative to government. Economic and political liberalization trends, beginning at the end of 1980s, shrunk the state's capacity to provide social welfare and security to its citizens and to impose and enforce rules within a specific territory. This facilitated the opening and expansion of public space for non-state actors to intervene in sectors that were previously monopolized by the state (Mkandawire and Soludo, 1999).

This change in orientation resulted in NGOs becoming a key factor in the donor politics of resource allocation from the late 1980s. The donor's argument was that support to NGOs and professional groups would help open up a political space for associational life to participate in promoting democratic development. The World Bank (1989) captures this succinctly when it observes:

> ... every opportunity should be taken to support local, communal, and non-governmental organizations of all types—village associations, cooperatives, credit unions, professional associations, chambers of commerce and industry, and the like.... The challenge is to build on this solid indigenous base, with a bottom-up approach that places a premium on listening to people and on genuinely empowering the intended beneficiaries of any development programme.

The overwhelming interest of donors agencies in civil society as an alternative vehicle for delivering development and poverty alleviation, good governance, etc., has led to the mushrooming of non-governmental organizations (NGOs) and community-based organizations (CBOs) in most African countries. As well, the end of the Cold War and the process of democratization have inaugurated an upsurge of social movements responding to the rising number of claimants to socio-economic and political rights. Indeed, the very concepts of entitlement and citizenship have undergone profound shifts (Ndegwa, 1996).

Meanwhile, new forms of inequalities unleashed by globalization and Africa's marginalization in the official international economy have resulted in a dramatic intensification in the struggles over resources, territories and access to funding sources. Furthermore, setbacks in the democratization process have brought their own forms of violence manifested in the privatization of security and the extra-judicial administration of justice, as well as renewed struggles over property rights and security. Involved in these processes are multiple organized forces of social control that include local militia, vigilante groups and death squads. These and others represent the unpleasant ('uncivic') face of civil society (Ninsin, 2000; Hirst and Graham, 1999; Nzomo, 2000).

Trends in Civil Society and Governance

The data and analysis in this section is based on empirical research findings from case studies of civil societies that the author coordinated in 12 African countries[1] during 1998-1999. The findings generally indicate that neither the state nor civil society is a paragon of virtue with regard to their governance structures and their democratization and development agendas. The studies also show that most African civil societies lack adequate capacity to network, raise awareness, and focus on certain common development goals.

All studies concur that since the early 1990s, there has been a dramatic increase in civic awareness and hence greater participation in the enlarged public space arising out of state retreat and democratization trends. However, it is not clear whether this expansion is just another rent-seeking industry, fuelled by the accelerating economic crisis and lack of alternative forms of livelihood in various African countries.

Some studies have noted that some strengths of civil society associations include their resilience, flexibility and close proximity to the community. For example, it was noted that civil society in Nigeria has a strong streak of resistance, creativity and robustness, which offers a concrete basis for a strategy for poverty alleviation based on participatory and sustainable development within a pan-African context. Thus, Nigerian civil society contains strong groups that cannot be easily written off. These groups have defended their autonomy and carried out broad democratic struggles directed at empowering the people to demand for and obtain their rights: human, group (minority), environmental, political, social, economic, etc. (Obi and Adjekophori, 1999: 76). This concurs with Zartman's (1995: 268-9) observation that this quality of resilience is demonstrated with civil society organizations that continue to exist following state collapse.

In Burkina Faso, also, it was observed that one of the main strengths of civil society lies in its diversity and the ability of its organizations to fund various development activities and hence become partners with government to provide support for the people. The participatory approaches used by many civil society organizations allow them to adjust their programs to the real needs of the people, thus giving them a comparative advantage over the state (Sawadogo and Kabore, 1999).

Most studies, however, indicate that Africa has rapidly expanding but weak civil societies with inadequate capacity to shape democratic change. They identify numerous weaknesses that include:

- poor coordination of activities, with minimum connectivity and functional relationship between and within various sectors of civil society;
- weak financial bases with a high dependency on Western donors;
- inadequate flows of information within and between civil society groups, resulting in high duplication of efforts, as well as unnecessary competition and rivalries;
- poor organizational and managerial skills; and
- weak civic and democratic cultures.

The authors of the Zimbabwean study note that although some significant progress has been made especially by some larger human rights NGOs in pushing for civil and political rights, some basic weaknesses remain. The author of the study summarizes some of the basic weaknesses of civil society organizations, particularly community-based associations (CBOs) (Saunders, 1995: 24):

> Civil society is littered with the wreckage of countless failed self-help organisations, training programmes, savings clubs and other schemes which never established a consistent regime of operation, nor attracted a regular membership. Even in better financed and staffed organisations like the trade unions, the heavy pressures of operating with small budgets undercut the practical communication of ideas, grievances and aims amongst the grassroots, thereby severing the possibility of full-fledged participation from below.

The Nigerian case study echoes a similar concern:

> ... serious challenge is posed to civil society in Nigeria by its own internal contradictions: poor institutional capacities, overblown expectations, its fractious and complex nature, state suspicion, penetration and subversion of associative groups, inadequate resources (human and material) and the near-absence of a co-ordinated social dialogue on the pressing need to reduce poverty. Personality differences, ethnicity, the struggle for resources, corruption and problems of accountability, ideological/tactical differences. In other instances, some actors have 'dual' identities, straddling between the state and civil society. NGOs in Nigeria are also constrained by excessive dependence on donor grants, and centralisation around one individual, which makes sustainability uncertain in the event of the incapacitation of the patron (Obi and Adjekophori, 1999: 78).

One of the manifestations of poor governance noted both within Nigerian civil society and elsewhere has been the lack of a culture of transparency, accountability and democracy within the 'rank and file' of civil society itself. A situation in which a group revolves around one individual, or in which the handling of accounts is 'hidden' and members are unaware of funding, is undesirable and could lead to the abuse of the essence of civil society, thereby hindering its capacity. Furthermore, many NGO staff members lack managerial and technical skills for running their organizations. Indeed, the majority of NGO leaders lack prior, specialized training in the areas in which they rush to work. Consequently, strategic planning for such programs is left to consultants who feel responsible only for their consultancy ideas, and not for the practical results to which they lead (Cheaka and Nangbe, 1998: 17). Furthermore, the high dependency on foreign donor funding compels Nigerian NGOs to design their programs in line with donor priorities and specifications rather than with local aspirations. Under these circumstances, the sustainability of projects is rendered uncertain since it is contingent on continued donor support. In addition, unhealthy competition with the state for foreign funding does not augur well for the promotion of good governance.

The problem of NGO dependency on donors is highlighted further by Kenyan case study, which notes that many of the country's formal civil society organizations are wholly dependent on international donors, with the result that donors rather than the civics dictate the agenda. The study found evidence indicating that donors were too focussed on reports and financial accounting and not focussed enough on program quality and impact. Two of the NGOs surveyed worried about the intellectual role played by donors in setting the civil society agenda. They said in some cases the process of revision eventually led to a situation where the program that is finally funded is that of the donor not the NGO.

On the other hand, donors complained about a lack of financial probity and discipline on the part of NGOs, and claimed that some NGOs gave fraudulent accounts and shirked on performance. Indeed, the study revealed a lack of transparency in the governance structures and processes of some NGOs in Kenya. The study noted that 'civil society' had become a rent-seeking activity, with cases of over-invoicing, fraudulent receipting for seminars and faking of participants' names. Personal and institutional competition for funding and territorial behavior had become very pronounced among funded civil society groups. This problem is compounded by the fact that many civic organizations are small and intensely dominated by either their founders or their executive directors, resulting in such enterprises being nicknamed MONGOs (my own NGO) and NGIs (non-governmental individuals).

The Kenyan data also reveals fraternization and coalition-formation between donor organizations and some NGOs that were regarded as donor favorites and which, as a result, had significant funds from each of the key civil society donors. For example, one such organization received more than a quarter of a donor's total funding to civil society over a two-year period. In another case, an organization received more than 50% of the donor's support for capacity-building in civil society (Musambayi and Maina, 1999). Some donors readily admitted that the reputation of the leaders of these organizations was an important consideration in the funding decision. The Kenyan study concludes on this point that aid is an addiction, fostering financial and, more perniciously, intellectual dependency. The key challenge for donors is to ensure that they give principled and sustainable support to civil society. The study suggests the need for donors to broaden as well as deepen their knowledge of African civil society, paying particular attention to what might sap or energize it.

The Malawi study makes similar observations when it points out that the organizations and institutions of civil society are based on weak political and economic foundations, compounded by dishonesty and lack of transparency. As a result, the country's civil society remains weak in terms of structure, size, content, and operational strategies. Its institutions and organizations suffer from poor funding, inadequately qualified professional personnel, bad strategies and lack of focussed visions. Strengthening the capacity of these institutions is thus a major challenge for the country (Ngirwa and Chirwa, 1999).

The above notwithstanding, donors continue to put money into civil society, even while being unclear about what impacts they are having. Concerns about this issue were expressed by Van Rooy (1998: 70) in a study on civil society and the donor industry:

> ... we are wary about wholehearted encouragement of donors to delve into a civic area where the preconditions for success are so far beyond an outsiders' reach. Armed only with a menu of projects and tight timelines and accountability rules, what can donors reasonably do? ... The danger is that enthusiasm over civil society's theoretical potential will push caution aside. Along with the promise of civil society, and the hope placed in the work towards social justice undertaken by fragile civil society organizations throughout the world, there are real perils.

Impact of State-Civil Society Relations on Governance

Current relations between civil society and the African state in the countries studied are generally characterized by tension and mutual mistrust. This is attributed to a number of factors, including a lack of well-developed frameworks for cooperation and limited understanding by members of the respective sectors of each other's divergent mandates. This, combined with competition for limited donor financial resources, causes governments to tighten control over national policies and institutional frameworks, thus curtailing the autonomy of the civic sector and undermining prospects for collaboration and good governance.

Indeed, some of the weaknesses of the civic sector are attributed to this poor relationship with the government. In Kenya, for example, the state has fragmented and dissipated the energies of the civic groups it distrusts, thus constraining their capacity for self-organizing, self-direction and autonomous action. State authorities manipulate the registration of societies' laws against groups they distrust. Annual licensing requirements are often the occasion for chastising those who have not stuck to the government's interpretation of the mandate for which they were registered. Indeed, the government's draconian powers of de-registration of 'dissident' NGOs, constantly hangs over all registered civic organizations. As a result, NGOs tend to 'torture their language' into euphemisms that the government finds acceptable (Musambayi and Maina, 1999; Nzomo, 1998).

In the Nigerian case, studies found that in dealings between the state and civil society, the former treats the latter as a junior partner. However, although the state has continually sought to dominate civil society and hijack the programs of its organizations, the latter have, to a large measure, preserved their autonomy and relevance. It was also noted that both state and civil society often interpenetrate, even while appearing as distinct entities. The implication of this is that state-civil society relations are complex and can be a condition of strength as well as weakness.

It is perhaps because of the structural civic weaknesses and the unfavorable political framework for civic action elaborated above, that most studies caution that we should not romanticize the role of civil society and its capacity for democratizing governance. As noted above, some organizations in the civic sector suffer from some of the same weaknesses as government—lack of accountability, transparency, weak institutional capacity, and undemocratic tendencies. Civil society should therefore not be viewed as the paragon of virtue or as an antithesis of corrupt authoritarian and collapsing African states. Analyses of African democratization therefore need to resist the unwarranted theoretical jump from 'the state is not viable' to 'civil society is the key to Africa's success' and vice versa. There is clearly a need for greater reflection on state–civil society relations and their impacts on governance.

Civil Society, Ethnic Associational Life and Governance

One of the ways of understanding the weaknesses of African civil societies is by drawing a historical linkage between civil society organizations and ethnic and associational life in general. Undemocratic governance in Africa was in part ensured by the demobilization and muzzling of those non-state actors which could have challenged the status quo. Indeed, much of the institutional and structural weaknesses of civil society noted in this review can largely be explained by the colonial and post-colonial political history characterized by exclusion from public political space of most non-state civic actors.

A typical approach of governments was to co-opt the leadership of the most strategically placed civic institutions, such as the national umbrella bodies of unions, labor and farmers' co-operatives, women's associations, etc. Those who resisted co-optation were demobilized and rendered ineffective. At the same time, the state encouraged the mushrooming of ethnically-based associations that could be employed as a basis of politicizing ethnicity, thereby engineering ethnic rivalries and tensions that in some countries have led to full-scale civil wars.

Kenya is a typical case of a country where the two post-colonial regimes of the late President Kenyatta (1963-1978) and current President Moi (1978-present) have employed this political strategy to its fullest. Both regimes adopted retrogressive laws that have constricted the associational space and spawned ethnic differentiation by aggravating social cleavages and inequalities in resource distribution. To consolidate his control over the state, Kenyatta initiated several constitutional amendments, which when enacted, constricted the associational space and constrained the ability of civil society groups to organize outside the state. The state, through its politics, differentiated the society and mutated the growth of civil society by selectively bestowing political and economic citizenship on some while marginalizing and de-recognizing others. The 'ethnic card' was played out in a manner directed towards realizing the leader's desired political outcome. Major trade unions were merged to form a Central Organization of Trade Unions (COTU) under state patronage. At the same time, the regime actively encouraged and allowed ethnic associations to mushroom and facilitated factional patronage networks. Mass institutions and radical nationalists were increasingly sidelined and focus shifted to ethnic political balancing, through a carefully calculated political strategy of dispensing or withholding patronage (Ngunyi and Gathiaka, 1993; Muigai, 1995; Aseka, 1999). The result was that until the end of the 1980s, apart from ethnic associations, only a handful of civil society organizations continued to operate in Kenya—mainly church-led organizations, the National Women's umbrella bodies whose leadership had long been co-opted by the state (Nzomo, 1998), and some legal NGOs.

The above suggests there is no ideal-type civil society waiting to be discovered. Instead, civil society is contextual and the forces both of class and kinship can animate its capacity to fight for and help root democracy. There can be no *a priori* assumption that only functionally differentiated civil society can serve democracy. Moreover, in the context of an increasingly mobile and deracinated African professional class, ethnic identity provides social anchorage and orientation. Many urban-based professionals are members, if not senior officials, of their clan and tribal associations. If they intend to pursue a political career, clan and ethnic support may make the difference between failure and success.

Are ethnicity and ethnic associations problems or assets for advancing governance in Africa? To answer this question we need first to address the divergent conceptions of tribe and ethnicity. Some view ethnicity as a subjective perception of common origins, historical memories, ties and aspirations. For them, the term, 'ethnic group' pertains to organized activities by persons, linked by a consciousness of a special identity, who jointly seek to maximize their corporate political, economic and social interests. This perspective further argues that, as a subjective basis for collective consciousness, ethnicity gains relevance for the political process when it spurs group formation and underpins political organization. The capacity to stimulate awareness and a sense of belonging among the potential membership of a group—the psychological dimension of ethnicity—complements and buttresses the political dimension of interest-oriented social action. Thus, a sense of 'people-hood' may be instrumental to group formation and participation in the political process. Nevertheless, initiative on the part of an elite remains indispensable to the promotion and defense of group interests (Chazan, et al., 1992: 106).

Arguing from a global perspective, Raikes (1992) contends that in the contemporary world, ethnicity has become a most significant expression of cultural difference and a most powerful investigator of political action. Challenges to the hegemony of states are breaking loose and ethnic identity is playing a double role in both an outward and inward social expansion. Under the auspices of ethnicity as a way of politicizing culture, people actively seek to defend and promote their own culture in opposition to that of others. Ethnicity's most salient feature from a political perspective is that it seeks to link images of a distant past with the present and, by so doing, construct a culturally-informed vantage point from which to report on and respond to the contemporary situation.

Mamdani (1996: 187) argues that ethnicity (tribalism) is a curse from which Africa must rid itself. In sum, whereas 'conspiracy' theorists view tribalism as a kind of cancer introduced from without and above, 'primordialists' regard it as an ahistorical original sin afflicting African peoples from below.

Ethnic associations are therefore historically neither a colonial nor a post-colonial government creation. Ethnicity, or a sense of people-hood, has its foundations in combined remembrances of past experience and in common aspirations, values, norms and expectations (Raikes, 1992).

Furthermore, class and tribe are not always opposed categories and this may be an important factor for the practice of politics and governance in some contexts. The individual member of an ethnic group, variously involved in economic roles such as worker, professional, businessperson or administrator develops cross-cutting ties of economic class, religion, gender, etc., that modify the exclusivity of primary group obligations. Insofar as the ethnic group, as a culturally-based social organization, interacts with other ethnic, economic and social groups, it promotes the salient interests— political power, economic resources, public positions, status, protection—of the dominant coalition among the membership at a particular time. Thus ethnicity, like socio-economic class, is a political category that places claims upon the state to which it normally responds. Ethnic group participation in this dynamic struggle over scarce state resources is a continuing element in contemporary African political life. It reflects the political imperatives of the times and cannot be wished away. This argument was corroborated in the specific case of Kenya. As Musambayi and Maina (1999) observed in their study of Kenyan civil society:

> many urban based professional are members, if not senior officials of their clan and tribal associations. And if they intend to pursue a political career, clan and ethnic support may make the difference between failure and success. This is because it is the tribe and ethnic identity that gives groups a political language, which in turn unites them over what to argue about and provides the images on which they can base their ideologies and their philosophies about power, justice and entitlement. Furthermore, substantial distrust of the state and other official institutions makes the family, clan and tribe not only high trust institutions, but also the site of significant political activity. Furtherstill, in Africa, class and tribe are not always opposed categories. Ethnicity supplies the grammar and metaphor of African politics, even for the middle classes. It frames the political and social demands that they make on the state. Thus, rather than see ethnicity as the rupturing force of African politics it should be seen as the proper starting point for the study of African social movements and of civil society. Indeed, democratization will not advance unless we explore 'the interior architecture of tribe'.

The Kenyan case, however, acknowledges ethnic cleavages in civil society where civic organizations are divided sharply by both vertical (territory, ethnicity) and horizontal (urban/rural divide and class). Some NGOs are dominated by a few ethnic groups, typically those that also dominate opposition politics. Frequently, these civic groups are further divided by policy and programmatic differences, patterning themselves on the larger cleavages between opposition and government. In this regard, the study cautions against the orthodox belief that civil society is an arena for negotiating interests and for democratic deepening. Instead, civil society can and often does feed into and aggravate existing social and political cleavages. The twin cleavages of class and ethnicity find voice and sustenance in civil society. Aseka (1999) concurs with this analysis. He argues that politicized ethnicity is a problem and one of the main setbacks to democratization in Africa. Furthermore, while a democratic multicultural civil society is imperative for the prospect of societal democratization, civil society must not be left to itself. Fractions of civil society are bound to become too self-centered and create protective shields for the interests of their co-ethnic comrades instead of the broader interests of the polity. Civil society left to itself can produce severely unequal power relations which can only be changed and rectified by a strong and wilful political class. In Nigeria, the politicization of ethnicity and the resultant stalling of democratic governance has persisted since the early 1960s. But here, ethnicity is said to be just one of several factors that have contributed to this situation. In this connection Osaghae points out that the stalling of democratization in Nigeria is a consequence of the many-sided nature of this militaristic struggle for spoils. Ethnicity and regionalism along with religion, statism and other lower-level communal sectarianism were key aspects of this dynamic, but both remain only a part of a much wider drama (Osaghae, in Musatapha, 1998: 16).

Senegal is an example of a country where the failure of policy-makers to respond to and harness diverse ethnic aspirations and demands has resulted in secessionist demands by the affected ethnic communities. Diaw and Diouf (1999) note that the post-colonial government has for a long time experienced a serious problem of governance due to the failure adequately to respond to the demand of the ethnic groups living in the Casamance region of Senegal:

Casamance separatism cannot be understood outside the national context that is, without taking into consideration the difficulties of building a post-colonial state, considering that the state-building procedures breed ethnicity, which destroys national and territorial modality. The territorial rupture demanded by Casamance separatists is based on three elements: the linguistic element, the sociological element and the religious element.

Diaw and Diouf conclude that no democratic society project can be viable in Senegal without dealing with this complex problem. The democratic consensus cannot operate exclusively in the center without running the risk of an explosion of the whole system.

Ethnicity: A Liability or an Asset for Democratic Governance?

The critical question remains: is ethnicity a problem *for* democratic governance or a problem *of* democracy? Some analysts view politicized ethnicity as a problem and argue that one of the main setbacks to democratization in Africa is the politicization of ethnicity. But most recent studies on this subject seem to argue that ethnicity need not necessarily hinder the democratic process. This paper shares the view of Glickman (1995) who asserts that ethnic conflict is not incompatible with the institutions of democratic government if it finds expression as a group interest among other interests and if the means of expression provide opening for rewards and not merely certain defeats. Sithole (1994) concurs, asserting that multi-ethnicity is facilitator of democracy and refutes the argument that the existence of many ethnic groups in the polity gives rise to authoritarian rule. He insists that what leads to dictatorship in both ethnically-pluralistic and ethnically-homogeneous countries is the tendency of men or women who are in positions of leadership to want power indefinitely. Indeed, accepting the existence of ethnic loyalties is the surest way of finding ways and means of taming ethnicity rather than denial and artificial suppression. Muigai (1995) also affirms that ethnicity ought to be one of the many factors that shape democratic development but it needs to be understood, harnessed and integrated into the political framework, if need be, by constitutional and legal mechanisms.

The challenge therefore is not to wish away ethnicity, but to address it as the potential cause of great social conflict that can nullify democracy or, if harnessed, as a source of enrichment of democratic political life. However, a danger remains in the historical tendencies in Africa to identify the state with narrow ethnic interests and to establish state-based ethnic hegemonies that deliberately exclude other groups from the process of governance.

Conclusions

As I noted at the outset, ethnicity and ethnic-based associational life can be both an asset and a hindrance to democratic governance depending on the way the policy-makers respond to and harness diverse ethnic aspirations and demands. In this regard, ethnic associations have potential as agents of democratic development. The shrinking of government involvement in the economy has enhanced the mobilization of local/grassroot non-governmental organizations as effective rural development agents. Moreover, the failure of governments to meet basic social economic welfare and greater levels of human insecurity, in general, have created a heightened ethnic consciousness in a majority of the people (urban and rural alike) as they retreat to their ethnic communities in search of security and social welfare support. Hence, for many African communities, ethnic identity is an important reference point for shaping political involvement. Democratic governance in Africa must therefore utilize, as its building blocks, ethnic and other social identities, including gender, religion and race. Such social identities, when harnessed, contribute to democratic governance and the development project in general. But, as the analysis in this chapter indicates, they can also be dysfunctional, if politicized in a manner designed to invoke hatred and animosity towards the 'other'.

Civil society organizations are clearly composed of a hybrid of diverse social institutions and actors and overlapping social identities of class, race, gender, ethnicity, etc. The richness and plurality of civil society organizations can provide important checks and balances on government power. They also have the potential of helping to monitor the environment, social abuses, and equitable distribution of benefits and economic resources within the society. With adequate capacity, which they now lack, they can play an important role in engendering and channelling participation in economic and social activities while mobilizing people to influence policy.

Ideally, civil society should therefore have both demand- and supply-side governance functions. On the demand side, civil society should monitor the state's exercise of power and facilitate the broadening of citizens' participation in public policy-making. On the supply side, civil society should share governance functions with the state assisting in the implemention of public policy outside of, but with the sanction, of state institutions. These governance functions apply at all levels—from grassroot organizations vis-à-vis local governments, up to alliances of civic organizations with a mandate to act in global fora.

Civil societies everywhere are now confronted with defining their role in this rapidly evolving global system of governance. In Africa, most civil societies having only recently gained a degree of acceptance and legitimacy as participants in national-level policy-making have not yet given any thought as to how to promote and defend the interests of their members beyond the national level. African civic institutions have not contemplated what role they could play in promoting global security in the context of an ascending global system of free markets with trade regimes and investment flows. This is despite the fact that globalization increases threats of disease, narco-terrorism, environmental disaster and ethnic conflicts, all of which spill across borders, destabilize populations, and bring unimaginable suffering.

A key question, therefore, for the future role of African civil society is how it will participate as a legitimate partner in the globalized processes and institutions that increasingly govern world affairs and that are also shaping national affairs in this new millennium. This is an issue that requires reflection, as governance has become a very complex set of interactions that crosses sectors, borders and hierarchies to an extent inconceivable until very recently. Separations of sectors and jurisdictions taken for granted for quite a long time are now giving way to a much more integrated world. And, despite the fact that much is still uncertain in terms of the future balance of power and the nature of new institutions of governance that are yet to emerge, there is no doubt that an empowered civil society could constitute a core ingredient alongside government and business, in shaping the 'new world order'. One might hope that, for the first time in history, the 'world order' may be shaped not by a power elite, but by millions of informed, self-conscious, and active citizens.

Note

1.   These countries are Senegal, Mali, Burkina Faso, Nigeria, Kenya, Zimbabwe, Malawi, Uganda, South Africa, Cameroon, Rwanda, Democratic Republic of Congo.

9 Post-Settler State-Society Relations in Zimbabwe: The Rise of Civil Society and the Decline of Authoritarianism

ALFRED G. NHEMA

Introduction

Despite the Zimbabwean state's continued efforts to muzzle civil society from the time of independence in 1980, civil society organizations have emerged in the 1990s with some degree of independence—symbolized by the belated establishment of an opposition party in the violent mid-2000 general election. Indeed, from the late 1980s onwards, Zimbabwe has witnessed an historic awakening of new forms of social creativity and resistance in virtually all components of civil society. It is these 'new' forms of political mobilization which this paper will address.

My argument in this chapter is that militancy in civil society arose initially in direct response to the state's desire to create a one-party state and more recently due to unfavorable changes in the inherited economic structure. Stagnant economic performance and the subsequent embrace of a structural adjustment program in the early 1990s have thrown vast numbers of people into a condition of indigence. With the collapse of the welfare policies that were introduced during the first independence decade and the rising cost of living, many in the middle and working classes—only recently accustomed to a stable way of life—have been made worse off economically than they were in the early years of independence. The combined collapse of a way of life and the state's illiberal tendencies have acted as push factors propelling civil society to adopt a more militant stance than heretofore. Although differing ideologically, new movements are demanding a new way of conceiving and doing politics; they oppose corruption and favor a new constitution that enshrines transparency in politics.

The chapter pays particular attention to the role played by the media in the liberalization process. It asserts that the media played a 'catalytic role' and continues to be at the forefront of the political liberalization 'putsch'. Other groups in civil society as well as opposition political parties have found refuge in a sympathetic, critical media which manages to act as an avenue through which they can accelerate political communication with the state and their own followers.

The first section recaps briefly the theoretical and practical underpinnings of the economic and political liberalization processes in Zimbabwe. Following with a review of the economic policies of the Mugabe regime from independence to the early 1990s, I proffer some explanations of why the regime ended up swallowing the prescriptions of the International Financial Institutions (IFIs) after a decade of debating and rejecting them. The second part is devoted to analyzing the domestic, regional and international factors behind the democratization push from the late 1980s onwards. This provides a good background for understanding the factors that contributed to the rise of civil society from the late 1980s and beyond. The third section is devoted to an analysis of civil society's role in the democratization and liberalization process. With the pressures for more political space from civil society, the regime has found itself increasingly unable to control and manipulate civil society groups. The final part examines the current and future liberalization trends in Zimbabwe. It asserts that, despite the state's desire to control and manage the democratization process, Zimbabwe's society has progressively moved toward a higher degree of pluralism—witnessed particularly in the election process results in 2000.

Theoretical Considerations

The idea of a vibrant civil society has attracted scholarly attention in Africa as elsewhere (see Chabal, 1998; Clapham, 1998; Nzongola-Ntajala, 1997). Disillusioned with the excesses of the African state, state-society relations theorists now associate civil society with the prospects of limiting state power. As Diamond (in Elly Rijnierse, 1993: 658) puts it:

> the greater the number, size, autonomy, resourcefulness, variety and democratic orientation of popular organizations in society, the greater will be the prospect for some kind of movement from rigid authoritarianism ... toward ... democracy.

There is optimism in Africa that, if they are allowed to operate in an unfettered manner, civil society groups that were instrumental in ousting colonial rule can promote the democratization process in the sub-continent.

The local concern in Zimbabwe for civil society stems from the course of political struggle in the country. Spurred by the oppressive nature of settler practices, much of civil society's activities prior to independence centered on opposition to settler authoritarianism. Although still mired in their traditional loyalties, civil society groups were drawn to the liberation movement, united at higher ecumenical levels by their desire to oust settler rule.

At independence, civil society organizations came to face a state controlled by government representatives with whom they had been allied during the war. Hence, the notion of an independent civil society implied a change of roles. Constituted as 'vehicles for the assault on state power,' groups such as labor were now expected to 'represent civil society's fight for resources and power'[1] by becoming 'watchdogs' of their former allies. (See MacLean in this volume for discussion of the similar situation in South Africa.)

Political developments in Zimbabwe from the late 1980s to the present have been characterized by the processes of redefining actors and realigning alliances between the state and civil society. The resurrection, resurgence and restructuring of civil society have arguably been the most important developments during this period.

Democracy and Civil Society

A fundamental starting point is to define the terms 'democratization' and 'civil society'. In this chapter, I define democratization functionally, as a process of change toward more democratic forms of rule: that is, a process during which a political regime opens up and extends more civil and political liberties to individuals or citizens in an attempt to achieve basic goals of good governance, transparency, equality among citizens.

I use the term 'civil society' to refer to that sphere where social relations including private business, non-state institutions, family and personal life, could evolve without state interference. It is only through such organizations that citizens become acquainted with the values, ideals, norms and benefits of public participation that limit the totality of state control over citizens.

This definition of civil society builds on autonomy from the state and other actors in terms of goal formulation. A high degree of autonomy is a precondition for political initiative and change. Autonomy consequently is a crucial element in studies of democratization, for it emphasizes the importance of wresting political initiative from ruling regimes. Hence political change is unlikely to take place without the articulation of alternative political and democratic views.

In making the choice of which groups to include in the study, I took into account the 'national' as opposed to the local or 'ethnic' character of the various groups and their ability to mobilize large sections of the population across ethnic lines. Although it is generally accepted that settler rule failed to create a cohesive organic nation, it would be erroneous to state categorically that after 20 years of independence, Zimbabwe has not attained some form of national identity.

A nation can be defined as an aggregation of people(s) developing solidarity on the basis of shared customs and institutions. A state on the other hand is:

> an organization within the society where it coexists and interacts with other formal and informal organizations from families to economic enterprises or religious organizations. It is, however, distinguished from the myriad of other organizations in seeking predominance over them and in aiming to institute binding rules regarding the other organizations' activities (Victor Azarya, cited in Bratton, 1989: 408).

In situations where nation and state are coterminous, ethnic allegiance fuses with state loyalty, giving rise to an environment in which the state acquires legitimacy and political authority. Colonial settlers failed to create a firm foundation for the building of a strong post-settler state in which nationalism and not localism is the norm. Localism is simply viewed as a situation in which individuals still owe their primary allegiance to their ethnic or racial group rather than the nation.

Unlike many African countries that are inhabited by multiple ethnic groups, Zimbabwe has only two major ethnic groups: the Shona and the Ndebele. After independence, a war-weary society displaying cleavages along color and ethnicity lines was discernible. To date though, differences among ethnic lines have become blurred. A shared political culture cutting across ethnic lines has become the norm rather than the exception. For the majority of people a common national identity has become a major social and political reality. The struggle for democracy and democratization has united the nation. Ethnicity now seems to be a less important consideration than it was during the early years of independence.

Almost all the civil society groups under scrutiny in this study have had to take into account the issue of ethnicity in their configuration. How these organizations are composed, their form and nature reflect to a large extent how they are dealing with the issue of ethnic balance. In general, painstaking attempts are made to ensure that the top leadership of most of the civil society groups is drawn from across the major two ethnic groups, the Ndebele and the Shona. For the most part, in order for a civil society group or a political party to pass the 'national character' test, its leadership is expected to reflect invariably that ethnic character. In making the choice of which groups to include in the study, I took into account the 'national' as opposed to the local or 'ethnic' character of the various groups and their ability to mobilize large sections of the population across ethnic lines.

When civil society groups focus primarily on local or specific ethnic group interests events at the national level are often viewed with a certain level of disinterest. Such groups, therefore, should be encouraged to enhance their influence and profile by linking up with other major civil society groups. It is through such linkages that they can make an impact at the national level. My decision to focus on groups with a national character for this chapter has therefore been deliberate. The assumption is that, if such 'national' groups are allowed to operate in an unfettered manner, they can lead to tendencies favorable to the creation of a more pluralistic national society. To that end, the focus here is on the Forum, the Zimbabwe Congress of Trade Unions (ZCTU), the National Constitutional Assembly (NCA), the Zimbabwe National Liberation War Veterans Association (ZINLWVA) and the media.

However, before I direct my analysis toward the political actions of these organizations, I turn first to the post-independence changes in the economy which have spurred the recent activities in civil society.

Economic Policies from the Early 1980s to the Late 1990s

With the lifting of sanctions following majority rule, high levels of economic growth were recorded in the first two years of independence. The gross domestic product (GDP) grew in real terms by 11% and 9.7% in 1980 and 1981, respectively. However, the economic growth rate fell sharply to 1.5% following the onset of drought in 1982/83, recovering only by 1985 when the GDP accelerated to 7.3%. Growth slowed again—to 2%—by the end of 1986, trickling to a mere 0.7% in 1987, before picking up to a somewhat lacklustre performance of 3.8% at the end of the first independence decade.

For most of the 1980s the regime financed its huge recurrent expenditure by short-term loans from international private creditors. However, that 'honeymoon' period with international financiers ended in 1987 and the central bank, faced with severe foreign currency shortages, simultaneously reduced foreign currency remittances and allocations to the private sector (see Nhema, 1987).

The regime also ran into a multitude of other economic problems by the end of the 1980s. At the macro-economic level, GDP per capita had remained stagnant for much of the first independence decade. The balance of payments sank into deficit (ILO, Occasional Paper 16: 22) while the foreign debt-service ratio ballooned (Institute of International Finance, 1998). Subsidies to inefficient parastatals rose from around 40% of the budget deficit to 60% by 1987 (Hawkins, 1985; African Economic Digest, April 1987) leading one local observer to call for a serious re-evaluation of the nature and operations of state-owned enterprises in the country (see Nhema, 1986). Corruption thrived while the public payroll swelled to several times its previous size. The quality of administration declined because party sympathizers, qualified or not, occupied key positions in both state-owned enterprises and government ministries.

At the micro-level, unemployment rates reached crisis proportions. Estimates are that only 10,000 jobs were created annually in the formal sector from 1980 to 1990 with the figure declining further after the introduction of Zimbabwe's Structural Adjustment Program (SAP). When compared to the estimated 200,000 to 300,000 high school leavers joining the labor force every year, the question of unemployment became the most serious problem facing the nation.

Those fortunate enough to be employed did not fare well either. Real wages, which rose somewhat in the early years of independence, fell sharply over the years under the impact of inflation and shortages. By the early 1990s workers found themselves actually worse-off than they were in the early 1980s.

As the economy continued to register a downward trend, and as funds from private lenders dried up, the regime found itself in a precarious position. Some donor funds that had been promised at the ZIMCORD[2] conference did not materialize (Lehman, 1992: 23). Disillusioned with the country's political and economic policies, the United States terminated aid funds after a diplomatic debacle in 1986, and Britain—following the US lead—stopped its Commodity Import Program the same year. Given that trade with these two countries constituted a significant proportion of the country's gross domestic product, Zimbabwe had no option but to try and cement friendlier ties with these key donor countries. As it reached out to them, it conceded to their demands to open up its economy before further credit facilities could be extended. Reluctantly, the regime found itself knocking on the doors of the IMF and the World Bank—a move it had resisted before. An agreement was reached in Washington in 1990 culminating in the adoption of the Economic Structural Adjustment Programme (ESAP) in 1991 thereby ending a 25-year era of excessive state intervention.

The specific reforms are now quite familiar. They include, among others: stream-lining of the public sector investment programs; privatization; reduction of public sector employment through freezes on hiring; relaxation of controls on prices, exchange rates and interest rates; and the introduction of incentives for the increased role of the private sector (Zimbabwe Government, 1991).

It must be emphasized that discussion and policies related to ESAP were largely confined to the ruling clique and business interests. Popular groups encompassing unions, churches, NGOs, student movements, and community groups were not consulted.

Explaining the Democratization Push

By mid-1988, a series of problems and scandals embroiled the Mugabe regime. These started when a group of angry student demonstrators were barred from marching into the city center to demonstrate against both the one-party state agenda that the government was proposing and the growing number of corruption scandals and crimes within both the party and government. In a style reminiscent of the settler period, the police were sent to prevent the protesters from leaving campus. When students responded by throwing stones at law enforcement officers, a scuffle ensued, leading to several arrests and the deportation of one Kenyan lecturer. The scenes of the riot police officers in full military regalia fighting against students who at best were armed with rocks, were graphic manifestations of an oppressive regime.

This crackdown—similar in many respects to government tactics of the settler era—fuelled public opinion against the state. Public antipathy increased after another, similar clash with students in mid-1989, especially when the government hurriedly passed the severely criticized University of Zimbabwe Amendment Act giving more power to the regime and the university administration to deal with dissent.Meanwhile, political debate was intensifying on the issue of the government's proposal for a one-party state following the merger of the Zimbabwe African National Union-Patriotic Front

(ZANU-PF) and the Zimbabwe African People's Union-Patriotic Front (ZAPU-PF) parties. Within the ZANU-PF party itself, Edgar Tekere was an outstanding critic. Takere, a former Secretary-General, had won support with the students over his opposition to the creation of a one-party state as well as with his charge that corruption within government and the party had reached corrosive levels.

The party reacted to Tekere's outbursts by expelling him. However, when revelations came to light, a few months after his expulsion, about high-level corruption involving senior government officials in the purchase and sale of motor vehicles, President Mugabe appointed a Commission to look into the allegations. The investigation triggered a series of resignations of ministers implicated in the scandal—the first time government officials had ever resigned on their own accord.[3]

A few months after the findings of the judicial commission had been made public, Edgar Tekere opportunely launched his Zimbabwe United Movement (ZUM) in 1989. Formed at the height of ZANU-PF's campaign to impose a one-party state, ZUM's oppositional manifesto stated that:

a multi-party state facilitates the competition of ideas on public policy and on how society is going to achieve its goals. The one-party state tends to make leaders complacent because there is no opposition to fear (*Financial Gazette*, 16 March 1990).

As the first serious opposition party to be formed after nine years of independence, ZUM's formation was welcomed by many groups and individuals opposed to the introduction of a one-party state. The emergence of ZUM further complicated the situation for ZANU-PF. The former's commitment to democratization undermined the latter's efforts to assert its hegemonic control. And, in the county's third election, held in March 1990, ZUM's performance demonstrated that the party enjoyed considerable support among civil society organizations. Although it won only two out of the 120 seats, the party had become a rallying point for civil society groups challenging the state's attempts to further monopolize power.

Regarding the specific events which triggered the old and new civil society groups to adopt a more militant stance against the regime, three main factors can be identified.   First, events external to Zimbabwe were important. The decline of superpower rivalry, and the subsequent collapse of authoritarian regimes in Eastern Europe demonstrated to people that public opposition could force autocratic regimes to give way to democratic pluralism. As the 'winds of democratization' swept across the continent more and more countries found themselves opening up their political systems. Various examples of democratization occurred during this period, including the abandonment of Marxist-Leninism in Mozambique in 1989, the institution of multi-party elections in Côte d'Ivoire, Zaire, Tanzania and Gabon in 1990, in Benin in 1991, the successful conclusions to the liberation struggles in Namibia in 1992 and, especially, the institution of majority rule in South Africa in 1994.

Second, with the introduction of ESAP, the vast majority of people—only recently accustomed to a decent standard of living—were thrown into a state of indigence. The rapid withdrawal of subsidies in 1991 was not accompanied by policies that sought to break down the oligopolistic nature of the market, and their removal resulted in a steep rise in the prices of most basic commodities. Devaluation measures made all imports expensive, thus local industries were unable to acquire the necessary new capital goods to replace the antiquated and inefficient technology that was a legacy of Rhodesia's isolation during the period of the Unilateral Declaration of Independence (UDI). At the same time, however, with the removal of protectionist measures, a deluge of imported products flooded the market. Unable to compete, many local industries, particularly the small-scale ones, closed down and retrenchment figures escalated. With decreased allocation of funding to health, there have been shortages of imported essential drugs, and the introduction of cost recovery measures have led to a reversal of the great strides made in the 1980s following independence. Similarly, with regard to education, per capita expenditure has fallen significantly leading to increased teacher-pupil ratios, shortages of teaching materials and a drop in school enrolment, especially for the 6-12 year age group where cost recovery measures were implemented.

Third, the Zimbabwean mass media in general, and in particular the newspaper industry, played a prominent role in the liberalization process—a topic that shall be discussed in the next section.

The Decline of Authoritarianism and the Rise of New Social Movements and Alliances

Under worsening economic conditions, the Mugabe regime failed to secure the continued loyalty of its former allies in civil society. Its popular support crumbled as economic decline undercut its welfare policies of free health, free education and the land redistribution program. While talk of getting 'lean and mean' appears to have been more acceptable in rich industrialized countries, in Zimbabwe the SAP knife cut to the bone. As economic conditions worsened, new movements sprang up.

The Forum

Capitalizing on the unpopularity of the regime, the Forum for Democratic Reform Trust (Forum)—now the FORUM Party—was formed in 1992. With its launching, history was repeating itself in Zimbabwe. Naming the multi-racial organization 'The Forum', invoked memories of the Federation of African Native Welfare Societies' 'Open Forum' of the 1950s. Moreover, like its predecessor, the new organization was to be 'part think-tank, part pressure group, part debating society' (*The Financial Gazette*, 9 July, 1992: 10). Finally, like previous multi-racial societies, its membership was comprised of blacks, whites and people of mixed races and its chief patrons—Enoch Dumbutshena, Garfield Todd, Diana Mitchell—were all veterans of multi-racial adventures

The launching of the Forum on 30 May 1992 in Bulawayo was also significant in that it reinforced Bulawayo's status as the birthplace of major opposition civil society organizations. Bulawayo was the center of 'opposition' politics until the late-1950s. Up until that time, Bulawayo was the industrial capital in the country before being overtaken by Harare from the 1960s onwards.

Along with the emergence of new civil society groups such as the Forum, there was a shift of alliances as civil society took a more combative position in its opposition to the regime's economic and political policies.

The Zimbabwe Congress of Trade Unions

The Zimbabwe Congress of Trade Unions (ZCTU) movement, which had been closely associated with the regime previously, called for a redefinition of relations between the state and civil society along lines differing from official corporatism (see The Chronicle, 8 September 1992). Buoyed by the change in leadership after the election of Morgan Tsvangirai as the new secretary-general in 1988, the union began its campaign to transform itself from being a fractured organization to one that would assume a key role of defending working class rights and interests (Loewenson, November 1990).

Predictably, the ZCTU's new stance sent shock waves through to the regime. Realizing that their erstwhile grip on the ZCTU was crumbling, the government co-opted one of its vice-presidents by appointing her as a junior cabinet minister, but the move proved to be a last-ditch attempt by a beleaguered regime to maintain its atavistic controls on labor and it did not stop the alliance between labor and the state from crumbling. Massive unemployment, the adverse effects of ESAP, falling real wages, and the lack of democracy all acted as new stimuli uniting labor against the state.[4] Yet, faced with increased opposition in the late 1980s, the government made concerted efforts to weaken the labor movement. These measures included: new regulations making it an offence punishable by up to two years imprisonment for workers in 'essential services' to strike; a new Labour Relations Amendment Bill—legislated in mid-1992 without any consultations with the unions—which encouraged the formation of multiple competing unions; confering on the minister responsible for labor sweeping powers to control union activities; and granting more power to employers in any future negotiating procedures.

When the ZCTU predictably opposed the new Labor Bill, the government adopted outright intimidation tactics. However, despite measures to constrain opposition—beginning with attempts to ban a ZCTU demonstration in 1992—the tango between labor and the state has continued unabated. It appears that the continued strength of the labor movement will be largely determined by the performance of the economy. As the situation stands at present, labor seems to be gaining an upper hand—if the recent spate of strikes that almost ground the country to a halt are anything to go by. In the year 1999 alone, the labor movement called for three successful strikes that almost paralyzed the economy.

Buoyed by their success, the labor movement has now gone a step further by sponsoring its own political party. The new workers' party, the Movement for Democratic Change (MDC), launched in September 1999, recently won 57 seats out of 120 contested seats in parliamentary elections held in June 2000. The new party has emerged as the first post-independence party to pose a formidable challenge to the ruling party.

The National Constitutional Assembly

Another new entry that has attracted national and international attention is the National Constitutional Assembly (NCA). The NCA is a voluntary forum for Zimbabwean citizens, bringing together churches, trade unions, human rights groups, women's organizations, political parties, students and a host of other associations, professional bodies and interested individuals for the purposes of debating the current Zimbabwean constitution. The assembly, launched in June 1997 was spearheaded by a task force drawn from a wide array of civil society groups agitating for constitutional reforms.[5]

The NCA's four broad objectives are:

- to initiate and engage in a process of enlightening the general public on the current constitution of Zimbabwe;
- to identify shortcomings of the current constitution and to organize debate on possible constitutional reform;
- to organize the constitutional debate in a way which allows broad-based participation; and
- to subject the constitution-making process in Zimbabwe to popular scrutiny with a view to entrenching that constitutions are made by, and for the people.[6]

The NCA hopes to achieve its objectives through workshops or seminars on the key issues of the constitution. The workshops according to the NCA would ensure the involvement and participation of all Zimbabweans and in particular women, the youth, students, workers, disabled persons and rural people. Beyond that the NCA would utilize all the available resources and education strategies, including production and distribution of pamphlets and other educational materials, media campaign, public meetings, rallies, 'stay-away' actions, picketing and demonstrations.

The NCA has indeed played a pivotal role in the democratization process in Zimbabwe through its initiation for constitutional reform. The NCA has noble objectives and it has managed to convince the generality of Zimbabweans that it is an all embracing advocacy group inspired by the national interest to promote political diversity, democracy and good governance through legal and constitutional reform.

The organization was formed at a time when symptoms of institutional decay, leadership failure and the collapse of policy-driven national strategies were all too apparent and many people viewed it as one of the most well-run and efficient civil society groups in the country. Indeed the NCA must be applauded for forcing the Mugabe government to initiate a constitutional review process.

However, despite its invaluable role in raising public awareness about the shortcomings of the present Lancaster House constitution, the NCA refused to participate in the new constitutional commission set up by government. Instead, its members insisted on a commission that would be clearly non-partisan. They also demanded that the process must be inclusive and not be subject to the whims of the government in power.

The NCA's campaigns to boycott the country-wide consultations set up by the government's Constitutional Commission (CC) were unsuccessful and the latter eventually completed its consultations and produced a draft constitution. However, the draft was eventually rejected in a referendum held in February 2000. The NCA had been in the forefront of the campaign against the draft constitution. They contended that the whole process that gave birth to the Constitutional Commission was flawed and that the provisions of the new constitution were just as undemocratic as those currently enshrined in the Lancaster House-derived constitution.

The Zimbabwe National Liberation War Veterans Association

The Zimbabwe National Liberation War Veterans' Association (ZINLWVA)—a very distinctive non-state grouping—has also added impetus to the democratization process in Zimbabwe.

Formed by former liberation war fighters, the members of this organisation have three major objectives: compensation in the form of pensions and gratuities for their contribution in the liberation struggle; commercial land allocated to them at concessionary rates; and free education and health for themselves and their spouses and offspring.

While one salutes the sacrifices and the role played by ex-combatants in bringing independence, the way they have articulated their issues has been far from civil. After a series of public demonstrations in July 1997, the ex-combatants upped the ante and threatened to take the law into their hands by disrupting proceedings to commemorate Heroes' Day at the National Heroes Acre on 11 August 1997.

The Heroes Acre fiasco marked a turning point in their campaign. In the scuffle that ensued, the former fighters had to be blocked by the police from advancing on the President who was delivering his speech. Visibly shaken by the demonstration, the President quickly wound up his speech and ended up delivering one of his shortest Heroes Day speeches. In the discussions that ensued with the war veterans thereafter, the President was forced to make a costly unilateral decision. He announced that more than 50,000 former fighters would each get a Zim$50,000 lump sum payment plus Zim$2000 monthly pensions before Christmas of 1997—all tax free. He also promised free education for the ex-fighters dependents, free health, free land and interest free loans up to Zim$200000 for each successful applicant.

The country has still not recovered from the President's expensive decisions as these led to what is now known as the 'Black Friday' of 14 November1997 when the local dollar fell around 75% against the US dollar.

To a large extent, despite their disruptive tendencies, the war veterans managed to shake the insensitivity of the present regime especially on the most sensitive issues of land and the general economic plight of the ordinary citizenry. As a result of these demonstrations the government has gone back to the drawing board to work out the modalities on land re-distribution. (However, as indicated in MacLean's chapter in this volume, the government's apparent complicity in the recent illegal land occupations by veterans, throws doubt on the government's sincerity in implementing a just and equitable process.) Frantic efforts are also under way to minimize the disparities between the 'haves' and 'have nots' through the indigenization of the economy. On that note the war veterans should be credited for their role in the democratization process. They managed to remind state managers that the generality of the Zimbabweans also want to partake in the national economy.

The Role of the Media

To help elucidate the key role played by the media, a review of how it helped to trigger the political liberalization process is in order. A good starting point is the newspaper coverage of the 'Willowgate' scandal in 1988 as it provides a framework for understanding what later transpired.

A government-owned newspaper revealed the high level of corruption involving senior government officials in the purchase and sale of motor vehicles already referred to above. The excellent investigative journalism and the fearless manner with which the reporters pursued the matter marked a watershed in the development of standards for a professional media. Events after the scandal took on a momentum of their own, however. Taking advantage of their newly-found freedom, the media became much more aggressive while government, shaken by the corruption revelations and the subsequent suicide of a senior minister over the corruption charges, became less willing and able to put its foot down on civil society. For the first time since independence, government officials were made aware that as public officials they 'lived' in a gold fish bowl!

Since then, the frenzied media and a voyeuristic public craving for more uncensored information managed to break down the veil of secrecy surrounding government operations. Even the operations of the much-feared Central Intelligence Organization (CIO) which had operated in a 'black box' before were no longer immune from scrutiny.[7]

After the unity pact of ZANU-PF and ZAPU-PF in 1987, newspapers adopted a critical stance. In the absence of a viable and strong opposition party, the independent newspapers and magazines provided the most informed and effective opposition to ZANU-PF policies. Although the regime controlled the local television and radio networks to prevent people from receiving alternative information, shortwave radio, satellite television, computers and fax made it difficult to control information reaching the middle class about developments in other countries.

While the dominance of the government-owned Mass Media Trust (MMT) has continued, this had not acted as a major impediment to the liberalization process. In fact, the MMT itself has had to liberalize, in view of the competition from independent newspapers. Although its papers, namely The Herald, The Chronicle, Mutare Post and The Sunday Mail continue to reflect the views of those in power as they did in the days of Rhodesian rule (Rosario, December 1993/January 1994: 29) after the Willowgate scandal they too have had to take a more critical stance. Since then, there have been several instances in which even MMT newspapers have offered blunt criticisms of the government. In some instances the editors were victimized.

A significant independent media player is the Associated Newspapers of Zimbabwe (ANZ) headed by Geoff Nyarot. The ANZ now runs the Daily News, in addition to three other provincial newspapers. Other independent influential weeklies include the Zimbabwe Independent, the Sunday Standard, the Financial Gazette and the Zimbabwe Mirror. Given their incessant opposition to state policies, government officials often refer to these papers as the 'opposition papers'. Despite occasional threats from such officials,[8] the papers have maintained a stance critical of government operations since the late 1980s. Many other magazines and newspapers have mushroomed since then.

As the number of private newspapers increased so did the competition for readership. Topics which were previously off-limits came to be extensively covered. Today, newspapers treat a whole range of issues from national affairs, international events, labor, women and religious issues in a 'no holds barred' approach. The independent media's revelations of corruption has been impressive. Examples include revelations about the peasant land re-settlement exercise which has been hijacked by senior government officials, the looting by senior government officials of a housing scheme meant for the average wage earner, the abuse of District Development Funds allocated to peasant farmers, diversion of funds to undeserving politicians from a low-interest World Bank loan facility designed to assist nascent private sector entrepreneurs, the abuse of the War Veterans fund, manipulation of tender procedures, and customs officers being arrested for bribes.

It cannot be denied that the media managed effectively to mobilize and orchestrate popular protest against the regime. The media provided a forum through which civil society could debate issues affecting them. Other than providing the forum for public discussion, the media also acted as an avenue through which groups in civil society made their demands known to the state. During much of the period under study, the major newspapers and magazines contained regular contributions on democracy and democratization from individuals and civil society groups. Letters to the editor were also very common with authors offering a diversity of views in a candid and forthright manner.

Why did the government fail to control this new 'glasnost' in the media? The first obvious reason is that, with the new wave of democratization sweeping across the world, most of the ruling elites were forced to commit themselves to the process of democratization. Any attempts to muzzle the press would have called into question their commitment to democracy both domestically and internationally. Furthermore, after its unsuccessful attempts to establish a one-party state as a result of the formation of ZUM and the Forum, the momentum created by the wave of democratization was difficult to halt. In other words, once the 'floodgates' of democracy were opened, the tides of autocracy could not control them. Indeed, although the mid-2000 elections were clearly neither free nor fair, the level of forceful opposition for the first time after two decades of independence did lead to the MDC winning half the votes and almost half the contested seats.

Conclusion

Faced with heavy opposition from civil society the state was not only forced to abandon its goal of establishing a one-party state by the end of 1990. It has also been compelled to repeal the notorious emergency regulations that had been in force from 1965 as pressure mounted especially after white-ruled South Africa had upstaged the regime by repealing its own in mid-1990. Previous controls on organized interests were also relaxed.

As the winds of political liberalization now blowing across Zimbabwe maintain their unabated onslaught, the ruling party's decreasing iron grip on organized interests will dwindle further. Also, as the army of privatization, ever on the march, continues its search for new fields to conquer, statist policies that have been the cornerstone of a command political structure will have to grapple with the chill winds of the market.

That noted democracy in Zimbabwe is still not secure. If the historical evidence supporting the hypothesis linking a vibrant civil society and a stable democracy is taken as a valid thesis, then one can understand why the Zimbabwean political system of more than 19 years' standing has been unable to legitimate itself fully. It needs to be continuously managed and defended or else it will decay.

This is not so much a function of inherited political and social structures as it is of political will. No matter how well structured political institutions are, they cannot act as insurance against natural 'despotic' Hobbesian tendencies. These can only be tempered when those in positions to change things start to battle in earnest for a decent political system that cherishes space for organized interests.

Notes

1. This observation by Steven Friedman in his study on social movements in South Africa is a good characterization of the problems facing Zimbabwean social movements during the early post-independence era. For more on this see, Friedman (1991: 9).
2. The first major post-independence Zimbabwe Conference on Reconstruction and Development (ZIMCORD) was held in 1981 with a view to soliciting funds from donors for its reconstruction projects. At that conference pledges amounting to Z$2 billion were made by various international donors. However, over the years those pledges were not matched with deeds. Only a tiny amount of the total pledge was ever disbursed.
3. Maurice Nyagumbo, one senior minister who was implicated—and a veteran of the nationalist struggle—felt so dishonored that he committed suicide.
4. Under such conditions, the state failed to secure the continued loyalty of its erstwhile allies, including civil servants. The latter who had been excluded from unionizing by inherited legislation demanded that they be allowed to operate their own unions. The formation of unions in this sector of over 200,000 employees boosted the strength and image of the labor movement.
5. The organization's leader, Thoko Matshe, is from Matabeleland while its vice-chairman is Shona. The issue of ethnicity in the organization came to the fore when elections for top posts were held in late 1999. The current vice-chairman alleged that he had been out- maneuvered from clinching the top post because of his ethnic background.
6. This is a summary of the objectives in a document produced by the NCA entitled 'Debating the Zimbabwean Constitution', June 1997.
7. It was through the investigative reporting of the media that the Midlands Central Intelligence Organization chief, Alias Kanengoni, and a provincial party leader were eventually taken to court and convicted to seven years each for shooting a Gweru businessman, Mr Patrick Kombayi, in the heat of the campaign on the eve of the 1990 elections. The judgement by the regional magistrate Wilbert Mapombere was seen as a victory for the press.
8. In September 1992, two journalists from *The Financial Gazette* were summoned under the

inherited 1971 *Parliamentary Privileges, Immunities and Powers Act* before a parliamentary committee to name the sources of a story alleging that senior members of the government had received favors from a corrupt business executive in deals involving the state owned Zimbabwe Banking Corporation and the Lorac group of companies. Despite the public outcry from members of the public and newspapers across the country, Parliament went ahead with the hearing. This action by Parliament is an indication that the rights and privileges of journalists are constantly contested in Zimbabwe. Recently, two journalists working for *The Sunday Standard* were detained by the military after they published an unsubstantiated story about a foiled military coup attempt in Zimbabwe.

10 Ethnicity and Race in the Changing Political Economies of South Africa and Zimbabwe

SANDRA J. MACLEAN

Introduction

On 8 May 1996, Thabo Mbeki, then Deputy-President of South Africa, opened a speech to the Constitutional Assembly in Cape Town with the memorable assertion, 'I am an African'.[1] This simple four-word sentence conveyed a message of communalism that transcended boundaries of both nationality and ethnicity. It was an appropriate beginning to an eloquent and powerful address that decried the 'destruction of all sense of self-esteem, [and] ... the corruption of minds and souls, [that occurs] when race and colour are used to determine who is human and who is sub-human'.

Mbeki's speech carried an obvious message of inclusion and belonging. Yet, paradoxically, it also held a provision for exclusion and separateness. In limiting the construction of his own identity to the complex of relations among peoples, land and environment of the African continent, Mbeki set firm geographic and cultural boundaries for the community of which he considered himself to be a member. Interestingly, at a time when the broadly communitarian ideals he expressed are often associated with notions of *global* cosmopolitanism, Mbeki chose margins of identity which set Africa distinctly apart from the rest of the world. The speech is revealing therefore, not only because it signaled the soon-to-be President's visionary and racially conciliatory stance, but also because its paradox of inclusion and exclusion featured one of the important dilemmas of our present age—that of defining/imaging boundaries, whether they are of identity or political jurisdiction.

Current debates on boundaries range from the end of sovereignty and/or the Westphalian order to predictions of and prescriptions for new forms of governance from local through global jurisdictions. Much of this scholarship is concerned ultimately with issues of the subjective and empirical limits of personhood, citizenship and state. It is not certain that the Westphalian system can accommodate the changes in the ways people are beginning to define themselves; in short, identity for many people now involves multiple loyalties that transcend national boundaries, thereby challenging the political rationale and moral justification for national sovereignty.

Individuals have no doubt always possessed diverse, competitive and sometimes incommensurable loyalties: to family, ethnic group, religious community, etc. However, in the past, different allegiant interests were mediated by the state, albeit with varying degrees of success and democracy. With globalizations, successful mediation is much more difficult and, indeed, may no longer be possible, nor perhaps even desirable, given that the many associations and communal relations which now transcend national boundaries appear to be associated with a sense of belonging to global or regional communities. These new regional and global identities emerging within civil societies tend to coalesce especially around issues of human rights and security that often exceed national interest or jurisdiction. At the same time, globalizing pressures appear to contribute to the fractionalization of civil societies, as is particularly evident in the proliferation of ethnic rivalries and conflicts. At present, then, as Robert Cox (1999: 27) has argued, while 'civil society has become the crucial battleground for recovering citizen control of public life', in many recent cases, civil societies have degenerated into conditions of group hatred and social anomy: battlegrounds quite literally!

As in much of the rest of Africa, identification along ethnic and racial lines has strongly influenced the political histories of Zimbabwe and South Africa. Issues of race and ethnicity were central features of the struggles in both countries for black majority rule: achieved in 1980 in Zimbabwe following a struggle for independence from British colonial rule and in 1994 in South Africa with the end of the Afrikaner-dominated system of apartheid. And, in both countries, race and ethnicity have continued to shape political cultures.

The degree of social tension related to identity politics has been determined largely by political economy in both Zimbabwe and South Africa. In Zimbabwe, the ruling regime has used race and ethnicity as political tools in its attempts to establish and then maintain corporatist rule. In some instances, the purpose and effect has been to minimize difference; in others, to highlight it. In South Africa, the new government has attempted to reduce ethnic and racial divisions, yet some of its policies—affirmative action, for instance—may actually accentuate differences, at least in the short term. Moreover, economic problems and social inequalities are serious impediments to reconciliation and reconstruction. This chapter argues that globalization pressures have intensified these contradictory processes of social integration and disintegration in both countries.

Zimbabwe: From Nationalism/Optimism to Globalization/Despair

Zimbabwe's political culture is characterized by a history of social divisions. Race, in particular, has been, and continues to be, a source of tension in the country. Although whites constitute only 2% of the population, their disproportionate control of the economy is a source of resentment for the 98% who are black. Ethnicity has also been a source of cleavage, particularly surrounding the two main 'African' ethnic groups: the dominant Shona comprising approximately 80% of the population and the Nbele making up another 17%, that is, most of the remainder. There has been conflict around both race and ethnicity, the most intense over the latter in the first post-independence decade, the most recent over the former in the pre-election period this year. The sources of these 'politics of identity', whether around race or ethnicity, are located in the dramatic, and largely negative, changes in Zimbabwe's political economy since independence.

Zimbabwe's present situation is perhaps best summed up by the title of Villalón and Huxtable's recent book, *The African State at a Critical Juncture: Between Disintegration and Reconfiguration*. As these authors point out, the potential for disintegration or for reconfiguration in many African states depends largely upon 'the latitude elites possess to manage changes in their political environments' (Villalón and Huxtable, 1998: 279). Throughout the continent, the degree of latitude has shrunk over the past two decades, often largely because of structural adjustment programs (SAPs). Nevertheless, latitude does vary across countries: some elites are better positioned or predisposed to take advantage of opportunities presented by structural change, while others have been adroit in finding ways to maintain their hold on power despite civil society pressures for reform. In Zimbabwe, it appears that the options available to President Robert Mugabe and the Zimbabwe African National Union-Patriotic Front (ZANU-PF) Party he leads have been considerably reduced of late. Increasingly unable to gain any advantage from globalization, the regime has met growing opposition from labor, intellectuals, human rights organizations and an appreciably more independent and vocal local media. As Alfred Nhema argues in another chapter in this volume, these pressures for democratization coupled with a recent escalation in racial tensions are contradictory, but related features of a growing crisis of governance in the country. This crisis has been symbolized most emphatically by the strong support for the opposition in the mid-2000 elections despite the government's failed efforts to coerce the electorate.

The Growing Rift between State and Society

Zimbabwean civil society is well developed in the sense that numerous non-state organizations representing a variety of social interests have been in existence for several decades. However, until recently, most organizations have had little strength relative to the state. At the beginning of the 1990s, for instance, Raftopoulos (1992: 57) described labor as being as being 'weak, and characterized by divisions on racial lines; sectionalism; low national density; political factionalism; and elitist and undemocratic structures'. Similarly, following independence, other civil society organizations—the media, most indigenous NGOs, student associations—tended to be co-opted or coerced by the government.

Yet, in the first post-independence decade, the regime rarely resorted to repression. Indeed, the interests of the government and civil society generally coincided since many civil society organizations had originated as part of the independence struggle and in support of the ZANU-PF. Moreover, the government's 'developmentalist socialism' policy and the impressive social improvements that were achieved won strong approval in civil society in the early 1980s (Sachikonye, 1995: 184).

By the end of the decade, however, a combination of recession, debt and drought made it increasingly difficult for the government to sustain the high level of investment in social development and therefore maintain the corporatist system of governance that had been constructed. To complicate matters, ethnic problems erupted between Shona who supported ZANU-PF and the Nbele who supported the minority ZAPU-PF Party.

Long-standing rivalries between the two main groups had temporarily been put to rest during the war of liberation, but competition resumed after independence and culminated in violence in the Nbele area of Matabeleland in the early 1980s. The government sent troops to quell opposition but conflict continued until 1987 when Joshua Nkomo, who had fled the country in the midst of vicious fighting in 1984, returned to merge his party with ZANU-PF and accept the vice-presidency (Sithole and Makumbe, 1997: 134).

The political solution on ethnicity has held since then. However, recently, racial politics have been more volatile. From the outset, ZANU-PF had promised to redress the inequities, especially in land holdings, which were the legacy of the former Rhodesian government.[2] However, the national income relied heavily upon export earnings from the agricultural sector that was dominated by the white settler community. And since growth was a precondition for any meaningful redistribution, the government had little choice but to continue to support the business interests of the white elite, even despite the objections of the poor black majority.[3]

The Mugabe regime was able to balance the interests of the predominantly white productive sector, the demands of an increasingly influential black bourgeoisie and the basic needs of the black majority quite successfully throughout the 1980s when the economy was growing at least slightly. As a consequence, generally peaceful race relations were maintained. The exception was during periods leading up to the national elections held every five years. Preceding each election Mugabe has used race as a tactic for winning votes, employing inflammatory rhetoric to condemn white domination of the economy and threatening to expropriate white-owned land for redistribution among poor black farmers. Following several years of economic decline, this strategy was particularly damaging in the election held in June 2000. In the prelude to the election, groups led by war veterans began to occupy white-owned farms demanding immediate settlement of land claims. To date, the violence associated with the land occupations has resulted in the loss of several lives, but has been excused, even condoned, by Mugabe and largely ignored by the police.

The Slide to Crisis

Renewed racial tensions are undoubtedly exacerbated, if not directly caused by the deterioration in the economy. Although the problems which plunged Zimbabwe into crisis pre-date the implementation of the first economic structural adjustment program (ESAP) in 1990, they have worsened since. From the mid-1990s on, there has been a steady trend of currency devaluation, deindustrialization, wage decline, retrenchments, and escalating unemployment rates (Sachikonye, 1995: 193; FMB, 1999). The social effects have been devastating, with funding cuts to health, education, and other social services. Drought in the early 1990s compounded the problem. Moreover, although post-apartheid South Africa's entry into the regional economy offered some potential for Zimbabwe's growth in the long term, it has created uncertainty and downturn in some sectors in the short term.

Despite the worsening conditions, ZANU-PF won the 1995 election. Support, however, has since waned in direct proportion to the downward spiral in the economy. Although some causes of decline have been external, the government bears a large share of the blame (FMB, 1998). Indeed, some policy decisions have been outrageous—and intensely unpopular! The malignant deterioration in both economy and governance since 1995 has dominated headlines in Zimbabwe's increasingly critical newspapers.[4] They have reported on: a scandal involving huge sums of money paid as reparations to war veterans; a moratorium on loans from the International Monetary Fund (IMF) because of the government's inability/unwillingness to make economic adjustments; unpopular military involvement in the war in the Democratic Republic of the Congo (DRC); arrests (and alleged torture by military personnel) of the publisher, the editor and a reporter of *The Standard*;[5] an attempt by the government to push through unpopular constitutional change; and the regime's heavy-handed, possibly illegal, and ultimately explosive, treatment of the land acquisition issue.

Opposition in civil society has ignited in the past two years. The mobilization of local civic organizations, non-governmental organizations (NGOs), churches, students and trade union members led at first to strikes and public demonstrations and eventually to the establishment of a new labor-led opposition party, the Movement for Democratic Change (MDC). The MDC's formation of the National Constitutional Assembly (NCA) last year appears to have been a critical point heralding the new level of organization and maturity within the Zimbabwean NGO community. Comprised of a broad range of voluntary associations which came together to protest the partisanship and the lack of openness and transparency exhibited in the government's Constitution Committee, the NCA managed to defeat the government's constitutional referendum in February 2000. This set-back provoked intense backlash from Mugabe and his supporters, but also generated a new resolve for democratization in civil society. The level of resolve became even more evident when the MDC won nearly half the seats in the June 2000 election (despite ZANU-PF's gerrymandering, stuffing of ballot-boxes, and threats and violence against opposition candidates and voters).

Zimbabwe's 'Politics of Difference' in a Changing Political Economy

Although Mugabe had previously been able to gain electoral support among the black, rural electorate by inciting racial hatred, this strategy is not likely to be so successful—nor as easily put aside following the election—in the present incendiary atmosphere of economic, political and social change (Taylor, 1999). In short, the patterns and problems of governance in Zimbabwe may be largely out of Mugabe's control, if not from his ability to sway events. Certainly, governance issues around economic crisis, regional war-mongering and social distress/unrest are the results of the government's policy choices and increasing authoritarianism. However, they are influenced also by changing relations among state, business and civil society in regional, international and global as well as national contexts.

In other words, the effects of globalization(s) on countries' political economies are relational and multi-level, and the current crisis of governance in Zimbabwe involves the convergence of several factors that extend beyond the national. First, the economic problems are the result not only of government mismanagement, but also of the declining competitiveness in the global and regional economies of a small, largely agriculturalist country with underdeveloped human capacity.

A second important issue is the intervention of Zimbabwean troops in the DRC. Some observers have argued that this was a diversionary tactic designed to distract attention from mounting tensions at home. However, Mugabe, wily politician that he is, likely would have foreseen that the action would exacerbate domestic problems. Therefore, regard for popular opinion was probably not the main reason behind this decision. An alternative explanation was that the action was a 'sop' to the military: a ploy to keep the officers and troops loyal to Mugabe should i) ZANU-PF lose the 2000 election and need military assistance to stay in power; or ii) military officers be planning a coup as was reported last year. This is credible, but probably not the whole story. Instead, 'new security' issues, for example, the regional and transnational connections of state and business actors surrounding trade (informal as well as formal) in minerals, are perhaps a factor in Zimbabwe's involvement in the DRC. Certainly, there have been reports that DRC President, Laurent Kabila, has given 'mineral rights' to Zimbabwean officers in exchange for their assistance. This suggests 'shadow state' proclivities and activities described by Reno (1998) and hints at the possibility that Zimbabwe's involvement in the DRC and, to some extent its constrained economic circumstances, are features of the networks of kleptocracy described by Bayart, et al. (1999).

A third 'globalization' issue affecting Zimbabwe's present circumstances and future prospects involves the interaction of local civil society groups with the international donor community. Strengthened opposition to the government is evidence of a maturation of the country's civil society. Yet, just as the economic failures cannot be blamed totally on the government's policy choices, neither should external contributions to the new activism in civil society be dismissed. Indigenous NGOs are dependent upon international donors for much of their financing and therefore are directed toward the issue-areas promoted by funding agencies. Hence, the campaign which Zimbabwe NGOs waged on the constitutional issue undoubtedly gained support from the emerging set of international norms of which the international donor community's current preoccupation with 'governance' is a feature. Moreover, regional links among NGOs—such as between Zimbabwe's NCA and Kenya's Citizen's Coalition for Constitutional Change—may be catalysts for social activism. Likewise, regional NGOs like MWENGO (Mwelekeo wa NGO) and Africa-wide research institutions like CODESRIA (Council for the Development of Social Science Research in Africa) help to construct and connect civil societies through their extensive research networks.

Ethnic and Racial Dimensions of the Changing Political Economy

It is interesting that with the recent escalation in racial tensions in Zimbabwe, there has not (yet, at least) been a corresponding exacerbation of ethnic rivalries. Joshua Nkomo's death in June 1999 did cause some to speculate that old rivalries between the Nbele and Shona would resurface. Indeed, the Vice-President commented that Nkomo had played a crucial role in maintaining peace, and that ethnic killings were 'certain' in the loss of his stabilizing presence. However, the NGO community, as well as other government leaders, were swift to rebut this prediction and, to date, there has been little evidence of significant ethnic tension in the general society.

Ethnic politics may yet ignite if the post-election situation deteriorates. To date, NGOs may have played a role in mitigating ethnic tensions in civil society. Identity politics did not emerge as a focal point for the voluntary sector, perhaps because many were initially engaged in building a national identity in the first post-independence decade, then capturing the national constituency in the second. Also, international and transnational connections established around the global 'norm' of 'good governance' may have helped to mediate ethnic divisions within NGOs and, through them, in the larger civil society. However, these benign influences may be overshadowed by more pernicious forces in the wake of the 2000 election and the violence surrounding the challenge to the government.

Also, there has been some speculation that increased dissension within ZANU-PF ranks may indicate a breakdown along sub-ethnic lines. Inter-Shona tensions have traditionally been a feature of political struggles within the party and it is possible that old rifts may be deepening as the party faces mounting opposition from civil society and, at the same time, is pondering Mugabe's succession.[6]

The Politics of Identity in South Africa

While Zimbabwe's future is uncertain at best, South Africa's prospects appear to be more hopeful. When the country held its first multi-racial, democratic election in 1994 after several decades of racist, authoritarian government—the last four under the legally institutionalized system of *apartheid* (apartness)—hopes for more equitable and peaceful governance were unbounded. And, by 1997, then Vice-President Mbeki was still sufficiently optimistic to suggest that South Africa might be the locus for an African Renaissance.

Certainly, transformation—whether or not it amounts to 'renaissance'—is the most striking characteristic of post-apartheid South Africa. Yet, the possibilities for 'good' governance in the face of such change remain uncertain as they depend on reducing inequities and insecurities: i) in a deeply divided society with entrenched cleavages of race, ethnicity, class and gender, and ii) in a neoliberal environment in which inequalities tend to be exacerbated.

The 'politics of identity' have been the singularly most notable/notorious of modern South Africa's attributes. Race has been the most polarized locus of identity because of the apartheid system, under which people were legally separated, often quite arbitrarily, into categories of Whites, Blacks, Coloreds and Indians. While it is true that political struggles based on identity did not begin with apartheid and are not confined to race (for instance, ethnic tensions pre-dated the arrival of whites on the Southern African landscape), colonialism and rivalries between the British and Dutch (Afrikaner) colonial groups often exacerbated divisions among indigenous groups and the institutionalization of apartheid in 1948 entrenched racial politics. Apartheid also contributed to various competitions and cooperations among ethnic groups. For instance, the National Party's politics of exclusion propelled several black ethnic groups (and parties) to unite as the multi-ethnic African National Congress (ANC), but it also helped to drive a wedge between the latter and the Zulus and the Zulu nationalist Inkatha Freedom Party (IFP).

The Political Economy of Transition

With the collapse of apartheid at the end of the 1980s, the idea of peaceful transition to a multi-party, multi-racial democracy was enthusiastically embraced in South African and abroad. Optimism prevailed when the newly elected ANC's Reconstruction and Development Programme (RDP) introduced in 1994 signalled that the government intended to honor its mandate to reduce social divisions and inequities.

Meeting the ambitious goals of the RDP—embedding democracy, disentangling the legacy of apartheid, accelerating economic growth, delivering affordable services equitably, and 'fundamentally transforming society, the economy and all spheres of government' (Goldin and Heymans, 1999: 109)—has been excedingly challenging. All areas of governance— political, legal, economic and security—have required policies to maintain a delicate balance between growth and equity, justice and reconciliation, pragmatism and hope. In no area has the need for balance been more obvious (or daunting) than with economic policy. GEAR (Growth, Employment and Redistribution), the government's major macro-economic strategy, has pitted the main business organization, the Southern African Foundation (SAF), against labour (Nedlac),[7] the former favoring privatization and market-oriented policies (including labour-market flexibility) and the latter arguing that the state should be more interventionist to ensure greater social equity (Nattrass, 1999).

The business position reflects the prevailing view that national policies must be in alignment with the international economic order/orthodoxy. As one SAF document argued:

> The increasingly free movement of money across political borders has magnified the link between economic policies and investment. If policies are appropriate, the enormous capital resources of the industrialised world become available; if policies are wrong, even a country's own citizens will hesitate to invest....With the right policies South Africa can grow much faster than would

otherwise have been possible, but with the wrong policies it will be punished harshly and quickly (in Nattrass, 1999: 84).

Given the trend towards conformity in economic policy—the 'globalization of politics' (Held, et al., 2000: 49)—South Africa (or any other country, for that matter) may appear to have few options. Therefore, it was perhaps inevitable that the SAF position would triumph and that South Africa would join the emerging 'competition state' ranks (Cerny, 2000). However, an overly strict market orientation for GEAR may create labor dissatisfaction that could derail reconstruction and reconcilation, especially when it is by no means certain that 'moving to the market' is all that it takes to attract international business.

Whether the open-market experiment in South Africa will eventually pay off remains to be seen, but certainly, to date, economic indicators have been equivocal at best. Toward the end of 1999 the *Financial Times* reported that economic growth (and confidence) was increasing, but foreign investment had declined, a low savings rate persisted and the unemployment problem has been particularly intransigent (Maphologela, 1999; Grawitzky, 2000; Hall, 2000). Some sectors and companies, as Shaw notes in this volume, are taking advantage of the new openness, but general outcomes are uncertain in the complex economic climate that includes the 'internationalization' of a range of institutions, services and pursuits, 'new technologies', 'new competitors', 'new corporate strategies', 'new positive sanctions' and 'new vulnerabilities'. At present, it seems that vulnerabilities tend to outweigh opportunities and corporate weaknesses are intricately tied to social fragility. Unemployment rates that hover around the 50% range are among the most significant indicators of corporate vulnerability and social stress. Very high crime rates also persist, serving as a deterrent to investment as well as both measure and source of social tension.

These economic and social problems are exacerbated by the situation in the region. Notwithstanding the optimistic symbolism of African renaissance, and despite the impressive growth rates of some Southern African countries like Botswana and Mauritius, the region as a whole is wrestling with new (in)security problems of economy, ecology and conflict. Retrenchments, unemployment and low wages in neighboring countries are producing severe migratory pressures and heightened levels of xenophobia (in short, a new 'identity' issue with origins in the changing regional political economy). New security connections and divisions are manifested also in informal and often illegal transnational transfers of goods and, increasingly, they are being identified and addressed with respect to the connections between conflict and the trade in minerals, particularly diamonds. Finally, 'new' regionalisms are emerging around health issues such as AIDS, and ecological issues of climate change, water availability and soil erosion, highlighting the inter-relatedness of the external and domestic political economies. These new complex arrangements of state, business and society extend governance beyond the national jurisdiction and/or competency range to the regional, international and global.

Civil Society in the Changing Political Economy

Despite the pressures of the new regionalisms, most actors within the governance 'triangle' have not responded particularly creatively to the new security agenda. As Vale (1997) argues, the government continues to conduct foreign policy within a traditional realist framework. Likewise, most civil society groups, having been preoccupied until recently with winning majority rule in the national constituency, tend to focus on domestic issues. Meanwhile, although international donors, NGOs, etc. have turned their attentions to the 'new' security issues of peacebuilding in Southern Africa and have begun to identify the regional/global and security/development connections, there is often a disjuncture between the discourse and practice. For example, although it is generally accepted that 'building capacity' in civil society is a necessary component of 'peacebuilding', there is little evidence that the resources supplied by international donors actually improve conditions at (or even reach) the grassroots. Moreover, the focus, if not always the rhetoric, of external agencies tends to be on the national. This was quite appropriate in apartheid South Africa when winning the national constituency was critical to furthering development and security objectives. In post-apartheid South Africa, however, 'good governance' cannot be separated from regional and global contexts (MacLean, 1999).

There have been limitations to the extent and direction of civil society's role in governance in the national as well as regional context. This is despite the existence of an actively engaged network of trade unions, churches and an estimated 50,000 NGOs, including numerous local associations or 'civics'. There are several reasons for this, but the most controversial has been the ANC-civics relationship. The organization and politicization of South Africa's civics was advanced during the struggle against apartheid when most of these local associations emerged in support of the ANC. While this collaborative state-society relationship facilitated the party's smooth entry into office in 1994, it also created some problems. In particular, there was considerable concern, at least initially, that the close association would impede the democratic functioning of these civil society organizations: that is, they would not be an effective check on the state.

Although these fears have been borne out to some extent and for some types of organizations,[8] several scholars detect a new vitality in civil society. For instance, Herman Kotzé (1999: 185) observes that 'toward the end of 1996, surviving NGOs slowly started to re-emerge after a fairly long period of painful organisation restructuring and refocusing'. Kuperus (1999: 659), similarly, remarks on a new energy in civil society, reporting that church organizations have opposed the government on GEAR's market orientation, its neglect of poverty issues, and the re-activation of the arms industry, while they have supported the Truth and Reconciliation Commission, the Employment Equity Bill and affirmative action policies. In short, they have attempted to hold the ANC accountable for policies that bear on its social welfare mandate. Steven Friedman, who has written extensively on South African civil society, also offers a more positive analysis of its possibilities than he did previously. At the beginning of the 1990s, he worried about civil society organizations' lack of autonomy. Then, he wrote: 'A key question for post-apartheid South Africa is, therefore, whether it is likely to enjoy voluntary associations diverse enough to express the full range of interests and values and strong enough to influence events' (Friedman, 1991: 15). Recently, however, he suggests that, if anything, space has opened up for civil society:

> There are no legal mechanisms which restrict civil society today. The government, in that sense, has made room for civil society. However, we're a polarized society that has obvious implications. There are parts of civil society the government will listen to and others that it won't, but this is part of any society.... Our country has a diverse civil society arrangement that has a complex relationship with the government (cited in Kuperus, 1999: 650-1).

Similarly, in another article, Friedman (1999: 12) asserts:

> Among the racial majority as well as minorities, civil society may wield countervailing power: COSATU [Congress of South African Trade Unions]... has shown that it is possible both to support the majority party (as most citizens do) and to present differing perspectives.

Such observations suggest that much of the anxiety of the early post-apartheid years surrounding civil society's ability to serve a 'watchdog' role has been dispelled. It appears that a robust pluralism is developing and that South Africa's civil society boasts a fair degree of autonomy from the ruling ANC government. However, some scholars believe that open pluralism is not necessarily a good thing at the present time. For instance, Webster and Adler (1999: 371) argue that South Africa's future depends upon the ability to construct a new corporatist arrangement among the main central stakeholders in state, business and society. Echoing Friedman, they note the energy and democratizing potential of civil society. They argue, however, that:

> these forces do not have the capacity to impose their alternative ideas on either the state or domestic and international capital. Nor is the government and capital able to satisfy the economic demands of this constituency through GEAR. Neither can they crush opposition. In other words, South Africa has entered a class stalemate ... [and compromise will not be possible unless] all key actors recognize the need to bargain and make concessions (Webster and Adler, 1999: 371).

Webster and Adler's ideas of compromise, or 'bargained liberalization' have been controversial; critics have argued that they are advocating workers' 'capitulation to the dictates of global capitalism' ('Editorial', *Southern Africa Report*, 2000: 1-2). Nevertheless, their analysis needs to be taken seriously; whether compromise is preferable or even possible, it is sobering that informed observers such as Webster and Adler argue that this is the only way to prevent a descent into violence.

Issues of Class, Race and Ethnicity

Given the integration of class, race and ethnicity in South Africa, the debate over compromise versus capitulation may provide insight on the 'politics of identity' in the future.

Unlike the Mugabe regime in Zimbabwe, which has deliberately politicized race to win votes, the ANC has made a sincere effort to minimize race and ethnic differences, both by defining the party in inclusive and non-racial terms and by introducing policies designed to minimize inequalities. Yet, despite positive signs—such as a diminishing tendency to vote along lines of race or ethnic group (interview with Acting Director, IDASA, June 1999)—racial and ethnic antagonisms persist. For example, developments in the Western Cape following the national elections in 1999 revealed that racial tensions still remained not far below the surface. When three white-dominated opposition parties formed a coalition on terms that virtually forced the exclusion of the ANC, which had won the majority of votes in the Cape region, some observers worried that white politicians were willing to kindle smoldering racial rivalries for their own political gains. As Merton and Barrel wrote in the *Mail and Guardian* on 11 June 1999:

> The coalition partners may well be correct in the letter of the law, but their actions have disregarded the social and economic factors in a province where votes were broadly cast according to race.

Beyond electoral politics, some government policies have had mixed results in minimizing difference, despite good intentions. Affirmative action, for example, which was clearly designed to reduce inequalities has exposed, and perhaps exacerbated, racial tensions. Considering the institutional barriers that existed for non-whites under apartheid, there is a logical, rights-based rationale for affirmative action. However, many qualified whites believe that their growing lack of job opportunities is the result of the program. And according to Amichand Rajbans, an Indian politician, 'many Indians [also] believe they have now become victims of affirmative action.' (Price, 1997: 169). The program has even, according to some of its critics, intensified divisions within the black community since it promotes educated blacks, but does little to help the poorest members of the black communities (Murray, 1997).

It is not surprising that affirmative action is controversial; after all, it designates job eligibility on the basis of visible differences at a time when high unemployment rates are creating dissatisfaction and heightening competition among members of all races and ethnic groups. The important question is whether the program ultimately will reduce the racially defined class divisions that apartheid created or whether a government policy that highlights race or ethnicity will have the contrary effect and actually deepen the social divisions. Price (1999: 171-72) argues that the latter will occur because, in elevating the 'salience of race', it becomes 'a significant basis of mobilization', hence stimulating 'racially exclusive forms of political association'. Furthermore, social mobility is linked to group membership under affirmative action, 'thus reifying race groups by linking them to the allocation of significant social rewards'.

The degree to which race and/or ethnicity becomes reified as a political and social division in the new South Africa is dependent upon various contingencies, some paradoxical. Clearly, economic growth is central to the prospects for reconstruction and reconciliation, and the ability to attract external investment is therefore crucial. Yet, as Price (1999: 173) observes:

> One of the great ironies in the South African situation is that international business is holding back investment partly out of a concern that the inability of the government to deliver immediate benefits bodes ill for political stability. On the one hand, international business demands economically orthodox fiscal and monetary policies that preclude rapid improvement in the black majority's material conditions of life; on the other hand, it refuses to invest heavily because those benefits have not been forthcoming.

Clearly, the tyranny of neoliberalism has created a 'double-edged sword' for the government of South Africa. The problem has deepened because of recent events in Zimbabwe. Business leaders, who are concerned that violence in the neighboring state will scare off potential investors, have put pressure on South African President Mbeki to intervene and, most importantly, to register his disapproval of Mugabe before the international community. Mbeki, however, has been very circumspect in his approach to the crisis, arguing that 'quiet diplomacy' is the most effective strategy. Others, however, believe Mbeki's reticence is motivated by other concerns. One explanation was recently outlined in an article in the *Financial Gazette* (18 May 2000) which quotes a member of the National Institute for Economic Policy, Johannesburg who suggests: 'A similar crisis could unfold in South Africa in future. If the president condemns the land crisis in Zimbabwe today, what shall he say when a similar scenario evolves in his own backyard tomorrow?'

This hardly seems plausible; unlike the Mugabe regime, the South African government is unlikely to show the same disrespect for the rule of law even if problems around land should intensify. A more compelling explanation is that Mugabe's actions are an attempt to reduce fears in the rest of Africa regarding South African aspirations towards regional (or continental) hegemony. Just as Mbeki's 'I am an African' speech was undoubtedly designed, at least in part, to assuage anxiety about his intentions towards his continental neighbors, his silence on Zimbabwe has been seen by some as an attempt to pre-empt criticism by Africans who would see his condemnation of Mugabe as a sign that he was kowtowing to white business interests. Indeed, the 18 May article in the *Financial Gazette* maintains that it was widely assumed that Mbeki was directly rebuking the 'captains of industry' when he exclaimed that 'people motivated by their own racism have created a psychosis of fear in South Africa about the Zimbabwe crisis'.

Mbeki's resort to the language of racial recrimination tends to fuel claims that there has been a shift away from the ANC's inclusive multi-racialism toward a more race-conscious stance. According to the *New Statesman* (15 May 2000), 'we are now seeing, even within the ANC, a more openly Africanist emphasis. In recent months, it is quite apparent that this has taken an increasingly confrontational racial edge'. This attitude, the article reports, became clearly evident in a heated public discussion that was touched off recently by a white, anti-apartheid journalist who described himself as an Afrikaner and an African. The debate, in essence over who qualifies as an African, brought quiescent animosities to the surface and demonstrated that the hard-won, post-apartheid racial harmony could easily be disrupted.

The Mbeki government must tread very carefully to avoid exacerbating any of these tensions, especially given the unsettled issues of identity that have erupted in the region and the close attention being paid by the international community. Certainly, the events in Zimbabwe serve as bitter warning to any government leader who would invoke race as a political tool. In particular, as the 15 May article in *New Statesman* article points out, how the 'politics of difference' are played out in the new South Africa depends largely on economic prospects:

> President Thabo Mbeki announced what he called the 'African renaissance' as a signature theme of his period in office. So far, apart from vague talk about a renewal for the African continent, the outlines of that 'renaissance' have been left extremely blurry. The danger is that this void will be filled with hollow rhetoric about exclusivist ethnic traditions, leaving hard political questions of radical social change untouched.

Conclusions

The recent escalation in racial tension in Zimbabwe appears to be directly attributable to government policy; in particular Mugabe's deliberate and reckless use of race as an election strategy. In South Africa, on the other hand, the government has appeared to be sincerely committed to mitigating the distinctions of race and ethnicity. Yet, the problems of identity politics are not likely to soon abate in either country.

In both Zimbabwe and South Africa, pressures of globalization and regionalism diminish the level of control and maneuverability that these governments have to control the direction of events in racial and ethnic politics. In Zimbabwe, Mugabe has repeatedly introduced the race card in his re-election campaigns. At the present time, however, with tensions in society increasing because of structural adjustment and economic collapse, military involvement in the DRC, and regime corruption, this strategy is not only dangerous, it has not gained Mugabe the same level of electoral support as in the past. For South Africa, the competitive global environment presents perhaps more obstacles than opportunities for the fledgling economy, and certainly, the demands and exigencies of the neoliberal agenda are contrary to minimizing social disparities and inequities. Furthermore, reconciliation policies like affirmative action that explicitly attempt to minimize the inequities and distinctions based on race and ethnicity may, paradoxically, help to entrench the 'politics of difference'.

In both countries, propects for governance that would reduce social cleavages are contingent upon the level of democratic activism in civil society organizations, but present conditions (authoritarianism in Zimbabwe, pressures for compromise in South Africa) miminize the strength of voluntary associations.

Secondly, the interactions of state, market and civil society actors are embedded in regional and global as well as national contexts. Well-established civil society groups in both Zimbabwe and South Africa support democratization and hence the mitigation of racial and ethnic differences. The project has advanced significantly in recent years as labor, NGOs, student organizations, churches and media, often in interaction with networks of NGOs, educational institutions and think-tanks, work together in order to bring the Mugabe regime to account in Zimbabwe and to support reconstruction and reconciliation in South Africa. However, continued social progress requires that civics, NGOs, labor, etc. as well as government must begin to form not only an inclusive national identity, but a regional and global civic identity as well. Clearly, this is a rather formidable undertaking. And, as Swatuk and Vale (1999: 384) observe, civil societies in Southern Africa are not particularly well disposed for the assignment at present:

> the [Southern African] region is cleaved along myriad fissures of identity: race, class, state, nation, tribe. Unlike Dahl's understanding of pluralism, these forms of identity emerge in weak states not to strengthen society, but to strengthen particular groups of people. They remain forms of exclusion, not inclusion.

Presently, the effects of globalization are such that 'many chains of political, economic and social activity are becoming worldwide in scope [and] ... there has been an intensification of levels of interaction and interconnectedness within and between states and societies' (Held, cited in Bush, this volume). Ultimately, the interactions of states, businesses and civil societies in Zimbabwe and South Africa and within regional and global contexts economies will determine whether the politics of inclusion will replace those of exclusion, thus having profound implications for sustained human development and security.

Notes

1. The speech was given at the adoption of the 'Republic of South Africa Constitution Bill 1996'.
2. In a policy statement published soon after the new government assumed power, the latter promised to end the 'economic exploitation of the majority by the few, the grossly uneven infrastructure and productive development of the rural and urban and distribution sectors, the unbalanced levels of development within and among sectors and the consequent grossly inequitable pattern of income distribution and of benefits' (Government of Zimbabwe, 1981: 1).
3. A.K. Mhina (1987: 28) noted that over 40 white farmers have been killed in Matebeleland in the first seven years following independence and many more had emigrated.
4. See the section on the media included in Alfred Nhema's chapter in this volume in which he describes the important role it has played in the democratization process.
5. It appears that this action was prompted by the newspaper publishing an article on a foiled military coup attempt.
6. Another dimension of this problem is the disapproval of Mugabe's second wife. Considered to be excessively extravagant, which is appalling when so many Zimbabweans are facing severe hardship, Grace Mugabe is a member of the same Zezuru group to which her husband belongs. As Stephen Chan (1999: 64) points out, accusations of favoritism leading to deeper ethnic divisions in ZANU-PF might become evident should Mugabe's successor be a Zezuru.
7. The SAF (South Africa Foundation) is a coalition of top South African companies. Nedlac consists of the Congress of South African Trade Unions (COSATU), the Federation of South African Labour (FEDAL) and the National Council of Trade Unions (NACTU).
8. Hassim and Gouws (1998: 69), for example, found that the 'unprecedented level of organizational strength' that women's organizations had achieved from 1991-94 through membership in the Woman's National Coalition had declined significantly thereafter. The authors argue that both because effective and talented leaders of the women's movement have moved into government and the collapse of apartheid had removed the motivating purpose of the struggle, there has been a 'demobilization' of civil society.

PART IV

GOVERNANCE AND CONFLICT

11 The Political Economy of Angola's Ethnic Conflict

ASSIS V. MALAQUIAS

Introduction

Angola represents one of Africa's worst post-colonial tragedies. Once justifiably regarded as a potential sub-regional leader in southern Africa, due to its considerable natural resources, it is now regarded as a 'collapsed state' (Zartman, 1995: 3). Ironically, the abundance of natural resources—particularly oil and diamonds—that was expected to help thrust post-colonial Angola into a position of sub-regional leadership has, instead, helped to fuel a 25 year civil war. Now, the Angolan state struggles for domestic viability and international relevance. Internally, the state is yet to find the right mix of political, economic and symbolic measures to end the civil war. Consequently, it has little capacity to provide the security necessary for human and economic development. Additionally, the Angolan state must now rely on domestic and international non-governmental organizations (NGOs) to provide essential services like food assistance and health care to the country's 12 million people. Internationally, the intractability and complexity of Angola's conflict has frustrated all peace-making/building/keeping initiatives to bring security to this former Cold War battleground. Consequently, there is considerable frustration and resignation about the slim prospects to end this peculiarly intractable conflict.

The civil war in Angola broke out during the process of decolonization from Portugal in 1975 as a result of the anti-colonial forces' failure to find agreement among themselves on a blueprint for post-colonial development. Paradoxically, although the major ideological disagreements separating these forces have been rendered irrelevant by the end of the Cold War, the conflict rages on now fuelled by greed and fanned by ethnic divisions. It is, therefore, crucial to focus on the financial and ethnic aspects of the conflict to understand Angola's continuing tragedy. In other words, the war in Angola persists because it is highly lucrative to both government and rebel leaders.

The civil war has provided a most convenient cover for the government and the rebels to plunder the country's vast resources without regard for accountability, let alone the development needs of the people they purport to govern and/or liberate. Thus, most of the estimated USD $2 billion/year in government receipts from oil production are used to purchase war materiel, enrich the President and his entourage, and support the extravagant consumption habits of a small number of state functionaries. Similarly, according to the United Nations' *Report of the Panel of Experts on Violations of Security Council Sanctions Against UNITA*, the rebels are able to use about USD $500 million/year in diamond revenues almost exclusively to acquire the means to wage their guerrilla campaign against the government. In addition to the war's economic aspect, powerful underlying ethnic currents constitute additional barriers to a peaceful settlement of the conflict. Thus, insofar as the main causes of the war's longevity can be found at the critical intersection of Angola's political and economic realms—within the domain of political economy—a lasting solution to the conflict is unlikely to be achieved on the battleground. A new framework for peace must involve creative and innovative ways that ensure equal opportunities for all citizens to gain power and wealth irrespective of their ethnic origin.

This chapter suggests that Angola's civil war and the ongoing crisis of governance can be attributed primarily to the unwillingness and/or inability of the governing Movimento Popular de Libertacao de Angola (MPLA) and the rebel Uniao Nacional para Independencia Total de Angola (UNITA) to find mutually acceptable mechanisms to share power and wealth. This is a reflection of the important historical divisions that separate them. In other words, the reluctance of MPLA and UNITA to share power and wealth in the post-independence period is a direct result of the major cleavages among the main nationalist groups that participated in the anti-colonial war of liberation which lasted from 1961 to 1975. But these cleavages were only partly the result of deep animosities caused by ideological differences reflecting Cold War allegiances—i.e., the Marxist MPLA was supported by the former Soviet Union while the Frente Nacional de Libertacao de Angola (FNLA), and later UNITA, were supported by the United States. Likewise, although class and race were also important dividing factors, they did not determine the fundamental character of the anti-colonial nationalist movements. What divided these would-be liberation groups were mainly ethnic differences predating colonialism. Tragically for Angola, these differences were left unresolved and allowed to simmer during the long anti-colonial struggle. Unsurprisingly, the 'nationalist' label was used primarily to acquire legitimacy at home and abroad. In reality, the ethnic orientation of the various liberation movements was only thinly disguised. Thus, FNLA, MPLA and UNITA represented almost exclusively the Bacongo, Kimbundu and Ovimbundu ethnic groups respectively.

The overthrow of the colonial regime in Portugal by a group of disgruntled middle-level army officers in April 1975 placed Angola on the inevitable fast track to independence. Predictably, however, in the absence of a common colonial enemy and with their ethnic differences accentuated by the mistrust and animosity exposed in the anti-colonial struggle, the nationalist movements derailed the process of state-building and set the new state firmly on the path to fratricidal self-destruction. In this context, Portugal's feeble efforts to set up a transition government that included FNLA, MPLA and UNITA did not stand a chance of success given the long history of mistrust among them. Ultimately, all groups invited foreign forces to help them achieve supremacy in the initial phase of the civil war. Nevertheless, neither UNITA nor FNLA was able to take control of Luanda even with the assistance of invading armies from neighboring South Africa and Zaire. MPLA emerged victorious: it was able to drive its two main rivals from Luanda, keep them out, install a one-party Marxist regime and win international diplomatic recognition from most states except apartheid South Africa and the United States. However, although it also relied on foreign troops from Cuba and the Soviet Union, the key to MPLA's success in installing and maintaining its regime particularly in the crucial early period—both immediately prior and after independence—resided in its strategy of *Poder Popular*, or people's power. This entailed arming civilians of the predominantly Kimbundu group in the capital and surrounding regions. Groups of armed Kimbundus ensured that UNITA and FNLA sympathizers who might endanger the new regime were driven out of the capital region.

For more than two decades, the Kimbundu group has maintained MPLA in power even in the face of inept governance. This is not surprising inasmuch as the Kimbundu are the primary beneficiaries of the complex web of patron-client networks that have emerged to distribute the vast oil and diamond wealth. Other ethnic groups, including the majority Ovimbudu, have no more than token access to power or wealth. By relegating other ethnic groups to the margins of Angola's political economy, the governing MPLA unwittingly forced these 'have not' ethnic groups to search for their 'own' sources of wealth and, in the case of UNITA, power. Thus, since the late 1980s, UNITA has acquired considerable wealth by mining Angola's vast diamond deposits. UNITA hoped that this wealth could then be used to procure the military means to take over the state. Although this rebel group has failed in its attempts to overthrow the MPLA government, it has largely succeeded in severely curtailing the Angolan state's political and administrative space.

It can be argued, then, that two major consequences have emerged from the failure to share power and wealth. First, the state is regarded as illegitimate by a significant portion of the population that has no political voice within highly restrictive political and economic systems and consequently does not receive tangible benefits from it. Second, it legitimizes violence as a means to destroy these artificial, unfair and undemocratic constructs. These two factors have conspired to abort all attempts to create a political consensus upon which a viable state can be built.

On the basis of the argument presented above, this chapter suggests that contemporary analyses of the Angolan conflict which emphasize the ideological differences among the major politico-military forces, developed within the Cold War ideological confrontation, must be reassessed. The fundamental cause of the civil war in Angola resides in the division of power and wealth along ethnic lines. One ethnic group, in particular the Kimbundu, has benefited disproportionately from the *de facto* exclusion of all others from the centers of political and economic power. Thus, the civil war can be seen as an attempt by UNITA, a powerful force claiming to represent the largest ethnic group, the Ovimbundu, to redress the perceived unfairness of the system.

By focussing on the political economy of the conflict, this chapter also sheds some light on how the major politico-military forces, MPLA and UNITA, have used ethnic politics for different, yet equally destructive, purposes. For MPLA, informal ethnic networks kept it in power even after suffering two apparently crushing setbacks both internationally and domestically. Neither the collapse of the USSR, its main external ideological and military supporter, nor the implosion of the domestic economy outside the oil sector, significantly eroded its power base. But there are significant costs associated with keeping the MPLA ethnic network operational. To fulfill its function, this informal network must be perpetually greased with the vast oil revenues controlled unaccountably by the regime. This has fostered a culture of corruption.

UNITA, on the other hand, has succeeded in using ethnicity to rally and sustain popular support among the Ovimbundu. By highlighting the fact that the governing MPLA is dominated by Kimbundus, UNITA has consistently characterized failure of governance in conspiratorial terms. In other words, UNITA has attempted to portray MPLA misgovernance as a conscious effort by the Kimbundu to deny other groups the benefits of mineral and oil wealth. Thus, UNITA has been able to justify the use of military means to redress the inequitable distribution of power and wealth. This has fostered a culture of violence.

Given its central importance, therefore, the political economy of ethnicity provides an important optic for a clearer understanding of Angola's current situation. Equally important, it opens possibilities to contemplate and anticipate possible solutions. One of the central arguments in this chapter is that ethnicity is a formidable force especially when, as in Angola, it is manipulated to achieve political and economic goals. However, as will be suggested in the conclusion, this force does not have to be necessarily destructive; its power can be harnessed for more positive and constructive ends, including modern projects of state-building in Africa. Unless such new and more positive forms for managing ethnicity are found, governance in Africa will remain highly problematic. The 'conscious management of regime structures with a view to enhancing the legitimacy of the public realm', as Hyden (1992: 7) defines governance, cannot possibly be achieved in situations where, given their primordial allegiances, significant segments of the citizenry do not recognize the legitimacy of the state, let alone the regime.

Specifically, as will be suggested in the conclusion, a solution to the civil war and the crisis of governance in Angola will necessitate a new political architecture that takes into account ethnic differences and the need to undertake an equitable division of power and wealth within a decentralized, democratic state. This is a necessary first step in a long process to liberate society from the destructive brand of ethnic politics that, in Angola, has generated twin cultures of corruption and violence.

This chapter is divided into four parts. First, it reviews the practical and theoretical connections between and among ethnicity, nationalism and statehood. Second, it analyzes the impact of colonialism on ethnicity and highlights some of the negative consequences for Africa of the colonial imposition of artificial boundaries that ignored pre-colonial social and political formations that had developed along ethnic lines. Third, the elements discussed in the two previous sections are applied to the case of Angola where ethnic divisions have led to civil war. Fourth, I suggest that good governance is highly problematic in a divided society like Angola. The conclusion proposes that state reconstitution in Africa cannot be imposed from above, it must rest on sub-national formations.

Ethnicity, Nationalism, and Statehood

The notion of ethnicity is both amorphous and imbued with extreme doses of subjectivism. Kellas (1991: 5), for example, defines ethnicity as a 'state of being ethnic, or belonging to an ethnic group'. The literature on ethnicity is filled with such vague definitions of this concept. The vagueness that characterizes definitions of ethnicity points to the fact that it cannot be defined in isolation of other important social, political and economic factors. At a minimum, this phenomenon must be understood in conjunction with such crucial and related notions like ethnic groups and nations. More broadly, ethnicity acquires particular significance when ethnic groups use it as the instrument of choice to gain political and economic power. Schermerhorn (1970: 12) defines an ethnic group as:

> a collectivity within a larger society having real or putative common ancestry, memories of a shared historical past, and a cultural focus on one or more symbolic

elements defined as the epitome of their peoplehood. Examples of such symbolic elements are: kinship patterns, physical contiguity (as in localism or sectionalism), religious affiliation, language or dialect forms, tribal affiliation, nationality, phenotypical features, or any combination of these. A necessary accompaniment is some consciousness of kind among members of the group.

Unlike Schermerhorn, Hutchinson and Smith (1996: 6) de-emphasize the connection with the 'larger society'. They prefer the term *ethnie* or ethnic community to define:

a named human population with myths of common ancestry, shared historical memories, one or more elements of common culture, a link with a homeland and a sense of solidarity among at least some of its members.

Whether one adopts Schermerhorn's comprehensive definition or Hutchinson and Smith's more elegant version, it is hard to deny the importance of ethnicity in the contemporary post-bipolar international system where various ethnic groups, many masquerading as nations, claim the right to govern themselves as independent, sovereign entities. Indeed, much of the current instability in the international system can be attributed to these intra-state conflicts that arise precisely because many ethnic groups are claiming, prematurely, the status of nation-statehood.

Understandably, the international community is hesitant to recognize such claims because a nation is much more than a group of people with a sense of community derived from common bonds of history, culture and common ancestry. Nations, as Kellas (1991: 2) suggests, 'have "objective" characteristics which may include a territory, a language, a religion, or common descent (though not all of these are always present), and "subjective" characteristics, essentially a people's awareness of its nationality and affection for it'. However, in the current Westphalian system, nations matter little. Peoples conduct their international affairs through states, not nations. Therefore, for a people or nation to achieve international relevance, the attainment of statehood is a primary prerequisite. The problem for would-be states, however, is that the current international system is inherently conservative in the sense that it abhors, and therefore discourages, territorial mutations of its constituting units—the states. Furthermore, most states still uphold traditional notions of power that equate it primarily with landmass and population. Since power—acquisition, accumulation and use—is at the very center of a state's existence and survival, no state will voluntarily give up territory and population.

The current configuration of the international system has not prevented political leaders who, expressing the national will or pursuing their personal ambitions, have attempted to achieve domestic or international relevance for their nations. In most cases, this process involves politicizing ethnicity. For Rothschild (1981: 6), the politicization of ethnicity involves four elements, including:

> (1) to render people cognitively aware of the relevance of politics to the health of their ethnic cultural values and vice versa, (2) to stimulate their concern about this nexus, (3) to mobilize them into self-conscious ethnic groups, and (4) to direct their behavior toward activity in the political arena on the basis of this awareness, concern, and group consciousness.

As numerous contemporary examples in Africa and elsewhere illustrate, ethnicity, once politicized, becomes a powerful political force that may ultimately 'enhance, retard, or nullify the political integration of states, may legitimate or delegitimate their political systems, and stabilize or undermine their regimes and governments' (Rothschild, 1981: 6). However, as Gurr and Harf (1994: 118) suggest, the re-emergence of ethnicity as an important dimension in global, not simply African, politics 'may be the result of the alienation and frustration that accompany the decline of artificial states'. As the next section shows, the politicization of ethnicity in Africa has retarded and in some cases nullified political integration of states, delegitimized post-colonial African political systems and undermined most African regimes and governments.

Africa: Ethnicity and Colonialism

Attempts by European powers to graft the Westphalian system onto Africa have resulted in dismal failures. The evidence resides in the fact that, currently, only a handful of post-colonial African states can be considered viable. Most other African states continue struggling for domestic survival and international relevance. This pathetic condition was not entirely unpredictable especially given the role of ethnicity in pre-colonial society.

Pre-colonial Africa included hundreds of societies ranging from small bands of hunters and gatherers to large, agricultural-based communities with highly sophisticated and centralized political structures dominated by chiefs and kings. Most of these societies were held together by a strong sense of kinship and common territory. As Thompson (1989: 64-5) notes, despite their diverse forms of social, political and economic organization, pre-colonial Africa had several features in common. These included the fact that 'each society identified with a "homeland", a specific territory defined not in the legalistic sense of a modern state boundary, but in the equally forceful sense of a "common land" occupied since the beginning of the "people" themselves'. Even more important, as far as the problematique of ethnicity is concerned, Africans attached to each place 'an emotional and cultural significance that could only be regarded as sacred' (Thompson 1989: 65). This realm—the subjective domain of emotion, culture and spirituality—must have escaped colonial European perception. Or, what is worse, it fell victim to colonial ethnocentric expediency with devastating effects for post-colonial Africa.

The departing colonial powers bequeathed upon the leaders of 'independent' Africa a virtual ethnic time bomb. The boundaries of the new African states reflected colonial, not cultural or national divisions. The hastily arranged decolonization process, coupled with the personal ambitions of the would-be leaders of the new states, did not allow for a more sober assessment of the costs and benefits of undertaking the post-colonial state-building project guided by an essentially unaltered colonial blueprint. Thus, predictably, independence did not usher in a new era of freedom, peace and prosperity. Instead, irredentisms and secessions dominated the agenda of nearly all newly independent African states. Ironically, now nationalism took on a new meaning: it was no longer anti-colonial but anti-state. Its instrument of choice was no longer liberation war but inter-ethnic strife and sometimes genocide. Could this have been prevented? The answer is, unfortunately, no. The inherited boundaries are artificial lines on a map, not ethnic/national boundaries. From this perspective, the post-colonial states are in many respects just as artificial and illegitimate as the entities they replaced. In this situation, it is inevitable that political parties will develop along ethnic lines and 'liberation armies' will be formed to subvert/reconfigure the new states to take into account ethnic realities.

The latest evidence of an attempt to reconfigure an African state along ethnic lines comes from Namibia where a secessionist movement is demanding independence for the Caprivi strip! Before Namibia's current crisis several other African states—the Democratic Republic of the Congo (former Zaire), Chad, Ethiopia, Nigeria, and the Sudan—have experienced long civil wars involving separatists seeking to establish their own states.

The reason for these wars does not simply reside in the existence of numerous, often unfriendly, ethnic groups, tribes or nations. Civil wars in Africa, particularly of the secessionist type, reflect these new states' inability to develop an inclusive political system that takes into account the fact that the primary allegiances of African citizens are not always to states. Often, that allegiance is shared with the ethnic group, tribe or nation because the citizens' sense of self is intrinsically attached to such factors as kinship ties, race, language, locality, religion and tradition. This, as will be further developed in later portions of this chapter, has significant implications for governance. The African state lacks administrative and ideological capacity to govern and is, therefore, unable to manage, let alone reconcile, ethnic conflicts. Specifically, governance in Africa is still essentially a zero-sum proposition. Most African states have come under the control of one ethnic group, usually numerically dominant. The resources of the state and economy are then used for the benefit of that group, to the detriment of others. This causes resentment, particularly when other groups perceive themselves as holders of certain tangible attributes—like economic power, intellectual excellence, or a tradition of military prowess—that could be translated into political power. In such cases, when access to political power is denied, civil wars often result.

This should not come as a surprise especially in Africa where control of the state has become a vital political goal for ethnic groups, both dominant and subordinate, because it provides unobstructed access to jobs, scholarships, land, education, credit facilities and other highly coveted privileges. For dominant groups, control of the state ensures political supremacy and economic dominance. Subordinate groups seek control of the state to ensure that their social, cultural and economic interests are protected and their aspirations fulfilled. When the political arena does not accommodate ethnic groups as interest groups they become conflict groups with a mandate to insert the group's grievances, claims, anxieties and aspirations into the national agenda/debate by all means necessary, including war. In extreme cases of real or perceived exclusionary politics, ethnic groups will opt for their own state, even if small and insignificant on the world stage, to ensure political, economic, cultural and demographic survival. Alas, this conforms to the Westphalian logic that places the state, not the nation/tribe/ethnic group, at the center of world politics. In other words, in the current international system, the state is an indispensable vehicle for ethnic groups, particularly those which aspire to nation-statehood status, to realize their political aspirations both domestically and internationally. In practice, for post-colonial Africa as elsewhere in the world, the Westphalian logic often involves lethal zero-sum conflicts. Marginalized ethnic groups, in particular, often seek to develop a strong political, and occasionally military, apparatus not only to move closer to the centers of power and wealth within the state but often to destroy the state itself. The case of Angola highlights some of these issues. In this case, a political and military force claiming to represent the majority ethnic group can use the country's natural resources—especially diamonds—to finance its drive to overthrow the government and, ultimately, transform the state.

Angola: Ethnicity and (Mis)Governance

Angola's civil war has been caused by various factors. Undoubtedly, one of the most important is ethnicity. It must be pointed out from the outset that ethnic divisions in Angola pre-date colonialism. As in many other parts of Africa, the pre-colonial process of state formation was carried out mainly along ethnic lines. When Portuguese explorer Diogo Cao first arrived at the Kingdom of Kongo in the early fifteenth century he found a complex process of state formation underway. Specifically, what Cao found in what would become Angola was not one homogenous state but a large number of distinct ethnic groups varying considerably in size, economic development and political organization. Some were small 'tribes' while others constituted larger nations. For example, the kingdom of Kongo dominated the political landscape in the region. Ruled by a monarch, Kongo was divided into six provinces, five of which had their own subordinate rulers. The central province of Mpemba was governed by the king personally and contained the royal city of Mbanza Kongo. This city lay on a well-cultivated territory surrounded by many small villages. Its population was once estimated to be as many as 100,000 people. The surrounding provinces were Nsundi to the north, Mpangu to the northeast, Mbata to the southeast, Mbamba in the southwest, and Sonyo on the coast west of the capital (Birmingham, 1966: 2). The 'scramble for Africa' split this kingdom into three modern-day African states: the Republic of Congo (Brazzaville), the Democratic Republic of Congo (Kinshasa) and Angola.

There were other smaller powers south of Kongo, in present-day Angola, like the kingdoms of Ndongo (or Ngola) and Kasange, that achieved some prominence in the sixteenth century before succumbing to the destructive effects of the slave trade. Other important political entities included the Lunda empire which 'dominated the scene from afar during the eighteenth century' (Birmingham, 1966: ix), as well as the Bailundo and Benguela kingdoms.

The colonial presence added a significant layer of complexity to this process of interaction among Africans. Equally important, by forcibly including within their colonial possessions different ethnic groups with different histories and aspirations, colonialism set the stage for a very problematic process of state-building in Angola and elsewhere in Africa after independence. Alas, the main combatants in Angola's civil war claim to represent the major ethnic groups in the country—Bacongo, Mbundu and Ovimbundu—that once constituted distinct kingdoms: Kongo, Ndongo and Bailundo respectively.

Currently, the Bacongo represent about 15 percent of Angola's population and reside mainly in the northern provinces of Cabinda, Zaire and Uige. They have traditionally regarded Kinshasa, not Luanda, as their cultural, economic and political center. The Mbundu, representing about 25 percent of the population, occupy the areas around the capital city, Luanda, and east as far as the Cassange area of Malanje province. A distinct ethnic sub-group has developed within the larger Mbundu region. The impact of the colonial presence on the western part of the Mbundu domain, more specifically around Luanda, brought to the region individuals originating from all Angolan ethnic groups. Over time, they constituted a unique group—heavily influenced by the language and customs of the colonial power—which can accurately be described as *Luandas* (Redinha, 1965: 7). The Ovimbundu are, by far, the largest ethnic group. They represent 35 to 40 percent of Angola's population and dominate the areas with the highest population density in the country—the central plateau provinces of Huambo, Bie and Benguela.

This ethnic diversity has dominated politics and society in Angola since the first contact with Europeans. Unfortunately, it has consistently been a source of weakness, not strength. For example, the ethnically diffused nature of resistance against Portuguese encroachment and dominance facilitated the imposition of colonial rule. Although sporadic anti-colonial resistance took place during Portugal's presence in Angola, the various kingdoms and chiefdoms threatened by colonial domination were not able to create a united front. From this perspective, the disunity that characterized the anti-colonial movement after WWII and the inability to establish an inclusive political system after independence has long historical antecedents.

Unlike other colonial powers, Portugal did not participate in the European drive to de-colonize after WWII. Thus, an anti-colonial war was fought from 1961 until 1974. Three 'national liberation movements' participated in the struggle: MPLA, FNLA and UNITA. However, contrary to the experience of other former Portuguese colonies, the liberation movements in Angola never succeeded in creating a united front partly because they were unable or unwilling to overcome their ethnic differences.

MPLA was founded in 1956 to lead the struggle against colonialism. However, its appeal never reached much beyond the Kimbundu people living around the capital region from where most of MPLA leadership emerged. This movement also succeeded in attracting some *assimilados* ('assimilated' Angolans who had embraced the Portuguese language and way of life), *mulatos* (Angolans of mixed race), and even some members of the settler community.

FNLA was created in 1962 through the merger of several groups the main objective of which was the restoration of the ancient Kongo kingdom in northern Angola. Thus, FNLA's main constituency remained almost exclusively restricted to the Bakongo ethnic group. Attempts to expand this constituency to include elements from other ethnic groups consistently failed.

Similarly, the main rationale for creating UNITA in 1966 was primarily ethnic. The Ovimbundu believed that, as the major ethnic group in Angola, it was critical that they had their own 'liberation movement' to counterbalance the role and power of the movements representing other major ethnic groups. History has shown that the political project of these movements was not national but sub-national. In other words, beyond the rhetoric, they were primarily concerned with the aspirations of particular ethnic groups—Bacongo, Mbundu, Ovimbundu—not the creation of an inclusive Angolan state where ethnic diversity was celebrated.

Unsurprisingly, post-colonial politics in Angola quickly degenerated into ethnic conflict as Portugal attempted to implement a decolonization process based on a Western-type winner-take-all form of politics. However, even in a best-case scenario—involving an enlightened colonial power and visionary nationalist leadership—Angola's post-colonial state-building project was doomed for several important reasons. A closer look at the situation in Angola reveals several important facts. First, the major ethnic groups are not as homogeneous as they appear on the surface. Second, none of the nationalist movements represented the majority of the population. Finally, issues of class and race would have conspired against the new state even if the main ethnic groups shared a common political goal.

First, to speak of three major ethnic groups grossly over-generalizes a very complex picture of ethnicity in Angola. Furthermore, the so-called 'big three' ethnic groups include several sub-groups. This level of ethnic fragmentation has important implications for governance. Even if either UNITA or MPLA were finally to win the civil war and attempted to impose ethnic hegemony, it would not necessarily guarantee peace because the Ovimbundu-controlled UNITA is in turn controlled by the Bieno sub-group. The Bailundo and Uambo sub-groups, although numerically superior and traditionally more powerful politically, militarily and economically, have been overshadowed by Jonas Savimbi's sub-group. Similarly, in the absence of the threat posed by UNITA, the major divisions within the Mbundu ethnic group that dominates MPLA would come to the surface and might manifest themselves violently. In other words, the civil war in Angola is hiding potentially violent intra-group divisions.

A second factor that seriously undermined the post-colonial political project in Angola was the fact that no nationalist movement could ever truly claim to represent the majority of the population. Moreover, even the allegiance of their respective ethnic groups was never either absolute or spontaneous. In fact, all three major nationalist movements in Angola had to 'mobilize' the populations within their areas of operations.

Equally problematic, MPLA cannot claim to have achieved power in the transition period to independence in 1975 due to its popularity throughout Angola.

The departing colonial power simply regarded this movement as the lesser of the three evils. As mentioned previously, the bulk of MPLA's leadership was drawn from the Luandas. This group had several perceived advantages over the other ethnic groups due to its close contact with the Portuguese during the colonial period. As a mainly urban group, its members were fluent in Portuguese—the language of education, business and politics—which would be adopted as the official language of independent Angola. It also had well-established contacts with the outside world, often through family ties, as is the case with the *mulatos*. Therefore, the Luandas were expected to inherit the economic clout built by the settler community. In other words, colonial rule allowed the Luandas to attain a privileged position that could be translated into real political, economic and cultural power after independence. Both UNITA and FNLA resented, and were threatened by, this perceived unfair advantaged enjoyed by MPLA which, alas, materialized into a long stay in power after the end of colonial rule even in the face of armed opposition by both UNITA and FNLA.

In the aftermath of the colonial regime's collapse and as preparations were hastily made to devolve power to Angolans, the leadership of the nationalist movements used a variety of stratagems to capture the political power that was up for grabs. Thus, they used control of territory and population, roughly along ethnic lines, to bolster their claims of legitimacy vis-à-vis the departing colonial authorities. However, since ethnic support could not be taken for granted due to the lack of ethnic cohesion discussed above, it had to be 'mobilized' as in the war for independence. The main forms of mobilization were political rallies which often included extensive uses of local songs, dances and other forms of cultural expression to underline the ethnic connection between a given nationalist movement and the people. This was emphasized especially by UNITA and FNLA, the two mainly rural movements.

Initially, significant portions of the Ovimbundu and Bacongo responded to the ethnic appeals of UNITA and FNLA respectively because these ethnic groups perceived the two liberation movements as instruments that would eventually restore their lost power, wealth and honor. Later, as the transition to independence quickly and predictably descended into civil war, mobilization became increasingly more coercive. Within their respective ethnic zones of influence, the nationalist movements demanded complete, unquestioning allegiance from the populations. Support for a rival movement, even if only alleged, became the ultimate political crime, often resulting in death. Although UNITA claimed to represent the largest segment of the population and could, arguably, win the planned pre-independence elections, the departing colonial administration, in a desperate attempt to salvage the transition process that was being undermined by the civil war, handed over power to MPLA. Why? Was ethnicity a determining factor? The answer is, clearly, yes. The departing colonial administration could not hand over power to either UNITA or FNLA because these groups' claims of legitimacy were based on their purported representation of specific ethnic groups: the Ovimbundu and the Bacongo. MPLA, on the other hand, was perceived to represent the urban segment of the population that could transcend ethnicity.

Beyond ethnicity, another set of explosive issues—class and race— seriously compromised Angola's hopes to establish a stable, peaceful society after independence. On the issue of class, UNITA regards the Kimbundu as the dominant group, even though the group is numerically smaller than the Ovimbundu. The dominant group, to use Schermerhon's (1970: 12) definition, refers to 'that collectivity within a society which has preeminent authority to function both as guardians and sustainers of the controlling value system, and as prime allocators of rewards in society'. Conversely, UNITA sees itself as the legitimate representative of the majority of the population—the Ovimbundu—that has been relegated to a subordinate class status. This marginalization was accomplished initially through external intervention by Russians and Cubans who helped place and keep the dominant group in power. More recently, the Ovimbundu have been kept out of power by manipulation of the political and economic resources by the dominant group.

Issues of class in Angola are made even more complex when juxtaposed with race. The Kimbundu happen to share geographic and political space with two other groups that compete for dominance. The first group comprises descendants of Angolan indentured laborers who worked in Portuguese plantations in the island of Sao Tomé. Insistent rumors allege that Angolan president Jose Eduardo dos Santos was born in Sao Tomé, not in Angola. Likewise, the most influential members of his inner circle were born, or are descendants of people who were born, in Sao Tomé. Their ethnic ties with the Kimbundu population are, at best, frail. Thus, ironically, their legitimacy is questioned even by the people from which MPLA draws most of its support. It has become clear that dos Santos' rule is tolerated only because the alternative, Savimbi, is unthinkable for many Kimbundu. The second group that competes for political, economic and intellectual dominance includes mixed-race Angolans. Members of this group occupy key positions in the ruling party, security apparatus—especially the army—and, until recently, both the public and the secret police. Members of this group are also disproportionately represented in the private sector both as owners of recently privatized enterprises and as employees of foreign corporations operating in Angola.

Given the analysis presented above, therefore, the war in Angola is more than a straightforward ethnic conflict pitting the Mbundu against the Ovimbundu. It also involves important political economy dimensions. Specifically, the war is partly sustained by the political ambitions and financial greed of two elites. The governing elite includes a minority racial group that controls both the economy and the army, and the descendants of returning Angolan indentured laborers from Sao Tomé. This elite controls substantial oil revenues accrued from the exploration of Angola's vast offshore reserves. The President directly controls the offshore bank accounts where such revenues are deposited. Most influential members of the governing elite also own private diamond concessions in the mining areas not controlled by UNITA. The latter's leadership has also taken to plundering Angola's vast diamond deposits. It is estimated that, between 1992 and 1998, UNITA has sold $3.72 billion worth of diamond in international markets. In such circumstances, where the rapacity of elites dominates, good governance is highly improbable.

The Improbability of Governance in a Divided Society

The preoccupation with good governance in Africa is not new. Two decades ago, after the 'lost decade' of the 1970s, the International Financial Institutions (IFIs) diagnosed Africa's affliction as a 'crisis of governance' reflected in the extensive personalization of power, the denial of fundamental rights and freedoms, widespread corruption, and the prevalence of non-elected and unaccountable governments (World Bank, 1989: 60). The recommended prescription emphasized 'political renewal' premised in 'a systematic effort to build a pluralistic institutional structure, a determination to respect the rule of law, and a vigorous protection of the freedom of the press and human rights' (World Bank, 1989: 60-61). Even critics of adjustment policies in Africa accepted, if reluctantly, the Bank's diagnosis and prescriptions. For example, in its *African Alternative Framework*, the United Nations Economic Commission for Africa (ECA) suggested that governance was the key to fundamental change in Africa. For ECA (1989: 60-61), governance involved the 'democratization of the decision-making process at national, local and grassroots levels so as to generate the necessary consensus and people's support'. In this sense, governance serves two important purposes. First, it pushes African rulers to become more accountable to the populations over which they claim authority. Second, it can 'facilitate a relationship of bargaining through which the interests of the state and those in society can be adjusted to each other so that the exercise of state power might be regarded as legitimate by those subject to it' (Apter and Rosberg, 1994: 91). This, for Hyden (1992: 10), results in a situation 'where politics is a positive-sum game; where reciprocal behavior and legitimate relations of power between governors and governed prevail; and where everybody is a winner not only in the short run but also in the long run'.

From a practical perspective, good governance involves political and bureaucratic accountability, freedom of association and participation, freedom of information and expression, and a sound autonomous judicial system. It goes without saying that the effectiveness of a system of governance depends largely on how it is perceived. Those governments that acquire authority or legitimate power to govern through a credible electoral process have a better chance of becoming real agents of change. Similarly, good governance requires arrangements to make bureaucrats more accountable through regular monitoring of public agencies and officials. This is essential to achieve transparency in bureaucracies, particularly as far as financial management is concerned. Even more important, political and bureaucratic accountability cannot become a reality until citizens acquire the freedom to establish religious groups, professional associations, women's groups, and other private voluntary organizations to pursue political, social, or economic objectives under the protection of an objective, efficient, reliable and autonomous judicial system.

This ideal scenario depicted could not be farther from reality in Angola. There, due to civil war and kleptocratic mismanagement, a decaying state is no longer able to carry out the vital functions associated with governance, including forms of domination, the nature of surplus extraction, and the patterns of resource allocation. Most of these functions are now formulated and carried out by powerful private agents who are not accountable to the public.

The inability to establish a regime of good governance in Angola can be understood by analyzing the ways in which the post-colonial state was erected, particularly in terms of the exercise of state power. Only then can policy failures and the consequent loss of state legitimacy and authority be explained.

Although Angola achieved independence in extremely difficult conditions, the MPLA succeeded in gaining control of the government and was able to extend and consolidate its administration throughout the country with the help of Cuban troops and Russian advisers. Angolans expected, in retrospect unrealistically, that the winning side would introduce a system of good governance and impose measures to establish a viable political order which, in turn, could promote national unity and ethnic harmony, social and regional equality, and economic development. Instead, an intolerant, inflexible political order was created based on Marxism-Leninism.

After inflicting severe political and military setbacks to UNITA and FNLA in the initial stages of the civil war, the MPLA installed a one-party regime that attempted either to co-opt or destroy most elements of civil society. Political participation could only take place when mobilized and organized by the state to serve its own specific purposes. The governing party mandated revolutionary hostility to all forms of traditional authority and the aspirant petty bourgeoisie for alleged collaboration with the colonial regime. Supposedly mass organizations were created to mobilize workers, women, students, artists, painters, writers, peasants, even children.

Lost in the Marxist-Leninist ideological fog was the basic contractual relationship between state and citizen. Instead, the latter became mainly a potentially valuable element to be used in furthering the goals of an oppressive state. This resulted in ethnic favoritism and divisions, corruption and injustices, all within a broader context of economic decline. In combination, these factors constituted an immense reservoir of hatred that sustained an already devastating civil war. With most avenues for political participation closed by the state, and in the presence of highly centralized, yet dysfunctional and decaying political and economic structures, Angolan citizens became consumed almost exclusively by concerns affecting their immediate survival; i.e., the search for food, shelter and security. Meanwhile, as mentioned, the development of a powerful and usurping state elite helped to create an ever-widening gap between state and citizen.

This gulf between the state and civil society manifests itself in various domestic conflicts involving class, race and ethnicity within an overall context of poor governance and economic decay. Ironically, in the war against colonial domination and during its first years in power, the governing MPLA proclaimed itself to be a 'movement of the masses'. Gradually, however, an elite—composed predominantly of *mulatos* and descendants from returning indentured laborers from the former Portuguese island of Sao Tomé—used their superior education, political skills and economic power to take control of the party from the Kimbudu elite. But, instead of maintaining the existing strong ties with workers and peasants, the governing elites grew increasingly detached from the common citizen and used the repressive means of the state to preserve their privileged status.

From the ordinary citizen's point of view, the elite's grip on state power has assumed hegemonic proportions and represents a throwback to colonial times when power, prestige and privilege were closely associated with class and race. Given their pivotal position, members of the Angolan ruling elite have enormous resources of patronage. These resources have been put to use to create extensive and intricate patron/client networks. It is within these networks that most political deals are made and significant economic transactions take place. Such networks are an indispensable base to hold political office or seek public employment. Unsurprisingly, the networks of patron/client relationships have been used by the ruling elites for political control and financial aggrandizement. In the process, however, they engendered high levels of corruption and have eroded public trust in government.

Since, for the vast majority of Angolans, survival meant operating in competition with a coercive and predatory state, most citizens opted for ingression into the informal spheres outside the reach of the state. This seriously hampered the development of civil society. Predictably, Angola's brand of arbitrary governance is unsustainable. Ironically, as the state's survival is threatened by the weight of war and economic decline, it cannot count on the resourcefulness of the civil society because it has been marginalized, co-opted, or battered into submission. The situation is equally cruel for citizens living within territories controlled by UNITA.

Throughout the years of insurgency, UNITA did not demonstrate that it was better equipped to facilitate the development of a healthy civil society than MPLA. After losing its power struggle with MPLA in 1975-76, UNITA returned to the countryside and waged a devastating guerrilla war with the help of South Africa and the United States. By the time the Bicesse Peace Accord for Angola was signed in May 1991, UNITA controlled most of the southeastern portion of Angola where it installed a rival administration.

Political participation in the areas controlled by UNITA was even more restricted than in government-held zones. Several reasons account for this situation. Although UNITA portrayed itself as a democratic organization, its political orientation and practice are clearly Maoist. As such, UNITA created very centralized structures both at the political as well as at the military levels. In fact, military structures dominated the organization in the sense that few civilians were allowed to hold leadership positions. All members of UNITA's decision-making bodies—the Politburo and its Political Commission—have a military rank. The merging of military and political positions and functions gave UNITA a particularly rigid and disciplinarian character. In other words, UNITA was transformed into a powerful army under the facade of being a political party. This mutation had significant and negative consequences for democratization, or failure thereof, in the early 1990s.

Since achieving independence in 1975, Angola was unshackled only briefly during the period of political and economic liberalization leading to the signing of the Bicesse Peace Accords in 1991 and up to the resumption of the civil war after the elections of September 1992. However, Angola's version of *glasnost* and *perestroika* revealed important paradoxes in state-society relations that reflected the magnitude of this country's many problems. The would-be totalitarian regime had created both dissent and dependency. The dissent, which lay mostly dormant throughout the repressive years, served as the catalyst for the mushrooming of all types of organizations after the legal framework of the one-party state was abandoned. Paradoxically, however, most of these organizations continued to depend on the state or international organizations for resources. Thus, political parties, churches, cultural groups, women's organizations, and so on, have proliferated not so much as a counterweight to the state but mainly to benefit from it in terms of financial assistance and all the other benefits traditionally allotted to the state elites.

As mentioned before, during the single party regime, the MPLA relied on 'mass organizations' it created—for workers, youth, women and children—to ensure participation of officially sanctioned groups while making the formation of autonomous organizations illegal. Mass organizations were expected to provide unconditional support for the MPLA's broad political, economic and social programs. However, since the introduction of economic reforms in the late 1980s and political liberalization initiatives in the early 1990s—allowing the emergence of truly autonomous organized groups—the MPLA has tried to influence key groups in society by binding them into organizations that have become dependent on state patronage. Thus, the regime can continue to influence society—this time with the additional 'civil' label—by extending its organization, coordination and supervision of as much of the population as possible. In addition, it can also stave off mass opposition and ensure its continuing survival.

It has now become clear that in Angola the emergence of organized groups commonly associated with civil society and their dependent relationship with the state constitutes an integral part of a well-designed strategy by the regime to keep itself in power. The MPLA had not planned to liberalize the regime and institute a genuine democratization process that would eventually make the party-state genuinely accountable to common citizens. In fact, the reverse is closer to reality. The liberalization measures introduced at the time were cleverly manipulated to create enough 'maneuvering space'—especially in terms of providing sufficient economic/financial gains—to ensure that the party would remain in power.

The structures arising under this reordering may not amount to a civil society, but instead resemble 'state corporatism'. Their continued existence, not to mention degree of influence and well being, depend on the whims of the state, particularly the party controlling it. By restricting the space of civil society the MPLA is thus preventing alternatives from emerging and impeding further democratization. Furthermore, the party and the state—ruling over hybrid economic structures combined with centralized power—can remain unaccountable.

Conclusion

There is no end in sight for the civil war in Angola. In fact, a new round of fighting is underway, triggered by the government's military occupation of UNITA's two main strongholds—Bailundo and Andulo—in October 1999 and the rebels' return to more traditional guerrilla warfare. Clearly, the war that started due to the main ethnic groups' inability to establish a common platform upon which to build the post-colonial state has become a convenient cover for the state's gross failures in governance. Specifically, it conveniently shields the ruling elite from popular accountability while enabling it to plunder the state's resources. Thus, an indefinite continuation of the war is the best scenario for the governing elite. Paradoxically, it also facilitates UNITA's continuing plunder of Angola's diamond wealth. Eventually, however, more peaceful ways must be found to rebuild the state.

Since the state in Angola has historically been regarded as artificial and illegitimate, the project to rebuild the state will necessarily rest on sub-national formations. The rules of the political game cannot be imposed from above by the state. They must be devised and implemented from below. Specifically, for Angola, this would entail a radical devolution of power to the local level where people find innovative and peaceful ways to govern themselves. In fact, many ethnic groups in Angola had already developed forms of accountable, transparent, responsible governance.

Angola, like all other former colonies, cannot return to pre-colonial forms of governance. It must adapt according to the requirements of the modern state. However, this does not necessarily entail a rejection of ethnicity. Being an Angolan and an Ovimbundu must not be mutually exclusive. But this goal will only be realized when the Ovimbundu and other ethnic groups perceive the state to be an expression of their aspirations, translated as access to power and wealth. In the absence of an equitable division of power and wealth within a democratic system, Angola's future will remain grim.

12 Ethnicities in Crises of Governance in Africa: The Case of Uganda in the Great Lakes Region

PAMELA MBABAZI

Introduction

Human development and security in the Great Lakes Region (GLR) of Africa have been threatened in the recent past by civil strife. The democratization process in Africa has again brought to the fore the phenomenon of ethnicity and, even in Uganda where the democratization process has been attempted along 'innovative lines', human development may ultimately be threatened by ethnicity as a political force. Therefore, this chapter aims to examine the nature of the ethnic crisis in the GLR and in particular its effect on governance in Uganda, noting that changes in the global system have had diverse impacts on the country's political, economic and social relations.

The ethnic crisis in Uganda, as elsewhere on the continent, is linked to colonial intervention and the peculiar nature of state formation. As a result largely of colonial legacies, one group controls government offices, security organizations and dominates vital sectors of the economy. This state of affairs is considered unacceptable by those excluded and this has led to conflicts, often along ethnic lines. These ethnic rivalries have affected governance—that is, the links among the state, civil society and the economy—in most countries in Africa. Recently, issues of globalization involving transnational economic, technological, ideological and cultural exchanges have opened up the ethnic question to new thinking.

The chapter is divided into four parts. The first part examines alternative perspectives on ethnicity, globalization and democratization. The second part locates Uganda in the international context historically in order to give a background on how recent changes in the global economy have affected its government structures and social system. The third part briefly locates

Uganda within regional dynamics. The fourth part examines the impact of structural adjustment policies (SAPs) as a feature of economic globalization, and argues that the key elements of liberalization and privatization have enhanced ethnic divisions. This section also deals with the impact of globalization on state reform/policy, particularly the destruction of the welfare state, and looks at the impacts on civil society with regard to democratization, pluralism and the re-emergence of ethnic rivalry. The chapter concludes by pointing out the limited prospects for good governance/democratization in the face of continued ethnic tension in the state, economy and civil society in the wider context of globalization. Finally, some suggestions are made on how the ethnic question could possibly be addressed.

Ethnicity, Governance and Globalization: Towards a Theoretical Framework

Ethnicity

Ethnicity is a complex phenomenon. And, ethnic rivalry poses a challenge to global peace and stability and retards human development/security. According to Okwudiba Nnoli (1989: 2), ethnicity is characterized by ethnocentrism, common consciousness and identity exclusiveness. It can alter its form, place and role in the life of a society. Nnoli argues that it is not possible fully to understand the ethnic phenomenon in Africa without an adequate understanding of its historical origin and class character. A number of explanations—economic, cultural, political and historical—have been given for the causes of global ethnic tensions and struggles.

The economic argument asserts that ethnic conflicts are essentially struggles over material resources (Horowitz, 1985). The inferior-superior relations of the Hutu/Tutsi in Burundi and Rwanda, for example, are a clear manifestation of conflicts that have erupted because of leaders following ethnic lines to canvass support. In Uganda also, there is growing discontent due to a perception that those that live in the west of the country compete more favorably in terms of land ownership, business opportunities, jobs, incomes, political offices, access to education, etc., because the President hails from the west. This arguably explains the persistent war in the north of the country, an area that has registered limited progress and development since the current National Resistance Movement (NRM) government came to power.

Timothy Shaw (1986: 591) argues that ethnicity was advanced in Africa by the politics of nationalism which, in effect, involved attempts to integrate diverse nations into one anti-colonial movement. He notes that ethnicity is continuously redefined as the context changes. In the 1960s, ethnicity was a political demand with economic potential because there were resources to dispute and distribute. However, Shaw asserts that in the 1980s, ethnicity was redefined as an ethnic response with political implications and the issue became economic sustainment. In other words, the politics of ethnicity were succeeded by practical economics. To date, with the pressures of globalization and 'good' governance, the trend seems to be continuing and the ethnic problem is becoming even more aggravated, with many ethnic conflicts emerging as a result of unequal distribution of resources.

Although African leaders have avowed the unity of their countries within the borders inherited from the colonial powers, the realities of ethnic diversities continue to mask and prevent any efforts toward achieving this goal. The disintegration of the 'Great Lakes Region' is a clear manifestation of this. According to Francis Deng (1991: 1), the genesis of these ethnicity crises is found in the colonial intervention and peculiar nature of state formation in Africa. The modern nation-state in the African context is an alien concept, which was imported and transplanted by the colonial powers. Groups were torn apart and others brought together by the colonial demarcation of state and, arguably, this has resulted in the creation of pluralistic communities, with many disparities.

While the struggle for independence was initially seen as a collective challenge that unified all the national forces, the critical question of distribution surfaced as an acutely divisive issue following independence. Deng (1991: 1) argues that the divisive issues have a regional dimension; that the demand for justice, equity and fair play generated tensions and even violent confrontations within and between countries as problems spilled over the borders of such countries as Rwanda, Burundi, Sudan, Democratic Republic of Congo (DRC), Eritrea, Liberia and Mozambique. All these conflicts have been chronic, deep-rooted and difficult to resolve either militarily or peacefully.

A continuing challenge for African states, non-state actors and regions, therefore, remains that of addressing the problems of diversities and inequalities between different ethnic groups and reconciling the principle of the preservation of colonial borders with the right of self-determination for sub-national groups. The challenge is now much greater within the contexts of globalization and pressures for good governance.

Globalization, Democratization and Governance

Globalization has been conceptualized variously by different scholars, but few have described the phenomenon from the perspective of developing countries. One exception is Rajni Kothari (1997) who defines globalization as a phenomenon of increasing colonial interdependence, of technological advances that diminish space and time, of cultural homogenization, and of emerging global, social and political identities. The underlying assumption here is that the nation-state is an outmoded institution, which tends to be in the way of world markets and borderless transnational corporations. At best, it is little more than a low-cost provider of infrastructure and public goods for global business.

Two main conclusions can be drawn from these conceptions: first, the traditional conception of the role of the nation-state is obsolete in the current process of globalization; and second, the state can only act in the interest of globalization as opposed to its own interests or the interests of its citizens.

The other major theoretical issue in the globalization debate is democratization and the related issues of governance and civil society. Good governance is now seen as a key to reconstruction in Africa, including Uganda. Democratic governance requires a system that guarantees citizens the right to .change bad governments and, on the part of governments, the responsibility to enforce law, provide essential services and raise revenue (Brett, 1997a: 215). The ability of citizens to participate in matters of governance largely depends on an open, autonomous and competitive political process, which allows citizens to organize and challenge existing regimes.

For democracy and good governance to be achieved, Brett (1997a: 214) argues that rulers must respect the right of people to pass judgement on their performance, respect the law, refuse corrupt payments and meet the obligations vested in their office. He further argues that citizens must obey the law, respect property rights, recognize the obligation to pay taxes, exercise only those rights which they are prepared to recognize in others, and sacrifice personal to social interests where this is necessary. In other words, a modern state should constitute a guarantee of political participation without prejudicing political order.

To understand clearly the nature of ethnic crisis and the prospects for governance in the GLR, a closer look at Uganda both in the international and regional contexts will help to bring the issue of ethnicity into clear focus and contextualize the impacts of globalization.

Uganda in the International Historical Context

Colonial Uganda

The colonial government encouraged ethnic divisions through indirect rule. Using both administrative and economic measures, groups in society were pitted against one another. In demarcating districts, for example, great care was taken to ensure that as much as possible one ethnic unit was constituted into a district.

Colonial authorities encouraged the tribal chiefs to rule their ethnic units by giving these chiefs special privileges and the latter's loyalty was 'bought' by offering them land measured in square miles (mailo-land). In Ankole, where there was a basic division in society between agriculturalists (Bairu) and pastoralists (Bahima), as in neighboring Rwanda and Burundi, all pastoralists were exempted from taking part in public labor known as *oruharo* (communal work). This involved activities like building roads, fighting animal pests and digging valley dams, among others. The Bahima were exempted from such work because they belonged to the same ethnic group as the King, a Muhima. Such activities were instead earmarked for the Bairu who were the traditional cultivators.[1]

Ankole was not unique. In Buganda too, the practice of giving the Royal family (Balangira) special place and preferential treatment as opposed to the peasant class (Bakopi), created antagonism in the local setting of the Buganda Kingdom. And, in the rest of Uganda, tribes, in particular 'non-Bantu' speaking ethnic groups of the north, were regarded as foreigners in Uganda as opposed to the 'Bantu' ethnic groups from southwestern, central and eastern Uganda. This gap between the Bantu and the non-Bantu groups created ethnic tensions in the governance of Uganda over the years and is still evident as the root cause of the Lord's Resistance Army (LRA) rebellion in the north under Joseph Kony and the previous 'Lakwena' crisis. Both rebellions/insurgencies reflect the resistance of northerners to the domination of the country by the Bantu ethnic group of western Uganda.[2]

Evidently, the origins of ethnicity as a negative or divisive political force can be located in the colonial politics. It is very obvious that British colonialism, through indirect rule undoubtedly bred much hatred and antagonism and encouraged and aggravated negative ethnic wrangles among the population, which came to be manifested in all spheres of life in Uganda. However, the single most important factor in entrenching ethnicity in the body politic of Uganda was the arbitrarily-set colonial boundaries. They brought, within the fold of one country, peoples at different levels of social development and they split nationalities into or among several countries. As

Mamdani (1983: 10) states, 'Every institution touched by the hand of the colonial state was given a pronounced regional or nationality character. It became a truism that a soldier must be a northerner, a civil servant a southerner and a merchant an Asian.' Through divide and rule tactics, one region was pitted against another and one nationality (tribe) against another.

Due to the institutionalization of ethnicity, the initial resistance to colonialism in Uganda was fragmented along ethnic lines. Apart from the trade unions and cooperatives, the associations that emerged were ethnically oriented. The political parties that were to come on stage later also sprang up along religious lines with ethnic tendencies. These included the Democratic Party (DP) under the banner of Catholicism and comprised largely of Baganda, and the Uganda People's Congress (UPC) under the banner of Protestantism and comprised mainly of northerners and westerners. Kabaka Yekka, on the other hand, was openly sectarian and monarchist. At the time of independence, therefore, a clearly focussed and vibrant civil society in Uganda was almost non-existent. Ethnicity was advanced by the politics of nationalism, and this shortcoming can be seen as the basis of ethnic and anti-democratic practices in the post-colonial period.

Post-Independence Uganda

Events in Uganda after independence moved well within the parameters established by the bilateral domination of the British in the economy. In addition, the World Bank was invited into Uganda in 1962, the year of independence and this meant that all policies and plans that were designed right from independence would comply with foreign interests. On the recommendation and support of the World Bank, for instance, output in the commodity-producing sectors was increased so as to boost the export of raw materials. In addition, the Ugandan government was urged to open its doors to private foreign investment and to rely on foreign aid to finance development (Mamdani, 1983: 23). Thus, Britain and the West continued to influence the affairs of Uganda, and the 'independent' government had very little room for maneuver.

The crisis in governance that was to arise later in Buganda, for example, was inevitable. It resulted in the abolition of kingdoms and the running into exile of Kabaka Mutesa II, which in turn resulted in even more ethnic tensions.[3] It should be emphasized here that ethnic brotherhood and loyalty have influenced the outcome of successive governments in Uganda since independence with different ethnic groups supporting different regimes. Buganda's claim to a special status in post-colonial Uganda, for example, was based on a single ethnic group's competition against other groups and this led to the overthrow of the Kabaka (King) of Buganda in 1966. The Idi Amin coup in 1971 complicated the situation even more. Foreigners were expelled, foreign enterprises nationalized, and the 'militarization' of the state—coupled with the repressive character of the regime—led to the disintegration of Ugandan society, eventually resulting in the regime's downfall in 1979. A rapid succession of short-lived governments followed and the Obote II government did not bring about much change.[4]

During the Obote I and II regimes, ethnic tendencies were observed in the national army and in the demarcation of political constituencies. This has continued to be the practice with districts today and, similarly, with parliamentary election constituencies. The church in Uganda, too, appears to be riddled with ethnic tendencies especially in the election of bishops. Membership in a specific ethnic group is a necessary condition to be elected as a bishop for a particular diocese. For a long time now, the demand has been for a bishop who is a 'son of the soil'; that is, a person from the local area. There has also been pressure for the division of dioceses into smaller units representing homogeneous ethnic units. The diocese of South Rwenzori, for example, was created as a result of the long-standing antagonism between the Bakonzo people and the Batooro, in which the ethnic factor was an important issue (Kambere, 1995: 70).

All this goes to show how deeply enshrined is the issue of ethnicity in Uganda's body-politic—ethnicity can be found within all aspects of governance and religion. We shall now take a closer look at the situation since the National Resistance Movement (NRM) government of President Yoweri Museveni came to power.

The Coming of the NRM Government

The NRM government came to power in 1986 after a five-year guerrilla war with the ultimate objective of creating a broad-based government that would embrace all ethnicities and political parties. The major plank of Museveni's political program has been to remove tribalism/ethnicity and religious sectarianism from the political agenda of Uganda. One cannot discount the enormous success that the NRM government has had in achieving this. From the beginning, all tribes and divisions of Uganda were embraced and an attempt was made to accommodate them all in the Cabinet. During the mid-1980s, the Museveni government had one of the largest Cabinets on the continent at the time. This was a move towards appeasing every Ugandan ethnic group by bringing each of them into the new Ugandan government. However, due to World Bank prescriptions (to reduce government expenditures), the Cabinet had to be trimmed and the implication was obvious. Those groups—ethnic and religious—that retained more people in Cabinet were looked on as being favored by the government and once again tribal and ethnic questions re-emerged.

With regard to religion, it is interesting to note that in the presidential elections of May 1996, although candidates could not stand on a political party ticket, no one could disguise the fact that the three contenders were a Protestant (Museveni), a Catholic (Ssemwogerere), and a Muslim (Mayanja). Arguably, going by Uganda's history, the Protestant candidate had to win since religion has always been a determining factor in Uganda's politics and Protestants are a majority.[5]

Today, the NRM government is being accused of nepotism and corruption. Two ministers have so far been censored in Parliament on accusations of influence peddling and corruption. Furthermore, it is alleged that people from western Uganda make up the biggest percentage of employees in the so-called 'juicy' state institutions. This antagonism was confirmed by *The New Vision*[6] newspaper headline of 30 July 1999, which stated, 'West Leads in Top Jobs: imbalance in lucrative parastatals angers MPs'. The article reported that according to the figures presented by the Minister of Ethics and Integrity, 'the west has 33% of the jobs in the institutions. The central region follows with 30%, eastern, 26% and northern region lags far behind with a mere 12%.' It is important to note here that the regional distribution of population in Uganda is fairly even. It is therefore not surprising that northerners feel sidelined especially with the slow pace of development evident in the northern part of the country, which may well explain the persistent civil war there. As an illustration, when expressions from President Museveni's language (Runyankore) are used in the central part of the country where the capital city, Kampala, is situated, Runyankore speakers are ridiculed by the non-westerners, particularly the northerners who feel they are ethnically marginalized and politically cheated. Even the word '*agandi*', a Runyankore expression of 'how are you?' has become equated with Banyankore overshadowing or taking the upper hand of government in Uganda. '*Agandi*' therefore is used by the non-westerners ironically to express their grievances for being ethnically deprived of political governance of the country. The ethnic group of Banyankore is resented by the non-westerners and this has resulted in conflict as evidenced by the persistence of the Lord's Resistance Army (LRA) rebellion in northern Uganda. This follows on the trail of the Holy Spirit Movement of Alice Lakwena in 1986, which was an ethnic faction of opposition also from the north.[7]

It is important now to take a look at Uganda in the regional context and illustrate how Uganda is similar to other countries in the region with regard to ethnic crises.

Regional Dynamics and Ethnicity

The other major countries in the region with conflicts relating to issues of ethnicity include Sudan, DRC, Rwanda and Burundi. In the case of the Sudan, its current civil war stands out as one of a kind in Africa. It differs from others in the region in that it combines elements of culture and religion, both of which determine the identity of a people and a nation (Deng, 1991: 4). The questions have always been whether the country is Arab, African, Afro-Arab or Arab-African, and whether it is to be considered Islamic and governed by *sharia*, or whether it has constitutional guarantees for religious freedom and equality. Historically, Arabization and Islamization in the north of the Sudan, were brought about through stratifying and discriminating processes that favored the Arabs, their religion and their culture over that of the Africans and this has created a lot of friction up to today.

Despite the difference between the countries, it is interesting to note that the manner in which southern Sudan has been marginalized by the north is very similar to the way in which northern Uganda (which borders the region) has been marginalized in Uganda. In both cases, the aggrieved parties have tried to win sympathy from across the borders (Sudanese People's Liberation Army (SPLA) with NRM and Lord's Resistance Army (LRA) with the Khartoum government), thus making the conflicts spill over the borders and become regional/international. Today, the Khartoum government offers support to the LRA rebels fighting in northern Uganda while the NRM government offers support to the SPLA which is fighting for autonomy in southern Sudan.

In DRC too, Uganda's relations are quite similar to the case of Sudan. The DRC has also harbored and supported Uganda's rebel groups over the years and consequently Uganda has come out in full support of DRC rebels who are also fighting for a share of power along ethnic lines. However, the explanation given by the Ugandan government to date is that Uganda's presence in the DRC is solely to fight the Ugandan rebels that have previously had their bases there. Critics have nonetheless argued that the presence of external armies in the DRC is largely linked to the struggle for the abundant mineral resources in the country.

In the case of Rwanda, its problems arguably have much to do with the position of Uganda as its close neighbor. When the Rwandese first had conflicts in the late 1950s, many Tutsis ran to Uganda as refugees. These exiled Rwandese eventually came to be associated with Museveni's guerrilla war of the early 1980s because many refugees were recruited by the NRA.[8] This resulted in the Obote II government persecuting the Rwandese, but the more they were persecuted the more they joined Museveni's guerrilla movement. Besides, these refugees were never accepted by the indigenous people in Uganda and could therefore not be assimilated. They were always seen as foreigners and never as part of the Ugandan society.

A political movement was eventually formed, mostly among the Rwandese exiles who had joined Museveni's guerrilla war, and this spearheaded the move towards returning to their motherland. When the demand by these exiles to return home was rejected by Rwandan President Habyarimana, they decided to use force and, hence, in 1993 there was an invasion of Rwanda by exiles from Uganda. To date, however, the relationship between the RPA government and the NRA government seems to be fragile, as evidenced by their recent clashes in the DRC, partly because of their support for rival factions, but perhaps more because of the struggle for mineral resources in the DRC.[9]

Having established the nature of ethnic crisis in Uganda and the region as a whole, we shall now examine closely the impact of globalization and try to ascertain whether or not the ethnic problem has been exacerbated.

Uganda and the Challenge of Neo-liberalism

Structural adjustment policies (SAPs), as features of the neo-liberal agenda which is integral to globalization, have made free markets central to the development process. And, the neo-liberal values of individualism and of open and competitive markets in association with minimal government have found expression in the privatization and liberalization of literally all sectors of Uganda's economy.

The political will portrayed by the Ugandan government in implementing the structural adjustment policies is undeniable. According to Brett (1997a: 219), the NRM leadership has among other things, incorporated opposition representatives into the regime, compromised its own ideological beliefs and maintained economic discipline, so as to ensure that these policies are implemented. The government, because of enjoying patronage and leverage from several donors and the West in general, has been able to manage and control the development change process in the country and mitigate the social effects of SAPs to manageable proportions.

Since coming to power, the NRM has implemented several economic reform programs. These are aimed at opening up the market and promoting growth and development of the country. In particular, foreign exchange was liberalized, marketing monopolies were reduced and state control was minimized. This has resulted in a tremendous growth of private economic activity arising largely from foreign investment, but a sizeable number of Ugandan entrepreneurs have also benefited. However, the ironic fact is that most of these so-called successful 'Ugandan' entrepreneurs are of Asian origin, which of course raises the question of race. In addition, most foreign investments in Uganda's economy are in secondary industries, with limited investment taking place in the agricultural sector, where the majority of Ugandans earn a living.

SAPs are the clearest economic indicators of the impact of globalization on Uganda. The major SAPs implemented in Uganda include liberalization of the economy, the return of expropriated properties, and the reduction and control of government spending. The focus here is on privatization of public enterprises, an exercise that has been implemented in the country, amidst lots of euphoria and controversy. There was no policy put in place to ensure that domestic entrepreneurs also benefited from the divested enterprises and, due mainly to lack of capital, most enterprises have ended up in the hands of foreigners, thus perpetuating the external dominance of Uganda. Unlike Zambia, for example, in Uganda there was no law put in place to limit foreign participation and ensure that distribution of ownership of divested enterprises is spread out among a broad section of the population. Instead, in Uganda's case, there are no restrictions and when public enterprises are privatized they are taken by the highest bidder regardless of whether the bidder is indigenous or foreign (Hansen and Twaddle, 1998).

Several parastatals that were formerly owned partly or wholly by the state have now been sold off to foreigners and a few indigenous entrepreneurs. For example, out of a total of 17 lease agreements signed between Uganda National Parks (UNP) and private companies to run tourist and hotel services formerly run by UNP, only five were leased to Ugandan entrepreneurs while the remaining 12 have gone to foreign companies. The accusations are that Westerners and cronies of the incumbent government are the ones who have supposedly benefited from this privatization exercise since they own most of these indigenous companies. An additional issue is the questionable practice of selling most of these enterprises for less than their full value when it is the people with state power who are purchasing or taking ownership of them. As indicated in *The Monitor Newspaper* (30 July 1999: 2), Lira MP and leader of the opposition faction UPC, Cecilia Ogwal, in reference to the corruption in government, alleged that 'As a matter of fact, enterprises formerly owned by all Ugandans are now owned by his [the President's] friends and henchmen'. This has no doubt tarnished the image of President Museveni and his current NRM government and accentuated the issue of ethnicity and inequality in the regions and population of Uganda. Worse still, the proceeds from the sale of public enterprises have not been earmarked for poverty alleviation programs. Instead, as Mamdani (1996) contends, the reality of privatization in Uganda is that it has exacerbated a new and more vicious round of corruption from which only foreign nationals and the state benefit. The privatization program is at present on hold as it resulted in the censure of two ministers following numerous accusations and counter-accusations of corruption. Since the state in Uganda is ethnically organized and particular ethnic groups dominate the central sectors of the economy and state, the privatization process has led to rising ethnic consciousness.

Arguably, a narrowly defined conception of privatization as advanced in the neo-liberal agenda may not end the problems of repression and corruption. In a critique of this agenda, Mamdani (1996) contends that the real object of privatization is not to eliminate the abuse of the state, but to dismantle the state that colonized people's resources, won and built through hard-fought nationalist struggles. Western powers know too well from their history that markets do not just exist in a vacuum, waiting to be freed; they have to be created and defended. Markets are created by either increasing the purchasing power of working people within a country or by conquering foreign markets. It is well known that while markets may be efficient they are not equitable. In the defence of the human conditions of living, only a strong state can ensure the reform of markets in the face of the private thirst for profits. Even Western capitalists know that they need a strong state to defend their markets, let alone win new ones, and also to defend the citizens from excesses of the market.

Therefore, for meaningful development to take place (i.e., to realize good governance and ensure human security), states must be reconstructed to become effective, not dismantled. As Mamdani (1996) argues, rather than pursuing 'market friendly' policies, the state should pursue policies that make the market 'people-friendly'. Government should provide a legal framework, maintain law and order, enforce contracts and pursue correct macro-economic policies. Government must encourage competition, intervene to prevent extreme interpersonal and spatial inequalities as well as promote the development of human resources as the UNDP's *Human Development Report 2000* and the World Bank's *World Development Report 1999/2000* both suggest.

The proponents of globalization and unbridled privatization and the dismantling of the state must confront the unfinished debate on the role of the state in development and the continuing relevance of the nation-state in the international economy. For the proper working of the market, my argument is that strong and, in many cases, expanded state intervention of the right kind is still necessary (but must be accountable as part of governance).

Uganda's experience shows that globalization has led to the dismantling of the state. SAPs have no doubt dramatically compromised the position of the Ugandan state as the bastion of national sovereignty and have revealed the state's weak and dependent character vis-à-vis foreign powers and institutions.

State, Civil Society and Ethnicity in Uganda: Globalization Pressures from Above and Below

> Long-term growth and national integration cannot depend on changes in macro-economic policy alone. The willingness of governments to accept and implement rational policies depends upon their accountability to their citizens and their capacity to protect their autonomy from pressure from vested interests (Brett, 1997b: 26).

Over the last decade, globalization has led to a number of changes in Uganda's state policy, market relations and civil society. Given global pressures, 'good governance' is now seen as the key to the reconstruction of Uganda and other Third World countries. How does all this affect the ethnicity question? Are the army and civil service, for example, still composed along ethnic lines? Has tribalism re-emerged? Is the opposition, taking on ethnic tendencies? These are some of the questions this section seeks to answer.

As earlier revealed, post-independence Uganda has been defined by political instability. Constitutions designed to guarantee open government and safeguard ethnic pluralism were overthrown by military dictatorships which promoted plunder and exploitation. Museveni's 'movement' revolution of 1986 clearly marked the entrance of new social forces into dominant positions within the state. These forces have tried to control the state by putting in place structures and activities that have largely been responsible for the opening up of the economy.

Policy reforms such as decentralization, privatization, rehabilitation of the country's infrastructure, agricultural promotion, and *entandikwa* (a credit extension scheme) have been undertaken by the present NRM government in an effort to promote growth and development. Consequently, both Ugandans and foreigners have been encouraged to participate in public programs, invest in new businesses, acquire new skills, increase productivity and bring back overseas assets, among other undertakings (Brett, 1997b: 28). Through persuasion, sensitization and consensus building, the government has been able to implement the reform programs in a fairly calm and conducive environment at least for the larger part of the country. The question, however, is whether the state will be able to ensure sustainability of its reforms in this new era of increased globalization. Arguably, Uganda's long-term progress will depend upon its ability to develop economic, administrative and political institutions of governance at the domestic level to the point where they can eliminate the need for external support. Whether this will be possible is a big question indeed, especially with the re-emergence of ethnic divisions in society, which arguably have been a result of the failure to respect democratic rights and ethnic pluralism.[10]

A strong civil society is considered to be a prerequisite for sustainable democracy. It is a reservoir of political, economic, cultural and moral resources to check the excesses of the state. The 1980s and 1990s witnessed increased donor funding for NGO activities, making civil society more vibrant across Africa. They were seen as agents of democratization and facilitators of economic liberalization.

Economic progress can only be achieved if stable democratic arrangements are created and this requires the development of appropriate social and economic institutions in civil society (Brett, 1997b: 28). An immense array of international and local voluntary organizations has emerged in Uganda since the NRM came to power. Interest groups of all kinds have blossomed (women's groups, the aged, environmental, youth, professional associations, etc.), a wide range of newspapers, often highly critical of the state, are being published and traditional cultural rights and assets that were removed in 1967 have been restored.

Alongside all the above, however, the NRM government has been able to operate a no-party system since 1986. According to the NRM, the movement system of governance is 'an organization for all', non-partisan, accommodative, and is based on the 'lived experiences' of Ugandans. This has inadvertently affected the growth of civil society in the country. NGO activity for example, is highly controlled by the state and because societies are divided along ethnic lines, most of the NGOs have taken on ethnic tendencies. If the state controls all activities in society, democracy is hindered because citizens cannot organize effectively to oppose the actions of government or powerful officials.

Nevertheless, private voluntary agencies, cooperatives, NGOs and community-based organizations are increasingly playing a fundamental role in Uganda's economic, social and political life; that is, in the inter-related processes of 'governance'. International NGOs rather than the state are now increasingly being used by donors to provide services to the population. The church, too, continues to provide education and health services as it did during the colonial era. Cooperatives, which had emerged originally to market export crops in the 1950s, now have to compete on an open market due to liberalization and many are likely to disappear. The number of NGOs, both local and foreign, has grown since 1986 in response to the open-door policy practiced by the NRM (World Bank, 1993b). The major setback, however, remains the ethnic tendencies these NGOs seem to be enhancing and this poses a big dilemma to the question of the sustainability of their activities.

In the 1990s, the globalization process came with both internal and external pressures. However, as earlier noted, despite fervent calls for multi-partyism, the NRM government has insisted that the 'movement' type of government is the best system of governance for Uganda, at least for the time being. The reason for the postponement of multi-party democracy reflects fear of the re-emergence of ethnicity but, ironically, ethnicity remains a problem even under the movement system. According to Mamdani (1998), Museveni's claim that the opposition in Africa tends to be ethnic and therefore, by implication, illegitimate, explains little because where the opposition is ethnic it is more than likely that the government is no less ethnic. He argues that a legal ban on organizing tends to drive it underground. However, given the uniqueness of Uganda's experiment, Mamdani's generalization may not be appropriate or even relevant. Arguably, under the movement government, the salience of ethnicity in national politics has to some extent been checked.

Changes towards good governance have not only originated from without. The Local Council (LC) system of governance has been a major innovative measure of the NRM government in its quest for good governance. This is a representative, popular, participatory administrative structure from the district level to the lowest level. The question, however, still remains: has this attempt by the NRM government to dismantle the central state and give power to the people removed ethnic tensions? The answer is no. Despite the existence of these apparent democratic structures, ethnic conflicts continue to emerge in Ugandan society.

The NRM government has also implemented a decentralization policy by giving power to local governments to make their own decisions. The participation of the local people is the driving principle. However, reports that have been received from several parts of the country indicate that some local councils are very hostile to officials who are not 'sons or daughters of the soil'. Instead, particular districts (which now are responsible for recruiting members of the civil service) have shown preference for natives in processes of personnel recruitment, award of tenders, etc., evidently bringing issues of ethnicity to the forefront again. In addition, given the view that districts are ethnically demarcated, most societies are now increasingly becoming inward looking. Undoubtedly, ethnic tensions seem to be rejuvenating, making it increasingly difficult to predict the future of the country, more so within the context of globalization.

Conclusion

Overall, the implications for ethnicity in Africa, with the sweeping changes in globalization, democratization and governance, need to be addressed by the social science community. What structures presently exist? How democratic are structures that have been put in place to address the ethnicity question? What impact have these had on governance and civil society in the broader context of globalization? How do we mainstream the ethnicity question in both public and NGO sectors? These are some of the questions and gaps that this chapter has been able to raise.

Evidently, the colonial system crystallized or consolidated ethnic differences, which acquired a regional complexion through differential policies in development. As revealed before, the British in Uganda encouraged cash-crop production in the south and migrant labor in the north, permitted intensive education in the south and relatively neglected the north. This led to recruitment into the army from the north while training for civilian bureaucracy and professionals was concentrated in the south. A polarization between the north and south inevitably occurred and arguably, the civil strife that has riddled Uganda over the last 20 years has been a result of this ethnic imbalance.

The forces of globalization have also increased imbalances in Uganda's society and this is gradually breeding discontent and antagonism. In spite of the current emphasis on democratization and 'good governance', the ethnicity crisis continues and it still has an overwhelming influence on policy or statecraft. A democratic government must be sensitive to imbalances in distribution of resources among its citizens, districts and regions. However, as earlier revealed, the NRM government seems to have failed to infuse its policies (and SAPs) with a reasonable dose of equality— especially regionally—and this appears to be triggering off a resurgence of the ethnicity question as evidenced by a recent uproar in Parliament (see *The Monitor Newspaper*, 30 July 1999: 1-2) and conflicts around the borders.

Ethnic struggles are influenced and exacerbated by uneven material access and this is evidently the case in the entire GLR. What then is the way forward? What prospects are there for Uganda's future (and that of the Great Lakes) in this new era of globalization? Posing these questions is in no way denying the urgent need to call for all conflicting parties to bury their differences and put on a united front, but whether this is possible is another question. As Doornbos (1988: 264) rightly predicted, the possibilities of fragmentation in the case of Uganda (and the GLR in general) seem to be getting higher. It is now very important to treat the ethnicity question not as a taboo topic but rather to consider its potential implications more closely. The only plausible solutions to the ethnicity problem seem to be twofold: first, ensure that different ethnic groups have a sense of representation and participation in the political life of their society; and second, there is a need to have power-sharing arrangements in which all ethnic groups are represented in government and centers of socio-economic resources. Even in this era of globalization, the lives of people everywhere need to be enriched. New regional approaches for collective action and negotiations have to be adopted and national policies should be made to capture opportunities in the global market, which can then be translated more equitably into human progress. The challenge, however, is to ensure that the benefits are shared equitably and interdependence works for people, not just for profits. Such measures would ensure stability and consensus in the region via new forms of governance and hence peace and development.

Notes

1. The Bahima (cattle keepers) were seen to be of a higher status than the Bairu, because in Ankole, the cow has always been a symbol of status and wealth and therefore those who did not own cows (the Bairu) were seen as inferiors and therefore regarded as serfs, supposed to do all the manual work for Bahima. This division was largely entrenched by the British colonialists.
2. The 13 years LRA rebellion in the north, led by Joseph Kony has often accused the NRM government of being sectarian and not favoring northerners.
3. The Kingdoms were abolished by Obote in 1966 and the Kabaka went in exile. This made the Baganda very bitter and they gradually withdraw their support from Obote. It is not surprising therefore that when Amin came to power, the Baganda were among his strong supporters.
4. Uganda was under dictatorial rule during the Amin era and the country was in total chaos. Amin himself was illiterate and his reign of terror claimed the lives of an estimated 1,000,000 Ugandans. Amin openly favored his ethnic tribesmen by appointing them to high-ranking positions both in government and in the army. The Obote II

government that came to power in 1980 after a number of short-lived governments was also openly sectarian and northerners (from Obote's ethnic group) dominated all the spheres of government.

5. For analysis of religion and politics in Uganda see Mudoola (1993).

6. The *New Vision* is the leading daily newspaper in Uganda.

7. The LRA insurgency in northern Uganda led by Joseph Kony developed from the Holy Spirit movement of Alice Lakwena (a cousin to Kony). The Lakwena group was comprised mainly of former army men and northern supporters of the overthrown Obote II regime. When it was defeated in 1987, the remnants of the group fled to the Sudan, where they later regrouped and formed the LRA under a new leader. It is this group that continues to destabilize northern Uganda with support from the Sudanese government.

8. Museveni first went to the bush with 26 companions to start a guerrilla war against the Obote government in Feburary 1981. Among the 26 were two Rwandese refugees who were later to play an important role in recruiting a larger number of Rwandese exiles into the NRA and eventually lead them back to Rwanda (Prunier, 1995).

9. It has been argued that the main reason for the involvement of foreign governments in the DRC crisis is their greed for the vast minerals in the Congo. Likewise, the fighting that took place in Kisangani in August 1999 and also in May 2000 between RPF and NRA has been attributed to the desire by both armies to control the mineral-rich areas.

10. There will be a referendum in Uganda in July 2000 to decide whether to adopt multi-party politics or remain under the movement system of governance.

13 Ethnicity, Power, Governance and Conflict in the Great Lakes Region

ABILLAH H. OMARI

Introduction

To talk of 'new security' let alone 'security community' in the Great Lakes Region (GLR) of Africa is to talk about the political economy of ethnicity, power, governance and conflict in the GLR countries and beyond. While the current conflict seems to be confined to the GLR, power relations and spill-over effects are actually felt in the entire Eastern and Southern Africa, albeit in different proportions.

Insecurity and instability, as well as an actual and latent loss of development, reached a climax in the 1994 Rwandan genocide. Yet this event did not mark the beginning of violence in the area, nor, unfortunately, the end. Conflict continues, peace is precarious, and economic development remains an illusion. And, the sub-continent's future remains difficult to predict, at least in part because of the emergence of numerous and complex state and non-state alliances and counter-alliances. Among the most prominent of the extra-African powers that have been involved, the United Nations (UN), and its continental subordinate, the Organization of African Unity (OAU), have appeared powerless to do anything to curb the situation.

This chapter seeks to highlight several inter-related factors in the conflict of the GLR, with a view to provoke robust discussions on these issues, and maybe establish nodal points for further research. In outline, I look at what is meant by the concepts, 'ethnicity', 'power', 'governance' and 'conflict'; then I explore the way they are applied in the GLR. I also focus on regime patterns, explaining the similarities among them, following which, I survey the influence of extra-African powers in the region. The focus then turns to the topical issue of the Great Hima Empire.[1] Its purported re-creation may symbolize (an ethnic?) form of a security community, albeit lopsided. However, alternatively, that empire could have more of a destabilizing effect thus impeding the construction of a sustainable regional security. Some tentative conclusions are offered at the end.

Ethnicity: A Primary Explanation?

It is now more relevant to discuss ethnicities in relation to crises of governance in Asia and Africa than it was a few decades ago. In the past, in these continents these identities were seen as static forces and were rarely understood in their wide and dynamic scope. The dynamics of such factors in Asia and Africa, which until recently were embedded and understood in terms of Cold War ideologies, did not affect other continents to any appreciable extent. The current appreciation of the impacts of both ethnicity and governance is a result of globalization. Economic integration of the world depends on good governance. And, apparently some nationalisms, including ethnic-nationalisms, affect good governance and economic development. While nationalisms seek to define and redefine identities, good governance includes concerns about the production and distribution of the economic 'cakes'. The combination of the two forces of globalization and nationalisms has produced conflict in most parts of Asia and Africa—thus the rationale to revisit concepts like ethnicity.

Ethnicity and rivalries have always existed in the GLR. Nevertheless, the new surge in tensions related to ethnicity has produced an impact of international proportion. If human security is to be enhanced, that surge cannot be ignored.

What then are ethnicity, power, governance and conflict? Are these concepts crucial in explaining what takes place in the Great Lakes? Are such notions region-specific or global in their application? In other words, are these concepts developed sufficiently to explain the phenomenon of ethnic conflict in the GLR? Although these 'umbrella' concepts have become commonplace parlance, all—ethnicity, in particular—require some explanation on their application. Although old notions of security remain, the form and content of security has changed. As I have noted elsewhere (Omari and Vale, 1995), old security questions have been interposed with 'new security issues', such as in (Eastern and) Southern Africa where there has been a surge of new nationalisms, manifesting themselves as ethnicities (Omari, 1995).

I argued previously that this surge in nationalism was the result of the failing state (Omari, 1995). In some parts of Africa the failure has been dismal. Because of poor governance practices and declining economic development, the state is not a viable rallying point and people revert to other identities—tribe, religion, race, regionalism, civil societies, etc. (Deng, 1995: 33-98). Somalia, where the state completely disintegrated, is a classic case of state failure in which a power vacuum was created causing state-societal relations to strain and conflict to ensue. More important, new political identities based on ethnicity tend to emerge. In most cases state institutions get replaced by systems of 'war lordism' of various types. In such situations ethnic feelings and the general tendency toward identity rediscovery permeate through to the grassroots. For example, when one parliamentarian in Tanzania was asked why he was displaying some ethnic tendencies, he responded: 'I never started it. I was born into my ethnic group, I had no choice. Don't blame me. I am what I am, you cannot change me.' Or, as one senior government official (in Tanzania) pointed out:

> In the 1960s and 1970s, if a civil servant died, the government knew where s/he came from and transported the body there for burial. Employment was a contract between the employer and the employee. Now if a civil servant dies the government looks for the deceased's relatives. It is important to have ethnically-based funeral associations.

Yet, despite the resurgence in ethnic politics at the turn of the century, there are still a few who are tied to the pan-nationalism of the 1960s, like one senior defense official in Tanzania who stated: 'I do not understand why people in Rwanda or Burundi would kill each other essentially because of the shape of their noses!'

For various reasons, including the failing state and declining economies, ethnicity is on the upswing. That ethnicity seems to be the method through which different sections of society relate may have provided some propensity for analysts and observers of the GLR to jump onto the bandwagon of this seeming reductionism; hence insecurity and conflict are looked at primarily at the level of ethnicity. What is important is to explain why ethnicity becomes a problem. As shown by the studies to which Nzomo refers in this volume, ethnicity and identity are not necessarily negative affiliations. They help to create bonds, which sometimes are essential for development. Ethnicities and ethnic-nationalisms only become stumbling blocks when they are exploited for selfish political ends—an increasingly common phenomenon with globalization.

Regime Patterns

What appears to be reductionism—that is, that events in the GLR can best be explained in terms of ethnicity—is compounded by regime patterns in the region. There is an obvious pattern unfolding.

Between 1980 and 1992, there was something in the politics of the region which might be termed the 'Museveni syndrome' (Omari, 1998). Yoweri Museveni, the Ugandan President, had told Milton Obote, a fellow presidential candidate in the 1980 Ugandan elections, that he (Obote) was going to win the elections because he was going to rig them (see Mbabazi in this volume). He continued to contend that if Obote should win, it would be due to election-rigging and therefore the only option left for himself would be to take up arms and fight an Obote government from the bush. As it turned out, this is what Museveni did from 1980 when he lost the election until he assumed power through his National Resistance Movement (NRM) in 1986 (Museveni, 1997).

Put in simple language, the 'Museveni syndrome' refers to a situation where a contestant in an election declares that, in order for the electoral contest to be regarded as free and fair, he or she must win. Thus, not far from Uganda, and certainly resonating in the GLR, Jonas Savimbi, the leader of the National Unity for Total Independence of Angola (UNITA), used the same philosophy to disassociate himself from the election results in Angola in 1992. When Savimbi's party lost the election, the war resumed.

Certainly, that the conflict still continues is due to more than the 'Museveni syndrome' or to national politics in general. The political economy of the minerals trade—especially diamonds and oil—sustains the conflict in Angola as it does in governments—those of Obote II (ie., the second regime, 1980-84), Paulo Muwanga, and Tito Okello.[2] The Ugandan rebels are using similar reasons and tactics the conflict in the Democratic Republic of Congo (DRC). However, the 'Museveni syndrome' is significant. And it is multi-fold, as indicated in several examples below. In the first place, President Museveni's NRM government is haunted by rebels who are fighting against his regime in the same way that he fought previous and Uganda is far from being peaceful and stable, despite what the biased international media portrays.

Secondly, the 'Museveni syndrome' and the style of coming to power that is associated with it has become a fashion adopted by others. Thus, the Rwandese Patriotic Front (RPF) fought the government of the late President Juvenal Habyarimana of Rwanda from 1990, using Uganda as a launching pad, to 1994 when the Front established itself as a government in Kigali. Similarly, in the Republic of Congo (Congo Brazzaville), former President Dennis Sassou-Nguesso, who had been defeated in the 1993 election, initially accepted the results then later retreated from his acquiescence. Soon after, Nguesso gathered his militia and launched a successful campaign to overthrow the democratically elected president, Pascal Lissouba.

Major Pierre Buyoya, likewise, accepted negative election results in the first multi-party elections in Burundi in 1992, which he had organized. He later used covert means to engineer a coup attempt in 1993. The coup was not successful in overthrowing the government, but the President, Melchior Ndadaye,[3] was killed. Following the unsuccessful coup attempt, Buyoya's machinations did not cease, and he persisted until he overthrew the remnants of the Burundi government in 1996, throwing the country back into turmoil, from which it still suffers. In 1997, Laurent Kabila and his rebels, then known as the Banyamulenge, launched attacks against the government of the late President Mobutu Sesse Seko in Zaire leading to a successful conclusion—the departure and final demise of Mobutu. Kabila changed the name of the country from Zaire to the ear-catching Democratic Republic of Congo, although the system of governance that was adopted had no resemblance to democracy. Before long, Kabila's government troops began to be attacked by rebels in the same way that Kabila's rebel forces had attacked the previous regime. Surprisingly, Kabila was now being attacked by the same people—the Banyamulenge—who had helped him to come to power.

So, there is an accepted fashion of coming to power—legitimated through the 'Museveni syndrome'—in Uganda, Rwanda, Burundi, Republic of Congo and the DRC. Yet, the fashion seems to have failed in Angola.

A third feature of the 'Museveni syndrome' that runs through all the above cases are two inter-related facts: i) these countries run on a no-party basis (including Uganda—the mentor); and ii) all of them are far from being stable. They are haunted by assortments of rebels as is characteristic of most post-guerrilla states.

Fourthly, there are clear inter-relationships among most of the surveyed cases. For example, Museveni's Uganda was the power behind the rise and the success of the RPF (Prunier, 1997). Historically, Batutsi in Rwanda and Burundi have allied against Bahutu in both, and in different periods, on different issues and in different proportions. Batutsi governments of Rwanda (and Burundi), and Museveni's government in Uganda were behind Kabila's success in the DRC.[4] And, at the present time, Uganda, Rwanda and Burundi are all against the Kabila government which they helped to create.

What has changed, and what is at stake? The interrelationships discussed above cannot by themselves make sense. Definitely, globalization has had an impact on the regional situation here as elsewhere, and the political economy of ethnicity has changed. Together, these two forces have helped to entrench ethnicity as a political factor by making it a contested core value throughout the region. Before looking at it more deeply, some statistical analysis is in order. The ethnic composition of Rwanda and Burundi (jointly) may explain Batutsi dominance even though they are the minority. The Batutsi are the dominant minority in all spheres of life in the both countries as Table 13:1 shows.

This distribution of power has been historically entrenched. It has certainly created some polarization, the 'haves' wanting to maintain the status quo and the 'have nots' wishing to change the equation. Statistics, of course, cannot be the rationale behind war and genocide. Such distribution points towards something else.

Table 13:1   Rwanda and Burundi: Batutsi Domination Over the Rest, 1962-98

	Bahutu %	Batutsi %	Batwa %	Total %
Population	85	14	1	100
Army	5	95	0	100
Civil service	20	80	0	100
Judiciary	5	95	0	100
Police	4	96	0	100
Education	20	80	0	100
Public enterprise	1	99	0	100
Diplomatic service	6	94	0	100

Source: Abillah H. Omari, 'Tanzania in the Great Lakes Region', A Briefing Paper for the Ministry of Foreign Affairs and International Cooperation, Dar es Salaam (October 1998)

The Great Hima Empire Recreated?

Having dealt with regime typology and patterns, and given the Batutsi dominance, the common denominator—ethnicity—cannot escape being part of the analysis. Ethnicity and regime patterns feed into each other to give credence to the concept of ethnicity, and hence the much publicized but also feared recreation of the Great Hima Empire in the GLR. It should be stated here that the countries concerned. share quite a number of historical roots: former interlucustrine kingdoms or parts thereof, ethnic composition and migration, and to date, regime similarities and war.

Is the recreation of the Great Hima Empire a mere fantasy or heresy? We may have no concrete evidence of this, yet some politicians have come to the fore to allay the fears and refute the idea as reported in the *Daily News* (Tanzania, 21 July 1991):

> Mr. Eriya Kategaya, Uganda's First Deputy Prime Minister and Minister for Foreign Affairs, has dismissed reports that President Yoweri Museveni and (the then) Vice-President of Rwanda, Paul Kagame, are masterminding a plan to establish a Tutsi empire. Mr. Kategaya said the reports were false, citing that the problems of the GLR especially in Rwanda and Burundi were more complex than the Tutsi and Hutu conflict reveal. He said Uganda's intervention in the DRC was based on protecting territory against rebel insurgents from the DRC. 'If there is anybody who opposed Buyoya when he seized power in Burundi then it is Uganda. We are the ones who mobilized the region to isolate Burundi under a Tutsi leader', he said. On the connection of Museveni and Kagame, Mr. Kategaya said the two leaders in their respective countries were struggling to protect their borders from foreign invasion.

Mr. Kategaya said the so-called Bahima people were not the majority in Uganda and wondered how they would influence others in the Central African states. He refuted claims that Kagame helped Museveni move into power in Uganda and said Kagame had no political and military base in Uganda and that he was then just a mere army officer.

This is tantamount to re-writing history as George Orwell did in his novel, *1984*: what purportedly happened did not actually happen. At any rate, this apology was not unexpected from Uganda's Foreign Minister. However, it is starkly contrasted by another report in *Mtanzania* (No. 1169, July 1999, Tanzania):

> Refugees from Burundi and Rwanda in Tanzania are said to be planning a Tutsi empire in the Great Lakes Region. The Hon. MP for Morogoro Urban and Chair of the Parliamentary Defense and Security Committee, Col. Ahmad Mazora said in Parliament, 'My Committee has reports to the effect that a Tutsi international power whose objective is political affiliation among Tutsi ... and activities to that effect have been reported and recorded in the refugee camps. We presented a report to the Hon. Speaker and we are sure the government is aware and vigilant.'

The long quotations above serve as a touchstone for this issue. Much of the personal history of President Museveni is well-known (Museveni, 1997). However, it is important to record two episodes. Museveni had a fighting force during the Uganda-Tanzania war of 1978-79 (Omari, 1980). This force, personal as it appeared, was no different from other forces at the time—those of Paulo Muwanga, Oyite Ojok, Tito Okello, etc. The tendency toward ethnically-based war-lordism continued in the period after Idi Amin and the Ugandan Army remained unified. When Museveni became the Defense Minister of Uganda, he made sure that his 'boys'[5] were trained by Tanzania, among other countries, and that he maintained command over them. They were subsequently the same 'boys' that went into the bush with him against the Obote and successive governments.

The boys, who actually were Batutsi, were characterized at the time as Banyankole people, Museveni's acknowledged ethnic group (Museveni, 1997; Omari, 1998), hence this loyalty to him in the context of Uganda's complex ethnic political equation. The same 'boys' appear as the RPF, organized in Uganda and attacking Rwanda from 1990 onwards, until they come to power in Kigali in 1994. It will be recalled that whenTanzania was facilitating mediation in Rwanda between 1992 and 1994, it was clearly known that the problem in Rwanda lay with President Museveni. Nevertheless, nothing could be done because Museveni was the head of state of a sovereign country.

Uganda, among other countries, is now deeply involved in the DRC crisis. Despite denials by Mr. Kategaya, President Museveni was recorded as saying that his troops are in the DRC to protect Uganda's vital national interests, which were not mentioned then.[6]

President Museveni is known as a Ugandan of Banyankole origin, coming from the Ankole area, where the Ugandan, Tanzanian and Rwandese borders meet. But his involvement with the 'boys', who later in Uganda and also in Rwanda were described as being Batutsi, leads to a number of speculations and stereotypes. One possibility is that President Museveni is actually an M-Tutsi, although he stands for everything that is Ki-Tutsi. The other possibility is that the 'boys' in question were Batutsi, like their mentor. Thus, the possibility looms large that there may have been a tacit understanding between the 'boys' and the latter—because of helping Museveni come to power in Uganda, he may assist them to return to Rwanda at a later stage. However, while this seems to complete the equation in Rwanda, it does not so fully explain the situations in Burundi and the DRC.

The events in the GLR, partly charted above, provide some evidence, not only of the surge of ethnicity, but also of the likelihood that something akin to the recreation of the Great Hima Empire will occur, especially among parts of Uganda, DRC and Tanzania, and the wholes of Rwanda and Burundi. This, of course, precludes the anthropological discourse on the differences and/or similarities among Batutsi, Bahutu and the rest, despite migrations and regionalism. In all these cases, the Tutsi element is prominent and evident.

Whether real or imaginary, the facts are clear; that is, the common features running through all the cases are the Tutsi questions of power-sharing and political and economic welfare. Having had successes in Uganda and Rwanda, Buyoya was assisted by his Batutsi colleagues to launch a coup and bust the sanctions in Burundi. Then, Kabila was assisted (Prunier, 1997) partly because he supported the Banyamulenge[7] who Mobutu was against. Given that, however, on coming to power Kabila ought to have found a solution for them.[8] It seems that Kabila had no intention to honor his part of the bargain; rather, he bit the very hand that fed him.

The Tutsi element, coupled with the history of the Bahima people, may help to explain the behavior of Uganda, Rwanda, Burundi and the DRC. There are some facts to substantiate this contention. Recent patterns show that Batutsi refugees in the GLR are not necessarily normal refugees seeking political asylum and ready to repatriate when the situation normalizes in their countries of origin. Rather, they are in fact in a diaspora, with a serious political agenda—however long it will take to capture the reins of power from Bahutu. Some members of the diaspora permeate the host societies, and several become quasi-naturalized. Others infiltrate government circles with a view to make and influence decisions later.[9] Thus, most Batutsi refugees are in fact alien citizens with no intention of going back soon. Batutsi and empire are inseparable. In addition to operating at the level of leadership, the dream of the empire operates among all Batutsi.

No one worries about the recreation of the Great Hima Empire for its own sake. Rather, worries center on the fact that the intended circle includes quite a number of countries with a substantial Batutsi refugee population. This has been vividly shown by van Eck (1999), who cautions about the question of 'boundary sovereignty':

> Because of the many conflicts over the past 30 years most countries have been directly affected by mass migrations across borders. While Tanzania and Zaire offered refuge to millions of Rwandan and Burundian refugees, Uganda sheltered hundreds of thousands of Rwandan refugees. Although most refugees eventually return, many settle in their adopted countries, forming bonds which impact directly on the question of boundary sovereignty.

Big Powers and the Great Lakes Region

Classic colonialism is a relic, but its absence does not mean there are no 'colonial' interests to safeguard despite increasingly changing norms given the impact of globalization. Interests among the big 'colonial' powers have changed with time, as have the nature and form of intervention to protect them. Thus, the apparent form is direct intervention or intervention by proxy. The GLR has attracted attention of the major powers in several ways.

France and Belgium have had historical connections in the GLR. In different proportions these two countries have had interests in Rwanda, Burundi and the DRC that have led to several state interventions. It is a cliché to state that the Belgian colonial administration took advantage of the ethnic equation in Rwanda and Burundi, thus cementing it as a political force. Belgium also had interests in the mineral-rich DRC. France, through culture and economic relations took it upon itself to prop up and maintain Mobutu until the latter became an embarrassment to the former. In 1994, that country, for myriad reasons, intervened in the GLR, to the extent that various observers have termed such intervention not only as unnecessary, but as a factor in fueling the genocide.[10] Prunier (1997) has amplified this:

> If we dismiss the strategic motive as having disappeared with the end of the cold war, then why would in this case France and the US engage in 'war by proxy'? The answer is largely cultural and has roots in France's colonial legacy which has given rise to a

complex nexus of pride, ideas on language and culture, dreams of former grandeur and memories of the past 'civilizing mission'. French leaders were extremely concerned about the possible disintegration of Zaire and interpreted Rwandan support for Kabila's ADFL as part of a plan to dismember Zaire and thereafter all of the French-speaking Africa with the support of the US.

I do not share the view that the strategic and economic motives have disappeared. The point is clear enough; there are traditional interests to protect. Britain and the United States have, of late, decided to conduct a back door 'quiet diplomacy'. Both of these countries intervene in the GLR through Uganda.

Of Ethnocentricism and Multiple Standards

Humanitarian aid operations during and after the 1994 Rwandan genocide have provoked a number of questions. First, some wonder if the administration of international humanitarian assistance itself is based on ethnocentric considerations. They ask why Western humanitarian operations are speedily conducted in Europe while responses to African crises are tardy and insufficient. More pointedly, the author of a Tanzanian newspaper article asks why a Kosovar refugee receives US$12 per day as opposed to one dollar per day paid or spent on an African refugee (*Mtanzania*, No. 1169, 13 July 1999). Issues of employment within the donor community and even corruption among Northern NGOs have been adequately analyzed (Salaita, 1998). Second, the whole question of withdrawing aid from Somalia to rush it to Bosnia at the beginning of the 1990s is still fresh in the minds of most Africans. And third, the issue that 'we could have done better' to halt or minimize the damage in the 1994 genocide in the GLR raises eyebrows (Annan). Running across all these examples is the feeling among Africans that non-Africans are preoccupied with their own ethnocentric and Euro-centric considerations, and are saying, in essence, 'let Africans butcher themselves'. However, it is not merely an issue of neglect.

African countries are profiled by the big powers according to yardsticks quite alien to the continent itself. Since the end of the Cold War, much of the economic assistance to Africa has been conditional upon democratic development and good track-records on human rights in the recipient countries. Many African analysts have wondered why such yardsticks were applied virtually overnight to certain countries—Kenya and Tanzania, for instance—but not to others. Among the latter, Uganda is the most conspicuous, Despite being heavily involved in civil wars at home as well as in the Sudan, Rwanda, and now the DRC, that country appears to be the 'darling' of the West (Omari, 1998). A country can hardly be involved in civil war and still observe human rights. And, to cap it all, Uganda like most countries in the GLR, is a no-party state.

These multiple standards applied by the West—predominately the United States and Britain with regard to Uganda—suggest the conclusion that Uganda has been chosen to be a custodian of the interests of these two big powers in the GLR. As Prunier (1997) observed:

> The US is concerned about instability in Zaire but is aligned with Uganda and Rwanda. The Americans need Uganda's support for their effort to overthrow the regime in the Sudan, which is charged with training Islamic militants and 'terrorists'. This includes $20 million in funds for forces seeking to overthrow [the regime in] the Sudan from bases inside Uganda, Eritrea and Ethiopia. American Special Forces have also been assigned to train the RPF in counterinsurgency techniques.

Thus allegations that Uganda fights some wars on behalf of the US and UK are not unfounded.[11] By so doing, both the US and UK are not only consciously entrenching ethnicity, they are also promoting the notion of the Great Hima Empire in the GLR, with President Museveni as its main pillar.

Economic Interests

Is President Museveni, the individual, enough to explain the fracas in the GLR? The answer, perhaps, is no. The major single economic interest in the region is mineral deposits in the DRC. The globalized economy of the twenty-first century no longer rquires a country to wage wars to protect mineral rights. Mineral wealth and possession are determined largely by competition for capital and investment inflows. Conflict and wars are prejudicial to such inflows. Unexpectedly, however, although that seems always to have been the case, it has only recently come to the attention of the transnational corporations which operate within a radius of about 300 km in territory that spans Burundi, Rwanda, parts of the DRC, parts of Uganda and parts of Tanzania. This area of about 300,000 km^2, which coincides with the envisaged area of the Great Hima Empire, contains rare minerals which lie outside the orbit of the present day global mineral and competition arrangements. Such rare minerals are important in space, computer and optical technology (Balati, 1999), so that whoever will control them will have an upper hand in those technologies.

Of Globalization, State, Market and Civil Society

The resources believed to be located in the sub-soil of the GLR attract external powers, big and small, and competition is tense. Hence, political economy explanations for the escalation of conflict and suspension of human rights and democracy considerations in the region are now more potent than before. Yet, the crisis is several generations old, and political economy approaches to analysis may not explain the situation entirely.

The future of the Great Lakes, like any other region is fused in the past and the present. The latter is heavily affected by globalization, while the past was conditioned both by ethnic relations and state (both colonial and post-colonial) performance. However, if the past role and nature of the state has largely determined the present, the future may yet be captured by the civil society, albeit by being linked to the market in an interesting way. In abstract theoretical terms, globalization has had an impact on the state-market-civil society triangle. On the ground in the GLR, this dynamic relationship is captured as an ethnicity-regime patterns-empire troika.

In recent times, the history of the GLR has been the history of struggle for control of the state. The relevance of the changing nature of the African state for explaining the current politics of the region goes beyond the erosion of its post-colonial role as the biggest employer. Rather, it extends to the degeneration of the state in two basic respects: i) the emergence of 'city-states' in the region,[12] and ii) the capture of the state by 'warlords' or other persons or groups who can deliver (including threats).

This is also related to the emergence of many fighting bands, whose aim is to capture the state.[13] And this is a situation which calls for subtle and sober analysis as to whether such soldiers constitute or represent civil society and what is the relationship between these two sectors; i.e., 'civil-military relations'? My own impression is two-fold. On the one hand, the soldiers and civil society are related through forms of nationalism, including the ethnic factor. On the other hand, they vie to fill the vacuum created by the disintegrating governance in terms of economic gains. The combination of the two factors has generated alliances and counter-alliances, which support the fighting and fuel the conflict.

On the whole, therefore, we have a confusing situation in the GLR. Globalization has unveiled a situation in which the state, market and civil society are fused but groups within each sector often compete, thus producing conflicts. At the same time, global forces extract the region's natural resources, which in turn finances the fighting. The GLR is one case where minerals which are in high demand in the global market finance wars, which partly are for economic gain, at least for the minority. We thus have a situation in Angola, where Savimbi's

UNITA survives, and indeed continues to fight not only for the control of, but also financed by the sale of diamonds.[14] The Angolan government is also able to survive and fight from the control, extraction and sale of oil. The market for both diamonds and oil is global and easily accessible, thus producing a stalemate in processes to end the fighting on the ground.

Another stalemate is found in the DRC. That country is now divided by a northwest-southeast line, the former controlled by the government and the latter by rebels. But each group has its own supporters, and both are dependent upon the extraction of minerals to keep the fighting going. This has led to cooperation and competition among supporters from other countries in the region in the looting[15] as the case between Uganda and Rwanda have shown.

Futures for the Great Lakes Region

As conflict simmers, prospects for peace and development remain in limbo. There are a number of factors by which the current conflict will seriously affect the future of the region. Briefly, these are refugees, ethnicity, economic losses, mineral wealth and poor governance. The sum total of these will be the nature of inter-state (and regional) relations in the future, and the type of a security community which will emerge and survive.

Refugees have been an important component of the conflict in the GLR. Africa hosts one-third of the world's refugees, most of whom result from the conflict in the GLR (Accord, 1999). In Tanzania, Ngara and Kasulu districts have more refugees than their host populations. In short, the effects of refugees are enormous. They include environmental degradation, the out-break of epidemics, small arms proliferation and crime, strain on the host countries' resources, and effects on inter-state relations (Omari, 1994; Salaita, 1998). Refugees will definitely affect the future of the GLR if their causes are not addressed.

Another factor is the rising tide of ethnicity in all its forms, as discussed above. The political economy of the GLR has begun to be modeled along ethnic lines (Griggs, 1999). There is a talk about the 'indigenization' of politics and economics in Tanzania,[16] where most political parties are established along ethnic lines. This also applies to Zanzibar, where the political problems are increasingly assuming religious and even racial overtones.[17] The Tanzanian example is given here because it is a country cherished for its peace, stability, and above all, national unity. However, life among Tanzania's neighbors is managed along ethnic lines and, therefore, it is difficult for Tanzania to be an exclusive non-ethnic enclave. Furthermore, as ethnicity seems to be condoned and promoted by some big powers, this may worsen the conflict in the future.

Economic loss resulting from the conflict in the GLR is a primary component to be considered. War and economic development are the antithesis of each other. Economic reconstruction following devastating wars in Rwanda, Burundi and the DRC will be an uphill task. The cost of armaments apart, economic ripples of this conflict may be felt far away in Namibia and Zimbabwe.[18] In the immediate neighborhood, Kenya and Tanzania are experiencing serious losses from the reduction of their transit trade with their huge landlocked hinterland, which is currently war-prone.

It can be anticipated that the struggle over common, precious and rare minerals, whether under the existing sovereign boundaries or under the Great Hima Empire, will be intense, and cannot be managed without wars. Such wars will dissipate energy and resources away from economic and social development.

Bad governance as a factor that can affect the future should be carefully looked at as well. Regime patterns, styles of coming to power and the existence of no-party states make democracy an empty and irrelevant phrase in many countries of the region. This is turning the democratic wheel backwards in the new millennium. It is increasingly becoming difficult to point to any democratic rule and regime in the region.

The nature of conflict in the GLR will generate long-term alignments and affect future inter-state relations. Refugees will continue to haunt some countries for quite some time. In addition, the current conflict has a negative impact on all established regional organizations.

Further, there have been discussions in some countries in East Africa about President Bill Clinton's visit to Uganda in 1998. There is some concern that the United States regards Uganda as the most favored country in East Africa and President Museveni as the most respected of all East African leaders. The concern goes to the extent that there are some feelings among those rejected of wanting to do something dramatic and positive enough to draw US attention, interest and favor. In short, with regard to the US position toward Uganda, many are asking: 'Why Uganda and not us?' (Omari, 1998).

Conclusions

As this chapter has tried to show, it is easier to destroy the peace than to rebuild it. At the helm, ethnicity and ethnic politics seem to have become major determinants in power sharing, governance, economic development and the outcome of the conflict itself in the GLR. Regime patterns and similarities among Uganda, Rwanda, Burundi and the DRC (also including the Republic of Congo) especially the common denominator of the Batutsi factor have lent credence to the fears that there is a move to recreate the old idea of a Great Hima Empire in the area which hitherto comprised the interlacustrine kingdoms. This recreation would be a recipe for continuing the conflict in the region. The interests of France, Belgium, Britain and the United States in the GLR seem to have sacrificed the usual norms and standards which are applied elsewhere; that is, good governance, democracy, human rights, liberalized economy and minimized state control. In this region, the big powers seem to condone 'ethnic' politics. This may be for economic reasons and interests. Otherwise, it is difficult to comprehend or even speculate about any other reason that would cause the United States or any other Western democracy to support no-party countries and leaders at the beginning of the millennium.

The conflict in the GLR has put any notion of sustainable regional economic and social development in jeopardy. As indicated, the signing of the East African Community was pushed forward, most likely to let Uganda sort out its problems. The war in the DRC has affected the Southern African Development Community (SADC), among other regional organizations, as its members have taken different sides and positions in that conflict.

The type of new regional security—human and national alike—expected to emerge in this millennium will be determined by these conflicts and realignments. Unfortunately, I envisage that the new security community which will emerge will not only be lopsided, but will engender contradictions, instability and insecurity in the whole of Eastern and Southern Africa.

Notes

1. The term Hima is used to mean a major ethnic grouping from which sub-groups such as Batutsi, Banyankole and others are part.
2. Uganda has had governments from the North, South and now West.
3. Melchior Ndadaye was the first Hutu president in Burundi since independence.
4. Nguesso's militia was assisted by Angola for different reasons, but the style remains the same.
5. The *boys*, were, in most cases boys, in the real sense of the word, meaning they were under age to fight. Museveni is one of those accused of recruiting and utilizing child soldiers, which constitutes a serious violation of human rights.
6. 'Invasion' notwithstanding, the political economy of diamonds exploitation is part of that interest.
7. Banyamulenge are Batutsi who migrated from Rwanda and settled in the DRC in the area around Kivu for the last 200 years. Following the Kivu Crisis of 1994, Mobutu's regime was all out to repatriate them to Rwanda.
8. Instead, legislation was passed to have their citizenship revoked, hence provoking a rebellion.

9. Solidarity among *Batutsi* and leaders of that origin is common. We have the example of Paul Kagame, a *M-Tutsi* Rwandese President, formerly Vice-President and Minister of Defense, being not only in the Ugandan Army, but also head of intelligence and the identification of Mobutu's last Prime Minister, Kengo wa Dondo, as having a M-Tutsi mother.
10. There has been a parliamentary inquiry in France to look into decisions made on Rwanda between 1990 and 1994.
11. For Britain's involvement, see Executive Intelligence Review, vol. 21, no. 43 (28 October 1994).
12. This is shown in the case of Luanda, Angola; Brazzaville, Republic of Congo; Kinshasa, Democratic Republic of Congo; Kigali, Rwanda; Bujumbura, Burundi; and to some extent Kampala, Uganda. In all these cases the government controls the capital and rebel groups hold the countryside. Thus, recognized governments govern city-states.
13. Including the child soldiers of the region. See also Note 5, above.
14. A similar case is found in Liberia and Sierra Leone.
15. 'The Zimbabwe Defense Forces, through a company registered in Harare as Osleg, has entered into a partnership with Comiex, a company believed to be President Kabila's personal wealth-generating agency' for diamond mining (see, Kahiya, 2000).
16. See debate in the Tanzanian parliament about indigenization of the economy, *Daily News* (Tanzania), No. 7252 (22 July 1999).
17. The main opposition party in Zanzibar is the Civic United Front (CUF), which has members of Arab origins, and enjoys popular support in Pemba.
18. These are on the side of the government in the DRC's civil war, while Uganda, Rwanda and Burundi are assisting the rebels. There have been demonstrations against the government in Zimbabwe, partly due to that county's involvement in the DRC, and partly because of economic difficulties.

14 The Peace and Conflict Impact of Overseas Development Assistance (ODA) in Sri Lanka

KENNETH D. BUSH[1]

Introduction

Sri Lanka is a country characterized by simultaneous integration and disintegration, as illustrated in a knot of anomalies and incongruities that confounds the critical observer and, more importantly, *serves to sustain* a crisis of governance which has degenerated into protracted, militarized violence.[2] Thus, Sri Lanka is a country which:

- enjoys high levels of literacy and life expectancy, but has seen over 70,000 people killed or disappear in political violence since 1983;
- saw 1,400 troops killed in one 36-hour battle in late 1998, but rarely sees such events make the front pages of the international newspapers;
- saw its economy grow by 6.4% in 1997, but has the second highest level of military expenditure as a percentage of GDP (6%);
- is a democracy where women have had the vote decades longer than their counterparts in some cantons of Switzerland, but emergency regulations govern public life, and the military makes the key decisions affecting the lives and livelihoods of the population in one-third of the island; and
- has an open market economy, but 32% of income transfers to rural areas come from army recruitment and compensation.

To further complicate matters, militarized violence on the island is not confined to a single conflict. Rather, the country has been wracked by multiple conflicts that have varied in intensity over the geography and history of the past 20 years. Often these conflicts intersect at international and very local levels, but sometimes they do not.

Where does this thumbnail sketch of Sri Lanka leave us?   First, it should, at a minimum, induce a considerable degree of caution in making categorical statements about the Sri Lankan experience.   Second, efforts to untie this knot of anomalies should draw our attention towards the principal concerns of the current edited volume: the examination of the shifting relations between states, markets and civil society at local, national, and international levels—in short, the 'nexus of governance'.   This chapter is an attempt to do just this through an examination of one particular facet of globalization: the impact of Overseas Development Assistance (ODA) in Sri Lanka, particularly, but not exclusively, on the dynamics of peace and violent conflict.   Thus, the central question guiding this chapter is: when, why, and how does ODA affect the structures and processes of peace and conflict in Sri Lanka?

To engage this question, the chapter is structured as follows: i) a general discussion of ODA and conflict; ii) an overview of ODA in Sri Lanka; iii) an examination of the peace and conflict impact of ODA at micro-, meso- and macro-levels; and finally iv) the consideration of the question of whether ODA subsidizes military expenditures and militarization in Sri Lanka.

ODA and Violent Conflict

ODA is an especially appropriate point of access for an examination of the theoretical interests of this volume because of its centrality in the political economies of most developing countries of Asia and Africa, and especially in Sri Lanka since its independence from Britain in 1949.   Further, it is increasingly evident that in all regions characterized by social, political or economic tensions, ODA *inevitably* effects the dynamics of peace and conflict—positively or negatively, intentionally or unintentionally, like it or not.   Decisions made in Washington, Paris and Tokyo have direct impacts on the lives of children, women and men in dusty, far-flung, villages around the world. In earlier times, the names of such places might have been known only to locals and marginalized foreign academics. However, in increasingly globalized worlds, we see *not only* the impact of the international on the local, *but also* the impact of the local on the international.   Thus, local-level struggles and events are increasingly able to transcend their immediate political geography and enter international arenas of articulation and contestation. This is illustrated in the increased prominence of such initiatives as: the network of resistance to the World Bank-supported Narmada Dam project in India; the international mobilization against British and American assistance to the militaries of human rights-abusing regimes, such as Indonesia, Colombia, Pakistan and Zimbabwe;[3] and the various movements to cancel the debt repayment of the most impoverished countries of the world (such as the Jubilee 2000 movement).

This chapter questions one of the most problematic and under-examined assumptions of the Northern 'development project', namely, that 'development equals peace', and by extension, that ODA invariably contributes to peace. In the past, peace and development were viewed as being synonymous or co-dependent. In some cases, this continues to be the dominant developmentalist dogma. While this is sometimes true, often it is not.

Logically, if 'development equaled peace', then conflict should diminish as a country 'develops', but this was not what has happened in Sri Lanka. Indeed, violence escalated alongside a steady and significant improvement in living standards for a large segment of the population. Despite the fact that the north of the country has been 'bombed back to the pre-industrial era', the economy has continued to grow strongly.[4] It appears that in many cases the very process of development aggravates conflict in a variety of ways, by: i) exacerbating perceived and real socio-economic inequalities; ii) privileging certain groups over others; iii) increasing the stakes in the competition for political control; iv) introducing new structures and institutions which challenge the old ones, and so on. Further, we need to bear in mind that under conditions of 'ethnicized conflict', identity is mobilized and politicized through violence. Consequently all social, political and economic life comes to be defined and strained through the lens of identity. Under such conditions, international interventions (developmental, humanitarian and economic) will *unavoidably* have an ethnic impact, due as much to the context as their content.

Given the theoretical interests of this volume, it is not sufficient to simply draw the connections between ODA and violent conflict—which is difficult enough given the problems in discerning causal relationships in increasingly complex, intersecting and messy social and political realities. There is the additional requirement to make the connections between globalization, governance and ethnicity or, more specifically, the politicization of identity. In the Sri Lankan case, as with all cases of identity-based conflict, the collective experiences of violence and the tit-for-tat of atrocity escalation across ethnic border lines, serve to forge a politicized sense of separate group identities. Whether the needs and demands of these groups are articulated through violence depends largely on whether there exist legitimate non-violent channels for their expression (see Bush, 1996a: 49-83). The politicization of identities tends to follow the institutionalization of violent and non-violent conflict as it is played out in the social, political and economic relationships within and between groups.

If one is to develop a more complete understanding of the impact of ODA, then it is necessary to examine this phenomenon at the micro-, meso- and macro-levels. Thus, this chapter analyzes three cases of ODA at each of these levels. While it dwells more heavily on the negative impacts of ODA, other examples of development projects might be cited which have had positive impacts. At this stage, however, the donor community has not yet developed or institutionalized the means of undertaking 'Peace and Conflict Impact Assessments' (PCIA) of development projects in conflict-prone regions, in a way similar to the assessment of the impact of development initiatives on the environment or on gender relations. Efforts are slowly under way to do so.[5] This chapter is intended to be a modest contribution to this effort within the context and contemporary debates within the field of international political economy.

Overview of ODA in Sri Lanka

In Sri Lanka, the volume of foreign development assistance has always been large relative to the size of the economy. Indeed, in the early 1980s, the Sri Lankan Finance Minister asserted that 'we have been able to obtain greater volume of foreign aid and foreign assistance *per capita* than perhaps any other Third World country' (Herring, 1998). This fact, combined with the universally recognized high quality of life (as measured by life expectancy, education, literacy, health, and so on), stands in stark contrast to the vicious spiral of violence on the island since the early 1980s.

Table 14:1 provides an overview of the volume and pattern of assistance in the recent past.

Table 14:1   Sri Lanka Total Receipts Net 1990-95

	1990	1991	1992	1993	1994	1995	Total
Japan	162.1	258.0	98.1	219.2	197.0	271.8	1206.2
UK	59.5	20.1	40.5	51.1	70.0	7.0	248.9
United States	72.1	78.0	52.0	77.0	37.0	26.0	342.0
Total DAC	420.2	443.9	285.8	466.1	430.3	431.1	2477.4
Asian Dev.							
Bank	112.4	150.8	129.9	120.3	89.2	83.1	685.7
IDA	123.0	182.0	68.4	123.4	70.6	98.3	665.7
IMF	56.5	76.1	157.7	71.9	67.5	-33.8	395.9
UNDP	7.7	10.0	12.3	8.1	6.2	5.4	49.7
Total for							
Multilaterals	321.3	426.9	387.2	337.6	249.5	176.8	1899.3

Source: World Bank 1998

It is fair to say that while the levels of violence escalated in Sri Lanka after 1983, most donors attempted to continue with their development programming as usual (see Warnapala and Woodsworth, 1987). Bilateral donors are quite frank about this in interviews. However, as the violence began to impinge on their programming, it became clear that development-as-usual was not always appropriate or possible. Initially, donor response was pragmatic, but off the mark. Instead of considering the peace and conflict impact of development and humanitarian programs, they framed the question as: how can we 'do' development in conflict situations? In Sri Lanka, this required a more self-conscious and politically sensitive approach to technical decisions on questions of *who* to work with (e.g., NGOs or the government of Sri Lanka), *how* to work (e.g., issues of access, monitoring, staff security, sustainability, communications and so on), and *where* to work (according to the ebb and flow of violence). While this was an improvement on earlier approaches, it was still focussed narrowly on the *developmental impact* of developmental initiatives. It did not yet systematically consider the *peace and conflict impact* of development initiatives. A narrow developmentalist perspective leaves critical questions unasked: What factors condition the peace and conflict impact of ODA, for better or for worse? How do development interventions legitimize/delegitimize certain actors, identities, and histories? How does this affect the potential for good governance or bad governance? More specifically, how do they affect the dynamics of peace or conflict?

To understand the contemporary impact of ODA on ethnicity and conflict/governance in Sri Lanka, we have to appreciate the degree to which the social, economic and political infrastructure continues to bear the past like an incubus.   Indeed, after 15 years of ethnicized violence, the past has come to define the present—shaping both the analytic lenses used to think about it and the institutional structures used to respond to it.   To the extent that ODA reinforces, rather than deconstructs, such institutions, then it may aggravate conflict.   Mick Moore has argued that the 'use of state power for the benefit of the ordinary Sinhalese has been, and remains, the primary legitimation, implicit or explicit, of all governments elected since 1956 at least, and arguably, since 1931' (Moore, 1985: 29).[6]   While there were winners and losers from within all ethnic groups as a result of the neo-liberal economic program of the UNP from 1977 onwards, it was particularly detrimental to inter-group relations. This was a corrosive process which was facilitated by the 'permeative' character of ethnic identity within conflict settings, described by Donald Horowitz as having 'a tendency to seepage' (Horowitz, 1985: 7). The 'ethnicization' of social, political and economic life coincides with the politicization of ethnicity, which together serve to ratchet up the tensions between identity and conflict, and raise the stakes sharply in all confrontations.   It adds volatility to every social, political and economic interaction across identity boundaries.

    In an effort to refine our understanding of the peace and conflict impact of ODA, this chapter focusses on three specific examples at the micro-, meso- and macro-levels.

ODA and Ethnic Politics at a Micro-Level: The 3,000 House Project

The 'Three Thousand House Project' on the east coast of Sri Lanka provides an insightful micro-level example of complex inter-connections between developmental interventions and the dynamics of peace and conflict. The arithmetic of the project appeared clear and straightforward.   The project sought to provide 3,000 houses in a community consisting of an equal proportion of Tamil, Sinhalese and Muslim populations. The decision by the community was to allocate the houses equally to each group, *i.e.*, 1,000 houses each.   While there were the typical complaints about this decision, it was accepted by the community as a whole and the houses were introduced.

    On the one hand, this illustrates how the communities made an explicitly political decision to allocate development resources in a way which was intended to maintain an equilibrium in the ethnic balance.   However, here is the problem: each community was not affected equally by the violence.

Those from communities which were harder hit, had a greater need for housing. Thus, this example illustrates how standard developmental criteria (needs-based decisions; efficiency-driven decisions; product-oriented rather than process-oriented approaches) may have to be subordinated to peacebuilding objectives. In this case, the principle of equity (needs-based allocation) was subordinated by the politically expedient of equality (arithmetic allocation). It gets more complicated yet: even if the decision was made by the communities themselves (as it was), did this development project reinforce politicized ethnic boundaries? In some ways it did. Was there an alternative? Perhaps the full example of success in this project would be when the communities themselves make their own decision based on the unadulterated criterion of need. The task which still confronts the development community is how to get there from here. The project underscores the point that donors might have to do their work differently—rather than to do different work—if they wish consciously to reinforce the positive peacebuilding impact of development programming. Importantly, the example also points to some of the developmental trade-offs that may be required in order to increase the likelihood of constructive peacebuilding trade-offs.

ODA and Ethnic Politics at a Meso-Level: The Gal Oya Project and the Accelerated Mahawelli Development Program (AMDP)

It is very instructive to compare the Gal Oya water project and the Mahaweli Program to develop a better sense of which such meso-level projects can have positive or negative impact on dynamics of peace and conflict.[7]

The USAID-supported Gal Oya water management project in Sri Lanka is an example of a project which generated both developmental and peacebuilding benefits. Interestingly, its peacebuilding impact was entirely incidental to the project which was designed and implemented according to developmental criteria. By cultivating the mutual interests of members from different ethnic and socio-economic groups, the project managed to thrive even in the midst of severe communal conflict. And perhaps more importantly, it resulted in the construction of ad hoc institutions of inter-communal cooperation beyond the scope of water management (Uphoff 1992; Uphoff 1992a). In other words, it had a significant, positive impact on the incentives for peace within a particular area of Sri Lanka.

One may look to another water program in Sri Lanka—the Accelerated Mahawelli Development Program (AMDP)—for an illustration of the dangers of not considering the peace and conflict dimensions of development projects. While this will be dealt with in greater detail below, it is sufficient to note at this stage that although the Mahaweli Program was designed to meet a number of developmental objectives, the failure fully to consider such highly political issues as population displacement and resettlement in the context of a communal civil war, ultimately led to the exacerbation of ethnicized tensions.

The Gal Oya Project

The Gal Oya Water project was one of the largest and most complex water schemes in Sri Lanka. It faced daunting obstacles—physical, infrastructural, bureaucratic and political. To top it all off, the project was confronted with an over-arching ethnic dimension: the up-stream areas were inhabited by members of the Sinhalese ethnic group, whereas the down-stream allotments were held by Tamil-speaking farmers. In other words, the Tamil-Sinhalese divide which constitutes the main battle line in the ethnic violence at the national level was paralleled at the local level of the project. In the context of ethnic tensions, if water did not reach the Tamil 'tail-enders', there would be good chance that this would be attributed to the 'maliciousness' of the Sinhalese 'head-enders' rather than to geographical or other factors. *In other words, the context within which the project was set was not especially conducive to cooperation between the communities; indeed, just the opposite.*

The project was not consciously designed to perform a peacebuilding function or to achieve peacebuilding objectives. However, it is an example of a development project with noteworthy peacebuilding spin-offs. In order to develop a thorough understanding of the potential peacebuilding role of international, national and local actors, these are the types of projects that should attract greater attention.

What does the Gal Oya teach us about ODA and positive peacebuilding impact? It appears that some of the factors that contributed to its success as a development project may also have contributed to its success in peacebuilding. The fact that it is a thoroughly participatory development project may be an important factor in explaining its success in both areas. The emphasis on promoting participation (as both a means and an end) generated a number of operating principles which have clear peacebuilding implications: i) ensuring continuity of personnel to make a learning process more feasible; ii) having a network of supportive, committed persons in a variety of positions; iii) avoiding partisan political involvement; iv) attracting and retaining the right kind of community leadership; v) going beyond narrow conceptions of self-interest; vi) an emphasis on capacity building which built up local capabilities for self-management and self-reliance in both resource use and communal relations; vii) the project was participatory from the start; viii) it incorporated learning from experience throughout; ix) it steered away from too much government involvement; and perhaps most importantly, x) it 'accept[ed], genuinely and fully, that intended beneficiaries have intelligence and social skills, not just labor and funds, that can be useful for project design and implementation. The poor can even usefully comment on technical design questions, but more important, they can help to plan and carry out the management of project activities' (Uphoff 1992a: 143).

The Accelerated Mahawelli Development Program (AMDP)

Prior to the escalation of violence following the riots of 1983, the dominant approach to development programming in Sri Lanka tended to emphasize large-scale infrastructural projects. The best known of these large-scale initiatives is the Accelerated Mahawelli Development Program (AMDP, 1977 to the mid-1980s). The large scale of the AMDP amplified its political impact and therefore justifies further examination.

The AMDP was a massive electricity and irrigation program for which the World Bank served as a major source of external financing and played the lead donor coordination role. The conspicuous absence of consideration of the project's possible negative impact on simmering tensions is striking— considering that it had glaring ethno-political implications, in particular: i) there was an ethnic overlay to the geographical areas which would benefit (or not) from the project; and ii) the government decision to resettle displaced Sinhalese villagers in traditionally Tamil regions. The decision by the Jayawardene government to compress and accelerate the 30-year program into six years further exacerbated ethnic tensions. The original version of the program had included irrigation projects in the Tamil-majority Northern Province, but this was removed from the accelerated program with the argument that it would be too expensive and problematic technically. Yet donors supported that program, as well as the government's national development program which included no specific initiatives for the Northern Province. In this environment, consideration of the possible negative impact of development programming on the conflict was not simply neglected, it was rejected. According to the World Bank, 'those donors who did raise concerns in the late 1970s and early 1980s about ethnic balance in the AMDP resettlement did not get a very sympathetic hearing' (World Bank, 1998a: 136).

In broad terms, we may ask what the impact of this was on the (dis)incentive structures for peace or conflict in this particular phase of ODA in Sri Lanka. It would appear that by supporting development programs that were perceived to be exclusionary, if not antithetical, to the interests of the Tamil community of the north and east, ODA exacerbated tensions between communities. The perceived exclusionary character of the government's development program created incentives for the Tamil leadership to be seen not to be working with the government—otherwise there was a risk that it would lose the support of its Tamil constituency. It also strengthened the challenge by the Tamil leadership of the legitimacy of the government's claim to represent the entire island, rather than just the Sinhalese south. The Tamil sense of alienation from the political process was formalized in 1983 when the democratically elected members of Parliament from the Tamil United Liberation Front (TULF) were expelled from government. By excluding the political party that had won every seat in every community with a Tamil majority, the government of J.R. Jayawardene marginalized democratic politics and pushed political expression out of the democratic arena. Political grievances were increasingly articulated through the violence of Tamil militant groups.

Particularly explosive were the Tamil militant responses to what they saw as government efforts to alter the demographic composition of the east coast by increasing Sinhalese settlement in, and control over, areas claimed by separatists to have been traditionally inhabited by Tamils. This so-called 'West Bank scheme' envisioned the resettlement of thousands of armed Sinhalese 'settlers' trained in self-defence on government-owned land in this area (Weaver, 1988: 67; FEER, 21 February 1985: 39). By 1985, over 50,000 Sinhalese had already been resettled on Tamil majority land(s) (Sinhalese settlers included ex-convicts, retired military personnel and families displaced by the AMDP). Unable to affect the government's colonization policy through non-violent means, some Tamil paramilitaries responded with terror and violence against these settlements—including the brutal massacre of whole communities including the well-publicized incidents at the Dollar and Kent Farms in 1984.

In an assessment of the Maduru Oya project of the Mahawelli Program, Gillies argues that at the planning stage 'virtually no attention was given to the project's impact on the fragile ethnic balance of Batticaloa District in which resettlement would occur' (Gillies, 1992: 55). And once the potential political volatility of the project became clear, aid officials found themselves in the awkward position of being committed to the project, but of having serious reservations about the fallout. They were further constrained by not wanting to be seen to be meddling in the 'internal affairs' of the country.

The AMDP illustrates that at this stage of the Sri Lankan conflict(s), there was not a shared understanding of the nature of the conflict. Indeed, there appears to have been widespread myopia that excluded the consideration of the conflict in development programming. There was a host of other aggravating factors amplifying the impact of the AMDP on the incentives for Tamil leaders to reject increasingly exclusionary rules of the political game. While the program did not create the conflict, it did exacerbate it in the areas in which it operated.

ODA and Ethnic Politics at a Macro-Level: Economic Liberalization

The program of economic liberalization that followed the election of the United National Party regime of J.R. Jayawardene in 1977 was fully encouraged and supported by the international donor community. With the defeat of the socialist regime of the Sri Lanka Freedom Party, ODA came flooding in. In an insightful paper on the detrimental impact of liberalization in Sri Lanka, Herring (1998) observes that one of the curious features of the liberalization program of the successive governments in Sri Lanka was that although some areas of public consumption were cut, public expenditures in the aggregate expanded. As Herring puts it, 'political praxis triumphed over economic policy rhetoric' (Herring, 1998: 14).[8] He continues:

> Capital and current transfers to public corporations, as well as revenue derived from the operation of Government enterprises, rose steadily in the early years of liberalization. Much of this expansion was driven by the strategy's reliance on attracting private foreign capital; expenditures on infrastructure were accelerated. Foreign aid, through project loans and grants, increased the size of the public sector, most significantly in the Accelerated Mahawelli project (irrigation and power). Total expenditures on public salaries and wages—one important measure of patronage—increased in both absolute terms and as a share of the GDP, reaching 9.9% in 1985. While the share of public investment more than doubled as a percentage of GDP in the 1978-82 period, compared to 1970-77 averages, international assistance (grants, loans) almost quadrupled as a percentage of GDP.

Although public expenditures expanded, they did not do so evenly or equitably—geographically, politically or *ethnically*. In keeping with the ethnicized political modus operandi in Sri Lanka, public expenditures became the means by which the UNP government dished out favors to curry political support. To the extent that the UNP disbursed its largess primarily to its Sinhalese supporters, then such patronage contributed to the sense that the government was not a national, but an ethnic, champion—a sense that was reinforced by the increasingly militarized responses of the state to dissent in Tamil majority areas. Certainly, the lion's share of rewards was delivered to government supporters in Sinhalese areas. Mick Moore (1990: 357) goes so far as to argue that the contradictions between the IFIs' principles of liberalization and the expansion of the public sector in Sri Lanka mean that external development assistance had changed from support *for policies* to support for the *government per se.* Moore concludes: 'I suspect that the UNP has undermined the democratic political system and perpetuated its own rule partly from the elemental desire to remain in clover'.

The impact of hardening and further politicizing the borders on ethnic identity was profound. The Tamil majority areas of the north and east were starved of government investment. According to the 1981 Central Budget, the capital expenditure in the Jaffna District (approximately 6% of the total population) was only 2.6% of the national capital expenditure. On a per capita basis, the capital expenditure in the Jaffna District was Rs313, while the national expenditure was Rs656. In addition, foreign aid allocation to the Jaffna District for the period 1977-82 was nil (CRD, 1984: 15). Furthermore, as late as 1975 almost 90% of industry on the island continued to be located in the Sinhalese majority Western Province (Shastri, 1990: 70). Of the 40 major government-sponsored industrial units, only five were located in predominantly Tamil areas—of these four were established in the 1950s and one in the 1960s (Manogaran, 1987: 130-34, 139). All of these figures are based on a period which was relatively peaceful. While such economic discrimination added to the disgruntlement of Northern Tamils and was criticized by Tamil politicians, it is the full-scale warfare since 1987 that has decimated the regional economy. A development worker who had just returned from Jaffna in May 1992 described the Northern Province as having been bombed and brutalized (by state and LTTE forces) back into a pre-industrial economy. In April 1993, Bruce Matthews, a Canadian academic reported: 'Meanwhile, the Jaffna Peninsula is locked off by the army, and life there is worse than ever. You will know that Jaffna has lost half of its population. Those that remain under the *de facto* Prabhakaran [i.e., the leader of the LTTE] government live hellish lives.'[9] By the late spring of 2000, an efficient and deadly offensive brought LTTE fighters to the gates of Jaffna (at the time of writing), further deepening the misery of the population.

The impact of economic liberalization on non-metropolitan regions of the country has, in relative terms, been consistently negative (see Dunham and Jayasuriya, 1998). In the north and east (which provides most support for the LTTE), mean incomes were almost on par with those in Colombo in the early 1970s but had almost halved by the early 1980s. Trade liberalization sharply reduced agricultural exports from the Jaffna Peninsula to the Colombo market and the area missed out on getting major projects. More recent data is not available, but it can reasonably be assumed that, with the on-going war, the region has become far more impoverished, with a large number of refugees effectively destitute.

In short, the donor push towards economic liberalization had negative impacts both developmentally and on the dynamics of ethnic conflict. The riots of 1983 provide a further example of how this played out in what is seen to be the liminal moment in the escalation of conflict in Sri Lanka (Bastian, 1990; Hyndman, 1988; Manor, 1984).

Does ODA Subsidize Military Expenditures and Militarization in Sri Lanka?

It is very interesting to compare the flow of international ODA into Sri Lanka with the military expenditures of the Sri Lankan government. Table 14:2 provides an indication of pattern and levels of military and security expenditure alongside ODA. One of the common questions that arises in conversations with the NGO and donor communities in Sri Lanka is whether ODA, in effect, subsidizes the war effort on the island by enabling the government to re-allocate resources from socially constructive activities to militarily destructive activities. This question is difficult to answer definitively since it requires us to rely on a counter-factual premise (which by definition is unverifiable empirically): that the government of Sri Lanka would not have allocated the same amount of resources to the war-machine in the absence of such development assistance. What is clear from Table 14:2 is that in the larger picture of public expenditure ODA is shrinking significantly as a proportion of military spending, so even if ODA was having a subsidizing impact, it would be diminishing over time.[10]

In considering the possible ways that ODA may subsidize militarization more generally, it should be noted that acquiescence itself may serve to reinforce disincentives to peace. Militarization is more than just the number of weapons circulating in the fields and streets of a country. In its most basic form, it is the tendency for non-military problems to be defined, and responded to, with military means. This process requires the institutionalization of violence within social, political and economic arenas. This is illustrated in a comment by a government official who described the incorporation of the Tamil paramilitaries into the government as 'the welcoming of terrorists into the heart of government'.

Table 14:2 Reported Military Expenditure and ODA (Rs. Million)

Year	Military Expenditures	Total ODA
1985	2770	3306
1986	5300	3648
1987	8000	4677
1988	6500	6588
1989	5800	6407
1990	9340	6697
1991	14130	7870
1992	17400	8280
1993	18270	8035
1994	22400	8257
1995	33200	9028
1996	39200	7739
1997	NA	7500

CHA 1998 from Accounts of the GSL
Source: JICA 1998

Militarization is a social process composed of both active and passive elements. Paradoxically, perhaps the most crucial element of this process is passivity. It is a willingness to accept (or at least not reject) the encroaching militarization of one's day-to-day life. In Colombo, this would include the acceptance of constant security checks and road blocks. It would also include the acceptance of a system which requires all Tamils who come to Colombo to register at the local police station in the neighborhood in which they are staying (this a version of the pass system in operation in Vavuniya). After a while, as Salman Rushdie once put it, all of this simply becomes 'part of the furniture'. However, the acceptance of such intrusions—whether unquestioningly or with security arguments—subsidizes and entrenches such practices in our mental, physical and political landscapes. After a while, the failure to reject may become a willingness to accept. From this point, acquiescence creates the political space within which the state military or the non-state paramilitary can push such intrusions to further and greater extremes. The challenge for the donor community then is to highlight the disincentives for inaction and the incentives for action in an environment which has subsidized and rewarded passivity.

To put a rather abstract argument in very concrete terms, we need only look at the acceptance of the War Defence Levy introduced in 1994 which imposed a goods and services tax of 4.5%. In January 1999 this was increased to 5.5%. And in May 2000, it was increased to 6.5%. This is a direct contribution to the war in Sri Lanka which is paid one way or another by all residents and organizations on the island. In other words, directly and indirectly, 5.5% of the ODA channelled into Sri Lanka will be allocated to the government's war in the north and east. It may well not be coincidental that expenditures on defence after the Levy was introduced increased from Rs 22.4 billion in 1994 to Rs33.2 billion in 1995 to Rs39.2 billion in 1996 (CHA, 1998). It seems more than a bit contradictory that ODA-supported activities with the stated objectives of development, humanitarian response, and peacebuilding would also contribute to the war effort through the War Levy. This is an issue which might be taken up in the annual meeting of the Consultative Group in Paris when donors meet to discuss their aid programs in Sri Lanka.

Conclusion

There is still much work to be done to develop a systematic and nuanced understanding of the ways in which ODA affects the dynamics of peace and violent conflict in Sri Lanka and elsewhere. Development workers— multilateral, bilateral and NGO—are increasingly aware of the limitations imposed on their work by the ebb and flow of violence in Sri Lanka. However, only slowly is attention being turned towards the systematic consideration and measurement of the peace and conflict impact of development work. And, there has been little change in the programming and monitoring logic underpinning development projects in conflict zones. Not only has it become clear that development does not necessarily equal peace, but often 'development' may generate or exacerbate violent conflict. Conversely, development projects may have positive peacebuilding impacts which are unintended, and thus undocumented and unable to inform future development work.

While some organizational and implementational changes are underway in some bilateral and multilateral development organizations, much more time needs to pass before their significance becomes apparent. Ultimately however, the primary point of reference in determining the magnitude and significance of such changes will be the impact on the lived experience of those in conflict and post-conflict zones. Development and peace mean nothing if they are not reflected in positive changes in the lived experience of those in, or returning to, conflict zones. It is clear in Sri Lanka and elsewhere that different groups may have different criteria—indeed, different understandings and expectations—concerning the means and ends of development initiatives in these settings.

Even if ODA was carefully conceived and implemented to increase its constructive peacebuilding impact, it alone will not resolve conflict in Sri Lanka. There are parallel political and economic initiatives which are also necessary for movement forward. Nonetheless, ODA has been shown to have both positive and negative impacts on structures and processes of peace and conflict. And for this reason, it cannot be neglected.

While the international community does appear capable of learning, there is a need for careful monitoring to assess whether it is learning the right lessons. The degree to which it may learn, and more importantly the types of lessons it may learn, are shaped by the range of experiences on which it draws. In this regard, the overwhelmingly Northern character of the development and peacebuilding 'projects' must be highlighted. Until Southern voices, experiences, and interests are included in a substantial and meaningful way, the potential for sustainable constructive impact will be compromised. There is a long way yet to go.

Notes

1. I wish to thank Tim Shaw, Fahim Quadir and Sandra MacLean at the Centre for Foreign Policy Studies of Dalhousie University for inviting me to participate in this project. I also wish to thank the Peacebuilding Program of the Canadian Department of Foreign Affairs and International Trade for supporting my research with the OECD DAC Working Group on Conflict, Peace and Development Cooperation upon which this chapter is based. My deepest thanks goes to my colleagues in Sri Lanka who, over 20 years, have taught me everything that one needs to know about theory, praxis and responsibility.

2. This paper uses the term 'militarized violence' rather than 'war' because it conveys a more accurate sense of the nature of violent conflict in Sri Lanka. While it includes conventional military engagements between organized forces of war, it also encompasses the full spectrum of abuses that defines 'dirty wars' around the world perpetrated by (primarily, though not exclusively) men, in or out of a uniform. It thus includes control through terror and the manipulation of fear, the systematic abuse of human rights, and a totalizing process by which all social, political and economic problems come to be defined as military problems—and, as military problems, the most suitable response is deemed automatically to be the application of the weapons of war.

3. On American assistance to Colombia, see Hodgson (2000: 7). On American assistance to Indonesia, see Vulliamy and Barnett (2000: 2). On British arms and spare parts to Zimbabwe while it was engaged in military adventurism in the Democratic Republic of Congo (DRC) and vicious repression of opposition movements and the illegal eviction of white farmers, see MacAskill (2000: 11 and 14).

4. Of course, this is not to suggest that economic growth is necessarily reflected in an increase in standards of living for all sectors of a population.

5. For an early effort to do just this, see Bush, 1998. See also Mary Anderson, 1999. For a very interesting effort to apply this idea, see WHO, September 1998. In the early 1990s I recall the blank look of a principal investigator of a medium-sized health research project

when I asked whether the research teams in his proposed Sri Lanka project would be mixed (Sinhalese, Tamil, Muslim) in an effort to facilitate access, trust, acceptance and inter-group professional linkages. No thought had been given to this issue. Such 'anthropological detail' was not considered necessary.

6. This comparison draws on a number of sources: For the Mahawelli/Madura Oya project see Gillies, 1992. For the Gal Oya Project see Uphoff, 1992; and Uphoff, 1992a.

7. International acclaim and material support were not so unconditional as the government seemed to think. After a 1980 budget deficit amounting to more than 26 percent of GDP, accompanied by a rate of inflation of at least 30 percent, the consortium of donors meeting in Paris in July pressured the government to cut current account and budget deficits and to raise more resources internally. Familiar aid budget disputes were repeated in meetings with the Aid Sri Lanka Consortium and IMF in the summers of 1982-1983; belt tightening was urged, the government cited domestic constraints and blamed external factors, and compromises were made (Herring, 1998: 11).

8. Bruce Matthews, personal correspondence, 29 March 1993. The area has suffered under the double burden of economic discrimination, and ultimately, war.

9. For an excellent study on the costs of war in Sri Lanka, see Arunatilake, Jayasuriya and Kelegama, January 2000.

10. Agence France Press reported on 14 May 2000: 'Sri Lanka is officially on a "war footing".' News is censored. Public meetings are banned, but life in the capital is as lively as ever and the only tension appears to be among visiting foreign journalists. As fighting between security forces and Tamil Tiger guerrillas escalated in the island's north, the government assumed war-time powers and imposed censorship on the media, while city authorities called for the curtailment of public celebrations. The government has raised the price of cigarettes and liquor by five to 10 percent and increased the 'national security levy' imposed on all goods and services by one percentage point to 6.5 percent, triggering across the board price increases.

References

Adam, Kanya (1997), 'The Politics of Redress: South African Style Affirmative Action', *The Journal of Modern African Studies*, vol. 35, no. 2, pp. 231-249.

Adam, Herbert (1998), 'Empowering the Fat Cats', *The Mail and Guardian*, 9-19 April.

Adedeji, Adebayo (ed.) (1993), *Africa within the World: Beyond Dispossession and Dependence*, Zed Books in Association with African Centre for Development and Strategic Studies (ACDESS), London.

Adejumobi, S. (1996), 'The Structural Adjustment Programme and Democratic Transition in Africa', *Law and Politics in Africa, Asia and Latin America*, no. 4, pp. 416-34.

Adler, Emanuel and Barnet, Michael (eds) (1998), *Security Communities*, Cambridge University Press, Cambridge.

Adler, Glenn and Webster, Eddie (2000), 'South Africa: Class Compromise...', *Southern Africa Report*, vol. 15, no. 2, pp. 3-7.

Africa News Online, (wysiwyg:29/http://www.africanews.org/o...abwe/stories/20000518/2000518_fe at2.html/20000504/20000504_feat31.html).

African Economic Digest (1987), 'Special Report: Zimbabwe' (April).

African National Congress (1994), *Reconstruction and Development Programme*, Umanyano Publications, Johannesburg.

Aina, Tade (1996), 'Globalisation and Social Policy in Africa: Issues and Research Directions', *CODESRIA Working Paper Series*, no. 6.

Alagappa, Muthiah (1995), 'The Asian Spectrum', *Journal of Democracy*, vol. 6, no. 1, pp. 29-36.

Alger, Chadwick F. (1994), 'Citizens and the UN System in a Changing World', in Yoshikazu Sakamoto (ed.), *Global Transformations: Challenges to the State System*, The United Nations University Press, Tokyo, pp. 301-29.

Almond, Gabriel A. (1990), *A Discipline Divided: Schools and Sects in Political Science*, Sage, Newbury Park, CA, pp. 173-188.

Amoore, Louise, Dodgson, Richard, Gills, Barry K., Langley, Paul, Marshall, Don and Watson, Iain (1997), 'Overturning "Globalization": Resisting the Teleological, Reclaiming the "Political"', *New Political Economy*, vol. 2, no. 1, pp. 179-195.

Anderson, Benedict (1983), *Imagined Communities: Reflections on the Origin and Spread of Nationalism*, Verso, London.

Anderson, Mary (1999), *Do No Harm: How Aid Can Support Peace—or War*, Lynne Rienner Publishers, Boulder and London.

Angel, David P. (1994), *Restructuring for Innovation: The Remaking of the U.S. Semiconductor Industries*, The Guilford Press, New York and London.

Apter, David and Rosberg, Carl (1994), *Political Development and the New Realism in Sub-Saharan Africa*, University of Virginia Press, Charlottesville.

Archibugi, Daniele and Held, David (eds) (1995), *Cosmopolitan Democracy: An Agenda for a New World Order*, Polity Press, Cambridge.

Armstrong, David (1998), 'Globalization and the Social State', *Review of International Studies*, vol. 24, no. 4, pp. 461-478.

Arndt, H.W. and Hill, Hal (eds) (1999), *Southeast Asia's Economic Crisis: Origins, Lessons, and the Way Forward*, Institute of Southeast Asian Studies, Singapore.

Aronson, Jonathan (2001), 'Global Networks and their Impact', in James N. Rosenau and J.P. Singh (eds), *Information Technologies and Global Politics: The Changing Scope of Power and Governance*, State University of New York Press, Albany.

Arquila, John and Ronfeldt, David (1997), *In Athena's Camp: Preparing for Conflict in the Information Age*, Rand National Defense Research Institute, Los Angeles.

Arudsothy, Ponniah (1994), 'New Strategies of Labour Control: The State, Transnationals and Trade Unionism in Malaysia', in Jackson Sukhan (ed.), *Contemporary Developments in Asian Industrial Relations*, University of New South Wales Studies in Human Resource Management and Industrial Relations in Asia, no. 3.

Arunatilake, Nisha, Jayasuriya, Sisira and Kelegama, Saman (2000), *The Economic Cost of the War in Sri Lanka*, Research Studies: Macroeconomic Policy and Planning Series No. 13, Institute of Policy Studies, Colombo, Sri Lanka (January).

Aseka, E.M. (1999), 'Ethnicity, Governance, and Prevention of Conflict: State of the Issue and Research Perspectives', *Africa Development*, vol. XIXIV, no. 3/4, pp. 71-102.

Athanasiou, Tom (1998), *Divided Planet: The Ecology of Rich and Poor*, University of Georgia Press, Athens and London.

Athukorala, P. (1998), 'Malaysia', in R. McLeod and R. Garnaut (eds), *East Asia in Crisis: From Being a Miracle to Needing One*. Routledge, London and New York, pp. 85-101.

Aulakh, Preet S. and Schechter, Michael G. (eds) (2000), *Rethinking Globalization(s): From Corporate Transnationalisms to Local Interventions*, Macmillan, London.

Balati, Albert (1999), 'The Dynamics of the Burundi Conflict', Unpublished MA Dissertation, University of Dar es Salaam, Tanzania.

Bangura, Yusuf (1994), *The Search for Identity: Ethnicity, Religion and Political Violence*, Occasional Paper No. 6, World Summit for Social Development, UNRISD, Geneva.

---- and Gibbon, Peter (1992), 'Adjustment, Authoritarianism and Democracy: An Introduction to Some Conceptual and Empirical Issues', in Peter Gibbon, et al. (eds), *Authoritarianism, Democracy and Adjustment: The Politics of Economic Reform in Africa*, Nordiska Afrikainstitutet, Uppsala, pp. 7-38.

Barber, Benjamin (1995), *Jihad vs. McWorld*, Times Books, New York.

Baxter, Craig (1997), *Bangladesh: From a Nation to a State*, Westview Press, Boulder.

Bayart, Jean-François, Ellis, Stephen and Hibou, Béatrice (1997), *The Criminalization of the State in Africa*, James Currey, Oxford.

Bazaara, N. and Nyago, Kintu (1999), 'Civil Society Empowerment and Poverty Reduction in Uganda: A Review Essay', *Research Report for CODESRIA-Civil Society Project*, CODESRIA, Dakar.

Bazaara, N. and Oloka-Onyango, J. (1999), 'Governance, Poverty and Globalisation', *Concept Paper for the 2nd Regional Meeting of the CODESRIA/UNDP Civil Society Programme*, Kampala (September).

Beckman, Björn (1993), 'The Liberation of Civil Society: Neo-liberal Ideologyand Political Theory', *Review of African Political Economy*, no. 58, pp. 20-33.

---- (1991), 'Empowerment of Repression: The World Bank and the Politics of African Adjustment', *Africa Development*, vol. XVI, no.1.

Bekker, Simon, Dodds, Martine and Ewert, Joachim (1999), 'A Strategic Social Analysis of the South African Wine Industry', Department of Sociology, University of Stellenbosch, Occasional Paper No. 9 (December).

Berger, Peter L. and Luckmann, Thomas (1966), *The Social Construction of Reality: A Treatise in the Sociology of Knowledge*, Anchor Books, New York.

Birmingham, David (1966), *Trade and Conflict in Angola: The Mbundu and their Neighbours under the Influence of the Portuguese 1483-1790*, Clarendon Press, London.

Biti, Tendayi (1997), 'Issues Facing Civil Society: A Southern Perspective', in Owen Stuurman and Riann de Villiers (eds), *Circle of Power: An Enabling Framework for Civil Society in Southern Africa*, The Development Resources Centre, Johannesburg, pp. 55-58.

Blair, Harry (1992), 'Defining, Promoting and Sustaining Democracy: Formulating an Aid Strategy for Development Assistance and Evaluation', mimeograph, USAID, Washington, DC.

Bobbio, Norbert (1979), 'Gramsci and the Conception of Civil Society', in Chantal Mouffe (ed.), *Gramsci and Marxist Theory*, Routledge, London, pp. 21-47.

Bornstein, David (1996), 'The Barefoot Bank with Cheek', *The Atlantic Monthly*, vol. 276, no. 6, pp. 40-47.

Botchwey, Kwesi (1999), 'Africa and Global Competitiveness in the Next Millennium', *Text of Vanguard's 15th Anniversary Lecture*, Vanguard (31 March).

Bowie, A. (1991), *Crossing the Industrial Divide: State, Society and the Politics of Economic Transformation in Malaysia*, Columbia University Press, New York.

BRAC (1999), *Annual Report: 1999*, BRAC, Dhaka.

Brass, Paul R. (1991), *Ethnicity and Nationalism*, Sage Publications, New Delhi.

Bratton, Michael (1989), 'Beyond the State: Civil Society and Associational Life in Africa', *World Politics*, vol. XLI, no. 3, pp. 407-430.

Brett, E.A. (1997a), 'Creating the Basis for Democratic Transition in Uganda', in P. Langseth, J. Katorobo, E. Brett and J. Munroe (eds), *Uganda: Landmarks in Rebuilding a Nation*, Fountain Publishers, Kampala, pp. 209-228.

---- (1997b), 'Adjustment Policy and Institutional Reform in Uganda', in *Ibid.*, pp. 26-34.

Bulpin, T.V. (1995), *Stellenbosch: Its Wine, Fruit and Flower Lands*, Northcliff, Gauteng, Fish Eagle. Discovering Southern Africa No. 2.

Bunch, Charlotte (1990), 'Women's Rights as Human Rights: Toward a Revision of Human Rights', *Human Rights Quarterly*, vol. 12, no. 4, pp. 486-98.

Bunch, Charlotte and Reilly, Niamh (1999), 'Strategic Planning: Global Campaign for Women's Human Rights', in Marilee Karl with Anita Anand, Floris Blankenberg, Allert Van Den Ham and Adrian Saldanha (eds), *Measuring the Immeasurable: Planning, Monitoring and Evaluation of Networks*, Women's Feature Service, New Delhi.

Burawoy, M. (1983), 'Between Labour Process and the State: The Changing Face of Factory Regimes Under Advanced Capitalism', *American Sociological Review*, vol. 18 (October), pp. 587-605.

Bush, Kenneth (1998), *A Measure of Peace: Peace and Conflict Impact Assessment (PCIA) of Development Projects in Conflict Zones*, International Development Research Centre, Ottawa.

---- (1996), 'Rocks and Hard Places, Human Rights Abuse, Bad Governance, and Population Displacement', *Canadian Foreign Policy*, vol. 4, no. 1, pp. 49-83.

---- (1996), 'Beyond Bungee Cord Humanitarianism: Towards a Developmental Approach to Peacebuilding', *Canadian Journal of Development Studies*, Special Issue (December).

Business Day (daily), Johannesburg

Business Report (daily), South Africa.

Callaghy, Thomas M. (1994), 'Civil Society, Democracy and Economic Change in Africa: A Dissenting Opinion about Resurgent Societies', in John W. Harbeson, et al. (eds) *Civil Society and the State in Africa*, Lynne Rienner, Boulder.

Campbell, Bonnie (2000), 'New Rules of the Game: The World Bank's Role in the Construction of New Normative Frameworks for States, Markets and Social Exclusion', *Canadian Journal of Development Studies*, vol. XXI, no. 1, pp. 7-30.

Campbell, Horace (1999), 'The Africa Search for Renewal in the Era of Globalisation', paper presented at the AAPS 12th Bi-Annual Congress, Dakar (22-25 June).

Carter Center (1990), *African Governance in the 1990s. Objectives, Resources and Constraints*, Carter Center, Atlanta.

---- (1989), *Perestroika and Glasnost in Africa*, vol. 1, no. 2.

Casaburi, Gabriel (1999), *Dynamic Agroindustrial Clusters: The Political Economy of Competitive Sectors in Argentina and Chile*, Macmillan, London.

Castells, Manuel (1998), *The Information Age: Economy, Society and Culture, Volume III, End of Millennium*, Blackwell, Oxford.

---- (1997), *The Information Age: Economy, Society and Culture, Volume II, The Power of Identity*, Blackwell, Oxford.

---- (1996), *The Information Age: Economy, Society and Culture, Volume I, The Rise of the Network Society*, Blackwell, Oxford.

Cawthra, Gavin (1997), *Securing South Africa's Democracy: Defence, Development and Security in Transition*, Macmillan, London.

Cerny, Philip G. (2000), 'Political Globalization and the Competitive State', in Richard Stubbs and Geoffrey R.D. Underhill (eds), *Political Economy and the Changing Global Order*, Oxford University Press, Don Mills, Ontario, pp. 300-309.

---- (1990), *The Changing Architecture of Politics: Structure, Agency and the Future of the State*, Sage, London.

Chabal, Patrick (1998), 'A Few Considerations on Democracy in Africa', *International Affairs*, vol. 74, no. 2 (April), pp. 289-295.

---- (1992), *Power in Africa: An Essay in Political Interpretation*, St. Martin's Press, New York.

---- and Daloz, Jean-Pascal (1999), *Africa Works: Disorder and Political Instrument*, James Currey, Oxford.

Chan, Stephen (1999), 'Troubled Pluralisms: Pondering an Indonesian Moment for Zimbabwe and Zambia', *The Round Table*, no. 349, pp. 61-76.

Chazan, Naomi, Mortimer, Robert, Ravenhill, John and Rothchild, Donald (1992), *Politics and Society in Contemporary Africa*, Lynne Rienner, Boulder.

Cheaka, A.T. and Nangbe, F.N. (1998), *NGOs and the Informal Sector in Africa: What Links and for What Purpose?* International Institute for Environment and Development, London.

Chen, Edward and Kwan, C. H. (1997), *Asia's Borderless Economy: The Emergence of Sub-Regional Zones*, Allen & Unwin, St. Leonards, Australia.

Chhachhi, Amrita (1998), 'Gender, Flexibility, Skill and Industrial Restructuring in the Electronics Industry in India', paper presented at the Regional Conference and Technology in Asia, Asian Institute of Technology, Bangkok (4-7 August).

Chhachhi, Amrita and Pittin, Renee (1996), 'Multiple Identities, Multiple Strategies', in A. Chhachhi and R. Pittin (eds), *Confronting State, Capital and Patriarchy: Women Organizing in the Process of Industrialization*, Macmillan Press, Basingstoke and London, pp. 1-42.

Childers, Erskine with Urquhart, Brian (1994), *Renewing the United Nations System*, Dag Hammarskjold Foundation, Uppsala.

Chin, Christine B. N. and Mittelman, James H. (1997), 'Conceptualizing Resistance to Globalization', *New Political Economy*, vol. 2, no.1, pp. 25-37.

Chole, Eshetu (1997), 'Prospects for Economic Recovery in Africa', *Eastern Africa Social Science Review*, vol. XIII, no. 1 (January).

---- (1991), 'Crisis and Adjustment in Sub-Saharan Africa', in Dharam Ghai (ed.), *The IMF and the South: The Social Impact of Crisis and Adjustment*, Zed Books, London.

---- and Ibrahim, Jibrin (eds) (1995), *Democratisation Process in Africa*, CODESRIA, Dakar.

Chossudovsky, Michel (1997), *The Globalization of Poverty: Impacts of IMF and World Bank Reforms*, Zed, London.
Chowdhury, Elora Halim (1997), 'Making a Difference: 25 Years of BRAC', *Star Magazine*, vol. 2, no 55, pp. 5-11.
The Chronicle (1992), Zimbabwe (8 September).
Cippolla, Carlo M. (1980), *Before the Industrial Revolution: European Society and Economy, 1000-1700*, Second Edition, W.W. Norton and Company, New York.
CIVICUS (1999), *Civil Society at the Millennium*, Kumarian, Connecticut.
Clapham, Christopher (1998a), 'Discerning the New Africa', *International Affairs*, vol. 74, no. 2 (April), pp. 263-69.
---- (ed.) (1998b), *African Guerillas*, James Currey Ltd., Oxford.
---- (1996), *Africa in the International System: The Politics of State Survival*, Cambridge University Press, Cambridge.
Clark, Ian (1997), *Globalization and Fragmentation: International Relations in the 20th Century*, Oxford University Press, New York.
Coate, Roger A., Alger, Chadwick F. and Lipschutz, Ronnie (1996), 'The United Nations and Civil Society: Creative Partnerships for Sustainable Development', *Alternatives*, vol. 21, no. 1, pp. 93-122.
CODESRIA Bulletin (1999), nos. 1, 2, 3, 4, CODESRIA, Dakar.
Coleman, William D. and Porter, Tony (1994), 'Regulating International Banking and Securities: Emerging Co-operation among National Authorities', in Richard Stubbs and Geoffrey R.D. Underhill (eds), *Political Economy and the Changing Global Order*, St Martin's Press, New York, pp. 190-203.
Commission on Global Governance (1995), *Our Global Neighborhood*, New York, Oxford University Press.
Consortium of Humanitarian Agencies (CHA) (1998a), *Yearbook 1997: Sri Lanka*, Consortium of Humanitarian Agencies, Colombo.
---- (1998b), 'Important Commitments on the Protection of Children made by Government and LTTE in Sri Lanka arising from the Visit of Mr. Olara Otunnu', *CHA Newsletter*, vol. II, no. 8 (May-June).
Coser, Lewis (1964), *The Functions of Social Conflict*, The Free Press, New York.
Cox, Robert W. (1999), 'Civil Society at the Turn of the Millennium: Prospects for an Alternative World Order', *Review of International Studies*, vol. 25, no. 1, pp. 3-28.
---- (1997), 'An Alternative Approach to Multilateralism for the Twenty-first Century', *Global Governance*, vol. 3, no. 1, pp. 103-116.
---- (1994), 'The Crisis on World Order and the Challenge to International Organization', *Cooperation and Conflict*, vol. 9, no. 2, pp. 99-113.
---- (1992), 'Global Perestroika', in Ralph Miliband and Leo Panitch (eds), *Socialist Register 1995*, Merlin, London, pp. 26-43.
---- (1991), 'The Global Political Economy and Social Choice', in Daniel Drache and Meric S. Gertler (eds), The New Era of Global Competition: State Power and Market Power, McGill-Queen's, Montreal, pp. 335-50.
---- (1981), 'Social Forces, States and World Orders: Beyond International Relations Theory', *Millennium*, vol. 10, no. 2, pp. 126-155.

---- with Sinclair, Timothy J. (1996), *Approaches to World Order*, Cambridge University Press, Cambridge.

Crawford, Neta C. and Klotz, Audie (eds) (1999), *How Sanctions Work: Lessons from South Africa*, Macmillan, London.

Crouch, H. (1996), *Government and Society in Malaysia*, Cornell University Press, Ithaca.

Culpepper, Roy and Caroline Pestieau (eds) (1996), *Development and Global Governance*, North-South Institute, Ottawa.

Cuny, Fred and Cuny, Christopher (1992), 'The Return of Tamil Refugees from Sri Lanka, 1983-1989', in Fredrick Cuny, Barry N. Stein and Pat Reid (eds), *Repatriation During Conflict in Africa and Asia*, Centre for the Study of Societies in Crisis, Texas.

Daily News (Tanzania) (1991), no. 7252 (21 July).

Daniel, W. (1987), 'New Technology: A Lubricant for the Reform of Industrial Working Practices', *Policy Studies*, vol. 8, no. 2 (October).

Deibert, Ronald J. (1997), *Parchment, Printing, and Hypermedia: Communication in World Order Transformation*, Columbia University Press, New York.

Deng, Francis M. (1995), *War of Visions: Conflict of Identities in the Sudan*, The Brookings Institution, Washington, DC.

---- (1991), 'Dilemmas of Nationbuilding: Racism, Ethnicity and Development in Africa', *Ethnic Studies Report*, vol. 9, no. 2, pp. 1-9.

de Tocqueville, Alexis (1959), *Democracy in America*, Vintage Books, New York.

Deyo, Frederick (1997), 'Labour and Industrial Restructuring in South-East Asia', in Garry Rodan, Kevin Hewison and Richard Robison (eds), *The Political Economy of South-East Asia*, Oxford University Press, Melbourne, pp. 205-224.

Diamond, Larry (1994), 'The Global Imperative: Building a Democratic World Order', *Current History*, vol. 93. no. 579, pp. 1-7.

Diaw, Aminata and Diouf, Mamadou (1998), 'Ethnic Group versus Nation: Identity Discourses in Senegal', in Okwudiba Nnoli (ed.) *Ethnic Conflicts in Africa*, CODESRIA Book Series, Dakar.

Dickson, Anna K. (1997), *Development and International Relations: A Critical Introduction*, Polity Press, Cambridge.

Dirasse, Laketch (1999), 'Conflict, Development and Peace in Africa: Gender Perspectives', *Conflict Trends*, vol. 2.

Doornbos, Martin (1988), 'The Uganda Crisis and the National Question', in Hansen Holger Bernt and Michael Twaddle (eds), *Uganda Now: Between Decay and Development*, James Currey, Oxford, pp. 254-266.

Dunham, David and Jayasuriya, Sisira (1998), 'Is All so Well with the Economy and with the Rural Poor?' *Pravada*, vol. 5, no. 10/11, pp. 22-7.

Dunleavy, Patrick and O'Leary, Brendan (1987), *Theories of the State: The Politics of Liberal Democracy*, Macmillan, London.

Duraiappah, K. (1999), 'The Role of Trade Union Education in Strengthening the Malaysian Trade Union Movement', in *1949-1999 Kongres Kesatuan Sekerja Malaysia Merayakan Limapuluh Tahun Pergerakan Kesatuan Sekerja di Malaysia*, MTUC, Kuala Lumpur.

Dyer, Susannah (1995), 'Stemming the Flow of Light Weapons', paper presented at the UNIDIR Workshop on *Proliferation of Light Weapons in the Post Cold War World*, Berlin.

Economic Commission for Africa (1989), *African Alternative Framework to Structural Adjustment Programmes for Socio-Economic Recovery and Transformation*, ECA, Addis Ababa.

Eckstein, Harry (1975), 'Case Study and Theory in Political Science', in F.I. Greenstein and N.W. Polsby (eds), *Handbook of Political Science*, vol. 7, Addison-Wesley, Reading, Massachusetts.

'Editorial: Capitulation?' (2000), *Southern Africa Report*, vol. 15, no. 2, pp. 1-2.

Edwards, Michael and Hulme, David (1992), 'Scaling-up the Development Impact of NGOs: Concepts and Experiences', in Michael Edwards and David Hulme (eds), *Making a Difference: NGOs and Development in a Changing World*, Earthscan, London, pp. 13-39.

Elias, Juanita (1999), 'Recruitment and Employment Practices in a Transnational Firm: Gendered Divisions of Labour in Malaysia and Britain', paper presented at the Second International Malaysian Studies Conference, Malaysian Social Science Association, Kuala Lumpur (2-4 August).

Embong, A.R. (1996), 'Social Transformation, the State and the Middle Classes in Post-Independence Malaysia', *Southeast Asian Studies*, vol. 34, no. 3 (December), pp. 524-547.

---- (1995), 'The Malaysian Middle Classes: Some Preliminary Observations,' *Jurnal Antropologi dan Sosiologi*, vol. 22, pp. 31-54.

Enemuo, Francis C. (1999), 'Restructuring State-Civil Society Relations for Economic Renewal in Africa', paper presented at the AAPS Biannual Congress, Dakar (22-25 June).

---- (1992), 'The Constitution of Civil Society in African History and Politics', in A. Caron, A. Gboyega and E. Osaghae (eds), *Democratic Transitions in Africa*, University of Ibadan Press, Ibadan.

Esman, Milton (1994), *Ethnic Politics,* Cornell University Press, Ithaca and London.

---- (1987), 'Ethnic Politics and Economic Power', *Comparative Politics* (July), pp. 395-418.

Ethical Trading Initiative, London (http:www.eti.org.uk).

Evans, Alison and Moore, Mick (eds) (1998), 'The Bank, the State and Development: Dissecting the 1997 World Development Report', Special Edition, *IDS Bulletin*, vol. 29, no. 2, pp. 1-84.

Evans, Peter (1997a), 'State Structures, Government-Business Relations and Economic Transformation', in Ben R. Schneider and Sylvia Maxfield (eds), *Business and the State in Developing Countries*, Cornell University Press, Ithaca and London, pp. 63-87.

---- (1997b), 'The Eclipse of the State? Reflections on Stateness in an Era of Globalization', *World Politics*, vol. 50, no. 1 (October), pp. 62-87.

---- (1995), *Embedded Autonomy*, Princeton University Press, Princeton.

Ewert, Joachim (1996), 'Labour Organisation in Western Cape Agriculture: An Ethnic Corporatism?', *Journal of Peasant Studies*, vol. 23, no. 2/3, pp. 146-165.

Ewert, Joachim and Hamman, Johann (1999), 'Why Paternalism Survives: Globalisation, Democratisation and Labour on South African Wine Farms', *Sociologia Ruralis*, vol. 39, no. 2, pp. 202-221.

Executive Intelligence Review (1994), vol. 21, no. 43 (28 October).

Falk, Richard (1997), 'Resisting "Globalization from Above" through "Globalization-from-Below"', *New Political Economy*, vol. 2, no.1, pp. 17-24.

---- (1995), *On Humane Governance: Towards a New Global Politics*, World Order Models Project Report of the Global Civilization Initiative, Polity Press, Cambridge.

Far Eastern Economic Review (FEER) (1985) (21 February).

Farrington, John and Lewis, David J. (1993), 'Background', in John Farrington and David J. Lewis (eds), *Non-Governmental Organizations and the State in Asia: Rethinking Roles in Sustainable Agricultural Development*, Routledge, London, pp. 3-8.

Farrington, John and Lewis, David J. (eds) (1993), *Non-Governmental Organizations and the State in Asia: Rethinking Roles in Sustainable Agricultural Development*, Routledge, London.

Farwell, Edie, Wood, Peregrine, James, Maureen and Banks, Karen (1999), 'Global Networking for Change: Experiences from the APC Women's Programme', in Wendy Harcourt (ed.), *Women @ Internet: Creating New Cultures in Cyberspace*, Zed Books, London.

Fatton, Robert (1995), 'Africa in the Age of Democratisation: The Civic Limitations of Civil Society', *African Studies Review*, vol. 38, no. 2, pp. 67-99.

---- (1992), *Predatory Rule: State and Civil Society in Africa*, Lynne Rienner, Boulder.

Featherstone, Mike (ed.) (1990), *Global Culture: Nationalism, Globalization and Modernity*, Sage, London.

Ferrnie, S., Metcalf, D. and Woodland, S. (1994), 'Does HRM Boost Employee-Management Relations?', working paper, Center for Economic Performance and Industrial Relations Department, London School of Economics.

Field, G. (1998), 'South Africa's Next Revolution', *WorldLink* (January/ February), pp. 108-115.

The Financial Gazette (2000), 'Zimbabwe Crisis Strains Relations Between South Africa Government', Harare (18 May).

The Financial Gazette (1990), Zimbabwe (16 March).

The Financial Gazette (1992), Zimbabwe (9 July).

Financial Mail (weekly), Johannesburg.

Finkelstein, Lawrence (1995), 'What is Global Governance?' *Global Governance*, vol. 1, no. 3, pp. 367-372.

First Merchant Bank of Zimbabwe Limited (FMB) (1998), *Annual Reports 1995 and 1998*, FMB, Harare.

Fishman, Robert (1990), 'Rethinking State and Regime: Southern Europe in Transition to Democracy', *World Politics*, vol. 42, no. 3, pp. 422-440.

Fowler, Robert (2000), *Report of the Panel of Experts on Violations of Security Council Sanctions Against Unita,* www.un.org/News/dh/latest/ angolareport_eng.htm

Franklin, M.I. (1998), 'The Political Economy of Informatics: Global-Speak and Gender-Power Relations', paper presented at the ISA Conference, Vienna (16-19 September).

Frenkel, Stephen and Peetz, David (1998), 'Globalization and Industrial Relations in East Asia: A Three Country Comparison', Centre for Corporate Change, Paper No. 87, University of New South Wales, Sydney.

Fridjhon, Michael (1992), 'Future of the Cape Wine Industry', in Michael Fridjhon, *The Penguin Book of South African Wine*, Penguin, Harmondsworth, pp. 276-282.

Fridjhon, Michael and Murray, Andy (1986), *Conspiracy of Giants: The South African Liquor Industry*, Divaris Stein, Johannesburg.

Friedman, Steven (1999), 'South Africa: Entering the Post-Mandela Era', *Journal of Democracy*, vol. 10, no. 4, pp. 3-18.

---- (1991), 'An Unlikely Utopia: State and Civil Society in South Africa', *Politikon*, vol. 19, no. 1 (December), pp. 5-19.

Fukuyama, Francis (1992), *The End of History and the Last Man*, Hamish Hamilton, London.

---- (1989), 'The End of History?', *The National Interest*, vol. 16, no. 2 (Summer) pp. 3-18.

Gamba, Virginia (1996), 'Controlling the Proliferation of Light Weapons: Problems and Linkages', paper presented at the UN Regional Workshop on *Small Arms and Light Weapons*, Pretoria.

Geertz, Clifford (1963), 'The Integrative Revolution', in Clifford Geertz (ed.), *Old Societies and New States*, Free Press, New York, pp. 105-57.

George, K. (1999), 'The Struggle for Trade Union Rights in Malaysia', in *1949-1999 Kongres Kesatuan Sekerja Malaysia Merayakan Limapuluh Tahun Pergerakan Kesatuan Sekerja di Malaysia*, Kuala Lumpur, MTUC.

Gibbon, Peter (1999), 'Some Reflections on State, Civil Society and the Division of Labour in Lake Tanganyika', paper presented at Workshop on *Dimensions of Economic and Political Reforms in Contemporary Africa*, Kampala (8-12 April).

---- (1996), 'Some Reflections on "Civil Society" and Political Change', in Lars Rudebeck and Olle Tornquist (eds), *Democratisation in the Third World: Concrete Cases in Comparative and Theoretical Perspectives*, The Seminar for Development Studies, Uppsala.

Giddens, Anthony (1999), *The Third Way: The Reversal of Social Democracy*, Polity, in association with Blackwell Publishers, Cambridge.

Gill, Stephen (1998), 'New Constitutionalism, Democratization and the Global Political Economy', *Pacifica Review*, vol. 10, no. 1, pp. 23-38.

---- (1995), 'Globalization, Market Civilisation, and Disciplinary Neoliberalism', *Millennium*, vol. 24, no. 3, pp. 399-423.

---- (1994a), 'Knowledge, Politics, and Neo-liberal Political Economy', in Richard Stubbs and Geoffrey Underhill (eds), *Political Economy and the Changing Global Order*, St. Martin's, New York, pp. 75-88.

---- (1994b), 'Globalization and the Emerging World Order', paper presented at workshop on 'Globalization: Opportunities and Challenges', Washington, DC (26-27 March).

---- and Mittelman, James H. (eds) (1997), *Innovation and Transformation in International Studies*, Cambridge University Press, Cambridge.

---- and David Law (1988), *The Global Political Economy*, Harvester/ Wheatsheaf.

Gillies, David (1992), 'Principled Intervention: Canadian Aid, Human Rights and the Sri Lankan Conflict', in Robert Miller (ed.), *Aid as Peacemaker: Canadian Development Assistance and Third World Conflict*, Carleton University Press, Ottawa, pp. 33-50.

Gills, Barry (ed.) (2000), Globalization and the Politics of Resistance, Macmillan, London.

---- (ed.) (1997), 'Special Issue: Globalization and the Politics of Resistance', *New Political Economy*, vol. 2, no. 1, pp. 5-200.

Glaser, Daryl (1997), 'South Africa and the Limits of Civil Society', *Journal of Southern Africa Studies*, vol. 23, no. 3, pp. 5-25.

Glentworth, Garth (1993), *Practical Aid Assistance to Good Government*, mimeograph, ODA.

Goetz, Anne M. and Gupta, R.S. (1994), 'Who Takes the Credit? Gender, Power and Control over Loan Use in Rural Credit Programs in Bangladesh', *IDS Working Paper*, no. 8, Institute of Development Studies, University of Sussex, Brighton.

Goldblatt, David, et al. (1997), 'Economic Globalisation and the Nation State: Shifting Balances of Power', *Alternatives*, vol. 22, pp. 269-285.

Goldin, Ian and Heymans, Chris (1999), 'Mounting a New Society: The RDP in Perspective', in Gitanjali Maharaj (ed.) *Between Unity and Diversity: Essays on Nation-building in Post-apartheid South Africa*, Idasa, Cape Town.

Gomez, Edmund Terence (1999), *Chinese Business in Malaysia: Accumulation, Ascendance, Accommodation*, Curzon, Surrey.

Gomez, Edmund Terence and Jomo, K.S. (1997), *Malaysian Political Economy: Politics, Patronage and Profits*, Cambridge University Press, Cambridge.

Government of Zimbabwe (1981), *Growth with Equity: An Economic Policy Statement*, Government Printers, Harare.

Grameen Bank (1996), *Consolidated Cumulative Statement up to May 1996*, Grameen Bank, Dhaka.

Grameen Trust (1996), *Grameen Dialogue*, vol. 26 (April).

Grawitzky, Reneé (2000), 'Govt Urged to Focus on Job Creation', *Financial Times Business Day* (10 March) (http://www.bday.co.za/).

Grieder, William (1997), *One World, Ready or Not: The Magic of Global Capitalism*, Simon and Schuster, New York.

Grossman, Rachel (1979), 'Women's Place in the Integrated Circuit', *Southeast Asia Chronicle/Pacific Research*, SRC no. 66/PSC vol. 9, no. 5.

GSS (Gono Shahajjo Sanghstha) (1993), *Education and Social Mobilization Program: Five-Year Project Proposal: 1993-1998*, GSS, Dhaka.

Gurr, Ted Robert (2000), 'Ethnic Warfare on the Wane', *Foreign Affairs*, vol. 79, no. 3, pp. 52-64.

----and Harff, Barbara (1994), *Ethnic Conflict in World Politics*, Westview, Boulder.
Haas, Peter M. and Haas, Ernst B. (1995), 'Learning to Learn: Improving International Governance', *Global Governance*, vol. 1, no. 3, pp. 255-285.
Habib, A. (1997), 'From Pluralism to Corporatism: South Africa's Labour Relations in Transition', *Politikon: South African Journal of Political Studies*, vol. 24, no. 1, pp. 57-75.
Hale, David (1997), 'Is Asia's High Growth Era Over?', *National Interest*, no. 47 (Spring), pp. 44-57.
Hall, James (2000), 'Jobless Figures on the Rise', *Financial Times Business Day* (10 March) (http://www.bday.co.za/).
Hansen, Holger Bernt and Twaddle, Michael (eds) (1998), *Developing Uganda*, James Currey, Oxford.
Hansen, Holger Bernt and Twaddle, Michael (eds) (1988), *Uganda Now: Between Decay and Development*, James Currey, Oxford.
Haque, Mahfuzul (1998), *Ethnic Insurgency and National Integration: A Study of Selected Ethnic Problems in South Asia*, University Press, Dhaka.
Harbeson, John W. and Rothchild, Donald (eds) (1995), *Africa in World Politics: Post-Cold War Challenges*, Second edition, Westview, Boulder.
Harcourt, Wendy (1999), *Women @ Internet: Creating New Cultures in Cyberspace*, Zed Books, London.
Harris, Simon (1999), 'Evaluating the Potential Role of Peacebuilding in Development Programming', presentation to the NGO Donor Forum, UNDP, Colombo (28 January).
Hart, G. (1994), 'The New Economic Policy and Redistribution in Malaysia: A Model for Post-Apartheid South Africa?', *Transformation*, no. 24, pp. 44-59.
Hassim, Shireen and Gouws, Amanda (1998), 'Redefining the Public Space: Women's Organisations, Gender Consciousness and Civil Society in South Africa', *Politikon: South African Journal of Political Studies*, vol. 25, no. 2, pp. 53-76.
Hawkins, A. (1985), *Public Policy and the Zimbabwe Economy*, USAID, Harare.
Hedrick-Wong, Yuwa, et al. (1997), 'Experiences and Challenges in Credit and Poverty Alleviation Programs in Bangladesh: The Case of Proshika', in Geoffrey D. Wood and Iffath A. Sharif (eds), *Who Needs Credit? Poverty and Finance in Bangladesh*, University Press, Dhaka, pp. 145-170.
Held, David (1997), 'Democracy and Globalization', *Global Governance*, vol. 3, no. 3, pp. 251-267.
Held, David (1995), 'Democracy, the Nation State and the Global System', *Economy and Society*, vol. 20, pp. 38-172.
Held, David, McGrew, Anthony, Goldblatt, David and Perraton, Jonathan (1999), *Global Transformations: Politics, Economics and Culture*, Polity Press, Cambridge.
Helleiner, Eric (1994b), *States and the Reemergence of Global Finance: From Bretton Woods to the 1990s*, Cornell University Press, Ithaca, NY.

Helleiner, Eric (1994b), 'From Bretton Woods to Global Finance: A World Turned Upside Down', in Richard Stubbs and Geoffrey Underhill (eds), *Political Economy and the Changing Global Order*, St. Martin's, New York, pp. 163-75.

Henderson, Jeffrey (1989), *The Globalization of High Technology Production: Society, Space and Semiconductors in the Restructuring of the Modern World*, Routledge, London.

Herring, Ron (1998), 'Carrots, Sticks and Ethnic Conflict: Explaining Civil War in Sri Lanka', Draft paper, Cornell University (November).

Hettne, Björn and Inotai, András (1997), *The New Regionalism: Implications for Global Development and International Security*, UNU/WIDER, Helsinki.

---- Inotai, András, and Sunkel, Osvaldo (eds) (1999), *Globalism and the New Regionalism*, Macmillan, London.

---- and Frederik Söderbaum (guest eds), 'Special Issue: The New Regionalism', *Politeia*, vol. 17, no. 3, pp. 4-142.

Hing Ai Yun (1995), 'Automation and New Work Patterns: Cases from Singapore's Electronics Industry', *Work, Employment and Society*, vol. 9, no. 2 (June), pp. 309-327.

Hirst, Paul and Thompson, Grahame (1996), *Globalization in Question: The International Economy and the Possibilities of Governance*, Polity Press, Cambridge.

Holcombe, Susan (1995), Managing to Empower: The Grameen Bank's Experience of Poverty Alleviation, Zed Books, London.

Holloway, Richard (1998), *Supporting Citizen's Initiatives: Bangladesh's NGOs and Society*, University Press, Dhaka.

Hoogvelt, Ankie (1997), *Globalisation and the Postcolonial World: The New Political Economy of Development*, Macmillan, London.

Horowitz, Donald L. (1985), *Ethnic Groups in Conflict*, University of California Press, Berkeley.

Hout, Wil (1997), 'Globalization and the Quest for Governance', *Mershon International Studies Review*, vol. 41, pp. 99-106.

Hughes, Dave, et al. (1983), 'The Wine Industry Today' in Dave Hughes, et al., *South African Wine*, Struik, Cape Town, pp. 27-35.

Hugo, Pierre (1998), 'Transformation: The Changing Context of Academia in Post-apartheid South Africa', *African Affairs*, vol. 97, no. 386 (January), pp. 5-27.

Hulme, David (1990), 'Can the Grameen Bank be Replicated: Recent Experiments in Malaysia, Malawi and Sri Lanka', *Development Policy Review*, vol. 8, no. 3, pp. 287-300.

Hutchful, Eboe (1995-6), 'The Civil Society Debate in Africa', *International Journal*, vol. 51, no. 1, pp. 54-77.

---- (1991), *A Perspective from Africa: Reintegration of Eastern Europe and the Soviet Bloc: Implications for Developing Countries*, The North-South Institute, Ottawa.

Hutchinson, John and Smith, Anthony D. (1996), 'Introduction', in John Hutchinson and Anthony D. Smith (eds), *Ethnicity*, Oxford University Press, Oxford, pp. 3-14.

Hyden, Goran (1992), 'Governance and the Study of Politics', in Goran Hyden and Michael Bratton (eds), *Governance and Politics in Africa*, Westview, Boulder, pp. 1-26.

INFORM (various years) *Sri Lanka Information Monitor B Situation Report*, INFORM, Colombo.

Institute of International Finance (1998), *Zimbabwe Country Report*, Washington.

International Labour Organization (1993), *Structural Change and Adjustment in Zimbabwe*, Occasional Paper 16, Geneva.

Islam, Nasir and Morrison, David R. (1996), 'Introduction: Governance, Democracy and Human Rights', *Canadian Journal of Development Studies*, Special Issue, pp. 6-18.

Jesudason, J. (1989), *Ethnicity and the Economy: The State, Chinese Business and Multinationals in Malaysia*, Oxford University Press, Singapore.

JICA (1998), *JICA in Sri Lanka 1998*, Japan International Cooperation Agency Sri Lanka Office, Colombo.

Jomo, K.S. (ed.) (1998), *Tigers in Trouble: Financial Governance, Liberalization and Crisis in East Asia*, Hong Kong University Press, Hong Kong.

---- (1998), 'Malaysia: From Miracle to Debacle', in K.S. Jomo (ed.), *Tigers in Trouble: Financial Governance, Liberalisation and Crises in East Asia*, Zed Books, London, pp. 181-198.

---- (ed.) (1995), *Privatizing Malaysia: Rents, Rhetoric, Realities*, Westview Press, Boulder and London.

---- (1994), *U-Turn? Malaysian Economic Development Policy After 1990*, Centre for East and Southeast Asian Studies, James Cook University of North Queensland, Townsville, Queensland, Australia.

---- (1990), *Growth and Structural Change in the Malaysian Economy*, St. Martin's, New York.

---- et al. (1997), *Southeast Asia's Misunderstood Miracle: Industrial Policy and Economic Development in Thailand, Malaysia and Indonesia*, Westview Press, Boulder.

---- and Todd, Patricia (1994), *Trade Unions and the State in Peninsular Malaysia*, Oxford University Press, Oxford.

Jones, R. J. Barry (2000), *The World Turned Upside Down? Globalization and the Future of the State*, Manchester University Press, Manchester and New York.

JSE Handbook 1997 (1997), Flesch for JSE, Johannesburg.

Kabemba, Claude (1999), 'Central Africa: Mediating Peace Where There is None', *Conflict Trends* (September) (http://www.accord.org.za/publications/ct3/centrala.htm).

Kabir, Mohammad Humayun (1998), 'The Problems of Tribal Separatism and Constitutional Reform in Bangladesh', in Iftekharuzzaman (ed.), *Ethnicity and Constitutional Reform in South Asia*, University Press, Dhaka.

Kabwegyere, Tarsis (1995), *The Politics of State Formation and Destruction in Uganda*, Fountain Publishers, Kampala.

Kambere, David (1995), *The Bakonzo Rwenzururu War 1962-82: Its Effects on the Growth of the Anglican Church in South Rwenzori*, ATIEA, unpublished BD thesis.

Kane-Berman, John (1999), 'Leave Well Alone: The Role of NGOs in the Process of Democratization', in Hennie Kotzé (ed.), *Consolidating Democracy: What Role for Civil Society in South Africa?*, Centre for International and Comparative Politics, Stellenbosch, pp. 159-64.

Kaplan, Robert D. (1994), 'The Coming Anarchy', *Atlantic Monthly*, vol. 273, no. 2, pp. 44-75.

Karl, Marilee with Anand, Anita, Blankenberg, Floris, Van Den Ham, Allert and Saldanha, Adrian (eds) (1999), *Measuring the Immeasurable: Planning, Monitoring and Evaluation of Networks*, Women's Feature Service, New Delhi.

Karugire, Samwiri (1996), *Roots of Instability in Uganda*, Fountain Publishers, Kampala.

Kaushikan, Bilahari (1997), 'Governance that Works', *Journal of Democracy*, vol. 8, no. 2, pp. 24-34.

Keck, Margaret E. and Sikkink, Kathryn (1998), *Activists Beyond Borders: Advocacy Networks in International Politics*, Cornell University Press, Ithaca, New York.

Kellas, James (1991), *The Politics of Nationalism and Ethnicity*, St. Martin's, New York.

Keohane, Robert O. (1991), 'International Relations Theory: Contributions of a Feminist Standpoint', in Rebecca Grant and Kathleen Newland (eds), *Gender and International Relations*, Indiana University Press, Bloomington, Indiana.

---- (1988), 'International Institutions: Two Approaches', *International Studies Quarterly*, vol. 32, no. 4 (December), pp. 379-396.

Keohane, Robert O. and Nye, Joseph S. Jr. (1998), 'Power and Interdependence in the Information Age', *Foreign Affairs*, vol. 77, no. 5, pp. 81-94.

Khan, Naveeda and Stewart, Eileen (1994), 'Institution Building and Development in Three Women's Organizations: Participation, Ownership and Autonomy', *The Journal of Social Studies*, vol. 63 (January), pp. 53-82.

Khandker, Shahidur R., Khalily, Baqui and Khan, Zahed (1995), *Grameen Bank: Performance and Sustainability*, World Bank, Washington, DC.

King, Gary, Keohane, Robert O. and Verba, Sidney (1994), *Designing Social Enquiry: Scientific Inference in Qualitative Research*, Princeton University Press, Princeton, NJ.

Klare, Michael (1995), 'The Trade in Light Weapons and Global Conflict Dynamics in the post-Cold War Era', paper presented at the UNIDIR Workshop on *Proliferation of Light Weapons in the Post-Cold War World*, Berlin.

Kofman, Elenore and Youngs, Gillian (1996), 'Introduction: Globalization—The Second Wave', in Elenore Kaufman and Gillian Youngs (eds), *Globalization: Theory And Practice*, Pinter, New York, pp. 1-8.

Kojima, Kiyoshi (1977), *Japan and a New World Economic Order*, Westview Press, Boulder.

Korhonen, Pekka (1994), 'The Theory of the Flying Geese Pattern of Development and its Interpretations', *Journal of Peace Research*, vol. 31, no. 1, pp. 93-108.

Korten, David C. (1987), 'Third Generation NGO Strategies: A Key to People-Centred Development', *World Development*, vol. 15, supplement, pp. 145-159.

Kothari, Rajni (1997), 'Globalization: A World Adrift', *Alternatives*, vol. 22, no. 2 (April-June), pp. 227-267.

Kotzé, Herman (1999), 'Swimming in a Wild Sea: The New Challenges Facing Civil Society', in Gitanjali Maharaj (ed.), *Between Unity and Diversity: Essays on Nation-building in Post-apartheid South Africa*, David Philip Publishers, Cape Town, pp. 171-98.

Kramsjo, Bosse and Wood, Geoffrey D. (1992), *Breaking the Chains: Collective Action for Social Justice among the Rural Poor of Bangladesh*, University Press, Dhaka.

Ku, Charlotte and Weiss, Thomas G. (1998), *Toward Understanding Global Governance: The International Law and International Relations Toolbox*, ACUNS Reports and Papers, no. 2, Brown University, Providence, RI.

Kumar, Radha (1995), 'From Chipko to Sati: The Contemporary Indian Women's Movement', in Amrita Basu (ed.), *The Challenge of Local Feminisms: Women's Movements in Global Perspective*, Westview, Boulder, Colorado.

Kuperus, Tracey (1999), 'Building Democracy: An Examination of Religious Associations in South Africa and Zimbabwe', *The Journal of Modern African Studies*, vol. 37, no. 4, pp. 643-68.

Krugman, Paul (1998), 'What Happened to Asia', Paul Krugman Homepage, January (http://web.mit.edu/krugman/www/).

---- (1997), 'Whatever Happened to the Asian Miracle?' *Fortune*, Internet Text Edition, 18 August (http://www. Fortune.com).

Kwan, C.H., Vandenbrink, Donna and Chia Siow Yue (eds) (1998), *Coping with Capital Flows in East Asia*, Nomura Research Institute, Tokyo.

KWV (http:www.kwv.co.za).

Labour News (1998-1999, various issues), MTUC, Kuala Lumpur.

Landes, David (1969), *The Unbound Prometheus: Technological Change and Industrial Development in Western Europe from 1750 to the Present*, Harvard University Press, Cambridge, Massachusetts.

Lanegran, Kimberly (1995), 'South Africa's Civic Association Movement: ANC's Ally or Society's "Watchdog"? Shifting Social Movement-Political Party Relations', *African Studies Review*, vol. 38, no. 2, pp. 101-26.

Langseth, P., Katorobo, J., Brett, E. and Munene, J. (1997), *Uganda: Landmarks in Rebuilding a Nation*, Fountain Publishers, Kampala.

Laurance, Edward (1995), 'Gun Buy-Back Programs: A Step towards Micro Disarmament', paper presented at the UNIDIR Workshop on *Proliferation of Light Weapons in the Post-Cold War World*, Berlin.

Lehman, Howard P. (1992), 'The Paradox of State Power in Africa: Debt Management Policies in Kenya and Zimbabwe', *African Studies Review*, vol. 35, no. 2, pp. 1-34.

Lemarchand, Rene (1986), 'Ethnic Violence in Tropical Africa', in John F. Stack (ed.), *The Primordial Challenge: Ethnicity in the Contemporary World,* Greenwood Press, New York, pp. 185-205.

Levene, Mark (1999), 'The Chittagong Hill Tracts: A Case Study in the Political Economy of "Creeping" Genocide', *Third World Quarterly,* vol. 20, no. 2, pp. 339-369.

Lim, Linda (1978), 'Women Workers in Transnational Corporations: The Case of the Electronics Industry in Malaysia and Singapore', Michigan Occasional Papers No. 9, Women's Studies Program, University of Michigan, Ann Arbor, Michigan.

Lim, Mah Hui (1998), 'Contradictions in the Development of Malay Capital: State, Accumulation and Legitimation', in J.G. Taylor and A. Turton (eds.), *Sociology of Developing Societies in Southeast Asia,* Macmillan, London, pp. 19-32.

Lochhead, J. (1986), *Retrenchment in a Malaysian Free Trade Zone,* Project KANITA, Universiti Sains Malaysia, Penang.

Loewenson, René (1990), 'ZCTU Congress', *Parade* (November), p.10.

Loubser, S.S. (1999), 'The Marketing Environment. Part 1: The Wine Business', University of Stellenbosch Business School, Bellville (December).

Lovell, Catherine H. (1992), *Breaking the Cycle of Poverty: The BRAC Strategy,* Kumarian Press, West Hartford, Connecticut.

Lubeck, P.M. (1992), 'Malaysian Industrialization, Ethnic Divisions and the NIC Model', in R. P. Appelbaum and J. Henderson (eds), *States and Development in the Asian Pacific Rim,* Sage, Newbury Park/New Delhi, pp. 176-98.

MacLean, Sandra J. (1999), 'Peacebuilding and the New Regionalism in Southern Africa', *Third World Quarterly,* vol. 20, no. 5 (October), pp. 943-56.

Madi, Phinda Mzwakhe (1997), Black Economic Empowerment in the New South Africa: The Rights and Wrongs, Knowledge Resources, Randburg, South Africa.

Mafeje, Archie (1995), 'Theory of Democracy and the African Discourse: Breaking Bread with My Fellow-Travellers', in E. Chole and J. Ibrahim (eds), *Democratization Process in Africa: Problems and Prospect,* CODESRIA, Dakar.

---- (1993), 'On Icons and African Perspectives on Democracy: A Commentary on Jibrin Ibrahim's Views', *CODESRIA Bulletin,* vol. 2, pp. 19-21.

Maharaj, Gitanjali (ed.) (1999), Between Unity and Diversity: Essays on Nation-Building in Post-apartheid South Africa, David Philip Publishers, Cape Town.

Mahathir, Mohamad (1991), *Malaysia: The Way Forward,* Center for Economic Research and Service, Malaysian Business Council, Kuala Lumpur.

Mahbubani, Kishore (1998), 'Can Asians Think?', *National Interest,* vol. 52, no. 2 (Summer), pp. 27-35.

Malaysia (1999), *Mid-Term Review of the Seventh Malaysia Plan, 1996-2000,* Economic Planning Unit of the Prime Minister's Department, Kuala Lumpur.

---- (1996), *Seventh Malaysia Plan,* Economic Planning Unit of the Prime Minister's Department, Kuala Lumpur.

---- (1971), *Mid-Term Review of the Second Malaysia Plan 1971-1975*, Malaysia Government Printers, Kuala Lumpur.

Malaysian Industrial Development Authority (MIDA) (1999), *Industry Briefs* (April).

---- Malaysia Electronics and Electrical Industries, A BT-MIDA Directory, Kuala Lumpur.

Mama, A. (1999), 'Dissenting Daughters? Gender Politics and Civil Society in a Militarized State', *CODESRIA Bulletin*, no. 3/4, pp. 29-36.

Mamdani, Mahmood (1998), 'Clinton, Museveni had Secret Agenda? What was the Trip All About?', *The Monitor Newspaper* (10 April).

---- (1996), *Citizen and Subject: Contemporary Africa and the Legacy of Late Colonialism*, Princeton University Press, London.

---- (1994), 'Pluralism and the Right of Association', in M. Mamdani and J. Oloka-Onyango (eds), *Uganda: Studies in Living Conditions, Popular Movements and Constitutionalism*, Jeep Book/2, Vienna, pp. 519-563.

---- (1983), *Imperialism and Fascism in Uganda*, Heinemann Educational Books, Nairobi.

Mandela, Nelson (1988), 'Report by the President of the ANC, Nelson Mandela to the 50th National Conference of the African National Congress', *The South African Journal of International Affairs*, vol. 5, no. 2 (Winter), pp. 156-215.

Mander, Jerry and Edward Goldsmith (eds) (1996), *The Case Against the Global Economy: And for a Turn toward the Local*, Sierra Club Books, San Francisco.

Mannan, Manzurul (1998), 'Culture, Cash and Credit: The Morality of Money Circulation', paper presented at the European Network of Bangladesh Studies Workshop, University of Bath, UK (16-18 April).

Manogaran, C. (1987), *Ethnic Conflict and Reconciliation in Sri Lanka*, University of Hawaii Press, Honolulu.

Manor, James (1989), *The Expedient Utopian: Bandaranaike and Ceylon*, Cambridge University Press, Cambridge.

Maphologela, Stan (2000), 'Economic Confidence Strengthens', *Financial Times Business Day*, 10 March (http://www.bday.co.za/).

Marais, H. (1998), South Africa Limits to Change: The Political Economy of Transition, UCT Press, Rondebosch.

Marshall, M. (1999), 'From States to People: Civil Society and its Role in Governance', in CIVICUS, *Civil Society at the Millennium*, Kumarian Press, Connecticut.

Matashalaga, N. and Makumbe, J. (1999), 'Civil Society Empowerment and Poverty Reduction in Zimbabwe', A Report for CODESRIA Civil Society Programme, Harare.

Mayall, James (1998), 'Globalization and International Relations', review article, *Review of International Studies*, vol. 24, no.2, pp. 239-250.

Mendelsohn, Oliver and Upendra Baxi (1994), 'Introduction', in O. Mendelsohn and U. Baxi (eds), *The Rights of Subordinated Peoples*, Oxford University Press, New Delhi, pp. 1-19.

Merton, Marianne and Barrell, Howard (1999), 'Storms in the Cape of Coalition', *Mail and Guardian*, 11 June (http://wn.apc.org/).

Mhina, A.H. (1987), 'Liberation Struggles in Southern Africa after Zimbabwe', in Ibrahim S.R. Msabaha and Timothy M. Shaw (eds), *Confrontation and Liberation in Southern Africa: Regional Directions after the Nkomati Accord,* Westview, Boulder, pp. 19-31.

Mills, Greg, Begg, Alan and van Nieuwkerk, Anthony (eds) (1995), *South Africa in the Global Economy*, The South African Institute of International Affairs, Johannesburg.

Milne, R.S and Mauzy, Diane K. (1999), *Malaysian Politics under Mahathir*, Routledge, London and New York.

Minnear, Melvyn (1999), 'The Ethical Trade Initiative: Towards International Fair-trade', *Wynboer* (September), pp. 24-25.

Mitter, Swasti (1991), 'Computer-Aided Manufacturing and Women's Employment: A Global Critique of Post-Fordism', paper presented at conference on *Women, Work and Computerisation*, Helsinki (30 June-2 July).

Mittelman, James H. (ed.) (1996), *Globalization: Critical Reflections*, Lynne Rienner, Boulder.

---- (1994), 'The End of the Millennium: Changing Structures of World Order and the Post-Cold War Division of Labor', in Larry Swatuk and Timothy M. Shaw (eds), *The South at the End of the Twentieth Century*, Macmillan, London, pp. 15-27.

Mizan, Ainon Nahar (1994), *In Quest of Empowerment: The Grameen Bank's Impact on Women's Power and Status*, University Press, Dhaka.

Mkandawire, Thandika (1995), 'Adjustment, Political Conditionality and Democratization in Africa', in E. Chole and J. Ibrahim (eds), *Democratization Processes in Africa: Problems and Prospects*, CODESRIA, Dakar.

---- (1991), *Democratic Governance in Africa*, mimeo, Dakar (June).

---- (1988), 'Comments on Democracy and Political Instability', *Africa Development*, vol. XIII, pp. 5-31.

---- and Olukoshi, A. (eds) (1995), *Between Liberalisation and Repression: The Politics of Adjustment in Africa*, CODESRIA, Dakar.

---- and Soludo, C.C. (1999), *Our Continent, Our Future: African Perspectives on Structural Adjustment*, Africa World Press, Trenton.

Mohamed Ariff (1999), 'Unmistakable Signs of Recovery', *New Straits Times* (12 June), p. 11.

---- Mohammad Haflah Piei, Wong, Diana and Abubakar Syarisa Yanti (n.d.), 'Responding to the Economic Crisis in Malaysia: A Pro-human Development Perspective', a Malaysian country paper prepared for the United Nations Development Programme/Regional Bureau for Asia and the Pacific (UNDP/RBAP).

Monga, Celestin (1996), *The Anthropology of Anger: Civil Society and Democracy in Africa*, Lynne Rienner, Boulder.

The Monitor Newspaper (1999), 'Trial Imbalance in Lucrative Jobs in Uganda' (30 July), pp. 1-2.

Moore, Mick (1993), 'Declining to Learn from the East? The World Bank on Governance and Development', *IDS Bulletin*, vol. 24, no. 1, pp. 39-50.

---- (1990), 'Economic Liberalization versus Political Pluralism in Sri Lanka', *Modern Asian Studies*, vol. 24, no. 2, pp. 341-383.

Moto, June 1993.

Moyo, Jonathan (1993), 'Civil Society in Zimbabwe', *Zambezia*, vol. 20, no. 1.

Mtanzamia (1999), no. 1169, Tanzania (13 July).

Muda, M. (1996), 'Malaysia-South Africa Relations and the Commonwealth (1960-95)', *The Round Table*, vol. 340, pp. 423-439.

Mudoola, Dan M. (1993), *Religion, Ethnicity and Politics in Uganda*, Fountain Publishers, Kampala.

Muigai, G. (1995), 'Ethnicity and the Renewal of Competitive Politics in Kenya', in Harry Glickman (ed.), *Ethnic Conflicts and Democratization in Africa*, Zed Books, London, pp. 161-196.

Munro-Kua, A. (1996), *Authoritarian Populism in Malaysia*, Macmillan, London.

Murphy, Craig (ed.) (2000), *Civil Societies in the New Millennium: Comparative Analyses*, Macmillan, London.

---- (1994), *International Organization and Industrial Change: Global Governance since 1850*, Polity Press, Cambridge.

Murray, Martin J. (1994), *The Revolution Deferred: The Painful Birth of Post-apartheid South Africa*, Verso, London and New York.

Murray, Nancy (1997), 'Somewhere Over the Rainbow: A Journey to the New South Africa', *Race and Class*, vol. 38, no. 3, pp. 1-23.

Musambayi, Katumanga and Maina, Wachira (1999), 'Civil Society in Kenya: A State of the Art Review', a report for CODESRIA Civil Society Programme, Nairobi, Kenya.

Museveni, Yoweri K. (1997), *Sowing the Mustard Seed: The Struggle for Freedom and Democracy in Uganda*, Macmillan, London.

Mustapha, Abdul Raufu (1998), 'Stalled Transition and the Ambiguities of Ethnicity in Nigeria: 1986-1998', Research Report for CODESRIA, Multinational Working Group on Ethnicity and Democratization in Africa (July) Dakar.

Naidoo, Kumar and Tandon, R. (1999), 'The Promise of Civil Society', in CIVICUS, *Civil Society at the Millennium*, Kumarian Press, Connecticut, pp. 1-16.

Najam, Adil (1996), 'NGO Accountability: A Conceptual Framework', *Development Policy Review*, vol. 14, no. 4, pp. 339-353.

National Constitutional Assembly, The (1997), 'Debating the Zimbabwean Constitution, (June).

Nattrass, Nicoli (1999), 'Gambling on Investment: Competing Economic Strategies in South Africa', in Gitanjali Maharaj (ed.), *Between Unity and Diversity: Essays on Nation-Building in Post-apartheid South Africa*, David Philip Publishers, Cape Town, pp. 75-94.

Naved, Ruchira T. (1994), 'Empowerment of Women: Listening to the Voices of Women', *The Bangladesh Development Studies*, vol. 22, no. 2/3, pp. 155-178.

Ndegwa, Stephen N. (1996), *The Two Faces of Civil Society: NGOs and Politics in Africa*, Kumarian Press, Connecticut.

Ndlela, Dumisani (1999), 'Mass Protests Mooted', *Zimbabwe Independent*, 12 February (http://www.samara.co.zw/zimin/index).

Nel, Philip and McGowan, Patrick J. (eds) (1999), *Power, Wealth and Global Order: An International Relations Textbook for Africa*, UCT Press for FGD, Cape Town.

Nel, Philip, Van der Westhuizen, Janis, Cornelissen, Scarlett, Ratshilumela, B., and Hill, L. (1998), 'En Route to the Competition State? The South African Policy Elite and Globalization', a report of a research project undertaken as part of the Human Sciences Research Council of South Africa's Programme on Global Change and Social Transformation (August).

Nelson, Paul J. (1995), *The World Bank and Non-Governmental Organizations: The Limits of Apolitical Development*, St. Martin's, New York.

New Statesman (2000), 'The Rainbow Coalition Starts to Fade', London, 15 May (http:/proquest.umi.com/pqdweb?TS'9616056...C'1&Dtp'1Did'000000054864 567&Mtd'1&Fmt'3).

Ng, Margaret (1997), 'Why Asia Needs Democracy?' *Journal of Democracy*, vol. 8, no. 2, pp. 21-22.

Ng, Cecilia and Mohamed, Maznah (1997), 'The Management of Technology and Women in Two Electronics Firms in Malaysia', *Gender, Technology and Development*, vol. 1, no. 2, pp. 178-203.

NGO Affairs Bureau (1998), *Flow of Foreign Grant Funds through NGOAB*, Prime Minister's Office, Government of Bangladesh, Dhaka.

NGO Forum on Sri Lanka (1998), '50th Anniversary of Sri Lankan Independence', mimeo (4 February).

Ngunyi, Mutahi G. and Gathiaka, Kaman (1993), 'State-Civil Society Institutions Relations in Kenya in the 80s in the Socio-Political Context of Adjustment in Sub-Saharan Africa', in Peter Gibbon (ed.), *Social Change and Economic Reform in Africa*, Scandinavian Institute of African Studies, Uppsala, pp. 28-52.

Ngwira, Naomi and Chirwa, Wiseman (1999), 'Civil Society Empowerment and Poverty Reduction in Malawi: A State of the Art Review', a report for the CODESRIA Civil Society Programme, Lilongwe, Malawi.

Nhema, Alfred G. (forthcoming), *Democracy in Zimbabwe: From Liberation to Liberalization*, University of Zimbabwe Publications, Harare.

---- (1987), 'State Must Create Off-Shore Arm of the Reserve Bank', *Sunday Mail* (18 January).

---- (1986), 'For How Long Shall We Subsidize Parastatals?', *Sunday Mail* (22 June).

Ninsin, K.A. (2000), 'Globalisation and the Future of Africa', *Occasional Paper Series*, vol. 4, no. 1, Print Source (Pvt) Ltd., Harare.

Nissan, Elizabeth (1984), 'Some Thoughts on Sinhalese Justification for the Violence', in James Manor (ed.), *Sri Lanka in Change and Crisis*, Croom Helm, London and Sydney, pp. 175-186.

---- and Stirrat, R.L. (1990), 'The Generation of Communal Identities', in Jonathan Spencer (ed.), *Sri Lanka: History and Roots of Conflict*, Routledge, London and New York, pp. 19-44.

Nnoli, Okwudiba (1998), 'Globalisation and Democracy in Africa', paper presented at the 25th Anniversary Conference of the African Association of Political Science (AAPS) Mauritius (3 October).

---- (1989), *Ethnic Conflict in Africa*, Working Paper 1/89, CODESRIA, Dakar, Norway, Royal Ministry of Foreign Affairs (1998), 'Guidelines for Development Cooperation with Sri Lanka', photocopy, Oslo, Norway (April).

NOVIB (Netherlands Organization for International Development) (1993), *Going to Scale: The BRAC Experience, 1972-1992 and Beyond*, Aga Khan Foundation Canada, Toronto.

Nyang'oro, Julius E. (ed.) (1999), *Civil Society and Democratic Development in Africa*, Mwengo, Harare.

Nzomo, Maria (2000), 'Civil Society, Governance and Strategies for Poverty Alleviation in Africa', a concept paper for CODESRIA Civil Society Programme, Dakar, Senegal.

---- (1998), 'Kenya: The Women's Movement and Democratic Change', in L.A. Villalón and P.A. Huxtable (eds) (1998), *The African State at a Critical Juncture Between Disintegration and Reconfiguration*, Lynne Rienner, Boulder, pp. 167-184.

---- (1994), 'Women in Politics and Public Decision-Making', in U. Himmelstrand, (ed.), *African Perspective on Development: Controversies, Dilemmas and Openings*, James Currey, London, pp. 203-217.

Nzongola-Ntajaj,Georges. (1995), *Class Struggle and National Liberation in Africa*, Omerana.

---- and Lee, Margaret (eds) (1997), *The State and Democracy in Africa*, AAPS Books, Harare.

Obi, Cyril and Adjekophori, Emmanuel (1999), 'Civil Society and Poverty Reduction in Nigeria: A State of the Art Review', a report for CODESRIA Civil Society Programme, Lagos, Nigeria.

O'Connor, David (1993), 'Electronics and Industrialisation: Approaching the 21st Century', in K.S. Jomo (ed.), *Industrialising Malaysia: Policy, Performance, Prospects*, Routledge, London, pp. 210-233.

Olojode, L. (1999), 'Globalisation and the Development of Civil Society in Nigeria', paper presented at the AAPS Bi-Annual Congress on *Globalisation, Democracy and Development in Africa*, Dakar (22-25 June).

Olukoshi, A. (1992), 'The World Bank, Structural Adjustment and Governance in Africa: Some Reflections', *Nigerian Journal of International Affairs*, vol. 18, no. 2.

Oluwo, D., et al. (eds) (1999), *Governance and Democratisation in West Africa*, CODESRIA, Dakar.

Omari, Abillah H. (1998), 'Tanzania in the Great Lakes Region', briefing paper for the Ministry of Foreign Affairs and International Cooperation, Dar es Salaam, Tanzania.

---- (1995), 'Causes and Prevention of Coups in Southern Africa', *Southern African Perspectives*, no. 45.

---- (1994), 'Development and Security in Southern Africa: Non-Traditional Considerations', paper presented at the Commonwealth Assistance for Diplomatic Training in South Africa, Pretoria.

---- (1980), 'Uganda-Tanzania Relations 1971-1979: A Case Study in Inter-African Relations', Unpublished MA Thesis, University of Dar es Salaam, Tanzania.

Omari, Abillah H. and Vale, Peter (1995), 'Southern African Institute: A Forum for Security and Development Concerns', *The Arusha Papers*, no. 4.

Osaghae, E.E., (1994), 'Ethnicity in Africa or African Ethnicity: The Search for a Contextual Understanding', in U. Himmelstrand, et al. (eds), *African Perspectives on Development: Controversies, Dilemmas and Openings*, James Currey, London, pp. 137-151.

Osman-Rani, H. (1990), 'Economic Development and Ethnic Integration: The Malaysian Experience', *Sojourn: Social Issues in Southeast Asia*, vol. 5, no. 1 (February), pp. 1-34.

Ottaway, Marina (1999), 'Ethnic Politics in Africa: Change and Continuity', in Richard Joseph (ed.), *State, Conflict, and Democracy in Africa*, Lynne Rienner, Boulder, pp. 299-317.

---- (1996), 'Ethnic Conflict and Security in South Africa', in Edmond J. Keller and Donald Rothchild (eds), *Africa in the New International Order: Rethinking State Sovereignty and Regional Security*, Lynne Rienner, Boulder, pp. 119-33.

Oxfam (1995), *A Case for Reform: Fifty Years of the IMF and the World Bank*, Oxfam, Oxford.

Oyediran, O. and Agbaje, A. (eds) (1999), *Nigeria: Politics of Transition and Governance, 1986-1996*, CODESRIA, Dakar.

Padayachee V. and Valodia, I. (1997), 'Malaysian Money: Sustainable Investments?', *Indicator SA*, vol. 14, no. 2 (Winter), pp. 23-28.

Pauly, Louis W. (1997), Who Elected the Bankers? Surveillance and Control in the World Economy, Cornell University Press, Ithaca and London.

Peterson, Spike V. (1997), 'Whose Crisis? Early and Post-Modern Masculinism', in Stephen Gill and James H. Mittelman (eds), *Innovation and Transformation in International Studies*, Cambridge University Press, Cambridge.

Peterson, Spike V. and Sisson Runyon, Anne (1999), *Global Gender Issues*, Second Edition, Westview Press, Boulder.

Pettman, Ralph (1999), *Understanding International Political Economy: With Readings for the Fatigued*, Lynne Rienner, Boulder.

Piore, Michael and Charles Sabel (1984), *The Second Industrial Divide*, Basic Books, New York.

Platter, John (annually to 2000), *South African Wines, Platter Wine Guide*, Epping.

Price, Robert (1997), 'Race and Reconciliation in the New South Africa', *Politics and Society*, vol. 25, no. 2 (June), pp. 149-78.

Price, R.M. (1991), *The Apartheid State in Crisis: Political Transformation in South Africa 1975-1990*, Oxford University Press, New York.

Princen, Thomas and Finger, Matthias (1994), *Environmental NGOs in World Politics: Linking the Local and the Global*, Routledge, London.

Proshika (1998), *Freedom from Poverty: Another Step Forward*, Proshika, Dhaka.

---- (1995), *Doing Development the People's Way: The Proshika Praxis*, Proshika, Dhaka.

---- (1995), 'Proshika: A Centre for Human Development', leaflet, Proshika, Dhaka.

Proust, Alain and Knox, Graham (1997), *Cape Wines: Body and Soul*, Fernwood, Vlaeberg.

Prunier, Gérard (1997), 'The Geopolitical Situation in the Great Lakes Area in Light of the Kivu Crisis', *Writenet Country Papers*,
    (http:www.unhcr.chrefworl/country/writenet/uridrc.htm).

---- (1995), *The Rwanda Crisis 1959-1994: History of Genocide*, Fountain Publishers, Kampala.

Raftopoulos, Brian (1992), 'Beyond the House of Hunger: Democratic Struggle in Zimbabwe', *Review of African Political Economy*, no. 54, pp. 59-74.

Raikes, P. (1992), 'Monogamists Sit by the Doorway: Notes on the Construction of Gender, Ethnicity and Rank in Kisii, Western Kenya', Denmark: Centre for Development Research.

Rajah, Rasiah (1996), 'The Changing Organization of Work in Malaysia's Electronics Industry', *Asia-Pacific Viewpoint*, vol. 37, no. 1, pp. 21-37.

---- (1994), 'Flexible Production Systems and Local Machine-tool Subcontracting: Electronics Components Transnationals in Malaysia', *Cambridge Journal of Economics*, vol. 18, pp. 279-298.

Rana, Swadesh (1995), 'Small Arms and Intra-State Conflicts',UNIDIR Research Paper, no. 34.

Redinha, Jose (1965), *Distribuicao Etnica da Provincia de Angola*, Centro de Informacao e Turismo de Angola, Luanda.

Refugee (1993), 'Special Issue on Sri Lanka', vol. 13, no. 3 (June).

Reno, William (1998), *Warlord Politics and African States*, Lynne Rienner, Boulder.

Rijnierse, Elly (1993), 'Democratization in Sub-Saharan Africa: Literature Overview, *Third World Quarterly*, vol. 4, no. 3, 1993, pp. 647-664.

Robertson, Robert (1992), *Globalization: Social Theory and Global Culture*, Sage, London.

Ronen, Dov (1986), 'Ethnicity, Politics and Development: An Introduction', in Dennis L. Thompson and Doy Ronen (eds), *Ethnicity, Politics and Development*, Lynn Rienner, Boulder, pp. 1-10.

Rosario, V. (December 1993 and January 1994), 'Media Development in 21st Century Africa', *SAPEM*, Harare.

Rosecrance, Richard (1996), 'The Rise of the Virtual State', *Foreign Affairs*, vol. 75, no. 4, pp. 45-61.

Rosenau, James N. (2001), 'Information Technologies and the Skills, Networks, and Structures that Sustain World Affairs', in James N. Rosenau and J.P. Singh (eds), *Information Technologies and Global Politics: The Changing Scope of*

Power and Governance, State University of New York Press, Albany, New York.

---- (1997a), *Along the Domestic-Foreign Frontier: Exploring Governance in a Turbulent World*, Cambridge University Press, Cambridge.

---- (1997b), 'The Complexities and Contradictions of Globalisation', *Current History*, vol. 96, no. 613, pp. 360-64.

---- (1992), 'Governance, Order, and Change in World Politics', in James N. Rosenau and Ernst-Otto Czempiel (eds), *Governance without Government: Order and Change in World Politics*, Cambridge University Press, Cambridge.

---- (1990), *Turbulence in World Politics: A Theory of Change and Continuity*, Princeton University Press, Princeton.

Rosenbeger, Leif Roderick (1997), 'Southeast Asia's Currency Crisis: A Diagnosis and Prescription', *Contemporary Southeast Asia*, vol. 19, no. 3, pp. 224-51.

Rosenberg, Nathan, and Birdzell, L.E. Jr. (1986), *How the West Grew Rich: The Economic Transformation of the Industrial World*, Basic Books, New York.

Rothschild, Joseph (1981), *Ethnopolitics: A Conceptual Framework*, Columbia University Press, New York.

Ruggie, J.G. (1982), 'International Regimes, Transactions and Change: Embedded Liberalism in the Post-War Order', *International Organization*, vol. 36, no. 21, pp. 379-415.

Rupesinghe, Kumar (ed.) (1989), *Conflict Resolution in Uganda*, International Peace Research Institute, Oslo.

Sachikonye, Lloyd M. (1995), 'From "Equity" and "Participation" to Structural Adjustment: State and Social Forces in Zimbabwe', in David Moore and Gerald J. Schmitz (eds), *Debating Development Discourses: Institutional and Popular Perspectives*, Macmillan, London, pp. 179-200.

Sakamoto, Yoshikazu (1997), 'Civil Society and Democratic World Order', in Stephen Gill and James H. Mittelman (eds), *Innovation and Transformation in International Studies*, Cambridge University Press, Cambridge.

---- (ed.) (1994), *Global Transformations: Challenges to the State System*, United Nations University, Tokyo.

Salaita, John (1998), 'The Adminstration of International Humanitarian Assistance to Africa: Some Practical Considerations', paper presented at workshop *Conflict and Humanitarian Assistance to Africa: A Nordic-African Dialogue*, Arusha, Tanzania.

Sandbrook, Richard (1993), *The Politics of Africa's Economic Recovery*, Cambridge University Press, New York.

Santos, Eduardo (1965), *Maza: Elementos de Etno-Historia para a interpretacao do terrorismo no Nordeste de Angola*, Ramos, Afonso e Moita, Lisboa.

Saravanamuttu, Johan (1998), 'The Southeast Asian Development Phenomenon Revisited: From Flying Geese to Lame Ducks?', *Pacifica Review*, vol. 10, no. 2 (June), pp. 111-125.

---- (1988), 'Japanese Economic Penetration in ASEAN in the Context of the International Division of Labor', *Journal of Contemporary Asia*, vol. 18, no. 2, pp. 139-69.

---- (1986), 'Imperialism, Dependent Development and ASEAN Regionalism', *Journal of Contemporary Asia*, vol. 16, no. 2, pp. 204-22.

Saunders, R. (1995), 'Civics in Zimbabwe: Are They Making a Difference?' *Southern Africa Report* (March).

Sawadogo, S.M. and Kabore, T.S. (1999), 'Civil Society Empowerment for Poverty Reduction in Burkina Faso: A State of the Art Review', Report for CODESRIA Civil Society Programme, Ouagadougou, Burkina Faso.

Schaeffer, Robert K. (1997), *Understanding Globalization: The Social Consequences of Political, Economic and Environmental Change*, Rowman and Littlefield, Lanham.

Schermerhorn, Richard (1970), *Comparative Ethnic Relations*, Random House, New York.

Schmitter, Philippe and Lehmbruch, Gerhard (1979), *Trends Toward Corporatist Intermediation*, Sage, Beverly Hills, CA.

Schmitz, Gerald J. (1995), 'Democratization and Demystification: Deconstructing "Governance" as Development Paradigm', in David B. Moore and Gerald J. Schmitz (eds), *Debating Development Discourse: Institutional and Popular Perspectives*, Macmillan, London, pp. 54-90.

Schneider, Ben R. (1999), 'The *Desarrolista* State in Brazil and Mexico,' in Meredith Woo-Cummings (ed.), *The Developmental State*, Cornell University Press, Ithaca, pp. 276-305.

---- and Maxfield, S. (1997), 'Business, the State and Economic Performance in Developing Countries,' in B.R. Schneider and S. Maxfield (eds), *Business and the State in Developing Countries*, Cornell University Press, Ithaca and London, pp. 3-35.

Scholte, Jan Aart (2000), *Globalization: A Critical Introduction*, Macmillan, London.

---- (1997), 'The Globalization of World Politics', in John Baylis and Steve Smith (eds), *The Globalization of World Politics: An Introduction to International Relations*, Oxford University Press, New York, pp. 13-30.

Searle, Peter (1999), *The Riddle of Malaysian Capitalism: Rent-seekers or Real Capitalists?* Allen and Unwin and University of Hawaii Press, St Leonards and Honolulu.

Segal, S. (1998), 'Black Economic Empowerment', in James Wilmot and Moira Levy (eds), *Pulse: Passages in Democracy Building: Assessing South Africa's Transition*, Idasa, Cape Town.

Seligman, Adam B. (1995), *The Idea of the Civil Society*, Princeton University Press, Princeton.

Sens, Allen and Stoett, Peter (1998), *Global Politics: Origins, Currents, Directions*, International Thompson Publishing, Scarborough, Ontario.

Serrano, I.R. (1999), 'Coming Apart, Coming Together: Globalisation and Civil Society', CIVICUS, *Civil Society at the Millennium*, Kumarian, Connecticut, pp. 153-165.

Shah, Ghanshayam (1990), *Social Movements in India: A Review of the Literature*, Sage, New Delhi.

Shailo, Iqbal (1994), 'Genesis and Growth of NGOs: Their Achievement and Success in National Development', *Grassroots*, vol. 4, no. 13/14, pp. 9-30.

Shastri, Amita (1990), 'The Material Basis for Separatism: The Tamil Eelam Movement in Sri Lanka', *The Journal of Asian Studies*, vol. 49, no. 1, pp. 56-77.

Shaw, Timothy M. (1999a), 'Island Governance in the New Millennium', Dalhousie University. ISLE Programme, Halifax.

---- (1999b), 'Foreword: Global/Local: States, Companies and Civil Societies at the End of the Twentieth Century', in Kendall Stiles (ed.), *Global Institutions and Local Empowerment*, Macmillan, London, pp. 1-8.

---- (1999c), 'Africa's Third Way/Third Chance: From Regression to Renaissance in the New Millennium', paper presented at the International Workshop, 'Future Competitiveness of African Economies', Dakar (March).

---- (1986), 'Ethnicity as the Resilient Paradigm for Africa: From the 1960s to the 1980s', *Development and Change*, vol. 17, pp. 587-605.

---- and MacLean, Sandra J. (1996), 'Civil Society and Political Economy in Contemporary Africa: What Prospects for Sustainable Democracy?', *Journal of Contemporary African Studies*, vol. 14, no. 2, pp. 247-64.

---- and van der Westhuizen, Janis (1999), 'Towards a Political Economy of Trade in Africa: States, Companies and Civil Societies', in Brian Hocking and Steven McGuire (eds), *Trade Politics: Actors, Issues and Processes*, Routledge, London, pp. 246-260.

---- MacLean, Sandra J. and Nzomo, Maria (2000), 'Going Beyond States and Markets to Civil Societies', in Thomas C. Lawton, James N. Rosenau and Amy C. Verdun (eds) *Strange Power: Shaping the Parameters of International Relations and International Political Economy*, Ashgate, Aldershot, pp. 391-406.

Sheth, D. L. (1991), 'Nation-Building in Multi-Ethnic Societies: The Experience of South Asia', in Ramakant and B.C. Upreti (eds), *Nation-Building in South Asia*, vol. 1, South Asia Publishers, New Delhi, pp. 13-26.

SIDA (1997), 'Expectations and Reality: Challenges on Sri Lanka's Path of Development', Swedish International Development Cooperation Agency, Asia Department, Sweden (June).

Sinclair, Timothy J. (1997), 'Global Governance and the International Political Economy of the Commonplace', paper presented at the annual meeting of the International Studies Association, Toronto (March).

Singh, J.P. (1999), *Leapfrogging Development? The Political Economy of Telecommunications Restructuring*, State University of New York Press, Albany, New York.

Sithole, Masipule (1994), 'Is Multi-Party Democracy Possible in Multi-Ethnic African States? The Case of Zimbabwe', in U. Himmelstrand, et al. (eds), *African Perspective on Development: Controversies, Dilemmas and Openings*, James Currey, London, pp. 152-164.

---- and Macumbe, John (1997), 'Elections in Zimbabwe: The ZANU (PF), Hegemony and its Incipient Decline', *African Journal of Political Science*, vol. 2, no.1, pp. 122-39.

Smith, Anthony D. (1981), *The Ethnic Revival in the Modern World*, Cambridge University Press, Cambridge.

Smith, C. (1997), 'Working Capital', *Millennium* (September), pp. 111-116.

Somasundaram, Daya (1998), *Scarred Minds: The Psychological Impact of War on Sri Lankan Tamils*, Vijitha Yapa Bookshop, Colombo.

Soros, George (1998), *The Crisis of Global Capitalism: Open Society Endangered*, Little, Brown and Company, London.

South African Institute of Race Relations, Annual Surveys 1994-5;1995-6;1996-7, Braamfontein.

South African Wine Industry Directory 2000 (1999), second edition, Kenilworth, Ampersand.

'South African Wine Industry Statistics' (1999), South African Wine Industry Information and Systems, Paarl.

Southall, Roger (1997), 'Party Dominance and Development: South Africa's Prospects in the Light of Malaysia's Experience', *Journal of Commonwealth and Comparative Politics*, vol. 35, no. 2 (July), pp. 1-27.

Southern Africa Report (2000), vol. 15, no. 3 (3rd quarter).

Sowetan, The (2000), 'South Africa Media Takes Dim View of Zimbabwe', Johannesburg, *Africa News Online*, 4 May, wysiwyg:29/africanews.org/so...bwe/stories.

Spar, Debora and Bussgang, Jeffrey (1996), 'Ruling the Net', *Harvard Business Review* (May-June), pp. 19-27.

'Special Issue in Honor of Helleiner' (1999), *Canadian Journal of Development Studies*, vol. 20, no. 3, pp. 439-632.

Spegele, Roger D. (1992), 'Is Robust Globalism a Mistake?' *Review of International Studies*, vol. 23, no. 2, pp. 211-39.

Spencer, Jonathan (ed.) (1990a), *Sri Lanka: History and Roots of Conflict*, Routledge, London and New York.

---- (1990b), 'Writing Within: Anthropology, Nationalism, and Culture in Sri Lanka', *Current Anthropology*, vol. 31, no. 3, pp. 283-300.

Sphani, Pierre (1995), *The International Wine Trade*, Woodhead, Cambridge.

Stackhouse, John (1998a), 'Village Phones Ring Up Profit', *The Globe and Mail* (6 July), pp. A1 and A8.

---- (1998b), 'It's a New Form of Credit: Only Women Need Apply', *The Globe and Mail* (7 November).

STAR Online (1999a), 'Electronics Industry Bouncing Back' (20 July), pp. 1-3.

---- (1999b), 'Internet Said to have Sparked Rally' (20 July), pp. 1-4.

Stellenbosch Farmers Winery (http:www.sfw.co.za).

Stepan, A. (1978), *The State and Society: Peru in Comparative Perspective*, Princeton University Press, Princeton.

Stiles, Kendall (ed.) (1999), *Global Institutions and Local Empowerment*, Macmillan, London.

Streefland, Pieter, et al. (1986), *Different Ways to Support the Rural Poor: Effects of Two Development Approaches in Bangladesh*, The Royal Tropical Institute, Amsterdam.

Stubbs, Richard (1999), 'War and Economic Development: Export-Oriented Industrialization in East and Southeast Asia,' *Comparative Politics*, vol. 31, no. 3 (April) pp. 337-355.

---- and Underhill, Geoffrey D. (eds) (1994 and 2000), *Political Economy and the Changing Global Order*, first and second editions, McClelland and Stewart and Oxford University Press, Toronto.

Subramaniam, Pillay (1999), 'Politics, Economics and General Elections', *Aliran Monthly*, vol. 19, no. 6, pp. 2-4.

Swatuk, Larry A. and Vale, Peter (1999), 'Why Democracy is Not Enough: Southern Africa in Search of Human Security', in Nana Poku (ed), *Security and Development in Southern Africa*, Greenwood Press, New York.

Swilling, Mark (1990), 'Political Transition, Development and the Role of Civil Society', *Africa Insight*, vol. 20, no. 3, pp. 151-60.

Tandon, Yash (1995), 'The Challenge of Participatory Development: Experiences of Civil Society in Southern Africa', for the UNV-PDRCA Sub-Regional Workshop on Participatory Development (May).

Tang, Min and Thant, Myo (1994), 'Growth Triangles: Conceptual Issues and Operational Problems', Economic Staff Paper, No. 54, Asian Development Bank, Manila.

Taylor, Scott D. (1999), 'Race, Class, and the Neopatrimonialism in Zimbabwe', in Richard Joseph (ed.), *State, Conflict, and Democracy in Africa*, Lynne Rienner, Boulder.

Thompson, Richard (1989), *Theories of Ethnicity: A Critical Appraisal*, Greenwood Press, Westport.

Turok, Ben (1998), 'Save Us from the Crony Capitalists', *The Mail and Guardian* (25 August - 3 September).

---- (1997), 'The Case of the Black Bourgeoisie', *The Mail and Guardian*, 3-9 October.

Ueckermann, Steven Bernhard (1997), 'An Evaluation of the South African Wine Industry's Capabilities as a Producer and International Marketer of Natural Wine Products', unpublished MBA thesis, Stellenbosch University (June).

United Nations Chronicles (1997), vol. XXXIV, no. 1

Uphoff, Norman (1992a), *Learning from Gal Oya: Possibilities for Participatory Development and Post-Newtonian Social Science*, Cornell University Press, Ithaca and London.

---- (1992b), 'Monitoring and Evaluating Popular Participation in World Bank-Assisted Projects', in Bhuvan Bhatnagar and Aubrey C. Williams (eds), *Participatory Development and the World Bank: Potential Directions for Change*, World Bank Discussion Paper 183, World Bank, Washington, pp. 135-153.

Uvin, Peter (1998), *Aiding Violence. The Development Enterprise in Rwanda*. Kumarian Press.

Vale, Peter (1997), 'Peace-Making in Southern Africa: Time for Questions', in Gunnar M. Sørbø and Peter Vale (eds), *Out of Conflict: From War to Peace in Africa*, Nordiska Afrikainstitutet, Uppsala, pp. 39-53.

---- and Maskeo, Sipho (1998), 'South Africa and the African Renaissance', *International Affairs*, vol. 74, no. 2, pp. 271-88.

van den Berghe, Edda-Nathalie (1995), *Farm Labour Relations and the Regional Economy of the Western Cape*, unpublished DPhil, University of Cambridge Press, Cambridge (May).

van der Westhuizen, J. (1999), 'Malaysia, South Africa and the Marketing of the Competition State: Globalization and States' Response', PhD dissertation, Dalhousie University, Halifax.

van Eck, Jan (1997), 'Identity Crisis: Moving Past Partisanship', *Track 2*, vol. 6, no. 1 (April) (http://ccrweb.uct.ac.za/two/2/p15.html).

Van Rooy, Allison (ed.) (1998), *Civil Society and the Aid Industry*, Earthscan, London.

van Zyl, D.J. (1993), *KWV 1918-1993*, Human and Rousseau, Kaapstad.

Villalón, Leonardo A. and Huxtable, Phillip A. (1998), *The African State at a Critical Juncture: Between Disintegration and Reconfiguration*, Lynne Rienner, Boulder.

Viriri, Itayi (2000), 'ZANU PF Heading for Defeat', *Zimbabwe Standard*, 12 March (http://www.samara.co.zw/standard/index.cfm?pubdate'2000%2D03%2D12).

Wad, Peter and Jomo, K.S. (1994), 'In-House Unions: "Looking East" for Industrial Relations', in K.S. Jomo (ed.), *Japan and Malaysian Development: In the Shadow of the Rising Sun*, Routledge, London and New York, pp. 213-231.

Wahid, Abu N.M. (1994), 'The Grameen Bank and Poverty Alleviation in Bangladesh: Theory, Evidence and Limitations', *The American Journal of Economics and Sociology*, vol. 53, no. 1, pp. 1-15.

Wallerstein, Immanuel (1974), *The Modern World System*, Academic Press, New York.

Weaver, Mary Anne (1988), 'The Gods and the Stars', *The New Yorker* (21 March).

Weber, Max (1947), *The Theory of Social and Economic Organization*, Free Press, New York.

Webster, E.C. (1998), 'The Politics of Economic Reform: Trade Unions and Democratization in South Africa', *Journal of Contemporary African Studies*, vol. 16, no. 1, pp. 39-64.

Webster, Edward and Adler, Glenn (1999), 'Towards a Class Compromise in South Africa's "Double Transition": Bargained Liberalization and the Consolidation of Democracy', *Politics and Society*, vol. 27, no. 3 (September), pp. 347-85.

Weiss, Thomas G. and Gordenker, Leon (eds) (1996), *NGOs, the UN, and Global Governance*, Lynne Rienner, Boulder.

Weiss, Thomas G. and Smith, Edwin S. (eds) (1997), *UN Subcontracting for Security and Services: Burden-sharing with Regional and Non-governmental Organizations*, Macmillan for ACUNS, London.

Wendt, Alexander (1992), 'Anarchy is What States Make of It: The Social Construction of Power Politics', *International Organization*, vol. 460, no. 2, pp. 391-425.

Westergaard, Kirsten (1996), 'People's Empowerment in Bangladesh: NGO Strategies', *The Journal of Social Studies*, no. 72, pp. 27-57.

WHO Partnerships in Health and Emergency Assistance (1998), WHO/DFID Peace Through Health Programme: A Case Study prepared by the WHO Field Team in Bosnia and Herzegovina, WHO Europe, EUR/ICP/CORD 03 05 01 (September).

Wickens, P.L. (1983), 'Agriculture', in F.L. Coleman (ed.), *Economic History of South Africa*, HAUM, Pretoria, pp. 37-88.

Williams, David and Young, Tom (1994), 'Governance, the World Bank and Liberal Theory', *Political Studies*, vol. 42, no. 1, pp. 84-100.

Williams, G., Ewert, J. Hamman, J. and Vink, N. (1998), 'Liberalizing Markets and Reforming Land in South Africa', *Journal of Contemporary African Studies*, vol. 16, no. 1 (January), pp. 65-94.

Williams, Rockylin (1995), 'Small Arms Proliferation in Southern Africa: Problems and Prospects', paper presented at the UNIDIR Workshop on *Proliferation of Light Weapons in the Post Cold War World*, Berlin.

Wilson, F. (1992), 'Ethnicity and Gender in a Modernising World', Denmark: Centre for Development Research.

'Winds of Change' (1999), *Wynboer* (September), pp. 20-27.

Wine (monthly), Cape Town.

Winetech 2020 (1999a), 'Creating the Future of the South African Wine Industry', Study Leader, Philip H Spies, Stellenbosch (January).

---- (1999b), 'A Logistics System for the RSA Wine Industry. An Interim Report, by Barry Kruge', Stellenbosch (October).

Wiseberg, Laurie S. (1996), 'Resolution 1296 Revised A Done Deal on Consultative Status: Not Ideal but a Major Improvement', *Transnational Associations*, vol. 6, November-December, pp. 350-353.

Wolfe, Robert (1998), *Farm Wars: The Political Economy of Agriculture and the International Trade Regime*, Macmillan, London.

Wood, Geoffrey D. (1997), 'States without Citizens: The Problem of the Franchise State', in David Hume and Michael Edwards (eds), *NGOs, States and Donors: Too Close for Comfort?* Macmillan, London.

---- (1994), Bangladesh: Whose Ideas, Whose Interests?, University Press, Dhaka.

Woods, Ngaire (ed.) (2000), *The Political Economy of Globalization*, St. Martin's, New York.

World Bank (1999/2000), *World Development Report 1999-2000, Entering the 21st Century*, Oxford University Press, New York.

---- (1998a), *Country Brief: Sri Lanka* (September).

---- (1998b), *The World Bank's Experience with Post-Conflict Reconstruction, Volume V*, Operations Evaluation Department, Report No. 17769, May 4.

---- (1997), *World Development Report 1997: The State in a Changing World*, Oxford University Press, New York.

---- (1996), *Pursuing Common Goals: Strengthening Relations Between Government and Development NGOs*, World Bank Resident Mission, Dhaka.

---- (1995), *The Bank and NGOs: Strengthening Linkages to Increase Development Effectiveness*, World Bank, Washington, DC.

---- (1994), *Governance: The World Bank's Experience*, World Bank, Washington, DC.

---- (1993a), *The East Asian Miracle: Economic Growth and Public Policy*, Oxford University Press, New York.

---- (1993b), *Uganda, NGO Sector Study*, World Bank, Washington, DC.

---- (1992a), *World Debt Tables 1992-93*, World Bank, Washington, DC.

---- (1992b), *Governance and Development*, World Bank, Washington, DC.

---- (1992c), *Cooperation between the World Bank and NGOs: 1991 Progress Report*, World Bank, Washington, DC.

---- (1989), *Sub-Saharan Africa: From Crisis to Sustainable Growth*, World Bank, Washington. DC.

Young, Oran R. (ed.) (1997), *Global Governance*, MIT Press, Cambridge, MA.

Youngs, Gillian (1999), 'Virtual Voices: Real Lives', in Wendy Harcourt (ed.),*Women @ Internet: Creating New Cultures in Cyberspace*, Zed Books, London.

Zaman, Hassan (1998), 'Assessing the Poverty and Vulnerability Impact of Micro-Credit in Bangladesh: A Case Study of BRAC', working paper, World Bank, Washington, DC.

Zartman, I. William (1995), *Collapsed States: The Disintegration and Restoration of Legitimate Authority*, Lynne Rienner, Boulder.

Zimbabwe Government (1991), *Zimbabwe: A Framework for Economic Reform, 1991-95,* Government Printers, Harare.

Zimbabwe Standard (2000), 'Dabengwa, Chihuri Face Lawsuit', 12 March (http://www.samara.co.zw/ standard/index.cfm).

Zysman, John (1996), 'The Myth of the "Global" Economy: Enduring National Foundations and Emerging Regional Realities', *New Political Economy*, vol. 1, no. 2, pp. 157-184.

Some useful web sites on governance
www.apecsec.org.sg
www.dal.ca/-centre
www.dal.ioihfx/
www.globalknowledge.org
www.idrc.ca
www.ids.ac.uk/eldis
www.ids.ac.uk/index.html
www.imf.org
www.info.usaid.gov
www.nsi-ins.ca
www.oneworld.org

www.sidsnetmaster@sdnhq.undp.org
www.un.org/depts/los
www.unrisd.org
www.worldbank.org
www.wto.org

For additional web sites, see comprehensive lists in:

Clemens, Walter C. Jr. (1998), *Dynamics of International Relations: Conflict and Mutual Gain in an Era of Global Interdependence*, Rowman and Littlefield, Lanham, Md.
Nel, Philip S. and McGowan, Patrick J. (eds) (1999), *Power, Wealth and Global Order: An International Relations Textbook for Africa*, UCT Press for FGA, Cape Town.

Index

312

non-governmental development
organization (NGDO) 129, 131-3
non-governmental institutions (NGIs) 157
non-governmental organizations (NGOs)
advocacy 130, 141-5
civil society and 150-4, 156-8
Delhi 124
first generation 132
gender-based 109, 110, 112, 113,
116-22
grassroots 119
impact on governance 158-9
Indian 109, 116, 117, 122, 124
micro-finance 129, 139, 140, 141,
144, 146: nt. 5 *(see also*
ASA, BRAC, GB, and Proshika)
mosque-based 132
South Africa 196, 202
super 124
types 118
Uganda 238, 239
Zimbabwe 188, 190, 192
see also international non
-governmental organizations NGOs
Norwegian Agency for International
Development (NORAD) 14

Obote I and II regimes 248
Official Development Assistance (ODA)
14, 265, 266-75
oil in conflict 207, 208, 210, 221, 248,
257
Organization for Economic Co-
operation and Development
(OECD) 11, 14
Overseas Development Administration
(ODA) 14, 27

Parti KeADILan Nasional (PKN) 48, 49,
50
Parti Raykat Malaysia (PRM) 49
peace and conflict impact assessments
(PCIA) 264
peacebuilding 267, 268, 275,
276,
peacekeeping and peacemaking 6, 9, 10,
18, 28
people's organizations (POs) 129, 132,
138, 140, 141, 144
Perusahaan Otomobil Nasional Bhd 47

Petronas 46, 47, 48
Plaza Accord/ Agreement [1985] 38, 39,
77
pluralism 3, 4, 18-20, 23-7, 30: nt.11
definition of 18
Poder Popular (people's power) 209
populist authoritarian 85
post-apartheid South Africa 70, 80, 190,
193, 196, 197, 201
changing political economy 194-8
expansion and changes 90, 92, 97
see also apartheid
post-colonial society 35
post-Fordism 79
post-neoliberal governance framework 5
poverty
alleviation of 129, 131-3, 135, 137
and underdevelopment 141
Prabhakaran 272
public call offices (PCOs) 116, 117

race 185, 187, 189, 193, 198-201
Ramaphosa, Cyril 84
Real Africa Investments Limited (RAIL)
81
Reconstruction and Development
Programme (RDP) 194
Reformasi movement 65, 69: nt. 5
regionalisms, new 6, 10, 29
Renong 72
rent-seeking 86, 88: nt. 5
rentier capitalism 70, 76, 77, 85
Republic of South Africa (RSA) 95, 102,
103
retrenchments 55, 57-61, 63
Rushdie, Salman 274
Rural Development Program (RDP) 137-
138
see also BRAC
Rwanda 226, 229, 233, 234, 242: nt. 8

Sakhi 125
Sanhita 118, 119, 125
Savimbi, Jonas 218, 220, 248, 256
Second Industrial Master Plan [1996-
2006] 37
second movement 6, 30: nt 2
Second Outline Perspective Plan (OOP2)
36
security, new 4, 9, 18